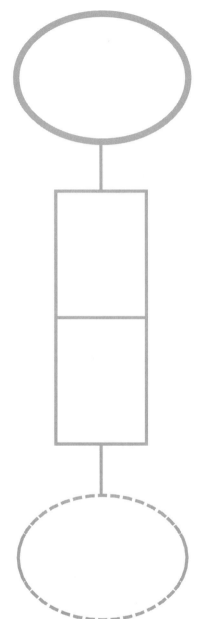

Database Modeling with Microsoft® Visio for Enterprise Architects

Terry Halpin
Northface University
Salt Lake City, Utah

Ken Evans
Perpetual Data Systems
Lincolnshire, UK

Patrick Hallock
In Concept, Inc.
Lake Elmo, Minnesota

Bill MacLean
Orthogonal Software
Corporation
Scottsdale, Arizona

MORGAN KAUFMANN PUBLISHERS

AN IMPRINT OF ELSEVIER

AMSTERDAM   BOSTON   LONDON   NEW YORK
OXFORD   PARIS   SAN DIEGO   SAN FRANCISCO
SINGAPORE   SYDNEY   TOKYO

Senior Editor: *Lothlórien Homet*
Editorial Assistant: *Corina Derman*
Publishing Services Manager: *Simon Crump*
Project Manager: *Sarah Manchester*
Full-Service Provider: *Kolam USA*
Cover Design: *Ross Carron*
Interior Printer: *The Maple-Vail Book Manufacturing Group*
Cover Printer: *Phoenix Color*
Cover Photo: *Nino Mascardi/The Image Bank*

Morgan Kaufmann Publishers
An imprint of Elsevier
340 Pine Street, Sixth Floor
San Francisco, CA 94104-3205
www.mkp.com

07   06   05   04   03   5   4   3   2   1

Library of Congress Control Number: 2003104297
ISBN: 1-55860-919-9

This book is printed on acid-free paper.

Contents

C
25.1.05

Database Modeling with Microsoft® Visio for Enterprise Architects

C
2

The Morgan Kaufmann Series in Data Management Systems

Series Editor: Jim Gray, Microsoft Research

Database Modeling with Microsft® Visio for Enterprise Architects
Terry Halpin, Ken Evans, Patrick Hallock, Bill MacLean

Designing Data-Intensive Web Applications
Stephano Ceri, Piero Fraternali, Aldo Bongio, Marco Brambilla, Sara Comai, and Maristella Matera

Mining the Web: Discovering Knowledge from Hypertext Data
Soumen Chakrabarti

Advanced SQL: 1999—Understanding Object-Relational and Other Advanced Features
Jim Melton

Database Tuning
Dennis Shasha and Philippe Bonnet

SQL: 1999—Understanding Relational Language Components
Jim Melton and Alan R. Simon

Information Visualization in Data Mining and Knowledge Discovery
Edited by Usama Fayyad, Georges G. Grinstein, and Andreas Wierse

Transactional Information Systems
Gerhard Weikum and Gottfried Vossen

Spatial Databases
Philippe Rigaux, Michel Scholl, and Agnes Voisard

Information Modeling and Relational Databases
Terry Halpin

Component Database Systems
Edited by Klaus R. Dittrich and Andreas Geppert

Managing Reference Data in Enterprise Databases
Malcolm Chisholm

Data Mining: Concepts and Techniques
Jiawei Han and Micheline Kamber

Understanding SQL and Java Together
Jim Melton and Andrew Eisenberg

Database: Principles, Programming, and Performance, Second Edition
Patrick and Elizabeth O'Neil

The Object Data Standard: ODMG 3.0
Edited by R. G. G. Cattell and Douglas K. Barry

Data on the Web
Serge Abiteboul, Peter Buneman, and Dan Suciu

Data Mining: Practical Machine Learning Tools and Techniques
Ian Witten and Eibe Frank

Joe Celko's SQL for Smarties Second Edition
Joe Celko

Joe Celko's Data and Databases
Joe Celko

Developing Time-Oriented Database Applications in SQL
Richard T. Snodgrass

Web Farming for the Data Warehouse
Richard D. Hackathorn

Database Modeling & Design, Third Edition
Toby J. Teorey

Management of Heterogeneous and Autonomous Database Systems
Edited by Ahmed Elmagarmid, Marek Rusinkiewicz, and Amit Sheth

Object-Relational DBMSs Second Edition
Michael Stonebraker and Paul Brown, with Dorothy Moore

A Complete Guide to DB2 Universal Database
Don Chamberlin

Universal Database Management
Cynthia Maro Saracco

Readings in Database Systems, Third Edition
Edited by Michael Stonebraker and Joseph M. Hellerstein

Understanding SQL's Stored Procedures
Jim Melton

Principles of Multimedia Database Systems
V. S. Subrahmanian

Principles of Database Query Processing for Advanced Applications
Clement T. Yu and Weiyi Meng

Advanced Database Systems
Carlo Zaniolo, Stefano Ceri, Christos Faloutsos, Richard T. Snodgrass, V. S. Subrahmanian, and Roberto Zicari

Principles of Transaction Processing
Philip A. Bernstein and Eric Newcomer

Using the New DB2
Don Chamberlin

Distributed Algorithms
Nancy A. Lynch

Active Database Systems
Edited by Jennifer Widom and Stefano Ceri

Migrating Legacy Systems
Michael L. Brodie and Michael Stonebraker

Atomic Transactions
Nancy Lynch, Michael Merritt, William Weihl, and Alan Fekete

Query Processing for Advanced Database Systems
Edited by Johann Christoph Freytag, David Maier, and Gottfried Vossen

Transaction Processing
Jim Gray and Andreas Reuter

Building an Object-Oriented Database System
Edited by François Bancilhon, Claude Delobel, and Paris Kanellakis

Database Transaction Models for Advanced Applications
Edited by Ahmed K. Elmagarmid

A Guide to Developing Client/Server SQL Applications
Setrag Khoshafian, Arvola Chan, Anna Wong, and Harry K. T. Wong

The Benchmark Handbook for Database and Transaction Processing Systems, Second Edition
Edited by Jim Gray
Camelot and Avalon

Edited by Jeffrey L. Eppinger, Lily B. Mummert, and Alfred Z. Spector

Readings in Object-Oriented Database Systems
Edited by Stanley B. Zdonik and David Maier

Foreword

I am delighted to write the foreword for this important and useful book on Microsoft's product for database modeling and design. When Microsoft acquired Visio Corporation a few years ago, it gained not only a suite of two-dimensional drawing technologies, but also state-of-the-art technologies for both database and software modeling that could be extended and adapted to blend harmoniously with Microsoft software environments.

These modeling solutions are now available in Microsoft Visio for Enterprise Architects (VEA), which is incorporated in the Enterprise Architect edition of Visual Studio.NET. While the software modeling solution focuses on the Unified Modeling Language (UML), the database modeling solution uses Object-Role Modeling (ORM) for conceptual analysis and varieties of Entity-Relationship (ER) and relational modeling for the logical design of relational tables. The functionality of the database modeling solution is quite deep, and this book provides a thorough and authoritative coverage of this functionality. To provide both an overview of the database modeling approaches themselves and a detailed treatment of Microsoft's database modeling solution within a book of economic length, the authors have omitted coverage of the UML solution— a topic addressed by other books.

Like most other database design tools, Microsoft's VEA product supports ER and relational modeling, allowing these logical designs to be forward engineered to physical database schemas for implementation in several popular database management systems, including Microsoft SQL Server, Microsoft Access, IBM DB2, and Oracle. The tool also supports reverse engineering from these physical schemas to logical models.

What really sets VEA apart from most other database design tools, however, is its deep support for the ORM conceptual modeling approach, which offers many advantages over traditional approaches. ORM can capture many more business rules in both graphical and high-level textual languages, where they can be easily validated by domain experts using the tool's automatic rule verbalization feature, as well as sample fact populations. Moreover, ORM's attribute-free approach allows all relevant information to be verbalized naturally in sentences, while making information models much more stable in the face of changes to the business.

To derive optimum benefit from VEA's database modeling solution, I encourage the reader to consider the ORM approach for conceptual analysis, where the data model of the business can be easily validated with the business experts who best understand the application domain. Such domain experts are often unfamiliar with and uninterested in lower level design details such as foreign keys and check clauses, but these experts can readily understand ORM models expressed clearly in plain language. The VEA tool is capable of forward-engineering ORM models to logical models and then onto physical database schemas and can also reverse engineer physical schemas directly to ORM models. Round-trip engineering is also supported, so that changes made at one level can be automatically propagated to other levels. For readers unfamiliar with the ORM approach, the authors have included a detailed overview of this methodology.

The book's main author, Dr. Terry Halpin, is the world's foremost authority on ORM and also worked as program manager for the database modeling solution in VEA before returning to academia at Northface University, which focuses its curricula on model-driven database and software development. While we miss Terry's expertise at Microsoft, we are delighted that Terry has documented within this book much of his knowledge and insights into both database modeling and the VEA database modeling solution.

The co-authors, Ken Evans, Pat Hallock, and Bill MacLean, are all experienced consultants in database modeling and implementation. As well as working for many years as modeling and database practitioners, they are also intimately familiar with VEA's database modeling solution. They know its strengths and current weaknesses and share many of their practical insights and hints on how to best use the tool. In addition, they provide practical advice on how to manage database projects in industrial settings.

While the functionality of VEA's database modeling solution is deep, not all of it is easy to discover. Since the first release of VEA, there has been a need for a publication that covers this functionality in detail. Not only is this the first book to comprehensively fill this gap, but it is written by experts in a style that is easily understandable. I heartily recommend this book to any practitioner or student interested in the science and art of database modeling.

Chandrika Shankarnarayan
Technical Product Manager
Microsoft Visual Studio for Enterprise Architects

Preface

This book explains how to model databases with Microsoft Visio for Enterprise Architects (VEA). Although primarily focused on tool features, this book also provides an introduction to data modeling and includes practical advice on managing database projects. We have all used VEA extensively in industrial database projects, and the principal author worked on the design of VEA's database modeling solutions.

Unlike most other database design tools, VEA allows you to model data at a truly conceptual level, using a fact-based approach known as Object-Role Modeling (ORM). For conceptual information analysis, ORM has many advantages over other methods such as Entity-Relationship (ER) modeling. ORM's attribute-free approach facilitates model validation by verbalization and population, and it helps to minimize the impact of changes to the application domain. Moreover, ORM diagrams can graphically display many more business rules than other approaches.

ER diagrams are also useful because they summarize the main features of a data model in a more compact form, and their structures are more closely related to those implemented in physical database schemas. The VEA tool enables you to display logical database models in a variety of notations, including IDEF1X, Information Engineering, and pure relational notation.

You can use the VEA tool to get the best of both conceptual modeling and logical modeling approaches by specifying the conceptual data model in ORM notation and then automatically transforming it to a fully normalized logical data model in ER or relational notation. You can also create a logical data model directly.

Once you have a logical data model, you can automatically generate a physical database schema for a relational DBMS such as SQL Server, DB2, or Oracle. The VEA tool also supports reverse engineering from physical databases and even round-trip engineering between conceptual, logical, and physical levels.

Given the considerable power and depth of VEA's database modeling solutions, there is much to learn in order to fully exploit its modeling features, and this is the main emphasis of this book. While some basic background in relational database modeling is assumed, a simple introduction to the ORM conceptual modeling approach is included so that you can enjoy the benefits of this approach even if it is new to you. A thorough examination of the ORM methodology is provided in a separate book (Halpin, 2001).

The book has four main parts. Part 1 provides an overview of the database modeling features in VEA, summarizes the different tasks involved in database modeling, explains how to install the product and get started with the Visio interface, and demonstrates how to forward engineer a data model from conceptual to logical to physical levels using a simple example. You should read Part 1 first.

Part 2 focuses on the conceptual modeling solution (ORM). It discusses how to construct an ORM model from object types, predicates, and constraints; how to configure, manipulate, and reuse ORM models; how to map ORM models to logical data models; how to reverse engineer physical database schemas to ORM; and how to generate reports that document ORM models. We recommend that you read Part 2 before Part 3. If you want to first explore the logical modeling solution, you may skip Part 2 until you feel ready to reap the benefits of conceptual modeling.

Part 3 examines the logical data modeling solution in detail. It shows how to create and edit a logical database model and how to generate a physical database schema from it. It also explains how to reverse engineer a physical database schema to a logical data model and how to generate reports that document the logical model.

Part 4 deals with advanced topics, and should be read only after you have digested Part 2 or Part 3. It examines how to deal with changes at any level (conceptual, logical, or physical) and how to perform round-trip engineering while keeping your models synchronized. It also discusses useful ways to customize and extend your models and provides practical advice on managing your database projects.

The *Glossary* summarizes the terms and ORM notations used by the VEA database modeling solutions. Use this to quickly check on the meaning of key concepts and the graphical symbols used in ORM models and logical database models.

The *Further Resources* section lists related texts and resources available in print and online. The author's website includes sample models that are used for discussion purposes at various stages in the book. You may freely download these models for your own personal use.

Acknowledgments

At Morgan Kaufmann Publishers, our editor, Lothlórien Homet, has been a delight to work with from the outset. Her patient professionalism and thoughtful consideration are much appreciated. Several passages in the book have benefited from detailed feedback by Dr. Andy Carver. Three consultants at InConcept Inc. (Necito dela Cruz, Dick Barden, and Patricia Schiefelbein) also provided valuable suggestions and reviews. Terry and Patrick thank their respective wives, Norma and Linda, for being so understanding and supportive during the writing task.

Finally, the development team at Microsoft is to be congratulated for creating such a productive tool for database modeling. If you are a Microsoft Developer Network (MSDN) Universal subscriber, the VEA tool is included in your subscription as part of Visual Studio .NET Enterprise Architect. We hope that this book will encourage others to exploit the vast potential of this database modeling tool.

Terry Halpin
Patrick Hallock
Ken Evans
Bill MacLean

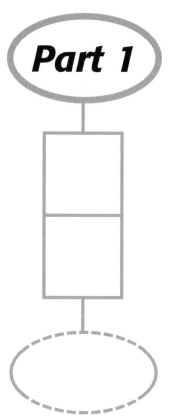

Part 1

Overview of Database Modeling and the Database Modeling Tool

This book has four main parts.

Part 1 provides an overview of the database modeling features in Visio for Enterprise Architects (VEA) and summarizes the different tasks involved in database modeling. Part 1 comprises three chapters.

Chapter 1 describes the scope of database modeling and what you can do with VEA. You learn how to best use this book and how to interpret its format conventions.

Chapter 2 explains the purpose of database modeling and the four different levels for working with data: external, conceptual, logical, and physical. It briefly reviews the main concepts underlying database modeling at the conceptual and logical levels.

Chapter 3 explains how to install the product and get started. You learn to use the Visio user interface and help facility. A worked example introduces you to the process of creating a data model and forward engineering it.

Parts 2 and **3** focus respectively on the conceptual and logical modeling solutions, and **Part 4** discusses advanced topics such as round-trip engineering and model management.

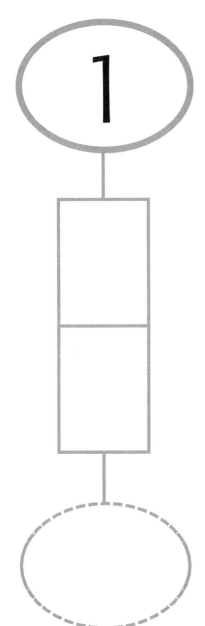

Introduction

If you have a well-designed database management system, you have
the keys to the kingdom of data processing and decision support.

Dr. E. F. Codd

This book will help business analysts, database designers, and database administrators to use the powerful database modeling facilities within Microsoft Visio for Enterprise Architects (VEA) to create and manage well-designed databases.

Process analysts, project managers, application development managers, and business experts will also benefit by understanding why data models are used and how they are built and maintained.

1.1   Why Read This Book?

Practical. This book offers a practical guide to VEA's powerful database modeling solution. Step-by-step instructions and worked examples help you learn how to specify, design, and build databases that accurately reflect your application domain.

You learn to reverse engineer a database into natural language facts. This function makes it easy for domain experts to check the database for conformance to business requirements.

You learn to model business rules as conceptual constraints or derivation rules and propagate them to a physical database. When you store business rules in a database, you need fewer lines of procedural code, which reduces development costs.

You learn to use domain-based data types. VEA generates physical data types for all columns that draw their values from a conceptual domain. This is a great timesaver and helps to ensure database consistency.

Clear. The examples in this book are illustrated by screen shots of menus, dialog boxes, and more. The glossary summarizes modeling terms and graphical symbols used.

Flexible. You can choose to begin with Object-Role Modeling (ORM), or you can create a logical model directly using Entity-Relationship Modeling (ERM).

Written by modeling experts and practitioners. The principal author, Dr. Terry Halpin, formalized the ORM methodology and worked as program manager at Microsoft for the database modeling solutions in VEA. Ken Evans, Pat Hallock, and Bill MacLean have managed and developed dozens of industrial projects involving conceptual, logical, and physical database design. Collectively, the author team has almost a century of practical experience in systems and modeling.

Unique. This book is the only through and practical guide to the comprehensive and powerful database modeling solution in Microsoft Visio for Enterprise Architects.

In summary, this book shows you how to use VEA's powerful database modeling solution to improve database quality and reduce development costs.

1.2   What Can You Do with Visio for Enterprise Architects?

In addition to the database modeling solution overviewed in the next section, VEA provides several stencils and templates for specific tasks that you may find useful in developing and managing applications. It is also a superb tool for general purpose drawing. The main "non-database" features of interest for application development are summarized below.

Software engineering. You can use the UML Model Diagram solution to model object-oriented applications, with forward and reverse engineering between class models and programming code. You can draw UML diagrams, document data flows, and component architectures and create user interface designs such as prototypes of dialog boxes, menus, toolbars, and wizards to explore user interaction.

Network engineering. You can forward and reverse engineer directory structures. When connected to a local area network, VEA can automatically discover an existing network and display an appropriate equipment symbol complete with serial number for each discovered network object.

Project administration. You can use the Project Schedule solution to document project information. You can use the Organization Chart to document organization hierarchies.

Website design. You can use the Web Diagram solution to design a conceptual website and to map an existing website.

Process and quality diagrams. VEA's Flowchart category has templates for Total Quality Management (TQM) diagrams, workflows, cross-functional flowcharts, Specification and Description Language (SDL) diagrams, and more.

General purpose drawing. VEA includes the drawing functions of Microsoft Visio Professional, which makes it easy to enhance your models by combining many kinds of shapes and documents. You can simultaneously open as many stencils as you like.

Some other possibilities.
Multi-application files. You can reuse non-VEA files, for example, by adding an Excel spreadsheet to your database diagram, adding an organization chart to your database project, or adding a voice recording of a domain expert's explanation.

Run a virtual modeling project. You can open or save documents stored on a SharePoint team Web site and have online discussions.

1.3   What Can You Do with the Database Modeling Solution?

Database modeling transforms the information structures of an application domain into data structures within a physical database. This process is normally divided into separate modeling phases. Figure 1–1 shows how the different types of model relate to each other and to each of the database modeling tasks on the right. You often find seemingly conflicting and vague definitions in an application domain, which is why it is represented by a cloud. Models are precise, which is why they are represented by rectangles. Your first step is to create an orderly conceptual model from the seeming chaos of the application domain.

Each database modeling task has a different purpose and requires different knowledge. Think of a database modeling task as a role to be played by a person with appropriate skills rather than as a job title. For example, the business analyst role is people-centered and requires skills in interviewing, presentation, and semantic modeling. In contrast, the database design role is technology-centered and requires extensive and up-to-date technical knowledge. To do both tasks, you need the skills for both roles.

Table 1–1 shows the meaning of the database modeling task names used in this book. Each task has a different purpose.

The following paragraphs outline four typical database modeling tasks: Each of the examples summarizes a step in the forward engineering process.

Task: Business Analysis

The business analyst and domain expert collaborate to create a semantically accurate conceptual model of an application domain, in terms easily understood by the domain expert. Object-Role Modeling (ORM) is best for creating a comprehensive definition of an application domain and its business rules.

Although pure Entity Relationship (ER) modeling can be used to model at the conceptual level, the versions of ER supported by VEA are more aligned with relational models than conceptual models. For example, a many-to-many relationship between entity types must be modeled indirectly by introducing an intersection entity type. Because entity types in the ER solution correspond to relational tables, models created with the ER solution are more accurately described as logical models rather than conceptual models. Hence, we often refer to such ER models as logical data models.

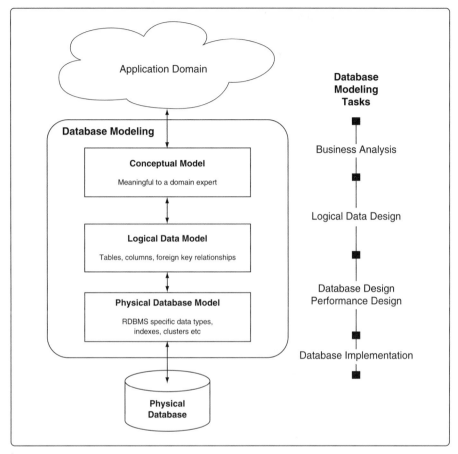

Figure 1–1　Database modeling in context.

Table 1–1　Database modeling tasks.

Database Modeling Task	What the Task Does
Business analysis	Creates a conceptual model of an application domain, using terms and language easily understood by business people.
Logical data design	Transforms a conceptual model into a set of relational tables and associated constraints.
Physical database design	Creates an SQL schema for a specific database management system, including physical data types and indexes.
Performance design	Tunes a physical model for optimum performance on the specific software and hardware platform.

Task: Logical Data Design

The business analyst and logical data designer create a normalized data model that accurately represents the conceptual model with tables and columns uniquely named. ER modeling is good for summarizing database table structures. If an ORM conceptual model was specified, the tool can use this to automatically create a fully normalized logical data model. ORM constraints are used to generate check clauses, stored procedures, triggers, and more. VEA applies domain-based data types from your conceptual model to the generated columns. You can also create a logical data model directly, without doing an ORM model first. You can choose relational notation or various ER notations (e.g., IDEF1X). If you don't start with ORM, you have to do many things yourself such as manually normalize the table structure, check all your column names for consistency, and manually cross-check data types on those columns that are drawn from a common domain.

Task: Physical Database Design

The logical data engineer and physical data engineer prepare a logical data model for use with a specific relational database management system (RDBMS) such as Microsoft SQL Server or IBM DB2. VEA helps by providing built-in, product-specific data types, triggers and stored procedures, database drivers, data source set-up tools, and more. To see if your physical model conforms to the rules of a specific database, simply select the relevant database driver (three mouse clicks) and run an error check (three mouse clicks).

Task: Performance Design

Database performance is affected by many factors such as RDBMS product characteristics, operating system characteristics, hardware characteristics, and application type (e.g., query/update pattern). Since database performance is implementation specific, it is not discussed in this book. You should seek product performance information in the relevant product manuals.

> *Caution:* When you change a database schema, you change what the database means. What may appear to be a "just a simple technical change" could have unintended semantic consequences. You should carefully check the semantic implications of each change to your database schema. Fortunately, ORM reports make it easy to check the semantic consequences of schema changes.

For conceptual modeling, VEA supports ORM via its ORM Source Model solution. With ORM, you specify what your database means before defining how your database is to be implemented. Focusing on semantics before system design helps to minimize specification errors and reduce development costs. The ORM Source Model solution is explained in Part 2.

For logical modeling, VEA supports ER and pure relational modeling, using its ER Source Model and Database Model Diagram solutions. The ER Source Model and Database Model Diagram solutions are explained in Part 3.

VEA makes it easy to design an application-neutral conceptual model that can be used to create and manage several different physical databases. The three shaded shapes in represent VEA's three modeling components. The database modeling tasks on the right cross-refer to Figure 1–1. The fourteen numbered arrows represent database modeling sub-tasks. Arrow 8 is dotted because this route is suitable only for creating models that you do not wish to reuse when building other models. The arrow functions are outlined in Table 1–2. The arrows are numbered for ease of reference. The number sequence is not intended to imply an activity sequence.

Table 1–2 gives a summary of the functions of the arrows in Figure 1–2. The arrows represent business processes and are provided to give you an idea of the different task sequences that you can choose through VEA's database solution. The chapter references on the right refer to the main chapters that deal with the function on that row. You can use Figure 1–2 and Table 1–2 to plan your own reading sequence.

The following paragraphs outline some activities that illustrate some of VEA's powerful capabilities. The numbers in parentheses refer to the arrows in Figure 1–2.

Create a source model. (2, 3). Use a conceptual model to define the scope and semantics of your application domain independently of your target database technology. Build a conceptual model using ORM's natural language approach or create a logical

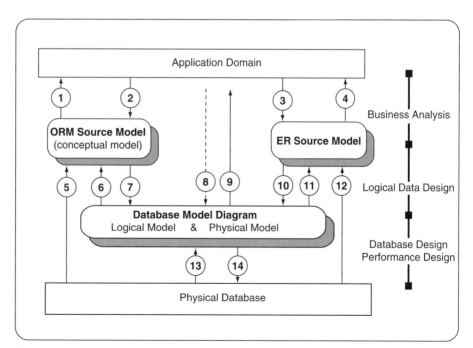

Figure 1–2   Database modeling and VEA.

Table 1–2   VEA sub-task summary.

Arrow	Function	Chapters
1	Review an ORM conceptual model.	9, 17
2	Create a conceptual model using ORM.	10, 13
3	Create a logical model using relational or ER notation.	Part 3
4	Review an ER model.	15, 17
5	Reverse engineer a physical schema into an ORM conceptual model. Update an ORM conceptual model to reflect changes in a physical schema.	8
6	Reverse engineer a logical model into an ORM conceptual model. Update an ORM conceptual model to reflect changes in a logical model.	7
7	Transform an ORM conceptual model to a logical model in fifth normal form. Update a logical model with changes to an ORM conceptual model.	7
8	Design a logical model directly. Update a logical model with changes to an application domain.	10
9	Review a logical model with domain experts.	15, 17
10	Generate a logical model from an ER model. Update a logical model with changes to an ER model.	10
11	Generate an ER model from a logical model. Update an ER model to reflect changes in a logical model.	10
12	Reverse engineer a physical database schema into an ER model. Update an ER model to reflect changes in a physical schema.	14
13	Reverse engineer from a physical database to a physical model. Update a physical model to reflect changes in a physical database schema.	14
14	Transform a physical model into a physical database. Update a physical database schema to reflect changes to a physical model.	11

model directly using ERM. Within the ORM Source Model solution, you may define portable data types that map to more than one database product, and you can define physical data types that map to a specific database product. These data types are domain level data types that help to ensure consistency between the data types in a logical model and the conceptual domains from which they are drawn. VEA's domain mapping feature helps you to ensure data type consistency across multiple databases even if they use different database products. If you have to do this manually, the bigger the model the harder it gets. Fortunately, VEA does this for you, which is a great time saver.

Transform a conceptual model into a 5NF logical model. (7) VEA can automatically transform an ORM Source Model into a logical model in fifth normal form—another great time saver! You can choose to display your logical model in either Relational or an ER notation (e.g. IDEF1X or Information Engineering).

Create a logical model. (3, 8) Create a logical model directly using the ER Source Model, the Database Model Diagram, or a combination of the two. VEA provides comprehensive features for editing logical models. You can edit names, definitions, indexes, stored procedures, formatting and much more.

Generate a physical database schema. (14) You can generate a physical schema from a logical schema. You choose a target database product by selecting a suitable driver and select from a drop-down box of built-in physical data types. VEA has database drivers for Microsoft SQL Server, Microsoft Access, Oracle Server, IBM DB2 Universal Database, Informix OnLine/SE Server, and Sybase Adaptive Server Enterprise. You will also find generic drivers for OLE and ODBC.

Validate models. You can periodically validate your model to keep it error-free.

Hint: Although the command sequence for model error checking is the same, you get different types of error messages depending on whether you are validating an ORM Source Model, an ER Source Model, or a Database Model Diagram.

Reverse engineer an existing database into a conceptual model. (5, 1) Many domain experts find logical models hard to understand. With VEA's ORM solution, you can present the semantics of a complex database using easy to understand English language facts. This is great for helping domain experts to identify conflicts between database semantics and their knowledge of the application domain.

Reverse engineer an existing database into a logical model. (13) VEA makes it easy to extract a detailed logical model from an existing database.

Convert from one database product to another. (5, 1, 2, 7, 14) You can convert a database from one database product to another. For example, an Oracle database can be converted to a Microsoft SQL Server database and vice versa. A typical conversion requires six main steps:

1. Reverse engineer the existing database schema.
2. Review and edit the conceptual model to ensure semantic accuracy.
3. Generate and edit the logical model to ensure correct normalization.
4. Edit the physical model to ensure data type and SQL code dialect accuracy.

5. Generate a new physical database schema in the target database product.
6. Migrate data from the source to the target database.

Prepare comprehensive and customized reports. (1, 4, 9) VEA's report wizard helps you generate the seven types of report named in Figure 1–3. The arrows indicate the different reporting options for different kinds of model. For example, you can generate an Objects report from an ORM Source Model and from a Database Model Diagram, but you can generate a Statistics report only from a Database Model Diagram. Chapter 9 shows you how to generate ORM reports for objects, facts, constraints, and subtypes. Chapter 15 shows you how to generate reports for statistics, tables, and data types.

VEA's natural language ORM reports help non-technical domain experts to check the semantics of a database schema. VEA's logical reports help database engineers to modify a physical database schema to meet performance or other technical requirements.

The New Report Wizard allows you to control the amount of detail in your reports using select, sort, and format. You can create summary reports that show the big picture or reports that show all the details. You can export your reports in .rtf format to make it easy for you to edit your report with a word processing program.

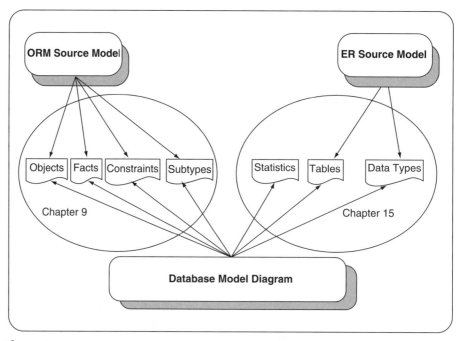

Figure 1–3 VEA reports.

Save your work as web pages. VEA's command File>Save as Web Page makes it easy to save your diagrams in .htm format so that you can publish them on the web.

Model databases with a team. Each team member can create a sub-model in either ORM or ERM. You can then create a single, comprehensive logical model by merging the teams' source model documents into a single project document.

Create reusable submodels. You can create a library of source model building blocks and then mix and match them to quickly build a large database model.

Manage naming conventions. You can define three different names for each table and column: a conceptual name, a physical name, and a name space. Modelers often find that two or more tables with the same meaning have been given different names and vice versa. VEA's name space feature helps you to assign a unique name to each table and each column even across multiple databases. If you have to merge two or more existing databases you will find the name space feature to be very useful.

Share your models with users who do not have Visio installed. The Visio Viewer is for those who do not have Visio but who want to view Visio diagrams (in the same way that Acrobat reader iss free for viewing .pdf files). You can find more information about Visio Viewer in the Further Resources section.

> ***Visio Viewer:*** Visio users should NOT install the Visio Viewer because it then becomes the default program for opening Visio files, and you have to go back and reset your default program for opening Visio documents.

Customize shape behavior. You can customize the behavior of the shapes that represent tables, columns, and relationships in your database model diagram. For example, you can specify what is to happen when you remove a table or foreign key in a database model diagram. You can specify how foreign keys are propagated; choose how name conflicts are resolved, and how default name prefixes are created.

Edit shapes. In addition to editing a logical model you can use Visio's "right click" menu to edit the display properties of shapes on the drawing surface.

> ***Note:*** Strictly speaking, a model is a schema plus a population of fact instances. Informally, this book often uses the term model as a synonym for schema.

And a word about indexes and performance tuning ...

> ***Note:*** Performance is product and application dependent so we don't say much about it in this book. Consult your product manuals and review your application objectives to understand how to tune a database schema for best performance. The ORM domain indexing feature does generate physical indexes, but its main value is to make it easy to manage index consistency.

1.4   How Can You Best Use This Book?

The following sample scenarios will give you an idea of how you can best use this book in your own situation.

Scenario and Question	Answer
Database Modeler Database modeling is my job. How can this book help me to do my daily work faster?	Import your existing database schema into a Database Model Diagram (see Chapter 14), then use your own models in parallel with trying each of the examples shown in this book.
Business Analyst I have to use data models as part of my requirements specifications. How can this book help me to be more efficient?	Reverse engineer an existing database schema into an ORM Source Model (see Chapter 8). Use the ORM Source Model to generate suitable semantic reports (see Chapter 9).
Student I know that database modeling is important. How can this book help me to learn more so that I can get a job as a database engineer?	Follow the book from cover to cover. Build some conceptual models in ORM and ERM, and use the New Report Wizard to prepare in-depth reports. Forward engineer your models to your preferred database product. Make changes to the physical database schema and reverse engineer it back into ER and ORM models and run the same reports as you did on the original models. Compare the before and after reports to see the effects of your changes.
Database Administrator I'm snowed under with management requests for explanations of our corporate database. How can this book help me?	Reverse engineer a database schema into an ORM Source Model (see Chapter 8). Run the reports described in Chapter 9 and export them to an .rtf file. Edit the .rtf file to fit your corporate standard and add appropriate ORM models or model fragments to support the reports (see Chapter 9). Consider using the Visio Viewer (see Chapter 17) for electronic model distribution. Ask the managers to confirm or deny the correctness of the ORM objects, facts, and constraints.

Scenario and Question—cont'd	Answer
Application Development Manager I have just been promoted from Chief Programmer and I need a better understanding of what my database engineers really do. They seem to take a long time to make simple user-requested changes and my programmers complain that database changes result in lots of unnecessary reprogramming and testing. Can I use this book to improve the effectiveness of my team?	Prepare ORM reports (see Chapter 9) and conduct a semantic review with domain experts (see Part 4). Use the reports described in Chapter 15 to review the potential impact of any changes on data elements (e.g., UML classes) in their application programs. Look out for duplications in your database schema caused by failure to correctly normalize or by unnoticed homonyms or synonyms. Review chapter 6 to see how to reuse model fragments to speed new development. Migrate business rules from application program code into SQL code stored in the database (see Chapters 5, 11, 13).
Program Manager, USAF Sub-Contractor I have just been appointed as program manager for new B3 bomber that is so stealthy that even I don't know where it is. The DoD insists that we use IDEF1X but I have never been able to fully understand the real meaning of all those lines, blobs, diamonds and boxes. How can I use this book to get a better understanding of what the IDEF1X data models really mean?	Reverse engineer your database schema into a Database Model Diagram (see Chapter 13) Set the IDEF1X notation options (Chapter 10) and print the IDEF1X schema. Run the reports described in Chapter 9 and compare them with the IDEF1X schema.

How you use this book depends on your desired result and on your level of knowledge. Here are some examples of how VEA can be used to support various job types. The examples are indicative rather than comprehensive.

Business analyst. Use the reports described in Chapter 9 to communicate with non-technical domain experts. Use the reports from Chapter 15 for database engineers. If you want to start a new requirements analysis project, make sure you understand the contents of Part 1 and then apply the methods described in Part 2 to your own project.

If you want to understand the semantics of an existing database, reverse engineer the database schema into an ORM Source Model (see Chapter 5) and run the reports described in Chapter 9.

Entity Relationship modeling expert. If you are an expert in ER modeling and want to get straight into logical modeling, make sure you understand the contents of Part 1 and then apply the methods described in Part 3 to your own project.

If you want to study the logical and physical structure of an existing database, you can reverse engineer a physical database schema into a Database Model Diagram (see chapter 13). Then you can use the reports described in Chapters 9 and 15.

Application development manager. Review the re-use section and have one of your database engineers try a small project using Part 4 as a guide.

Database administrator. You can reverse engineer multiple databases into a single conceptual model and use it to ensure that all relational columns that are drawn from a single domain use a common data type and naming convention.

Systems architect. VEA allows re-use of all or part of an existing model for future applications. This helps to reduce development costs. You can use a single conceptual model to manage domain level metadata across several applications. Business rules can be maintained in a single conceptual model and re-used in many applications. You can easily add new ORM objects to extend the scope of the conceptual model and quickly generate a new logical model in fifth normal form. VEA helps by eliminating the tedium of repetitive manual normalization.

Student. If you are new to database analysis and design, you should follow the natural sequence of the book. If you want to learn more about ORM and database design, look at papers on the ORM website www.orm.net and read the book, *Information Modeling and Relational Databases* (Halpin, 2001).

1.5   Format Conventions

Term	Meaning
Click	Left click of the mouse.
Press	Always refers to a key on the keyboard.
Choose	To select from a set of options, such as radio buttons or check-boxes.
1, 2	Numbered steps are a guide to an action sequences.
Actions and menus	Menu commands are often shown in parentheses after a statement of an action; e.g., Save As (File > Save As, Filename).
Shaded box	Shows a helpful hint, shortcut, or note.
A+B	A plus (+) sign between two keys means that you must press the keys at the same time (e.g., Press Ctrl+Shift).

Term—cont'd	Meaning
Code	Code examples and menu options are often shown in this font.
File> New>	Text with initial capital letters separated by ">" shows a menu selection sequence.
Caution	Shows that the action described may lead to irreversible consequences.
.erx	A period and three lower case letters refers to a file type.

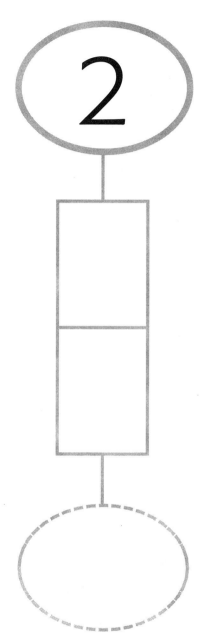

2

Database Modeling

2.1 Four Information Levels

A *database* is essentially a set of facts about an application domain. An application domain is also known as a "Universe of Discourse" (a term coined by the 19th century mathematician Augustus De Morgan), since it corresponds to those aspects of the world that we wish to talk or discourse about. The information content of an application domain may be viewed at four different levels: conceptual, logical, physical, and external.

The *external level* deals with the user interface. Here is where we design how information is presented to various user groups, and what operations they are allowed to perform. For example, Figure 2–1 displays two instances of a screen form that allows users to view and edit basic information about patients. Here, asterisks indicate mandatory fields: each patient must have a patient number and a name.

If known, a patient's country of birth and/or country of residence may be entered. Drop-down list boxes enable the user to choose from a list of countries (both country codes and country names are provided) that is displayed when the cursor is placed in the field. A question mark indicates that no selection has been made, so this detail is unknown to the system. Many alternate user interfaces may be used for this task, but a treatment of user interface design is outside the scope of this book.

Forms like this might be implemented using in-memory "business objects" that have been coded in a programming language such as Java or C#. The design of such transient models is also outside the scope of this book. What *is* in scope is the design of persistent models (i.e., databases) for storing such information. Such databases may be specified at conceptual, logical, or physical levels.

At the *conceptual level,* the information is specified naturally, using language and concepts easily understood by non-technical domain experts. For example, The Patient identified by patient number "1025" resides in the Country identified by the country code "CA." At this high level of communication, ORM provides the best approach.

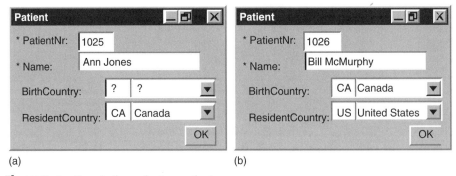

(a)   (b)

Figure 2–1   Sample forms for two patients.

At the *logical level,* you specify the information in terms of data structures supported by a logical data model. For this purpose, we choose the relational data model invented in 1969 by Dr. E. F. Codd. For example, the residence fact mentioned above might be stored in a resident Country attribute of a Patient table. Using VEA, you can also display this information in an ER style notation. At this level, VEA allows you to specify portable data types that can be mapped to a variety of physical data types depending on the target database platform. At the *physical level,* we choose a target database management system (DBMS) for implementing the logical model. In this book, we restrict our attention to relational DBMSs, such as Microsoft SQL Server, IBM's DB2, or Oracle. For example, using SQL Server 2000 we might choose to store resident Country values using the physical data type char(2).

The rest of this chapter summarizes the main, top level ideas behind conceptual and logical database design, using the Patient example in Figure 2–1 to illustrate the concepts. As you are probably more familiar with logical database modeling, we'll start with that before moving on to conceptual modeling. The main purpose of this chapter is to provide a quick review of the basic concepts underlying database design. For a thorough grounding in these concepts, you should refer to other books (e.g., Halpin, 2001).

2.2 Designing Databases at the Logical Level

A *relational database* is so-called because all its facts are stored in relations (tables), comprised of sets of tuples (rows). Care is required in designing the *relation schemes* (table structures) used to store the facts. For example, suppose we try to store all the facts on the patient forms in Figure 2–1 in a single table. The table scheme for this design is shown in Figure 2–2, using the default relational notation supported by VEA.

The table name "Patient" is shown at the top, and the names of its *attributes* (columns) are listed vertically below. Each table must have a *primary key,* which is a set of one or more columns whose values uniquely determine a single row of the table. In this case, the patientNr column is the primary key, as shown by the "PK" notation and the underline. *Mandatory* columns are displayed in bold type, and can contain only

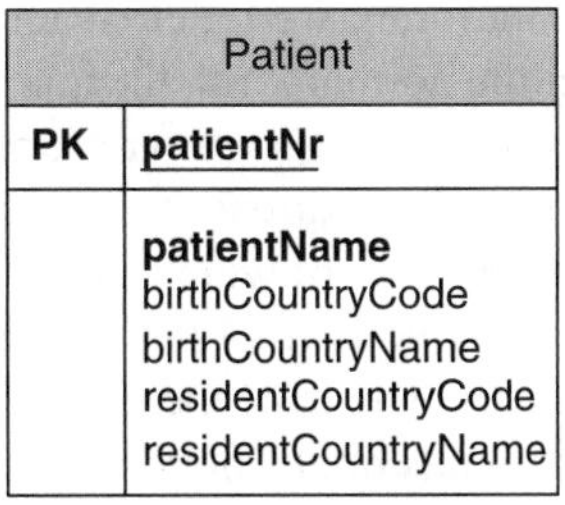

Figure 2–2   A poorly designed table scheme for capturing the data in Figure 2–1.

actual values. *Optional* columns are displayed in non-bold type, and may contain *null values,* indicating that an actual value is unknown to the system.

As you probably realized, this table design is flawed. Intuitively, relationships between country codes and country names are facts about countries, not patients, so they should not be bundled into a table about patients. This error is easily exposed by populating the table scheme with the sample data from Figure 2–2, as shown below.

Patient (<u>patientNr</u>, patientName,   birthCtryCode, birthCtryName, resCtryCode, resCtryName)

| 1025 | Ann Jones | ? | ? | CA | Canada |
| 1026 | Bill McMurphy | CA | Canada | US | United States |

Here, the table is set out horizontally, and some column names are abbreviated to fit in the space available. Null values are denoted by "?" Each row of a relational table contains one or more facts. The (CA, Canada) entries on the first row denote the fact that the country with the code "CA" has the name "Canada." But this same fact is represented by the (CA, Canada) entries on the next row. Since the same fact is stored twice, we have *redundancy*.

Although controlled redundancy may sometimes be used to improve performance, redundancy in a logical model is generally bad, mainly because it makes it much more difficult to avoid data entry errors. For example, unless we take pains to prevent it, we may associate different country names (e.g., "Canada," "Cameroon," "Cambodia") with the same country code 'CA' on different rows of the Patient table above, making the database *inconsistent*.

For users whose only access to the database is via the form template shown in Figure 2–1 this error is avoided, since the form provides read-only access to the country code-name facts in the drop-down list. However the database administrator who enters these facts into the database in the first place has no such protection. Moreover, such a table scheme would be very awkward for entering such facts in advance, since it requires patient details as well. In short, the table is badly designed.

One way to spot problems with the table design in Figure 2–2 is to realize that it contains *functional dependencies* unrelated to the primary key. For example, each birth country code must have only one birth country name, and each resident country code must have only one resident country name. The lack of enforcement of these dependencies is what gives rise to possible inconsistencies (e.g., a country code having more than one country name).

If you are designing a logical database model directly, you can use *normalization* theory to avoid such problems. Normalization by decomposition specifies rules about what kinds of conditions are required for a relation is to conform to a given *normal form*. The higher the normal form, the more protected the table is from data entry errors. The most important normal forms are summarized in Table 2–1.

The table scheme in Figure 2–2 is in first normal form (1NF) because it has a fixed number of attributes, each of which can hold only atomic values (not collections of values). It is also in second normal form (2NF), because each of its attributes is functionally dependent on the whole of the primary key (patientNr).

Given any attributes or attribute-sets X and Y of a table scheme, we say that X *functionally determines* Y (written $X \to Y$) if and only if, for each value of X there is at most

Table 2–1

Normal Form	Definition
1NF (First Normal Form)	All attributes are single-valued and fixed.
2NF (Second Normal Form)	In 1NF, and every nonkey attribute is functionally dependent on the whole of a key (not just part of it)
3NF (Third Normal Form)	In 2NF, and its nonkey attributes are mutually independent. Hence there are no transitively derived dependencies.
BCNF (Boyce-Codd Normal Form)	All its elementary functional dependencies begin at whole keys.
4NF (Fourth Normal Form)	In BCNF, and all its nontrivial dependencies are functional (single-valued) dependencies.
5NF (Fifth Normal Form)	For each nontrivial join dependency, each projection includes a key of the original table.

one value of Y (for any given population of the table scheme). A *nonkey attribute* is neither a key nor part of a composite key. The table scheme in Figure 2–1 has functional dependencies between some of its nonkey attributes. For example, birthCountryCode$\rightarrow$ birthCountryName, and residentCountryCode$\rightarrow$ residentCountryName. There are also functional dependencies in the opposite direction (from country names to country codes). Hence the table scheme is *not* in third normal form (3NF).

To obtain third normal form, the embedded functional dependencies must be removed by decomposing the table into multiple tables. In this case, we should remove the country name columns from the original table, and store the relationship between country codes and country names in a separate table, as shown in Figure 2–3.

The primary key declaration in the Country table captures the functional dependencies from country codes to country names. The "U1" mark on the countryName column declares that these values in this column are unique (each country name refers to

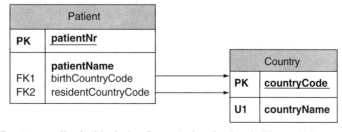

Figure 2–3 A normalized table design for capturing the data in Figure 2–1.

only one country). This captures the functional dependencies from country names to country codes.

The "FK1" and "FK2" marks in the Patient table declare that birthCountryCode and residentCountryCode are *foreign keys* (each of their column values must be included in the primary key column of some table). The arrows from the Patient table to the Country table display the connections from the foreign keys in the Patient table to the primary key of the Country table. The sample population shown below illustrates these foreign key constraints: each birth or resident country code in the Patient table is also a country code in the Country table. The country table has two candidate keys (underlined). Here a double underline is used to distinguish the "primary key."

Patient	(patientNr,	patientName,	birthCountryCode,	residentCountryCode)
	1025	Ann Jones	?	CA
	1026	Bill McMurphy	CA	US

Country	(countryCode,	countryName)
	AU	Australia
	CA	Canada
	US	United States
	. . .	. . .

Note that the foreign key connections between the tables denote constraints, not facts. For example, the fact that Ann Jones resides in Canada is stored in the patientName and residentCountryCode columns of the Patient table. The foreign key reference from the residentCountryCode column to the countryCode column of the Patient table merely ensures that resident country codes are legal country codes. Using VEA, you can redisplay the schema of Figure 2–3 in an ER-like notation, such as IDEF1X, and you can supply relationship names (e.g., "was born in," "resides in") for the foreign key references. But you cannot use these foreign key connections to actually store the birth and residency facts. These facts must still be stored in columns of the Patient table. The relational data model requires all facts to be stored in tables. In pure ER modeling, the Patient table would be replaced by an entity type Patient with just two attributes (patientNr and patientName), and the birth and residency facts would be captured by relationships between the Patient and Country entity types. Since VEA does not support pure ER modeling of this kind, its ER modeling solution is classified as logical modeling rather than conceptual modeling.

To obtain a correct database design for the Patient form, it was sufficient to use third normal form, because the Patient and Country tables are actually also in fifth normal form (5NF). There are many cases however where 3NF tables are still open to redundancy or update anomalies, and further decomposition is required to reshape them into 5NF tables. We have no space here to provide a full coverage of normalization theory. For a concise but thorough treatment of normalization by decomposition, see section 12.6 of Halpin, 2001. One advantage of using the ORM solution is that VEA can automatically generate 5NF table schemas from correct ORM models. So if you use ORM, there is no need to concern yourself with normalization theory.

2.3   **Designing Databases at the Conceptual Level**

For any given application, the domain experts who understand the meaning of the underlying information and business rules are often non-technical. Since these subject matter experts are the only reliable source for validating whether you have modeled the information correctly, you should communicate your model to them at the conceptual level, using concepts and language that they easily understand. Object-Role Modeling (ORM) enables you to do this using natural language sentences from which VEA can automatically generate a database model for implementation.

ORM also provides a rich, graphical notation that enables you as a modeler to visualize the semantic connections and business rules within a conceptual model. Although domain experts often find this notation easy to use, it is not necessary for them to see the graphical notation at all. If you wish, you may specify the model completely in natural language, making use of VEA's verbalization and reporting features to validate the model with the domain experts. How to do this is explained later in the book. For now, we content ourselves with a brief overview of conceptual modeling, using the Patient form example to illustrate some of the key ideas.

Besides its textual and graphical notations, ORM includes a design procedure to help you construct a conceptual model. An early step in this design procedure is to verbalize sample information in terms of elementary facts. For example, the form shown in Figure 2–1(b) contains five facts, which might be verbalized as follows:

> The Patient with patient number 1026 has the PatientName 'Bill McMurphy.'
> The Patient with patient number 1026 was born in the Country with code 'CA.'
> The Patient with patient number 1026 resides in the Country with code 'CA.'
> The Country with code 'CA' has the CountryName 'Canada.'
> The Country with code 'US' has the CountryName 'United States.'

This verbalization indicates that there are two *entity types* (Patient and Country) identified respectively by a number and code, and two *value types* (PatientName and CountryName). Unlike entities, values (e.g., character strings) are lexical in nature, so they identify themselves. In ORM, the term "object" is used for either an entity or value. The *reference schemes* for the four *object types* may be summarized thus:

> Patient(Nr); Country(Code); PatientName(); CountryName()

By removing the specific values from the five fact instances, we see that there are four *fact types* (kinds of fact):

> Patient has PatientName.
> Patient was born in Country.
> Patient resides in Country.
> Country has CountryName.

Fact types are comprised of object types, such as Patient and Country, and logical *predicates,* such as "was born in." The following *constraints* apply to these fact types:

Each Patient has **exactly one** PatientName.
Each patient was born in **at most one** Country.
Each Patient resides in **at most one** Country.
Each Country has **exactly one** CountryName.
Each CountryName refers to **at most one** Country.

This completes the specification of the conceptual schema. The next chapter shows you how to enter a schema like this into the VEA tool, and forward engineer it to a relational database.

If desired, you may display an ORM schema in graphical form, as shown in Figure 2–4. Here entity types are displayed as named ellipses, with their reference schemes in parenthesis. Value types are displayed as dotted ellipses. Each part played in a predicate is called a *role* and is displayed as a role-box. Predicates are displayed as a named sequence of roles, with each role linked to the object type that plays it.

A large dot attached to a role link indicates that the role is *mandatory*. For example, each patient and each country must have a name. For each fact type, a sample population of fact instances may be provided, with a column in the table for each role. An arrow-tipped bar besides a role is a *uniqueness* constraint, indicating that entries in the role's associated fact column are unique.

For example, Figure 2–5 includes sample fact populations for two of the fact types. Entries in the resident patient column are unique, in accordance with the uniqueness constraint for its role (each patient resides in only one country). The resident country column includes a duplicate entries for "US," demonstrating the lack of a uniqueness constraint (the same country may have more than one resident). The column entries for the country code-name fact type are both unique, indicating clearly the 1:1 nature of this relationship. Examples like this are very handy for validating constraints with domain experts. Chapter 4 explains how to add such examples to your models.

If you are familiar with ER, but not with ORM, you might find some of this discussion rather strange. For example, ORM makes no use of attributes, instead expressing all facts as relationships. This is quite deliberate, and has many advantages. For example, ORM models (and queries based on them) are more stable, because they are immune to changes that reshape attributes into entity types or relationships. Moreover, all facts and rules can be verbalized directly in sentences, and the role-based framework simplifies the expression of many constraints.

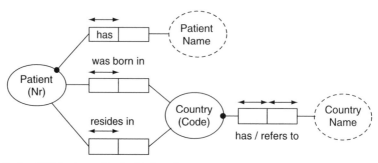

Figure 2–4   ORM schema for the Patient form.

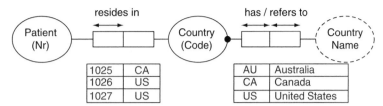

Figure 2–5 Two ORM fact types, with sample populations.

Although ORM models tend to consume more space than ER models, they typically reveal more semantics, and you can use VEA to automatically transform ORM models to compact, attribute-based models for relational implementation. For example, you can use VEA to map the ORM schema in Figure 2–4 to the relational schema shown in Figure 2–3. This forward engineering process is introduced in Chapter 3, and explained in detail in Chapter 7.

2.4 The Database Life Cycle

VEA's database modeling functions can help both individual database users and large corporate development teams. Individual database users do their own business analysis and database modeling. In a complex business environment many people with a wide range of skills are needed. However, the basic database modeling principles are the same for all environments. In a complex business environment, numerous people may work to define, apply and manage computer systems to meet business needs for efficiency and effectiveness. Tasks such as hardware selection, network management, and budgeting form part of the information systems life cycle.

The database life cycle is a core component of the information systems life cycle. The purpose of the database life cycle is to define database requirements and to manage database solutions to support the information system life cycle objectives. Tasks include managing data, and selecting and managing database products such as database server hardware and RDBMS software.

The database life cycle includes two main components: technology, and data. Computer systems proliferation and low cost desktop systems have created a wide awareness of computer technology. However, data itself is less tangible and is often harder to understand and manage.

The following paragraphs outline the phases in the database life cycle depicted in Figure 2–6. Each phase occurs within the context of the previous phase. The two-way arrows indicate that iteration takes place between adjacent phases. For example, in phase 4, a performance designer defines the physical model in collaboration with the database designer of phase 3. The names such as "business analyst" shown in Figure 2–6 reflect roles and skill sets rather than job titles. It is possible that the same person may perform many of these roles.

The arrows between each box represent transformations that change the appearance of the model whilst retaining its meaning. Ideally, the transformations are reversible.

Figure 2–6   Database Life Cycle.

For example you can transform a conceptual model into a logical model and back again without losing semantic information. You can transform a logical model into a physical database structure and back again without losing semantic information.

Phase 1: Define Business Needs

The first phase in the database life cycle defines the desired business results, project feasibility and business performance metrics. Phase 1 provides answers to business questions such as: Why should we build this database? Can this database be built in time to meet the business need? What is the scope of this database? The output is a set of business targets and a development plan.

Phase 2: Define Database Requirements

The second phase defines the scope of the database in terms of a conceptual information model. The business analyst defines a conceptual model in collaboration with domain experts. Phase 2 answers questions such as: What are the facts in the application domain? What things does the application seek to manage? What business rules apply to these things? The output of phase 2 is a transformable conceptual model.

Phase 3: Design Logical Model

During the third phase, you design a logical model that shows tables, columns and relationships. The database designer defines the table structure in collaboration with the business analyst. Phase 3 answers questions such as: What logical schema accurately represents the facts in the application domain? Ideally, the output is a fully normalized logical model.

Phase 4: Design and Build Physical Model

The fourth phase designs and builds a physical database for a specific DBMS in a specific technical environment to meet specific performance criteria. The database performance designer defines the physical database model in collaboration with the database analyst. Phase 4 answers questions such as: What information is needed to create a physical database that meets specific update transaction and query load requirements? What are the key update transactions and queries that require high performance? What performance will be achieved by a specific database product on a specific hardware platform? The output is a physical model adapted to meet the desired business performance using a specified technical solution.

Database performance tuning requires a thorough understanding of the technical characteristics of a specific set of products. A database performance specialist must keep up to date with product changes and maintain an awareness of the complex and changing interactions within a specific technical configuration. Database performance tuning optimizes the interaction between technical components such as the RDBMS product, the computer operating system and the systems hardware.

Phase 5: Maintain Database

This phase covers the post-implementation tasks that are usually done by the database administrator (DBA). For example, a change to a business rule is a semantic change and requires a corresponding change to conceptual, logical, and physical models. However, a change to performance requirements or technology requires changes to the physical model only. A well-designed relational database enjoys the property of data independence, which enables you to change database technology without changing your conceptual or logical models. Data independence protects investment in database application programs and reduces the cost of change.

The rest of this book is focused on the use of VEA to design databases at conceptual, logical, and physical levels. Chapter 17 includes some pragmatic advice on best practices. A useful coverage of database administration procedures and practices may be found in Mullins (2002).

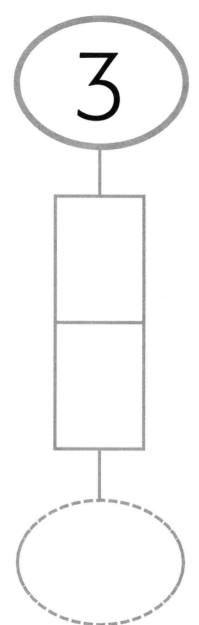

Getting Started

3.1   Product Editions and Versions

Microsoft Visio is available in three different editions: Visio Standard, Visio Professional, and *Visio for Enterprise Architects (VEA)*. Visio Standard is a powerful, general-purpose drawing tool. Visio Professional includes all the functionality of Visio standard and adds a logical database solution for working with databases, as well as a Unified Modeling Language (UML) solution for working with object-oriented software.

Although Visio Professional allows you to create new logical database models and reverse engineer existing databases to logical database models, it does not allow you to forward engineer logical database models to physical database schemas. The UML solution in Visio Professional supports UML diagramming and reverse engineering of program code to class diagrams but does not support forward engineering to code from class diagrams.

Visio for Enterprise Architects includes all the functionality of Visio Professional, as well as much more extensive modeling capabilities for both databases and software. On the database modeling side, it supports both forward and reverse engineering, conceptual data modeling using Object-Role Modeling (ORM), model error checking, database model reports, and model-database synchronization. On the software modeling side, it adds support for forward engineering from class diagrams to code skeletons, model error checking, and model report generation.

Although the standard and professional editions of Visio may be purchased as individual products, Visio for Enterprise Architects is currently available only as a component of *Visual Studio .NET Enterprise Architect*. Visual Studio is available in a number of editions (Academic, Professional, Enterprise Developer, and Enterprise Architect), but only the Enterprise Architect edition contains VEA.

The Visual Studio .NET products first became available in January 2002. Visio for Enterprise Architects 2002 SR-1, the first service release for VEA, became available in April 2002. As well as including updates for its underlying Visio Professional 2002, this service release included bug fixes for VEA's database and software modeling solutions.

Visual Studio .NET 2003, the second major release of Visual Studio .NET, has been announced to ship on April 24, 2003, so should be available by the time this book is printed. The tool discussion in this book is based on the VEA version contained in the final beta of the Enterprise Architect edition of Visual Studio .NET 2003, which was released in November, 2002, under the code name "Everett." This version of VEA included several important bug fixes.

To improve productivity, you should ensure that your version of Visio for Enterprise Architects is at least as recent as that contained in the Enterprise Architect edition of Visual Studio .NET 2003.

3.2   Installation

Before installing the product, ensure that your system meets the following minimum configuration: 600 MHz Pentium-III, 256 MB RAM, 750 MB free space on system drive, 2.5 GB free space on installation drive, recent operating system (Windows 2000,

Windows XP or Windows .NET Server), a CD-ROM or DVD-ROM drive, video resolution of at least 800×600, and a mouse or pointing device.

You may get by with a less powerful system, but if you intend to use the full power
of the Visual Studio package (not just the Visio component), you'll appreciate the added
performance provided by a powerful PC. The most recent requirements and installation
details may be accessed in the Visual Studio ReadMe file, or online at
http://go.microsoft.com/fwlink/?LinkId=8661.

To install VEA, you first have to install Visual Studio .NET Enterprise Architect. On
inserting the first CD or DVD, the auto-install process starts and the setup screen shown
in Figure 3–1 appears. If you wish to view the ReadMe file now, click on the View
ReadMe option.

Follow the instructions in the Install Wizard to complete the installation of Visual
Studio. This process typically takes at least two hours, even on a well-configured computer. By default, this installation *does not* install Visio for Enterprise Architects.

Figure 3–1   The opening screen for the Visual Studio installation process.

Figure 3-2   The opening screen of the Visio installation process.

Although not strictly required, it is recommended that you uninstall any previous version of Visio before installing VEA. To uninstall a previous Visio version, choose Start > Control Panel > Add or Remove Programs, select the Visio program from the list of installed program, press the Change/Remove button and complete the uninstall process.

Figure 3-3   Choosing either the default or a custom installation.

Figure 3–4   The final dialog for Visio installation.

Assuming you have installed Visual Studio for Enterprise Architects, you may now begin the Visio installation by inserting the CD or DVD with Visio for Enterprise Architects in its label. The auto-install process starts, and the Visio setup welcome screen appears, as shown in Figure 3–2. Edit the user name and organization fields as needed to match your personal details, then press the Next button to display the End User License dialog. If you accept the license terms, ensure the check box is checked, then press the Next button to display the installation dialog shown in Figure 3–3.

Unless you want to customize the installation in some special way, choose the default installation by pressing the Install Now! Button. If you instead press the Customize button, you can change the location for installing the software, and you can specify which features are to be installed. In either case, the installation process should then continue without further input to successful completion, as reported by the dialog shown in Figure 3–4. Press OK to complete the installation.

3.3   The Visio Interface

Once Visio is installed, you can run it from the desktop by choosing Start > All Programs > Microsoft Visio. If a Visio icon appears on your desktop, you can also run Visio by double-clicking this icon. If you wish to run Visio on an existing Visio document file, you can do so by double-clicking that .vsd file in the Explorer directory.

The first time Visio runs, it takes a while to update its directory cache before you can use it. This delay does not occur in subsequent runs. On running Visio for the first time, the opening screen appears as shown Figure 3–5.

When you select the Database category from the category list shown in Figure 3–5 you will see a window with five icons similar to that shown in Figure 3–6. The Express-G and ORM Diagram templates are standard Visio stencils and are also included in Microsoft Visio 2003 Professional. These templates can only be used for drawing diagrams so they are not further discussed in this book. The remaining three options are for database modeling, and form the main subject of this book.

Let's take a tour of Figure 3–6. On the left hand side, you will see the category list of Visio's non-database solutions that were summarized in section 1–3. When you design databases, you will use the database category exclusively so the other category options are not further discussed here. Beneath the category list you will see the tool tip that appears when you hover your mouse over one of the five menu icons.

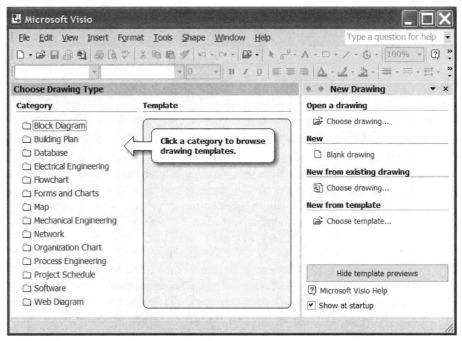

Figure 3–5   Visio's opening screen.

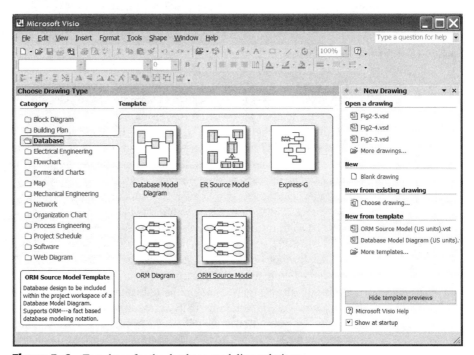

Figure 3–6   Templates for the database modeling solutions.

Along the top of the window you can see several toolbars. You can display the toolbar menu shown in Figure 3–7 by right clicking anywhere in the gray area at the top of the main window. You use the toolbar menu to set your working toolbar defaults.
In Figure 3–7 you can see the effect of selecting the toolbars for Standard and Formatting. You can easily view or hide a toolbar by clicking on its checkbox.

You can customize the toolbars by changing the buttons displayed on each toolbar or by adding a new toolbar and customizing that.

To customize a toolbar, click on Customize at the bottom of the menu shown in Figure 3–7 to reveal the toolbar customization dialog box shown in Figure 3–8. The Toolbars tab shown in Figure 3–8 gives you the same options as the right click list shown in Figure 3–7.

Figure 3–7 Toolbar Menu.

Figure 3–8 Customizing Toolbars tab.

You can add a new toolbar by clicking on the New button shown in Figure 3–8 to reveal the new toolbar naming dialog box shown in Figure 3–9.

When you have typed in a name for your new toolbar, click OK and the new toolbar name will appear at the bottom of the list of toolbars as shown in Figure 3–8.

You can adapt each toolbar to your needs by using the controls on the Commands tab shown in Figure 3–10 to add or delete toolbar buttons.

You can use the Options tab shown in Figure 3–11 to further personalize your menus.

If you unexpectedly get a screen that looks like Figure 3–12, you have accidentally hidden the database task pane and you should click on View > Task Pane to return to the database menu shown in Figure 3–6. When you reveal the View menu you will also see a "Toolbars" option that takes you to the toolbars menu previously discussed (see Figure 3–7).

Let's continue our tour of the main menu (Figure 3–6). The righthand side of your screen should look something like Figure 3–13.

Look at the list of files under the heading "Open a drawing". The file at the top of the list is the image of Figure 3–6 whereas the two files below it are the ORM Source Model examples used in this book. This list shows all the recently opened Visio files regardless of whether they are database related files or not. This makes Visio very flexible because you can switch from one category to another just by clicking on a filename. This is one place where you benefit from investing in a meaningful file naming convention of your own.

Figure 3–9   Naming a new toolbar.

Figure 3–10   Customizing Commands tab.

Figure 3–11 Customizing Toolbars—Options tab.

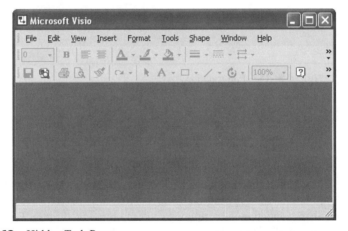

Figure 3–12 Hidden Task Pane.

If you do get lost here, you can close all your open files by repeatedly clicking on the black "×" in the top right hand corner of your screen and then start again by clicking on View > Task Pane. Be careful not to click on the red and white window exit button because that will instantly close Visio.

The "New" function opens the standard Visio drawing surface, which is useful if you need to make a quick Visio drawing to illustrate a point. The "New from Existing Drawing" function opens a file menu so you can select an existing file on which to base your next task. You can use the "New from Template" function to switch templates. If

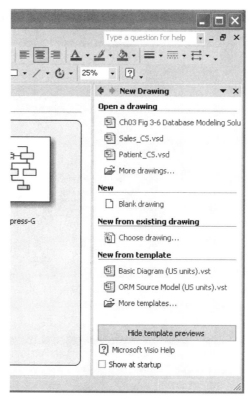

Figure 3–13   File functions.

you click the checkbox next to "Show at startup," then Visio will start in whatever template you had open when you checked the checkbox.

When you click on the small down arrow at the top of the right hand window you will see the menu shown in Figure 3–14.

Clicking on the "Search" button will change the right hand window to look like Figure 3–15. Clicking on "Search Tips" will reveal a Help window that explains the Search functions. To return to the main menu (Figure 3–6), just click on the "New Drawing" option as shown in Figure 3–14.

Let's now take a look at floating and docking windows. If you can access the sample model Patient_CS.vsd, open it now, and Visio will give you a display that looks something like Figure 3–16.

Here the screen displays a number of windows, including the ORM Source stencil, the Drawing window, and the Database Properties window. You can reposition any window by floating it. To *float a window,* right-click its title bar and choose Float Window from the context menu. Figure 3–16 shows the context menu for the ORM Source stencil.

You may now drag the window to another place on the screen. To *dock a window,* simply drag it to the edge of the screen where you want it. Figure 3–17 shows the ORM

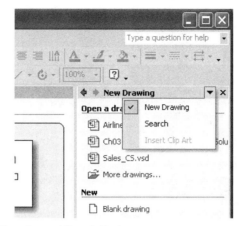

Figure 3–14   New Drawing and Search Options.

Figure 3–15   Search window.

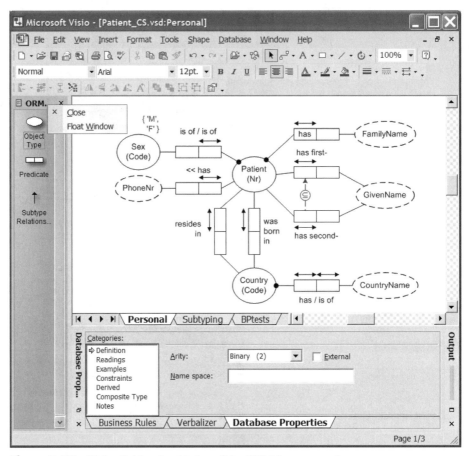

Figure 3–16   Right-clicking the title bar of the ORM Source stencil.

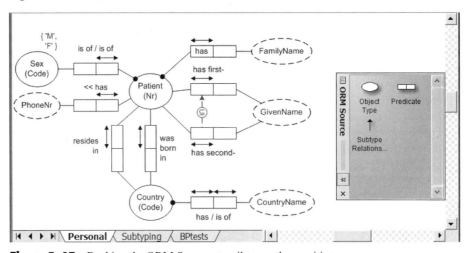

Figure 3–17   Docking the ORM Source stencil to another position.

Source stencil docked at the right of the screen. To save space here, only the Drawing and ORM Source stencil windows are displayed in the figure.

You may float and dock any window. If you are floating the Database Properties window, you may also dock it by right-clicking its title bar (on the left of its window) and choosing Dock Window from its context menu.

The Drawing window has horizontal and vertical scroll bars. To move the drawing within the window, move the scroll bars by clicking them with the mouse. If you have a wheel mouse, you may use the wheel to scroll up or down.

To change the *magnification* at which the drawing is displayed, choose the zoom level from the magnification drop-down list box in the Standard Toolbar. Figure 3–18 shows the magnification set to 200%. If the Standard Toolbar is not displayed, you can display it by choosing View > Toolbars from the main menu, and checking the Standard option. You can also zoom in on any area by holding the Ctrl and Shift keys down as you select the zoom region. To *pan and zoom* around any area, open the Pan & Zoom Window by choosing View > Pan & Zoom Window from the main menu. Then move this window to focus in on an area of interest, as shown in Figure 3–18.

3.4 Using Help

You can get lots of help from within Visio and from the Microsoft Office website. Figure 3–19 shows the result of typing "help" in the question box in the top right hand corner of your screen.

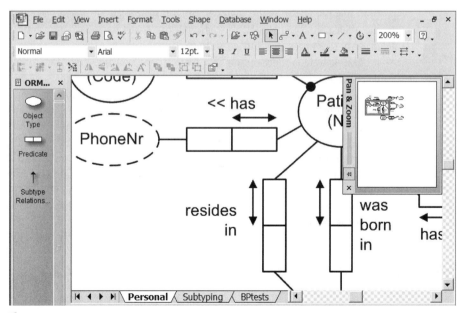

Figure 3–18 Panning and zooming.

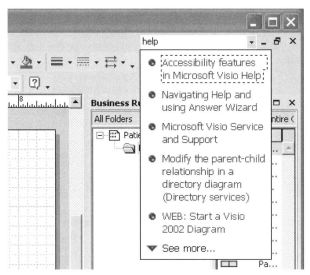

Figure 3–19   General Help.

If you click the small question mark shown in the top left hand area of Figure 3–19, you get the Visio specific help window. To show the Contents window, click the Show icon second from the left (which toggles it to a Hide icon). See Figure 3–20.

If you double click on Help on the main menu, you reveal the help menu shown in Figure 3–21. The Microsoft Visio Help option displays the help window shown in Figure 3–20. The Developer Reference is for those who want to program Visio's shapes. This option is not about database development. If you are connected to the internet, Visio on the Web takes you directly to Microsoft's Visio website. Office on the Web takes you directly to Microsoft's Office website.

The Activate Product option is a feature that you use when installing VEA. You can use Detect and Repair to automatically find and repair any errors in the Visio software. The About Microsoft Visio option shows version and license information.

A useful way to find help about the database modeling solution is by using the Answer Wizard tab that you can see on Figure 3–20. If you put "ORM" into the "What would you like to do" box and click on "Search," you will get a response similar to that shown in Figure 3–22. Have fun!

To activate Help at any time, you may also press the *F1 key*. This is especially handy when working within the database modeling solution, as the help displayed will often be context sensitive, displaying specific help related to the functional region where the cursor is currently positioned.

3.5   Pagination and Layers

When you view a large database model, it helps a lot to display different sub-areas of the model on different pages. If you look back at Figure 3–17, you'll see that the

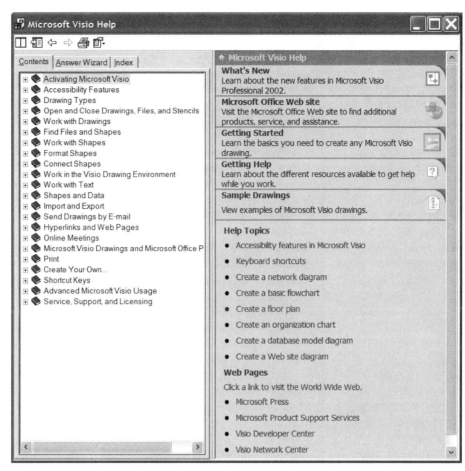

Figure 3–20   The Visio Help window.

Figure 3–21   Main menu help.

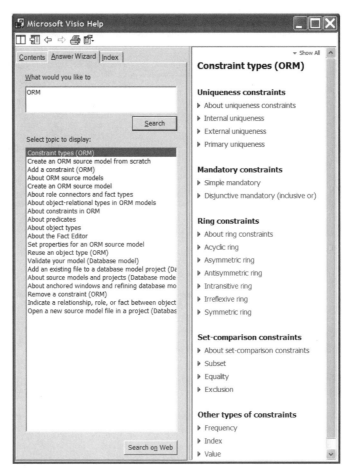

Figure 3–22   ORM help.

sample model Patient_CS.vsd is divided into three pages: Personal, Subtyping, and BPtests.

You can *add a new page* at any time using the Insert > New Page command on the main menu. To *rename a page,* simply right-click the relevant page tab at the bottom of the drawing window, choose the Rename Page option from the context menu, and enter the new name.

When you *print* the pages of your model, the page names are not included automatically. However you can print page names as well as other useful information by using *page headers and footers*. To add a header or footer to each page in your database model, choose View > Header and Footer from the main menu. This opens the Header and Footer dialog shown in Figure 3–23.

For the Left, Center, or Right regions of the header or footer, enter any text that you want to include in that region. Click the arrow to the right of the box, and then choose

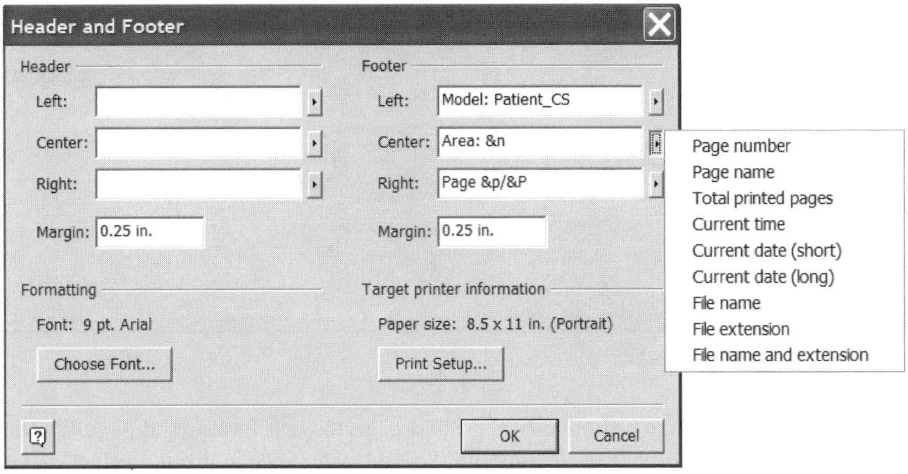

Figure 3–23   Adding a header or footer to pages for printing.

any tool-provided information that you want to include. For example, Figure 3–23 shows the footer entries for the Patient_CS model, including the pop-up menu options for adding details to the center area of the footer.

The left region of the footer contains the user text "Model: Patient_CS". The central region contains the user text "Area:", and the Page Name option has been selected to follow that text. The tool encodes the page name entry as the "&n" parameter. The right region of the footer includes the user text "Page" followed by the Page number (&p), then a slash "/", and then the Total printed pages (&P). For example, when printed, the first page of the Patient_CS model will include the following information in the footer: Model: Patient_CS, Area: Personal, Page 1/3. You can preview how the pages will look by clicking the Print Preview icon in the Standard Toolbar.

For Margin, type a value to specify how far the header or footer prints from the top or bottom of the page. To change the typeface, size, color, or other aspects of the header or footer font, press the Choose Font button and then make your choices.

You can add special *fields* to your drawings. To add a field you must first select the shape to which you want to add the field. Not all shapes allow you to add fields. You can always add a field to a text box created with the Text Tool from the Standard Toolbar.

Select the relevant shape, such as a text box, then select Insert > Field from the main menu to reveal the Field Dialog shown in Figure 3–24. Choose the relevant category from the Category list (e.g., Date/Time). In the Field list, select the field you want to add. (e.g., Print Date). In the Format list, click on the format you want to use. When you click OK, the field will appear on your drawing.

Each Visio drawing contains at least one foreground page and may also contain one or more *background pages*. You use a background when you want the same shape such as a project name or company logo, to appear on more than one drawing page. The background element appears on each page to which you assign the background. You

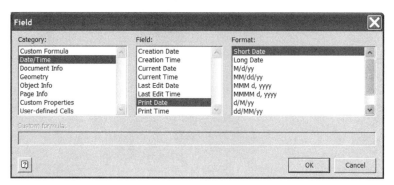

Figure 3–24   Field dialog.

can assign only one background page to each foreground page, but each background can also have a background, so you can create a layered effect. When you assign a background to a foreground page, the shapes on the background are visible when you display the foreground page, but you cannot edit them from the foreground page. To set background pages, choose File > Page Setup > Page Properties from the main menu.

If you want to selectively view, edit, print, or lock shapes in a drawing, or to have several layers of text and shapes within the same page, you should use *layers* instead of a background. You use layers to organize related diagrams and parts of diagrams. A layer is a named category of shapes. By assigning shapes to different layers, you can selectively view, print, color, and lock the different shape categories. You can also snap and glue a shape to a layer. You can assign a shape to multiple layers or to no layers at all. Every page in a drawing can have a different set of layers. Some shapes are already assigned to layers. When you drop a shape on a page, the corresponding layer is added to the page. To use layers, choose View > Layer Properties from the main menu.

You can use layers to present a database model layer by layer. The top layer can reveal just a few main ORM objects or tables, and each successive layer can be used to reveal extra detail. This gives you a very powerful way to present complex database models. You can introduce your audience to the main ideas on the top layer and then gradually drill down to the layers that reveal the details. As with most other topics, the Visio Help has lots of information about layers. As discussed in section 5.10, the ORM Source Model solution places different kinds of constraints on different layers, so you can hide or display them at will.

3.6   Simple Examples of Forward Engineering

In this section, you'll learn how to create a simple ORM model and map it to a relational database model. You'll also see how to create the relational model directly, without using ORM. Finally you'll see how to automatically generate the Data Definition Language (DDL) code for the physical database schema.

The main purpose of this section is to give you a quick overview of how the tool supports database modeling at various levels. To derive maximum benefit from this section, you should work through the examples using the Visio tool. In following the steps outlined, you'll be introduced to various components of the user interface. These will be covered in detail in later chapters. For now, just try to understand the main ideas being illustrated by these examples.

The examples in this section are based on a simple fragment of an application domain that deals with medical patients. Suppose that you need to build a database to store facts that can be entered via a simple patient form, two instances of which are shown in Figure 3–25. How would you do this using the Visio tool?

Creating a Simple ORM Model

To create a formal model of data, you must understand, at least informally, the semantics or meaning of the data. To facilitate this move from data to information, the ORM approach suggests verbalizing the information in terms of elementary facts. The facts on form (a) of Figure 3–25 might be expressed informally as "Patient 1025 is named Ann Jones, smokes and is allergic to penicillin and codeine". To ensure that objects are well-identified, and the facts are all elementary, this may be restated as the following four facts:

> The Patient with patient number '1025' has the PatientName 'Ann Jones'.
> The Patient with patient number '1025' smokes.
> The Patient with patient number '1025' is allergic to the Drug named 'Penicillin'.
> The Patient with patient number '1025' is allergic to the Drug named 'Codeine'.

Similarly, the following single fact is captured on form (b) of Figure 3–25.

> The Patient with patient number '1056' has the PatientName 'John B. Smith'.

You might argue that form (b) also tells us that patient 1025 doesn't smoke and doesn't have any allergies. Well, there's no need to store that information explicitly in the database, because we typically assume that if a fact is not included in, or derivable from, the database then it's false—this is called the closed world assumption.

The actual entries ("1025", "Ann Jones" etc.) on the form fields are called *values,* and are typically numbers or character strings. Values are often used to refer to other

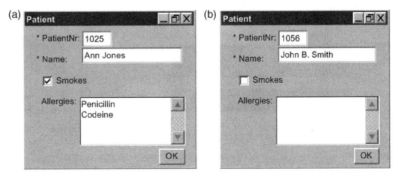

Figure 3–25   Two patient record forms.

things called *entities*. For example, the value "1025" is used here to identify a patient, or entity instance. In this example, the two different patients have different names ("Ann Jones" and "John B. Smith"), but in general two patients might have the same name, so we use patient numbers instead to identify them.

A set of all possible instances of a given kind is said to be a type. The set of all possible patient names is a *value type*. Let's call this "PatientName". The set of all possible patients is an *entity type*. Let's call this "Patient". Similarly the set of all possible drugs is an entity type. Let's call this "Drug". In ORM, values and entities are treated as objects, so value types and entity types are *object types*.

> *Note:* In languages like English that distinguish between singular and plural, it's good form to always use a singular term for an object type (e.g., "Patient" rather than "Patients").

When an entity can be identified using a single value, the manner or mode in which the value refers to the entity is said to be a reference mode. For example, "1025" refers to a patient by being a number for it, and "Penicillin" refers to a drug by being a name for it. Simple reference schemes may depicted by placing the reference mode in parentheses after the entity type name. The reference mode "number" is often abbreviated to "nr" or "Nr". For example, the entity types and reference schemes in our application may be set out as shown below:

Patient(Nr)
Drug(Name)

Because values refer to themselves, they are self-identifying, so do not have a reference scheme. This may be shown by placing empty parentheses after the value type. For example, the PatientName value type may be declared thus:

PatientName()

Collectively, the two forms in Figure 3–25 contain five fact instances. Assuming the reference schemes above are declared, these facts may be set out more concisely thus:

Patient '1025' has PatientName 'Ann Jones'.
Patient '1025' smokes.
Patient '1025' is allergic to Drug 'Penicillin'.
Patient '1025' is allergic to Drug 'Codeine'.
Patient '1056' has PatientName 'John B. Smith'.

By removing the instance values, you can see that there are just three kinds of facts involved. These *fact types* may be set out thus:

Patient has PatientName.
Patient smokes.
Patient is allergic to Drug.

Removing the object types from these sentence types leaves the predicates. As in logic, a predicate is just a declarative sentence with the object terms removed. An ellipsis "..." may be used as a placeholder for the object term. So the predicates for the above fact types are:

... has ...
... smokes ...
... is allergic to ...

The number of object-holes in the predicate is the *arity* of the predicate. The ... has ... and ... is allergic to ... predicates are *binary predicates* because they have two object holes. The smokes predicate is a *unary* predicate, because it has just one object hole. If a binary predicate is infix (its placeholders are at its ends), then the ellipsis symbols may be omitted. For example, the predicate has is implicitly the same as ... has ....

To complete the model, you need to add any relevant constraints on the fact types. For this application, the relevant constraints may be expressed formally in ORM thus:

Each Patient has exactly one PatientName.
It is possible that the same Patient is allergic to more than one Drug and that more than one
    Patient is allergic to the same Drug.

The set of sentences listing the reference schemes, fact types and constraints is an ORM schema, expressed in textual form. An ORM schema may also be depicted in graphical form. The following steps show one way to create the sample ORM schema in Visio for Enterprise Architects.

1. Run Visio (e.g., Start > All Programs > Microsoft Visio).
2. Open the ORM Source Model template (File New Database ORM Source Model).

    When you select the ORM Source Model template, a screen like Figure 3–26 appears. In addition to the menus and icons at the top, there is an ORM stencil, a Drawing window, and an area for displaying the Business Rules editor, and other windows you might open (e.g., Verbalizer). To reduce the space consumed by Figure 3–26, the display has been resized.

Note: Normally the drawing window occupies most of the screen. By default, the three shapes in the ORM stencil appear on the same horizontal row. You can give the drawing window more room by reducing the width of the ORM stencil so that the shapes line up vertically, as shown here. To do this, hover the cursor on the border between the stencil and the drawing window until the cursor changes to a resize cursor, then drag it to the left.

Further space for the drawing window has been reclaimed by turning off Rulers. For tidiness, grid lines have been suppressed. To control view aspects like this, open the View menu and toggle the relevant menu options.

You can add sentence types to an ORM model by dragging Object Type and Predicate shapes from the stencil to the drawing window. Alternatively you can add sentence types using the Fact Editor. For now, let's use the *Business Rules* editor to do this.

3. Move the cursor to the bottom row displayed in the Fact Types pane of the Business Rules window (in our example, there is only one row).

   The Fact Types pane now prompts you to start typing the new fact type. It also displays a New... button at the right, as an alternative way to start entering a new fact type. See Figure 3–27.

4. Press the New... button.

   This causes the Fact Editor to appear. By default, the fact editor's input style is Guided, which is easier for occasional users. The Freeform input style is

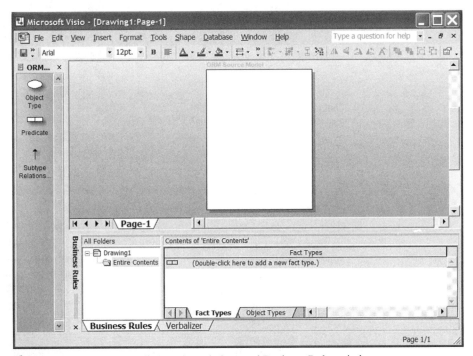

Figure 3–26   ORM stencil, Drawing window, and Business Rules window.

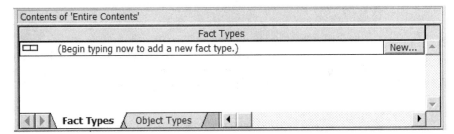

Figure 3–27   To enter a new fact type, press the New... button (or just type the fact type).

faster for experienced users. Let's be daring, and change the input style to Freeform.

5. Set the radio button for Input Style to Freeform, as shown in Figure 3–28.

The freeform setting allows you to enter fact types faster by using a formal syntax that can be parsed by the fact editor. If you choose Capitalized mode (the default), you must name each object type with a single word, starting with a capital letter, e.g., PatientName. If you want to start with a lower case letter, or embed spaces in the name, you must choose bracketed mode, e.g., [Patient Name].

Reference modes may be declared in parentheses after the entity type name, e.g. Patient(Nr). Value types are declared by appending empty parentheses, e.g. PatientName(). The rest of the sentence is parsed as the predicate.

6. Type the fact type Patient(Nr) has PatientName(), and select the Constraints tab.

This opens the Constraints pane, which allows you to enter constraints on that fact type. Constraint Question #1 prompts you to select one of four alternatives from a drop-down list box.

7. Select the Exactly One option, as shown in Figure 3–29.

The phrase "Exactly one" is short for "at least one and at most one", so this choice actually adds two constraints, which are automatically verbalized at the bottom. The default setting for Constraint Question #2 is correct, so leave it as is. The next chapter explains how to improve the wording of Constraint Question #2 by providing an inverse reading for the fact type, e.g., PatientName is of Patient.

8. Press the Apply button.

This enters the fact type and its constraints into the model, and prompts you for a new fact type starting with Patient. Once you have chosen a reference scheme for an entity type, you don't need to repeat the reference scheme when specifying subsequent fact types.

9. Complete the fact type Patient smokes, and press the Apply button.

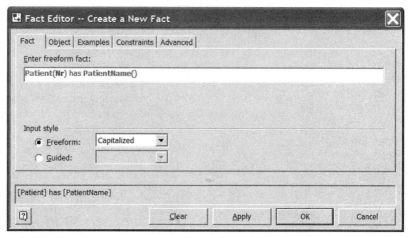

Figure 3–28 Entering a fact type in the Fact Editor using Freeform input style.

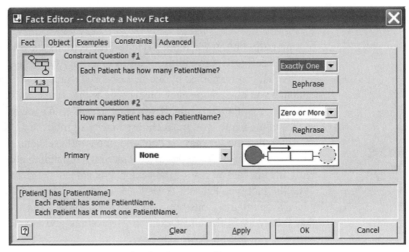

Figure 3–29   Adding constraints in the Fact Editor.

This enters the unary fact type into the model, and prompts you for a new fact type starting with Patient.

10. Complete the fact type Patient is allergic to Drug(Name), and select the Constraints tab. Now select the Zero or More option for Constraint Question #1, and press the OK button.

This enters the fact type and its constraint into the model, and closes the Fact Editor. The three fact types you entered do not yet appear on the drawing window, but they are now displayed in the Business Rules window.

11. Select the three fact types by placing the cursor on the first fact type, holding the Shift key down, and moving the cursor to the last fact type.

The first fact type is included in the selection even though it is not highlighted with the others (see Figure 3–30).

12. Now drag the fact types onto the drawing page where you want them displayed.

The model now appears in graphical format. You can finesse the display by moving the predicate text and object types around as shown in Figure 3–31. Entity types are shown as named, solid ellipses, with their reference mode in parentheses. Value types are shown as named, dashed ellipses.

Each predicate is shown as a named sequence of role-boxes. In ORM, a *role* is simply a part played in a relationship (which may be unary, binary or longer). Each role is connected by a line to the object type that plays it. If the role is *mandatory* for the object type, a black dot is added; otherwise the role is optional. For example, each patient must have a name, but needn't smoke or have allergies.

The arrow-tipped bars over predicates depict *uniqueness constraints*. The uniqueness constraint over the first role of Patient has PatientName, indicates that if you populate this fact type with a set of fact instances, each patient number occurs there at most once. So each patient has at most one patient name.

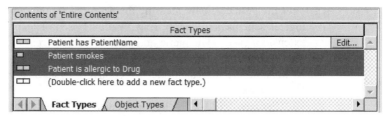

Figure 3–30 Selecting the fact types to drag onto the drawing window.

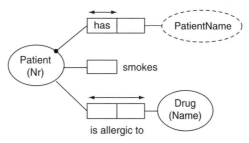

Figure 3–31 Graphical ORM model for the sample application.

The spanning uniqueness constraint on the allergy fact type indicates that only the patient-drug combination need be unique. So a patient may be allergic to many drugs, and vice versa. ORM uses mandatory and uniqueness constraints instead of cardinality or multiplicity constraints, because this facilitates constraint validation by sample populations, and also scales properly to associations with three or more roles.

13. To *save your model*, choose File > Save from the File menu, or click the Save (diskette) icon. This opens the Save-As dialog box. Choose the folder where you want to save the model, add a filename for the conceptual schema (e.g., Patient1_CS), press the Save button in the dialog, then press OK in the properties dialog. The file will be saved with the extension ".vsd" (Visio document).

Building a Logical Database Model from ORM

To transform an ORM model to a logical database model, you first add the ORM model to a database model project, and then build the logical model. Here's one way to do this for the ORM source model created earlier.

1. From the File menu, open the logical modeling solution by choosing File > New > Database > Database Model Diagram.
2. To create a *database model project*, choose Database > Project > Add existing document from the Database menu.
3. An Add Document to Project dialog box should now appear. Use the Look in: field to navigate to your saved ORM model, then press the Open button. The ORM model should now be listed in the project window.

4. Save the project file by pressing the Save icon on the main menu, and giving the logical schema a filename (e.g., Patient1_LS). The project file also has the extension ".vsd". The name and page of your current model is always listed in the title bar at the top of the screen.

5. Now *build* the logical model by choosing Database > Project > Build from the Database menu.

VEA now builds the relational database schema automatically. The Output window records the progress of the build process. If the build fails, you will see error messages in the Output window. If the build succeeds, the resulting table schemes appear in the Tables and Views window at the left of the screen. By default, so long as the ORM model is correct, the build process generates a relational schema in fifth normal form.

Figure 3–32 shows roughly what the screen should look like at this stage. For a compact, tidy screenshot, some windows have been resized, and the ruler and grid display have been suppressed (using View menu toggles)—there is no need for you to do this. Although the table structures have been created, they do not yet appear on a diagram. To see the logical database model in graphical form, you need to drag the table schemes onto the drawing page shown at the right of the project window. This is the next step.

6. To select the two table schemes, mouse-click the first table scheme, hold the Shift key down, and click the second table scheme. Now drag the schema onto the drawing page by holding the mouse's left button down as you move the cursor to the drawing page. The result is shown in Figure 3–33.

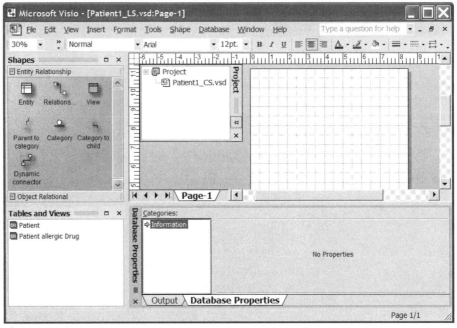

Figure 3–32   Building a logical database model from an ORM source model.

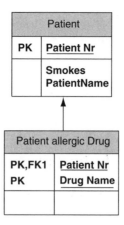

Figure 3–33   The logical schema built from the ORM schema.

There are two table schemes, with one foreign key connection between them. Each table has its name in the shaded header, with its columns listed below. Primary keys are underlined, marked "PK" and appear in the top compartment for the columns. Mandatory (not null) columns are in bold. Foreign key columns are marked FK*n* where *n* is the number of the foreign key with a table. In this case we have only one foreign key that targets the primary key of the Patient table. The foreign key connection itself is depicted as an arrow from the foreign key table to the target table.

In this example, the names of the tables, as well as the names and data types of the columns, are those that are generated automatically by default. Various options exist to control how table and column names are generated. In practice it's best to set the data types on the ORM model, where object types correspond to conceptual domains. The correct data types then automatically propagate to all the attributes based on these domains. A detailed coverage of such issues is provided in later chapters.

Creating a Logical Database Model Directly

Instead of deriving a logical database model from an ORM model, you can create the logical model directly using the Database Model Diagram template. For example, to create the relational model displayed in Figure 3–33, proceed as follows.

1. From the File menu, open the logical modeling solution by choosing File > New > Database > Database Model Diagram.

   The screen should now look similar to Figure 3–34. For a compact, tidy screenshot, some windows have been resized, and the ruler and grid display have been suppressed (using View menu toggles)—there is no need for you to do this.

   The *Entity Relationship stencil* to the left of the screen is used to construct a relational database schema. This stencil has seven shapes. If you hover the cursor over a shape, a Screen Tip appears to explain its purpose. Only the first two of these shapes are needed to construct the sample database model.

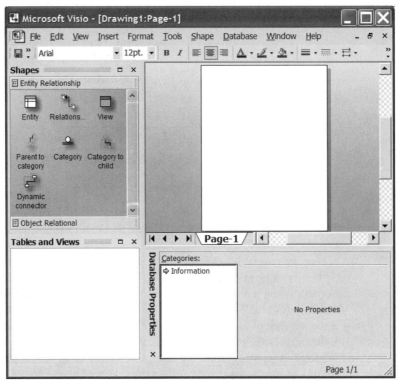

Figure 3–34   The Database Modeling Diagram template.

The *Entity shape* depicts a relational database table structure. This structure is technically called a table scheme, to distinguish it from an actual table, which includes a set of data rows. From now on however, we will often refer to a table scheme informally as a table.

The *Relationship shape* is used to establish a connection from a foreign key in one table to the column(s) that it references (typically a primary key in another table).

2. Select the Entity shape and drag it onto the drawing window. This creates a local instance of the shape, and names it Table 1.

When a table shape is selected, its *Database Properties window* is also displayed. You can use this to set all the properties of the table. In the Categories section, an arrow to the left indicates which category is currently selected for editing.

3. Check that the Definition Category is selected. Now edit the Table 1 entry in the Physical name field to rename the table as "Patient". This change is immediately applied to the shape in the drawing window, as shown in Figure 3–35.

4. Select the Columns category to bring up the properties pane to edit columns. In the Physical Name field enter the column name "patientNr". Leave the default data type unchanged. Check the Required check box to declare the column not null, and then check the PK check box to declare it a primary key column.

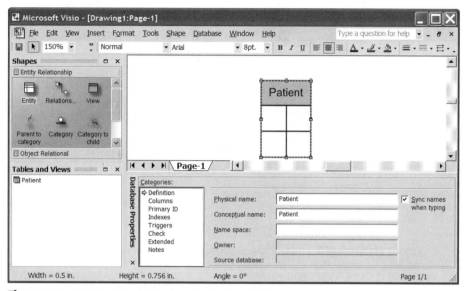

Figure 3–35   Using the Entity shape to declare a table scheme.

On the drawing surface, the primary key column is now displayed in the top compartment of the table shape, and marked "PK". The column name appears in bold type, indicating that it is a mandatory column.

5. Move the cursor to the second row, add the column name "patientName", and check the Required box.

The second column now appears on the table shape, below the primary key line.

6. Move the cursor to the third row, add the column name "smokes", and check the Required box.

The third column now appears on the table shape, below the primary key line. The table shape and properties sheet should now appear roughly as in Figure 3–36. In practice, you would normally make some changes to data types, but we'll postpone discussion of that till a later chapter.

7. Drag another instance of the Entity shape to the drawing window, edit its Definition category to rename the table as "Allergy", and then edit its Columns category to add the columns named "patientNr" and "drugName", and check both of these to be Required, PK columns. The drawing window should now show two table shapes as shown in Figure 3–37.

All that remains is to add the foreign key connection between the tables. Declaring the Allergy.patientNr column to be a foreign key referencing the Patient.patientNr column ensures that each patient for which an allergy is recorded is also recorded in the Patient table. From an ORM perspective, this is just a way to implement the mandatory constraint that patients have their names recorded.

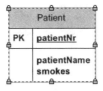

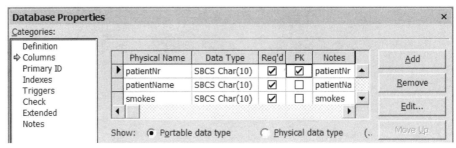

Figure 3–36   Adding column details to the Patient table.

Patient	
PK	patientNr
	patientName smokes

Allergy	
PK	patientNr
PK	drugName

Figure 3–37   The two table schemes are now defined.

8. Drag an instance of the Relationships shape in the Entity relationship stencil onto the drawing window. Move the end with no arrow-tip into the middle of the Allergy table, until the table is highlighted in red, and a red rectangle appears on the line end where it attaches to the table. This indicates that the line end is glued to the table shape.

9. Move the arrow-tip end into the middle of the Patient table, until the table is highlighted in red, and a red rectangle appears on the arrow tip indicating it is glued to the table shape. The foreign key connection should now be displayed by a connecting arrow as in Figure 3–38. The foreign key column Allergy.patientNr is marked FK1.

10. To *save your model*, choose File > Save from the File menu, or click the Save (diskette) icon. This opens the Save-As dialog box. Choose the folder where you want to save the model, add a filename for the logical schema (e.g. Patient2_LS), press the Save button in the dialog, then press OK in the properties dialog. The file will be saved with the extension ".vsd" (Visio document).

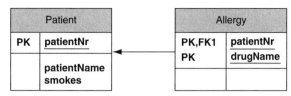

Figure 3–38   The foreign key reference is now displayed.

Generating a Physical Database Schema

Regardless of whether you created a logical database model directly, or derived it from an ORM model, you can use that logical model to generate the physical database schema for a target DBMS. Generation gives you the option to generate the DDL script instead of having the tool build the tables for you. It is usually best to first generate the DDL script, which you can later execute within your chosen DBMS.

1. Open the sample logical model in the Database Model Diagram template (e.g., double-click either Patient_LS.vsd or Patient2_LS.vsd).
2. Select Database > Generate from the Database menu. This invokes the Generate Database wizard.
3. Ensure the option Generate a text file of the DDL script is checked, and press the Next button.
4. In the Installed Visio drivers field, choose the target database driver (e.g., Microsoft Access), if needed using the Setup... options to configure it. In the Database name field, enter a database name (e.g., MyDB), and press the Next button.
5. Accept all the defaults for the next screens, and choose Yes when prompted whether you want to view the generated DDL script.

The DDL script now appears in a code editor. You may save it if you wish. The code shown below is extracted from a DDL script generated from the Patient1_LS file discussed earlier, choosing SQL Server 2000 as the target DBMS. This code has been reformatted and stripped of comments to save space. If you used Patient2_LS as the logical model, the names will differ slightly because different naming choices were made. Later chapters discuss how to control name generation and provide an in-depth treatment of the Generate wizard.

```
create database "MyDB"
use "MyDB"

create table "Patient allergic Drug"
    ("Patient Nr" char(10) not null,
     "Drug Name" char(10) not null)

alter table "Patient allergic Drug"
    add constraint "Patient allergic Drug_PK" primary key ("Patient Nr", "Drug Name")
```

```
create table "Patient" (
    "Patient Nr" char(10) not null,
    "PatientName" char(10) not null,
    "Smokes" bit not null)

alter table "Patient"
    add constraint "Patient_PK" primary key ("Patient Nr")

alter table "Patient allergic Drug"
    add constraint "Patient_Patient allergic Drug_FK1"
        foreign key ("Patient Nr") references "Patient" ("Patient Nr")
```

This completes the introductory overview of the tool. By now, you should have some basic understanding of how to employ the tool to create simple data models and use them to generate physical database schemas. The database modeling solution in Visio for Enterprise Architects is very powerful, and so far we have only scratched its surface. The remainder of the book examines VEA's functionality systematically and in detail.

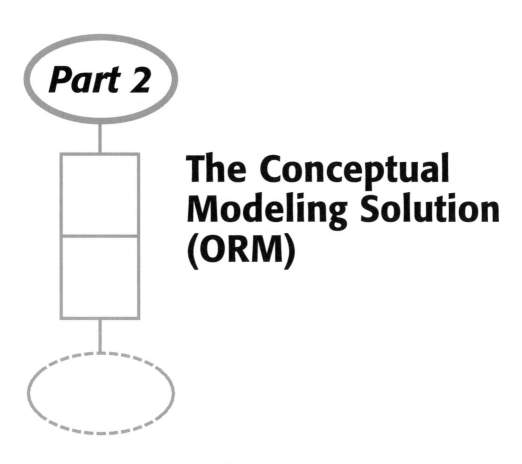

The Conceptual Modeling Solution (ORM)

Part 1 overviewed the database modeling features in Visio for Enterprise Architects, summarized database modeling tasks, and presented a quick walkthrough of forward engineering database models from conceptual through logical to physical levels.

Part 2 focuses on the conceptual modeling solution for Object-Role Modeling (ORM). You learn how to create ORM models, map them to normalized logical database models, reverse engineer physical databse schemas to ORM models, and produce conceptual model reports.

Chapter 4 explains how to construct basic ORM schemas from fact types, simple constraints, and derivation rules. You learn how to use the Fact Editor to enter fact types and sample fact instances. You see how to verbalize model elements, objectify associations, perform model error checks, and specify data types.

Chapter 5 shows you how to add many other kinds of constraints, in order to exploit the rich graphical notation of ORM for visualizing business rules. You also learn how to add subtypes, annotate models with indexes, and use Visio's layer mechanism to control which constraints are displayed or printed.

Chapter 6 shows you how to manipulate, configure, and reuse ORM models. You learn how to use the Show Relationships feature to display all the roles played by any given object type, and how to redisplay model elements. You learn how to clone, cut and paste, and reference model elements.

Chapter 7 shows you how to automatically transform an ORM source model into a normalized logical model. You are introduced to database projects and logical model editing. You learn how to migrate changes to a logical model back to an ORM source model. You learn to control how VEA generates the names for logical model elements when mapping an ORM model to logical model. You learn about the Code Editor for SQL constraint code, and how to apply different options for mapping subtypes.

Chapter 8 shows you how to reverse engineer a physical database into an ORM schema, which you then refine, and how to import models from some other tools.

Chapter 9 shows you how to generate comprehensive and customized reports for objects types, fact types, constraints, and supertypes. You learn how to display your reports on screen, print them, save them as an .rtf file for further editing, and how to copy diagrams and text from your reports to other documents.

Part 3 focuses on the logical modeling solution, and **Part 4** discusses advanced topics such as round-trip engineering and model management.

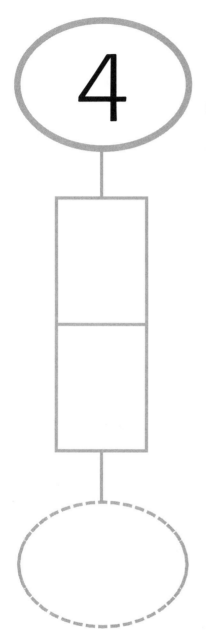

Object Types, Predicates, and Basic Constraints

4.1   **Object Types**

As discussed in the previous chapter, an ORM object type is either a value type or an entity type. A *value* corresponds to an entry in a table, and is typically a character string or numeric constant (e.g., "Ireland," 56). A value identifies or refers to itself, so there is no need to specify a *reference scheme* (identification scheme) for it.

An *entity* is identified by means of a reference scheme that uses one or more values. A simple reference scheme uses only one value (e.g., the Country with CountryCode 'US'). A good rule of thumb is "If you can write it down, it's a value." Clearly, you can write down the code 'US,' but you can't write down the actual country that is referred to by the code 'US.' Thus, the country code 'US' is a value, but the actual country (the United States of America) is an entity.

Entities and values in an ORM model correspond to real world objects in the application domain, not tables and columns in a logical database model. Trying to make this association will only lead to confusion.

A *simple reference scheme* for an entity type may be declared explicitly using a binary association (e.g., Country has CountryCode. This reference scheme may be abbreviated by using a reference mode displayed in parenthesis after the entity type name (e.g., Country(Code).

A *composite reference scheme* uses two or more binary associations, e.g., the State that has StateCode 'WA' and is in the Country that has CountryCode 'US.' Composite reference schemes are declared using an external uniqueness constraint (e.g., each StateCode, CountryCode combination refers to at most one State).

Table 4–1 summarizes the ways in which different kinds of object type may be referenced. This section discusses how to declare value types and how to use reference modes to provide simple reference schemes for entity types. It also shows how to delete object types. The next section explains how to declare sentence types, including binary associations used to reference entity types.

An object type may also be declared a *subtype* of another. For example, Woman might be declared a subtype of Person. Composite reference schemes and subtyping are discussed in Chapter 5.

The Visio tool also allows an object type to be declared *external*. This means that the object type has been previously defined (either as an entity type along with its associated reference scheme, or as a value type) in another model and is simply being reused, so there is no need to redefine it in the current model. External object types are discussed in Chapter 6.

Table 4–1   Object types and reference schemes.

Kind of Object	Reference Scheme	Reference Scheme Declaration
Entity	Simple	Reference mode
		Binary association
	Composite	External uniqueness constraint
Value	—	—

The Visio tool allows you to add new object types and edit them using the Business Rules window, the Fact Editor, or the ORM Source stencil. Existing object types may also be edited using the Database Properties Window. Figure 4–1 shows four object types displayed in the Drawing window, with details of their properties visible in the Business Rules and Database Properties windows. Let's examine some alternative ways to create these examples. If you have not already done so, open the ORM Source Model template (File > New > Database > ORM Source Model).

Adding Object Types with the Business Rules Window

1. If the Business Rules window is closed, open it (Database > View > Business Rules).
2. Select the Object Types tab of the Business Rules window, to view the Object Types pane.

    The Object Types pane displays a table with four columns, as shown in Figure 4–1. Each row of this table lists the main properties of an object type in the model. You can insert and update entries in this table directly. The Object Types column holds the name of the object type.

    The Physical Data Type column displays its data type in the currently selected DBMS. By default, the *physical data type* is set to char(10) (i.e. a fixed length string of ten characters). This column may also be used to display the *portable data type,* in this case SBCS(2), where "SBCS" means "single byte character set."

    Portable data types use generic names for corresponding physical data types in different back-ends. To toggle the display between physical and portable data types, right-click the table header, and select Show Portable Data Type or Show Physical Data Type from the context menu.

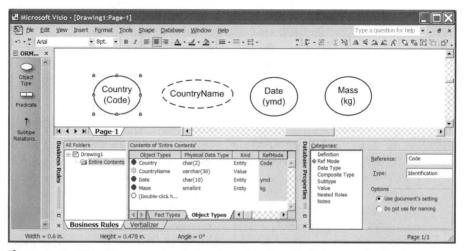

Figure 4–1 Object types may be displayed graphically, with their properties listed.

The Kind column classifies the object type as an Entity type, Value type, or External type. By default, Kind is set to Entity. The RefMode column holds the reference mode. An entry is allowed here only if the object type is an Entity type.

3. Position the cursor in the Object Types column, and type the name "Country."

   A solid circle with dark blue fill appears to the left of the object type name. This icon denotes an entity type. You can also double-click or press the F2 key before typing the name, but this is not needed. If ever you add a new row that you don't want, delete it by selecting it and pressing the Delete key.

4. Position the cursor in the Physical Data Types column, double-click the entry to enable in-place editing, and replace "10" by "2," so that the entry reads "char(2)."

   Selecting this column also causes a down-arrow to appear on the right. This can be used to display a drop-down list of data types for selection. However, in-place editing is usually faster. Data types are discussed in detail later in the chapter.

5. Place the cursor in the RefMode column and type "Code."

6. To display the object type on a diagram, select the dark blue entity type icon at the left of the row and drag it onto the drawing window.

7. Double-click the object type on the drawing window to display its Database Properties sheet. In the Categories section, select the Ref mode category.

   The settings for Country should now appear as in Figure 4–1. The Database Properties window allows you to specify all details about object types. The Type of a reference mode may be selected from a drop-down list, the default for Entity types 15 Identification. The choice for this type influences how the reference scheme is verbalized. The four radio buttons under Options allow you to control how table and column names are formed when building the logical model. For this example, just accept the default settings.

8. Select the Notes category, and enter any relevant details in the Notes field to explain how the term "Country" and its reference scheme are to be understood in the model. Figure 4–2 shows one possibility. The Database Properties window allows you to set many other properties for object types, but we'll ignore these until later.

Now let's look at *reference mode type* in more detail. Use the Business Rules window to add the three other object types shown in Figure 4–1, and assign them the property values shown. When entering the CountryName object type, change its Kind to Value by selecting that option from the drop-down list. A dashed circle with light blue fill appears to the left of the object type name. This icon denotes a value type. After adding CountryName, Date(ymd), and Mass(kg), display them on the drawing surface by dragging their object type icons onto the drawing window.

If the *Verbalizer* tab does not appear next to the Business Rules tab, open the Verbalizer (Database > View > Verbalizer), and select its tab to view the verbalization of the

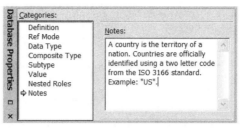

Figure 4–2 Notes may be used to provide further documentation.

current selection on the diagram. Select the Mass object type and change the Type of its reference mode to Measurement. The verbalization of the reference scheme should now read "Every Mass value is measured in kg," as shown in Figure 4–3.

This figure also includes an *Object Types window* in the lower left corner. To view this window, select Database > View > Object Types. This window provides a compact list of all the object types and their reference modes. You can float this window to any position by right-clicking its title bar and choosing Float Window. Although you cannot use it to edit properties, you can use it to drag object types onto the drawing window.

The type of reference mode has four settings: Identification; Measurement; Formatting; and No reference mode. Identification is the normal case, and is the best choice for Country(code). Measurement is the best choice for unit-based reference schemes, such as Mass(kg). Formatting may be used to describe the format in which values are displayed. For example, Date(ymd) indicates that date values used in exam-

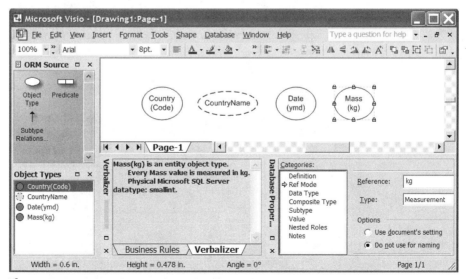

Figure 4–3 If the reference scheme is unit-based, set its type to Measurement.

Table 4–2　The type of reference mode influences the verbalization.

Example	Type of RefMode	Verbalization
Country(Code)	Identification	Every Country is identified by one distinct Code.
CountryName	None	—
Date(ymd)	Formatting	Every Date value is recorded as *ymd*.
Mass(kg)	Measurement	Every Mass value is measured in kg.

ples show the year first, then month, then day (e.g., 2002-08-14). The No Reference Mode setting is used for value types, or for entity types with no reference mode (e.g., compositely identified entity types).

The examples in Table 4–2 show how the type of reference mode influences the verbalization. Verbalizations may be included in reports, so choosing the type of reference mode can improve the documentation. However such choices have no formal significance and have no impact on the structure of the resulting database schema.

Adding Object Types with the Fact Editor

Object types and reference modes may also be added to a model using the *Fact Editor*. The fastest way to do this is to include the reference modes while entering fact types in Freeform mode, as discussed in the previous chapter. For example, open the Fact editor (Database > View > Fact Editor), set the input style to Freeform, and enter the fact type, with reference modes placed in parenthesis after the object types. Value types are followed by empty parentheses (). A simple example is shown in Figure 4–4(a).

Alternatively, you can enter the fact type first without the reference schemes, as shown in Figure 4–4(b). You can then add details about the reference modes by select-

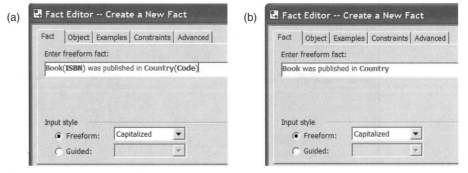

Figure 4–4　Reference modes may be (a) included or (b) excluded, while entering fact types.

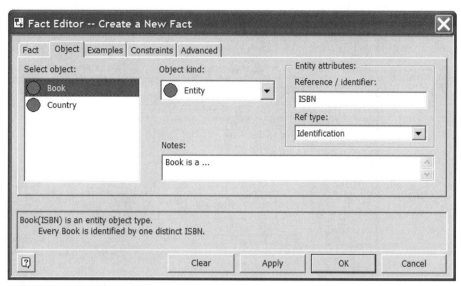

Figure 4–5 Reference schemes may be omitted while entering fact types.

ing the Object pane of the fact editor, and making appropriate entries, one object type at a time, as shown in Figure 4–5. Although this allows you to enter the type of reference mode, and notes for the object type, you need to specify the data type elsewhere (e.g., using the Business Rules window or Database Properties window).

Adding Object Types with the ORM Source Stencil

Object types may also be diagrammed directly by dragging shapes from the ORM source stencil and using the Database Properties sheet to set the properties. Let's see how to do this with an example.

1. Drag the Object Type shape from the ORM source stencil onto the Drawing window. By default, it has the name "Object."
2. Double-click the object type to display its Database Properties (see Figure 4–6).
3. Type the object type's name (e.g. "Region"). If you double-clicked before, this name replaces "Object" in the Name field of the Definition pane. If not, you need to move the cursor to this field before typing. As you type the name in the dialog box, the change is immediately displayed in the shape on the drawing window.
4. Select the Ref Mode category, and enter the reference mode (e.g., Code). You can also set the data type, and add notes as discussed earlier.

Displaying Object Types

Regardless of how object types were created, they are all listed in the Object Types and Business Rules windows. At any time, you may drag existing object types onto the Drawing window from either the Object Types pane of the Business Rules window or the Object Types window.

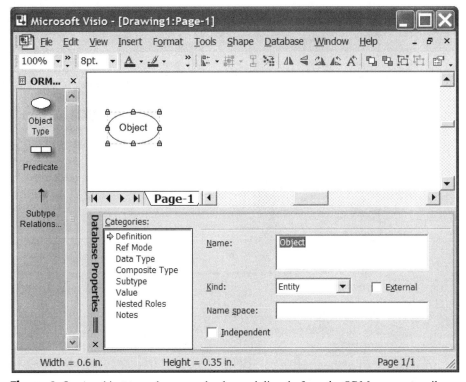

Figure 4–6   An object type shape may be dragged directly from the ORM source stencil.

The object types pane of the Business Rules window can also be used to *locate an instance of the object type in the diagram*. For example right-click the Country row of the table in Figure 4–1, and select Find Object Type in Drawing from the context menu. The Country shape in the drawing window is now highlighted. If multiple instances of the object type occur on the drawing surface, only one of these will be highlighted.

Deleting an Object Type

An object type may exist in the model without being displayed on a diagram. The same object type may be displayed in many places on the diagram, on the same or different pages. You can *delete* an object type shape from the drawing window by selecting it, and then pressing the Delete key. This invokes a message box with the prompt "Remove selected item from the underlying model?" If you answer Yes, the object type is removed from the model, so every shape depicting it on the diagram is also removed. If you answer No, the selected shape is removed from the diagram, but the object type still exists in the model (and any shapes depicting it elsewhere on the diagram remain).

You can also delete an object type from the model by selecting it in the object types pane of the Business Rules window, and pressing the Delete key. In this case, no prompt is issued. If you deleted the object type by mistake, immediately press the *Undo* icon on the main menu (or press Ctrl+Z) to restore it.

You can also delete an object type from the model by selecting it in the Object Types list window, and pressing the Delete key. This invokes a message box with the prompt "This will delete all instances of this object type from this diagram. Are you sure?" If you answer Yes, the object type is removed from the model and the diagram. If you answer No, the object type remains in both the model and the diagram.

Name Spaces

As shown in Figure 4–7, the Definition pane of an object type's Database Properties window includes a *Name* space text box. On rare occasions, you may want to allow different object types in the same model to have the same local name. For instance, you might use a Region object type in a Sales model to refer to sales areas (e.g., North). You might also use a Region object type in a Geography model to refer to geographical regions (e.g., Oceania). If you later merge the models, and want to retain the original names for these separate concepts, you can distinguish them by assigning them different name spaces (e.g., Sales and Geography).

As Figure 4–7 shows, the Object Types window displays the fully qualified names of object types (e.g., Sales.Region). The object types pane of the Business Rules window displays only their local names (e.g., Region), but you can find the corresponding shape by selecting Find Object Type in Drawing from the context menu. When you build a logical database model from a conceptual model, numbers are used instead of name-space names to provide distinct names (e.g., Region and Region1).

Independent Object Types

In ORM, an object type is said to be an *independent object type* if its instances can exist without playing other roles. Independent object types always map to a key, total table when the logical model is built (i.e., their identifier is used as the primary key of the table, and the table contains all their instances). One use of independent object types is to create reference tables. For example, if we want the database to include a table with all the region codes, we might declare the Region object type to be independent.

To declare an object type independent, open the Definition pane of its Database Properties window, and select the Check Box named Independent. The tool automatically appends " !" to the name of the object type to indicate its independent status (see Figure 4–7).

Note that if a region is identified by a code (e.g., 'N'), but we also record a region name (e.g., 'North'), then Region is not independent, since each instance plays a role other than that in its reference scheme. In this case, a two-column reference table is created, with one column for the code and another column for the name.

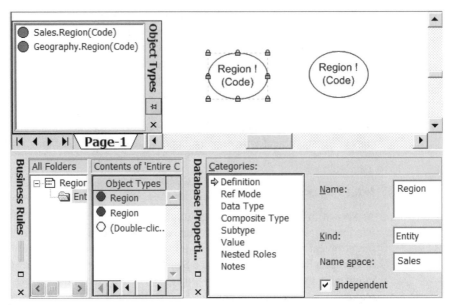

Figure 4–7   Object types may be declared Independent, and assigned a Namespace.

4.2   Fact Types

In ORM, a relationship type used to identity an entity type is called a reference type (e.g., Country has CountryCode). Other relationship types are called fact types (e.g., Country competed in Sport). Relationship types are also called sentence types or associations. In the Visio tool, all sentence types are informally called fact types, or simply facts.

You can add sentence types to an ORM model by entering their text into the Fact Editor. You can also add them graphically, by working with Object Type and Predicate shapes in the drawing window. You can edit existing sentence types using the Fact Editor or Database Properties dialog, and you can delete them with the Delete key. Most people find the Fact Editor to be the fastest and most natural way to add and edit sentence types, so let's consider these methods in turn.

Adding Fact Types with the Fact Editor

The basic operation of the Fact Editor was discussed in earlier sections. To invoke the Fact Editor from the Business Rules window, move the cursor to the bottom row of its Fact Types pane, then either start typing the fact type, or press the New... button, or press the F2 key. You can also invoke the Fact Editor by choosing Database > View > Fact Editor from the main menu.

By default, the fact editor's input style is Guided, and the relationship is Binary (it has two roles), as shown in Figure 4–8. You can enter a binary relationship giving both a forward reading (e.g., Employee works for Department) and an inverse reading (e.g.,

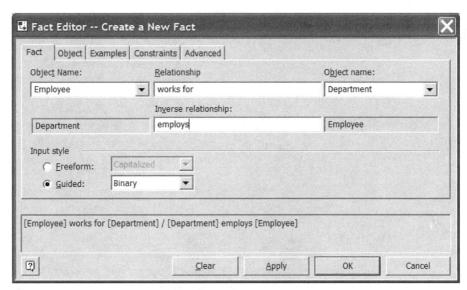

Figure 4–8   Adding a fact type in the Fact Editor using Guided input style.

Department employs Employee). To enter the forward reading, type the names of the object types in the Object Name fields, and the forward predicate name in the Relationship field. To enter the inverse reading, just type the inverse predicate name in the Inverse relationship field—the object type names are provided for you in the relevant order.

If you wish to add reference schemes or other details for the object types, select the Object pane of the Fact Editor, enter your choices as discussed in the previous section, and press the Apply key to return to the Fact pane.

If you wish to add more fact types at this stage, press the Apply button to add the current fact type into the model. The editor is now ready to accept another fact type, with the subject of the previous entry named in the first Object Name field. Selecting the arrow at the right of this field displays a drop-down list of all the object types in the model for your selection. If you want to introduce a new object type, simply type its name over the top of the entry.

If you have no more fact types to add at this stage, press the OK button to add the current fact type into the model and exit the Fact Editor. If you pressed the Apply button instead of OK, and have no further fact type to declare, press the Cancel button to exit the Fact Editor.

Once you are familiar with the Fact Editor, you will probably want to change its input style to *Freeform*. As discussed in the previous chapter, freeform input allows you to enter sentence types faster by using a formal syntax. You can use the radio button to change to Freeform. You can also make Freeform the default by opening the Database Modeling Preferences dialog (Database > Options > Modeling) selecting its Fact Editor pane and setting the preferred mode to Freeform.

With freeform input, you can enter fact types in either Capitalized or Bracketed form, as chosen from the Fact Editor's Freeform drop-down list box. With *capitalized form*, you name each object type using a single word that starts with a capital letter, and you avoid capitalized words in the predicate text. The sentence can now be easily parsed into object terms and predicate. For example: Vice President visited Country.

For languages where this doesn't work, or when the name uses multiple words separated by spaces, use *bracketed form*. In this case, you must enclose the object type names in square brackets. For example: [vice president] visited [country]. The verbalization shown at the bottom of the Fact Editor always uses bracketed mode. If an inverse reading is supplied, a slash "/" is used to separate forward and inverse readings.

Recall that the arity of a predicate is its number of roles. A unary predicate has one role, a binary predicate has two roles, a ternary predicate has three roles, and so on. With freeform input, the arity of a predicate is determined simply by the number of object terms included in the sentence. With Guided input, you can select the arity from the Guided drop-down list box. This is set to Binary by default, as shown in Figure 4–8.

As an exercise, try adding the following two fact types using either freeform or guided input: (Patient smokes; Patient was prescribed Drug by Doctor.) If using Guided input, set the arity to Unary for the smokes fact type, and Ternary for the prescription fact type. For ternary and longer fact types, Guided input provides extra fields to cater for more object terms and the rest of the predicate text, as shown in Figure 4–9.

To display a fact type on the diagram, drag it from the Business Rules window to the Drawing Window. For binary predicates with forward and inverse readings, both readings are displayed, separated by a slash. For ternary and longer fact types, only one reading can be displayed on the diagram. By default, a horizontal predicate is read from left to right, and a vertical predicate is read from top to bottom.

You can *flip* the direction of a predicate by selecting the relevant menu option (e.g., Shape > Rotate or Flip > Flip Horizontal), tool bar icon, or hot key. Flipped predicates are displayed with "<<" in front of the predicate name to indicate the normal reading direction is reversed.

Ternary and longer predicates are often called *n*-ary (*n* > 2). For n-ary fact types, only one reading can be entered in the fact editor. To add *alternative readings for n-ary fact types,* select the predicate shape and enter the other readings in the Readings pane of its Database Properties window. For example, Figure 4–10 includes two extra readings for the fact type Patient was prescribed Drug by Doctor.

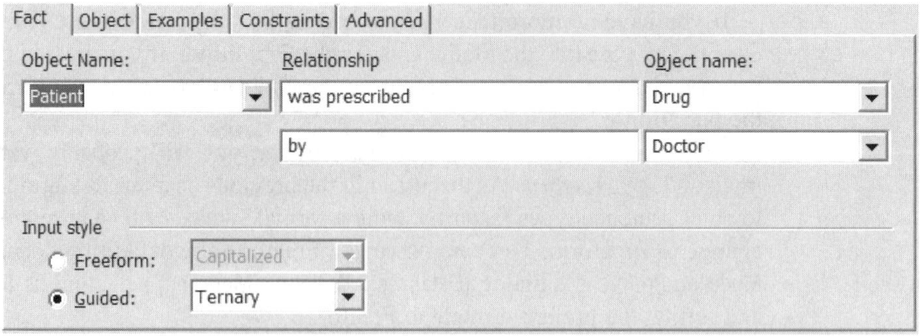

Figure 4–9   Entering a ternary fact type using Guided input.

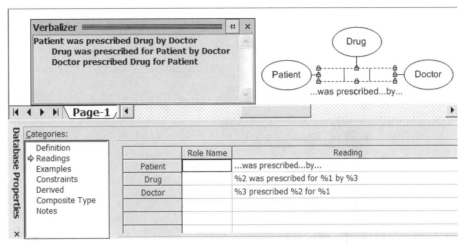

Figure 4–10 Adding alternative readings for n-ary predicates.

The object types are listed in a column, in the order in which they fill the "..." place-holders in the first predicate reading to provide the fact type reading. The tool assigns position names to the roles played by the object types, based on their order in the list. In this example, Patient = %1, Drug = %2, and Doctor = %3. Numbers are used because in general the same object type may play more than one role in the same predicate. When entering a second or later reading, you must associate this reading with the relevant order to traverse the roles in the fact type. You do this by using the position names to refer to the roles. In this example for instance, you enter %2 was prescribed for %1 by %3 to declare the alternate fact type reading Drug was prescribed for Patient by Doctor. Although the alternate readings are not displayed on the diagram, they can be viewed in the Verbalizer window, as shown in Figure 4–10.

Adding Fact Types with the ORM Stencil

Fact types may also be diagrammed directly by dragging shapes from the ORM source stencil and using the Database Properties sheet to set the properties. Let's see how to do this with an example.

1. Drag two Object Type shapes from the ORM source stencil onto the Drawing window, and use the Database Properties window to declare them as Patient(Nr) and Drug(name).
2. Drag a Predicate shape from the stencil onto the Drawing Window, and click one of its roles twice. The first click selected the predicate. The second click selected the role, displaying a control handle (yellow diamond) at the end of its role connector.
3. Select the role connector's control handle, and drag it onto the border of the Patient shape to glue it to a connection point. By default, connection points are not displayed, but the tool notifies you when it makes a connection.
4. Select the other role (two clicks) and glue its connector it to the Drug shape.

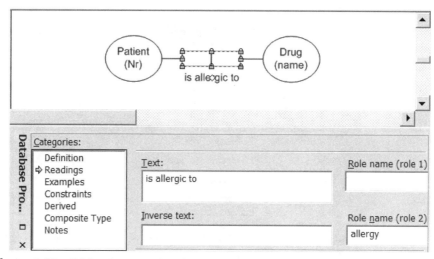

Figure 4-11   Editing the properties of a predicate shape

5. Select the predicate shape. In the Readings pane of its Database Properties window add the forward predicate text "is allergic to." Optionally, you may add an inverse predicate reading, and readings for one or both roles (see Figure 4–11).

If you need to define a unary predicate, or an *n*-ary predicate, use the Definition pane to set the relevant arity, as shown in Figure 4–12. This pane can also be used to declare a namespace for the predicate, or to declare it as external. You may add explanatory comments about the predicate in the Notes pane. Other panes are discussed later.

Displaying Fact Types

Regardless of how fact types were created, they are all listed in the Fact Types pane of the Business Rules window. At any time, you may drag existing fact types from this pane onto the Drawing window to have them displayed. To select a contiguous series of fact types, hold the Shift key down as you select the first and last fact type in the series. All but the first fact type will appear highlighted. You can then drag the fact

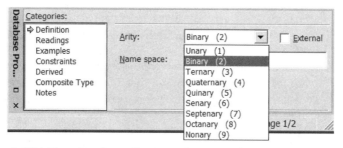

Figure 4-12   The arity of a predicate may be any number from 1 through 9.

types on to the drawing page where you want them displayed. You can finesse the display by moving the predicate text and object types around.

A handy alternative is to open the Object Types pane of the Business Rules window, drag out one or more relevant object types, and use the *Show Relationships* option. For example, if you drag the Patient object type onto any drawing page, right-click Patient, and select Show Relationships from its right-click menu, all the relationships in which Patient plays will be displayed on that page. This feature is extremely useful in schema browsing and in reverse engineering.

The fact types pane of the Business Rules window can also be used to locate *an instance of the fact type in the diagram*. Right-click any fact type listed in the pane, and select Find Fact in Drawing from its context menu. The tool highlights the first instance it finds of the fact type shape in the drawing window. In a multi-page model, it may need to change the active page to do this. If multiple instances of the fact type occur on the drawing surface, only one of these will be highlighted.

Editing Fact Types and Deleting Predicates

You can *edit an existing fact type* using either the Fact Editor or the Database Properties window. You can select the fact type's row in the Business Rules window, and press the Edit... button to bring up the Fact Editor. You can also select the fact type in either the Business Rules window or Drawing window and then open the Fact Editor on it (Database > View > Fact Editor). If the fact type is displayed on the drawing window, you can also select it to bring up its Database Properties sheet and edit it there.

A fact type may exist in the model without being displayed on a diagram. The same fact type may be displayed in many places, on the same or different pages. To *delete* a predicate shape from the drawing window, select the shape, and then press the Delete key. This invokes the prompt "Remove selected item from the underlying model?" If you answer Yes, the predicate is removed from the model, so every shape depicting it on the diagram is also removed. If you answer No, the selected shape is removed from the diagram, but the predicate still exists in the model; any shapes depicting it elsewhere on the diagram remain.

Note that deleting a predicate does not delete the object types that played in that predicate. If you want to delete them also, you need to select them before pressing Delete. If you select multiple elements on the drawing surface and press the Delete key, you are prompted "Remove all selected items from the underlying model?" Answer Yes or No according as to whether you wish to perform this bulk delete.

You can also delete a fact type from the model by selecting it in the fact types pane of the Business Rules window, and pressing the Delete key. In this case, no prompt is issued. If you deleted the object type by mistake, immediately press the Undo icon on the main menu (or press Ctrl+Z) to restore it.

4.3 Adding Basic Constraints in the Fact Editor

An *internal constraint* applies to just one predicate. External constraints apply to two or more predicates. The Fact Editor allows you declare the following internal constraints: internal uniqueness, simple mandatory, internal frequency, and ring constraints. It does not allow you to specify internal, set-comparison constraints (e.g., an exclusion constraint between two roles of the same predicate), external constraints (e.g., an external uniqueness constraint, or a set-comparison constraint between two predicates) or value constraints (e.g., restricting Sexcode values to {'M', 'F'}).

In practice, constraints declared in the fact editor are best restricted to simple internal uniqueness and simple mandatory constraints, as discussed in this section, and ring constraints, as discussed in the next chapter. Value constraints are added using the Database Properties window, and all other constraints may be added using the Add Constraints dialog, as discussed in the next chapter.

You can add internal *uniqueness* and *mandatory constraints* to a binary or longer fact type when you first enter the fact type in the Fact Editor. Alternatively, you can select an existing fact type on the drawing window, and open it for editing in the Fact Editor (Database > View > Fact Editor). Some examples were considered in the previous chapter. Let's look at a couple more now.

Open the Fact Editor on the fact type Employee works for / employs Department, and select the Constraints tab. For a binary fact type, the constraints pane by default combines uniqueness and mandatory constraints to make it faster to specify them. For instance, in Figure 4–13, choosing "exactly one" means both "at least one" (mandatory) and "at most one" (unique). If you don't want to use this default shortcut, open the Database Modeling Preferences dialog (Database > Options > Modeling) and uncheck the option that indicates combined uniqueness and mandatory. The constraint symbols and verbalization automatically appear below to help you see the result of your choice. If there are more than two constraints involved, only two of these are verbalized here. You can always see the full verbalization later by selecting the fact type on the diagram and opening the Verbalizer window.

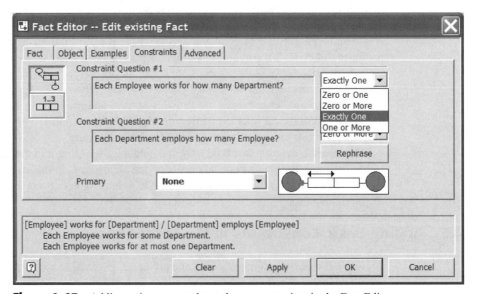

Figure 4–13   Adding uniqueness and mandatory constraints in the Fact Editor.

For a binary fact type, you are asked two constraint questions, one for each role. For each question, select the relevant choice from the drop-down list: Zero or One; Zero or More; Exactly One; One or More.

Including an inverse predicate reading often improves the clarity of the second constraint question. If the question is still unclear, press the Rephrase button to have the question formulated in a different way. Press the Apply button to enter the constraints into the model and leave the Fact Editor open. Press the OK button if you want to enter the constraints into the model and close the Fact Editor.

Caution: Don't declare a role to be mandatory for an object type unless each instance of that type in the database must play that role. It is rare for a role to be mandatory unless it also has a simple uniqueness constraint. It is very rare for a role played by a value type to be declared mandatory. For example, consider the fact type Patient(Nr) has / is of FamilyName(). If FamilyName plays no other role in the schema, its role is implicitly mandatory, so there is no need to declare this. If it does play another role in a fact type (e.g., Person formerly had Family Name), it may be possible to have an instance of Family Name that does not currently name a patient.

A uniqueness constraint may be declared *primary* by selecting the relevant role(s) from the drop-down list for Primary Figure 4–14 declares the primary reference scheme for Country explicitly, using a mandatory 1:1 association between Country and Country Code. Primary uniqueness constraints are marked with a "P". As discussed earlier, it's easier to declare the reference scheme implicitly using a reference mode.

If the fact type is ternary or longer, the Constraints pane is displayed differently. Figure 4–15 depicts entry of a uniqueness constraint that spans all three roles of the fact type Patient was prescribed Drug by Doctor discussed in Figure 4–10. To add a uniqueness constraint, select the uniqueness constraint button at the top left, then select the relevant constraint option, and press the Space key. To toggle the constraint off, press the space bar again. Unless the constraint spans all the roles, you may add more than one uniqueness constraint.

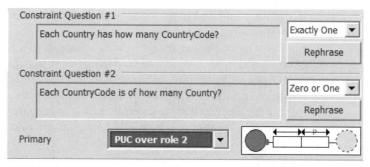

Figure 4–14   Declaring a primary uniqueness constraint.

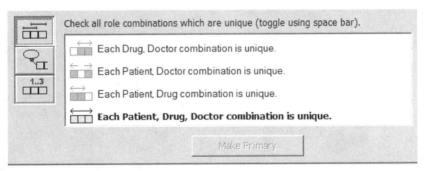

Figure 4–15   Declaring a uniqueness constraint on a ternary fact type.

It is rare for any role of an *n*-ary fact type to be mandatory. If you do need to add a mandatory constraint to a role, select the mandatory constraint button in the second-top left position, then select the relevant mandatory constraint option, and press the Space key. To toggle the constraint off, press the space bar again.

4.4   Populating Fact Types with Examples

It is a good idea to include *sample population* of fact instances for all fact types. You can do this when you declare the fact type in the Fact Editor, or later by selecting the fact type on the diagram and opening the Fact Editor for it (Database > View > Fact Editor). Click the Examples tab of the Fact Editor, and enter enough sample facts to illustrate the relevant constraints.

For example, Figure 4–16 shows three fact instances for the fact type Patient was born in Country. Here the patients with patient numbers 1001 and 1002 were born in the United States (CountryCode = 'US'), and patient 1003 was born in Australia (CountryCode = 'AU'). The population is consistent with the uniqueness constraint pattern shown on the fact type. Each role of the predicate corresponds to a column in the sample fact table. The first role has a simple uniqueness constraint, so the entries in the first column must be unique. This indicates that each patient was born in at most one country. The second role does not have a uniqueness constraint, so entries in the second column may be duplicated (e.g., 'US'). This illustrates the possibility that more than one patient was born in the same country.

For a binary fact type, you should include at least three rows of data to illustrate its uniqueness constraint(s). You can use the Analyze button to request the tool to induce the constraints from your examples, or to check for inconsistencies between your data and your constraint specification. For example, if you incorrectly replace 1003 by 1002 in the third row, the analysis leads to an error message noting that the examples suggest a uniqueness constraint spanning both roles, not just the first. In this case, close the analysis results dialog and correct the examples.

If the examples are significant however, you can press the Apply UC Constraints button to have the tool apply the uniqueness constraint pattern that is consistent with the

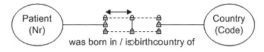

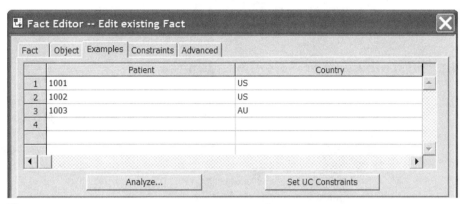

Figure 4–16   Adding a sample fact population to a fact type.

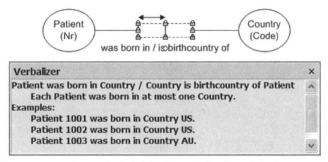

Figure 4–17   Fact examples are included in the verbalization of the fact type.

sample population. Try it out for yourself. This is a very useful feature for validating constraints with domain experts, since they find it easier to think about the rules using concrete examples.

If you select a fact type for which you have provided examples, and then you open the Verbalizer (Database > View > Verbalizer) the examples are also verbalized, as shown in Figure 4–17. As discussed later, fact examples may also be included in printed reports. You cannot delete an example row by clearing each of its cells, since the tool merely replaces the values by nulls, shown as "<???>" in the verbalization. To delete a fact example, right-click its row and select the option Delete Rows from the context menu.

4.5   Saving a Model

To save your model, choose File > Save from the File menu, or click the Save (diskette) icon. If the model has not been saved before, this opens the Save As dialog box. Choose the folder where you want to save the model, add a filename for the model, press the Save button in the dialog, then press OK in the properties dialog. The file will be saved with the extension ".vsd" (Visio document). If you previously saved the file, then the Save operation simply replaces the old copy with the latest version of the model without opening any dialog boxes.

4.6 Verbalization and Hyphenation

Both the ORM source model and the logical database model solutions provide automatic *verbalization* of any part of the model that you select, including any examples that you entered. This feature is very useful for communicating the meaning of a model to non-technical domain experts. To illustrate this feature, let's open the sample Employee ORM source model that comes with the product. To open this model, choose File > New > Browse Sample Drawings then select the Database folder and the Employee ORM source sample file, and hit the Open button.

The Employee page of the Employee source model should now appear. The full model is spread over three pages, called Employee, Project and Room. The name of the currently displayed page appears in a tab below the drawing window. By default, only the Database Properties and Business Rules windows appear below the drawing window. To open the verbalizer window, choose Database > View > Verbalizer from the main menu. This should now appear below the drawing window. If you ever have trouble seeing all the windows, choose Window > Tile from the main menu.

Now use the mouse to select the part of the model you want verbalized. To select a single model element, simply click on it. To select an area of the model to be verbalized, hold the left house button down and drag the cursor diagonally over the area. All aspects of the model within that area will be verbalized (including fact examples if you have added them). In Figure 4–18, the Employee has MobileNr and Employee has Room predicates and their constraints are selected. The verbalization appears in the Verbalizer window (shown here in a float position).

The Verbalizer window remains open until you close it. You can float or dock windows freely by right-clicking their title bars and choosing the relevant option from their context menu. For windows docked together, you can choose which of them are displayed at any time by selecting the relevant tab at the bottom of the combined window (e.g., Database Properties, Business Rules, or Verbalizer).

The tool verbalizes constraints mainly by inserting logical quantifiers (e.g., each, some, at most one) and operators (e.g., If ... then ...) into fact type readings. If you include an adjective in a predicate just before an object place-holder, you can often improve the constraint verbalization by appending a *hyphen* to the adjective.

For example, Figure 4–19 shows the verbalization of two fact types: Patient has first-GivenName; Patient has second-GivenName. Note the use of the *hyphen* in the predicates "has first-" and "has second-". This binds the adjectives "first" and "second" to GivenName when constraints on those predicates are verbalized, so that keywords like "some" or "at most one" are inserted before the adjective instead of after it. In this example, if you omitted the hyphens, the constraints would verbalize instead as "Each

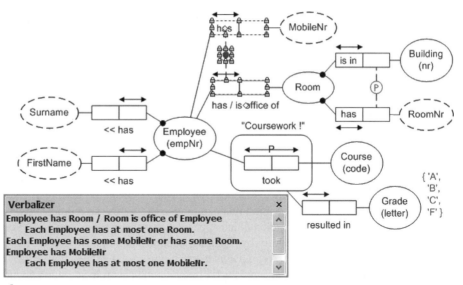

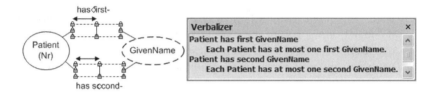

Figure 4–18   All model elements in the current selection may be verbalized.

Figure 4–19   Use of hyphens to bind predicate parts to object terms in the verbalization.

Patient has first at most one GivenName" and "Each Patient has second at most one GivenName", which is at best awkward and at worst unintelligible.

The use of hyphens does not have a direct effect on the logical model that the tool creates from the ORM model. However, the overall effect is potentially large, since hyphenation can help the domain expert to understand the verbalization and correctly validate your model.

4.7 Objectifying an Association (Nesting)

The sample model in Figure 4–18 includes the association Employee took Course. To record the grade (if any) that an employee gets for a given course, the association was *objectified* as Coursework, and the fact type Coursework resulted in Grade was added. The object type Coursework is said to be *nested,* since it nests an association inside it.

Nesting is specified using the Advanced pane of the Fact Editor. If you enter a new fact type (e.g., Employee plays Sport) in the Fact Editor, you can add the nesting before closing the editor. If instead you have a fact type on the diagram that you want to objectify, then first select the fact type and then open the Fact Editor (Database > View > Fact Editor). Now select the Advanced tab and enter a name for the objectified association in the field labeled "Objectify / Nest fact as:" For example, you might objectify Employee plays Sport as Play. Figure 4–20 shows the nesting declaration for the Coursework association in the sample model.

If the association is already on the drawing window, pressing the OK button in the Fact Editor causes the nesting envelope to be displayed around the association. You can also display a nested object type by dragging it out from the Business Rules editor. The name of the objectified association appears outside the nesting envelope, as in Figure 4–18. You can reposition this name by selecting the nested object type, and then dragging its control handle (which appears as a small, yellow diamond). You can also resize the envelope vertically by dragging a shape handle (small green square).

ORM currently requires that each objectified association either has a spanning uniqueness constraint, or is a 1:1 association. This rule is enforced when a model error check is performed (see next section).

When you create a nested object type, the tool automatically creates derived predicates between the nested object type and the object types involved in its defining predicate. This provides a uniform way of navigating from any object type (nested or un-nested) to the rest of the schema, and is mainly designed to facilitate conceptual queries. By default the derived predicates are named "involves" or "is involved in". If you wish, you may rename these predicates by double-clicking the nested object type

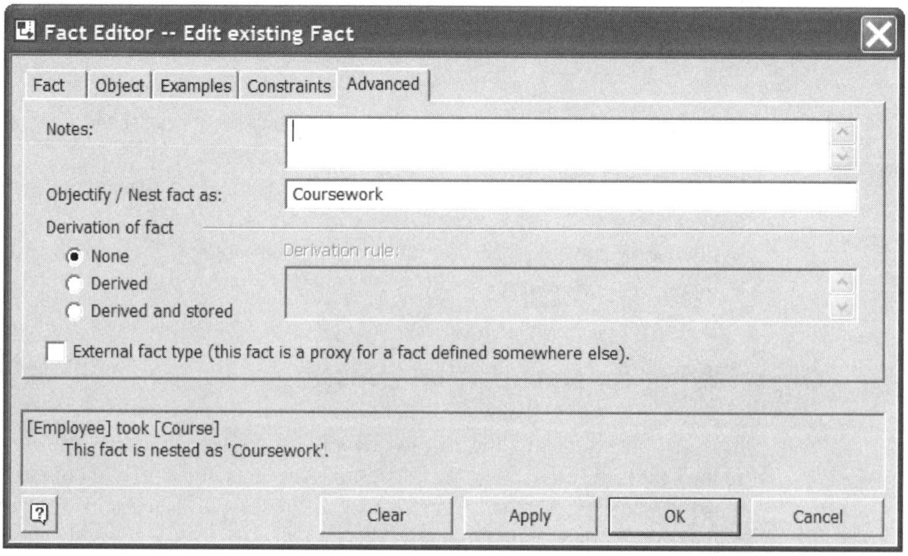

Figure 4–20   Nesting is declared using the Advanced pane of the Fact Editor.

on the diagram window to display its Database Properties Sheet, then selecting the Nested Roles category and renaming the nested role readings.

4.8 Model Error Checks

The tool allows you to create and save your conceptual schema in stages, even if the schema is incomplete or incorrect. However, before the tool can map your conceptual schema to a logical database schema, your conceptual schema must be syntactically valid—it must conform to the grammatical rules laid down by the ORM metaschema. The tool provides both basic and deep model error checking mechanisms to enforce these rules of grammar.

To request a *basic model error check* at any time, select Database > Model Error Check from the main menu. This test quickly scans your model to see whether it satisfies many basic rules to which all valid ORM model must conform. Any errors detected are displayed in the Output window. *Double-click the error message to highlight the model element causing that error*. For example, a model error check on the ORM model in Figure 4–21 generates error message 2006. Double-clicking that message highlights the offending fact type: Patient is allergic to Drug. If the predicate is not yet on the diagram, you are prompted to drag it there for viewing. If the error message is unclear, select the message and *press F1 to view the online help* topic for that error number. In this example, the error can be removed by adding a uniqueness constraint to the predicate.

The tool automatically performs a *deep model error check* whenever you attempt to build a logical model from the conceptual model. This procedure takes longer but is far more thorough, and can detect many kinds of errors that might not be detected by a basic model error check. Again, double-clicking an error message takes you to the ORM model element causing the error, so you can fix it before trying another build. The build will not succeed until you have fixed all the errors.

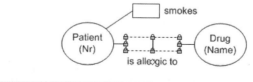

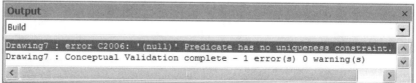

Figure 4–21   A Model Error Check displays errors in the Output window.

4.9 Derived Fact Types

If a fact type may be *derived* from one or more other fact types, you may specify this using either the Advanced pane of the Fact Editor or the Derived pane of the Database Properties window. Select the relevant radio button to set the derivation status of a fact type to be None (not derived), Derived or Derived and stored. If the fact type is displayed on the diagram, a single asterisk "*" is appended to the predicate name to indicate it is derived (but not stored).

A double asterisk "**" indicates the fact type is both derived and stored. This setting requires special care (e.g., a derived and stored fact should not be updateable unless the derivation rule is preserved), so should be chosen only in exceptional cases.

The ORM schema in Figure 4–22 includes the derived fact type Window has Area. Whenever you declare a fact type to be derived, you should also enter a derivation rule to declare how it can be derived from other fact types. Although ORM includes a formal language for specifying derivation rules, the tool does not yet support this language. So any derivation rules entered in an ORM schema are treated just as comments. To apply the derivation, you need to provide the relevant code yourself at either the logical or physical level. For example, you could create a relational view WindowView (windowNr, height, width, area) with the rule for computing area included in the SQL code for the view definition. Views are discussed in a later chapter.

If you declare a fact type to be derived and stored and request the tool to build the logical database schema, the tool will create one or more base table columns to store facts of this type. However, you still need to write the code to enforce the deriva-

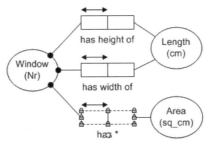

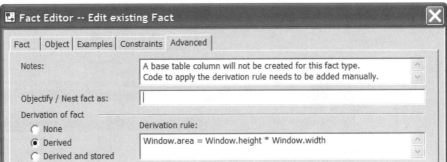

Figure 4–22   Specifying a derived fact type in the Fact Editor.

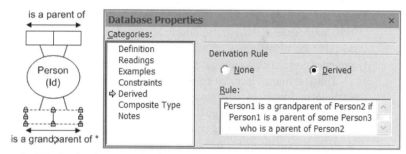

Figure 4–23   Derivation may also be declared in the Database Properties window.

tion rule. How you do this (with triggers or computed columns, etc.) depends on the DBMS.

The derivation for the area example involved simple arithmetic computation. In such cases, it's often easier to declare derivation rules in attribute style. If you assign the role names "height," "width," and "area" to the right-hand roles of the predicates, you can attribute these to the left-hand object type using dot notation (e.g.,(Window.area). This enables you to formally capture the derivation rule in attribute style.

If the derivation involves logical inference of a more general nature, it's often convenient to specify the derivation rule in relational style, as shown in Figure 4–23. Here numbers are appended to distinguish the object type variables Person1, Person2 and Person3. If you assign the names "parent," "child," "grandparent," and "grandchild" to the roles of the parenthood and grandparenthood predicates, you could declare the derivation rule in attribute style as Person.grandparent=Person.parent.parent.

Although compact, this has the disadvantage of being navigation-specific (e.g., it doesn't tell us how to derive someone's grandchildren). Moreover, the role names actually refer to sets in this case, and if you use plural names to distinguish such cases, the rule becomes unstable if the uniqueness constraint pattern may change over time.

If that last statement lost you, don't worry. The tool doesn't force you to specify the rules formally. Just write them down in any way that makes sense to those who have to validate or implement the rules.

4.10   Data Types

In the first section of this chapter, you saw how to specify a *data type* for an ORM object type using either the Object Types pane of the Business Rules window, or the Data Type pane of the Database Properties window. It's time now to look at data types in more detail.

Although data types for columns may be specified at the relational level, it is far better to specify data types at the ORM level. Why? First, it saves a lot of work, because data types in ORM correspond to the syntactic *domains* on which relational attributes are based. Typically each ORM object type plays many roles, each of which maps to one or more columns in a relational database. Setting the data type once for the object type propagates that data type to every attribute mapped from its roles. Second, this avoids type mismatch problems in the generated relational database (e.g. foreign keys are automatically given the same data type as the primary keys they reference).

Third, it makes it much easier to change data types. For example, a database might include hundreds of columns concerning dates (birthdate, hiredate, orderdate etc.). Suppose you need to change the data type for each of these columns from, say char(10) where dates were stored as character strings like '2002-07-06,' to a datetime data type with built-in support for date arithmetic. At the ORM level, all you need do is change the data type for the object type Date. At the relational level, you need to change all the hundreds of date column data types (unless your DBMS properly supports relational domains or user-defined types, and you have been disciplined in using this support). Of course, after changing the schema for a populated database, you still have the data migration problem but having the schema updated so easily is a major benefit.

If you have decided on the target DBMS, and you want to see the physical data types for that DBMS, you should *setup the relevant database driver*. To do this, choose Database > Options > Drivers... from the main menu to invoke the Database Drivers dialog box and select the relevant DBMS. Figure 4–24 shows the main pane of the dialog screen when choosing Microsoft SQL Server. Ignore the other panes for now. Press the Setup button to open the Setup dialog, and use the ODBC Drivers pane to select the relevant ODBC driver.

Microsoft provides ODBC drivers for many DBMSs. For some DBMSs (e.g., DB2), native ODBC drivers may be obtained from their vendors. If your DBMS is not on the list, you may use the ODBC generic driver. Use the Preferred Settings pane of the Setup dialog to make more specific choices (e.g., to set the SQL Server version to 2000). For further details about setup and ODBC, see Chapter 11.

By default, each object type in an ORM model is assigned a data type of char(10). Before mapping an ORM model to a relational model, you should declare the relevant data type for each object type. If the object type is displayed in the drawing window, you can double-click it to bring up its Database Properties sheet, select the Data Type pane, and then press the Edit button to enter the new data type. For instance, if you

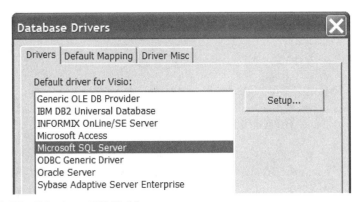

Figure 4–24   Selecting a DBMS driver.

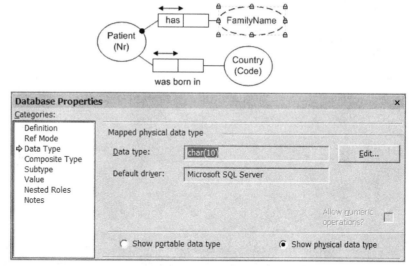

Figure 4–25   To edit the data type in the Database Properties window, press the Edit button.

select the FamilyName object type in Figure 4–25, the Data Type pane of its properties dialog appears with the default data type of char(10) as shown. Here the radio button is set to show the *physical data type* for the chosen DBMS, in this case SQL Server.

The data type field in the Database Properties sheet is read-only, so you cannot edit it directly. Instead, press the Edit button to invoke the Data Type dialog box specific to that DBMS. The Native type and Length fields display the defaults (char and 10). To store family names as variable length character strings, select the relevant item (e.g., varchar) from the Native type drop-down list (scroll down, or quickly type the initial characters until the item appears), as shown in Figure 4–26(a). Click the mouse to accept the change, then move the cursor to the Length field. To allow for family names of up to 30 characters, change the value from 10 to 30 (see Figure 4–26[b]), then press the OK button to accept the change. The Database Properties window now shows the data type as varchar(30).

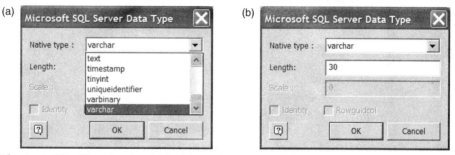

Figure 4–26   Changing the physical data type to varchar(30).

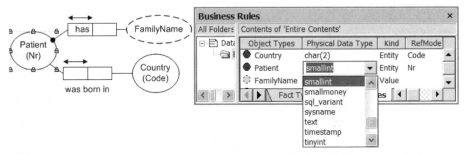

Figure 4–27   Basic data type settings may also be edited in the Business Rules window.

If you want to edit several data types, it's quicker to do this in the Object Types pane of the Business Rules Window. If needed, open this window (Database > View > Business Rules) and select its Object Types tab to display the Object Types pane. The data type field supports a drop-down list for selecting the native type and allows you to edit the length directly (see Figure 4–27). The whole field is editable, so you can simply type in the desired data type (e.g., varchar(30)) without accessing the drop-down list at all. The field is parsed as you go, with basic Intellisense support (e.g., if you type "varc" this is automatically expanded to "varchar"). If you enter an illegal data type, the Data Type dialog box is invoked for you to complete the entry there.

The reference scheme Country(code). abbreviates the association Country is identified by CountryCode, so when you set the data type for Country you are actually setting the data type for CountryCode. One standard way to reference countries is by their 2-letter ISO codes (e.g., 'AU' for Australia, and 'US' for the United States). This choice requires a fixed length character string of 2 characters in length, so the data type for Country should be set to char(2). Value types often have other constraints that can't be captured by simply declaring a built-in data type. For example, the characters in country codes must be letters, and social security numbers must match the pattern ddd-dd-dddd (where "d" denotes a digit). Currently, the tool does not support the specification of such pattern constraints, but they are easy to implement manually in most DBMSs.

If you know the DBMS in which your model will be implemented, you will proba- bly prefer to work with physical data types. If you haven't made that choice yet, or you intend to work with many kinds of DBMS, then you may prefer to use *portable data types*. When a portable data type is mapped to a given DBMS, it is replaced by a cor- responding physical data type. To display portable data types on the Data Type pane of the Database Properties window, select the "Show portable data type" radio button.

Use the drop-down lists to select the appropriate values. For example, Figure 4–28 shows portable settings that might be used in place of the physical data type var- char(30). The Text category is used for character strings, the Type is set to Variable Length, the Size is set to Single Byte characters (rather than Double Byte), and the Length is set to 30. As discussed earlier, you can toggle the display of data types

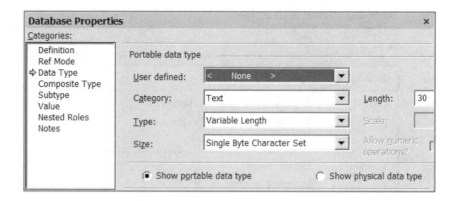

Figure 4–28   Portable data types may be used instead of physical data types.

between physical and portable in the Object Types pane of the Business Rules window by right-clicking the table header and selecting that option from the context menu.

The possible settings for portable data types are summarized in Table 4–3. You can access details about specific settings by using the on-line help. If you choose the Numeric category, one of the options is *Auto Counter*. This is used if you want the DBMS itself to provide a unique number for each entry in the relevant base table column, automatically incrementing the number for the next entry in the column.

Support for this feature depends on the DBMS as well as the tool. For example, in Microsoft Access this maps the Counter data type, and in SQL Server this is implemented as smallint with the *identity property* added. For SQL Server, if you display physical data types in the Database Properties window, you can add the identity property to any numeric type by checking the Identity option in the Data Type dialog. You can see this option in Figure 4–26(a), but it is grayed out because the data type is not numeric. For Oracle databases, the tool can be configured to create an Oracle Sequence object for all auto counter primary keys. The tool will also write the trigger for assigning primary keys to new rows based on the Oracle <SEQUENCE NAME>.NEXTVAL syntax.

If an ORM object type with the identity property is mapped to a logical schema, the identity property is incorrectly displayed as applying to all columns mapped from role of the object type, not just the desired primary key column. However this error is fixed when the actual DDL is generated for the physical schema. If you find this apparent inconsistency confusing, you may prefer to delay setting any identity properties until the logical level.

To define *user-defined data type,* choose the Database > User Defined Types from the main menu to invoke the User defined Types dialog. Press the Add button to enter a name for the type, then enter the settings for the type in the portable data type property fields. Physical data type settings cannot be displayed in this dialog. The example shown in Figure 4–29 effectively defines phoneNrType as a synonym for char(12).

Table 4-3 Portable data types.

Category	Type	Length/Precision (= default)	Scale (= default)	Size
User-defined	*typename*			
Text	Fixed length	Length = 10	—	1-byte char set
	Variable length	Length = 10	—	2-byte char set
	Large length	—	—	
Numeric	Signed integer	—	—	Small, Large
	Unsigned integer	—	—	Small, Large
	Auto counter	Precision = 10	—	Small, Large
	Floating point	—	—	Small, Large
	Decimal	Precision = 10	= 2	Small, Large
	Money	Precision = 10	= 2	Small, Large
Raw data	Fixed length	Length = 10	—	—
	Variable length	Length = 10	—	—
	Large length	—	—	—
	Picture	—	—	—
	OLE object	—	—	—
Temporal	Auto timestamp	—	—	Small, Large
	Time	—	—	Small, Large
	Date	—	—	Small, Large
	Date & Time	—	—	Small, Large
Logical	True or False	—	—	Small, Large
	Yes or No	—	—	Small, Large
Other	RowID	—	—	—
	ObjectID	—	—	—
	Unknown	—	—	—

Once defined, a user-defined type can be used like any other data type, and will appear in drop-down lists of data types. Because they are data types rather than object types, user-defined types do not appear as object types in the Business Rules window or in the Object Types window. In an ORM model, user-defined data types are of little use, because ORM object types themselves provide even stronger support for semantic domains, and allow value constraints to be specified (see next chapter). Once you define a data type for an ORM object type, this propagates to all relational columns mapped from those roles, along with any value constraints defined for the type.

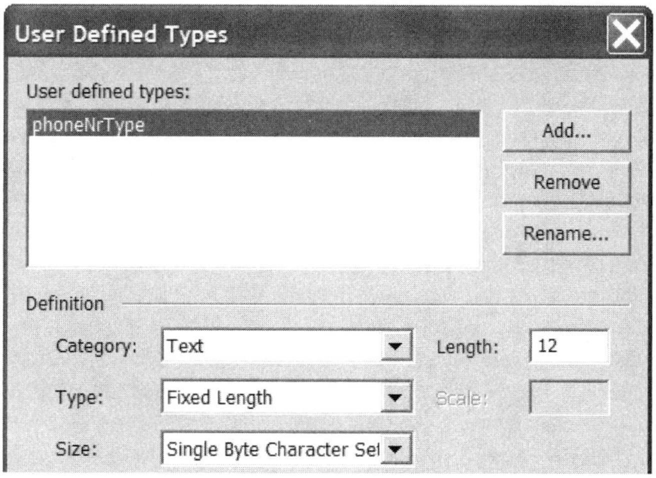

Figure 4–29   Defining a user-defined type.

If you don't use ORM, however, user defined types are useful at the logical level. You can define many columns based on the same user-defined type, so if ever you change that user-defined type, the change propagates to all the columns defined on it. Although the tool supports this concept of user-defined types, not all DBMSs do so. If you wish to avail yourself of this feature, ensure that your DBMS supports it, and check that the tool generates appropriate DDL for this feature.

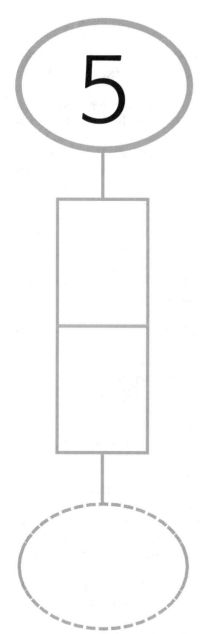

5 ORM Constraints

5.1   Value Constraints

ORM constraints apply either to an object type or to one or more roles. This section discusses how to add constraints to an object type. The rest of the chapter explains how to add all the role-based constraints.

The previous chapter showed how to constrain the possible values for an object type by associating it with a data type. You can further constrain an object type by confining its possible values to a list or range of values within its data type. For example: SexCode = {'M', 'F'}; Score = {1..100}; SQLchar = {'a'..'z', 'A'..'Z', 'O'..'9','_'}. These are called *value constraints* because they limit the allowed values for a value type. If you apply a value constraint to an entity type, e.g. Sex(Code), the constraint is understood to apply to the associated value type, e.g. SexCode.

To *add a value constraint* to an object type, first ensure it is displayed it in the drawing window. Select or double-click the object type to bring up its Database Properties window. Open the Value pane by selecting Value from the list of categories. To *add* a value to the constraint, type the value in the Value field and press the Add button. The tool immediately displays the current list of values in braces next to the object type. If the data type is character-based, the tool adds single quotes around each value. Do not add quotes yourself. Figure 5–1 shows how it looks for the Sex object type if you already added the value 'M' and just typed in the value 'F' but have not yet added it.

If you now press the Add button, the value list is updated to {'M', 'F'}, as shown in the lower left of Figure 5–2. To *reposition a value constraint* on the diagram, select the object type (not the constraint) and then move the control handle (small yellow diamond) that appears.

Now consider an application domain where buildings must have fewer than 20 stories, and floors numbered 13 are excluded because some people think this number is unlucky. If FloorNr is the value type for floor numbers, you could assign it a numeric data type (e.g., smallint) and then add the value constraint {1..12, 14..20}. This constraint includes two ranges. Let's see how to add this constraint using the tool.

To *add a range of values,* type the minimum value in the From field, and the maximum value in the To field, and press the Add button. For example, Figure 5–2 shows how the Value pane looks after adding the first range 1..12. The second range 14..20 has been typed in but not yet added. If you now press the Add button, the value list is updated to {1..12, 14..20} as required.

To *remove an entry from a value constraint,* select the entry in the Defined values/ranges field, and press the Remove button. To *delete a value constraint,* remove each of its entries in this way.

By default, the drawing window displays at most five entries in a value constraint. For example, if you enter the seven values 'Sunday' through 'Saturday' for WeekDay, the first five values are shown, and an ellipsis "..." is appended to indicate that other values are hidden (see Figure 5–3). To *change the maximum number of values displayed for an individual object type,* right-click the object type, choose Shape > Custom Properties from its context menu, and change the Value list size number in the Custom Properties dialog. This dialog can also be used to introduce new custom properties of

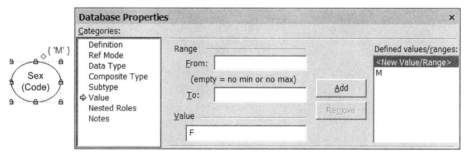

Figure 5–1 Half-way through adding an {'M','F'} value constraint to SexCode.

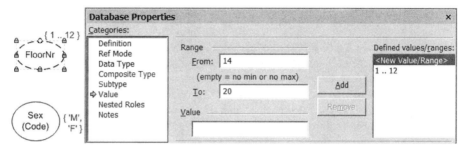

Figure 5–2 About to add a second range {14..20} to FloorNr.

your own. Regardless of how many values are displayed on the diagram, all the values
you enter in the constraint are included for DDL generation purposes.

> *Hint*: Declare a value constraint only if the list of values is stable. If the list of val-
> ues is likely to change over time, store the values in a look-up table where they can
> be referenced and modified as needed. For example, if you want a one-column table
> of country codes, declare Country (Code) to be independent. If instead you want a two-
> column table of country codes and country names, use the fact type: Country (Code)
> has CountryNameO.

5.2 Internal and External Uniqueness Constraints

The previous chapter showed how to use the Fact Editor to add uniqueness and mandatory role constraints to a single predicate. For these two kinds of internal constraint, the
Fact Editor usually provides the easiest way to add the constraints. All other role-based
constraints are best added and edited using the *Add Constraint dialog*. Although you

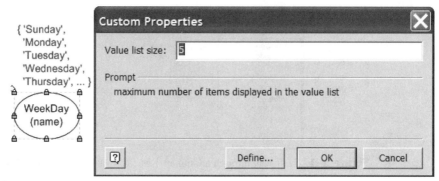

Figure 5–3   The maximum number of values displayed is editable in a custom property.

can use the Fact Editor to add frequency and ring constraints, it's easier to add these with the Add Constraint dialog. Moreover, the Fact Editor can't be used for constraints that involve more than one predicate. From now on, all examples of ORM constraint editing will use the Add Constraint dialog.

You can quickly add constraints to predicates in the diagram window by selecting the relevant predicate(s) and invoking the Add Constraint dialog to add constraints to one or more of those predicates. To select more than one predicate, hold the Shift key down as you click each predicate. To *invoke the Add Constraint dialog,* right-click the selection and choose Add Constraints from the context menu (or choose Database > Add Constraint from the main menu).

For example, suppose you wish to add constraints to the following associations: Room is in Building; Room has RoomNr. Hold the Shift key down to select both the predicates. The selection is highlighted, as shown at the top of Figure 5–4. Now right-click, then select Add Constraints from the context menu. The Add Constraint dialog appears with the constraint type set to Uniqueness by default.

The roles of the selected predicates are displayed as role boxes, followed by the sentence type verbalization. The message field at the bottom of the dialog prompts you to click on the role boxes to select roles. To apply a uniqueness constraint to the first role of Room is in Building, click the first role box. The tool automatically highlights and numbers the selected role and verbalizes the constraint corresponding to this selection, as shown in Figure 5–4. To apply the constraint and leave the dialog open, press the Apply button. The constraint now appears on the diagram, and the role selection is cleared ready for the next constraint.

If you press the OK button, the constraint is applied and the dialog closes. You can always clear the current role selection by pressing the Reset button. If you press the Cancel button, the selection is cleared and the dialog is closed.

With the dialog still open, apply a uniqueness constraint to the first role of the Room has RoomNr association by selecting its first role box and pressing Apply. By now, uniqueness constraints should be displayed on each of the two roles played by Room, as shown at the left of Figure 5–5. One more uniqueness constraint remains to be added. Here, the term "RoomNr" means a local room number used to identify a room within

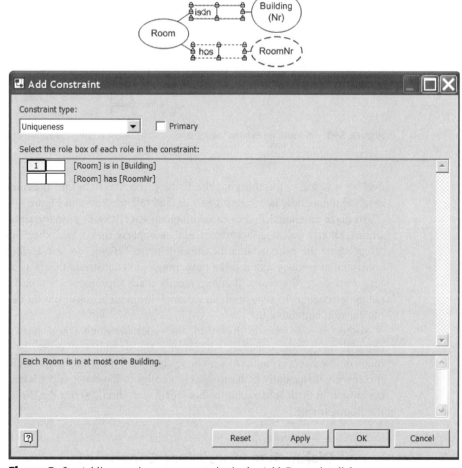

Figure 5–4   Adding a uniqueness constraint in the Add Constraint dialog.

the scope of a single building. For instance, building 40 and building 41 might each have a room with room number 6767, but the BuildingNr-RoomNr combination 40-6767 refers to at most one Room, as does the combination 41-6767.

To indicate that each BuildingNr-RoomNr combination refers to at most one room, add a uniqueness constraint that spans the roles played by Building and Room in these predicates. To do this, simply click both the roles in turn. The tool numbers these roles 1 and 2 as shown in Figure 5–5. The tool verbalizes the constraint automatically. This is an *external uniqueness constraint* because it spans roles from different predicates.

Press the OK button to apply the constraint and close the dialog. The external uniqueness constraint is displayed as a circled "U" connecting the two roles, as shown in Figure 5–6(a). If this constraint provides the primary way to identify Room, you may

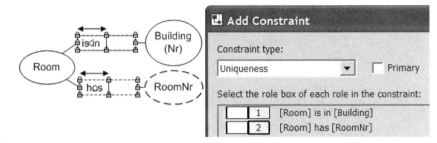

Figure 5–5   Adding an external uniqueness constraint spanning the right-hand roles.

declare it *primary* by checking the Primary check box before pressing OK. Primary external uniqueness is displayed as a circled "P" as shown in Figure 5–6(b).

To make an unqualified external uniqueness constraint primary, right-click the constraint, choose Database Properties from its context menu, and check the box labeled "Represents the primary identification scheme." If you do not declare a uniqueness constraint as primary and it is the only uniqueness constraint that is a candidate for primary reference, the tool will automatically mark it primary when building the logical database schema. To reposition an external uniqueness constraint on the diagram, simply select it and move it.

Although conceptually irrelevant, the order in which you specify the roles in an external uniqueness constraint determines the default sort order for any composite index defined over columns to which the constraint roles map in the logical schema. For this reason, it is usually better to select the roles in top-down order when specifying the constraint. In the Room example, this means you should select the Building role before the RoomNr role.

5.3 Simple and Disjunctive Mandatory Constraints

The ORM schema in Figure 5–7 is based on the Employee ORM source example that comes with the tool. In addition to five uniqueness constraints (four internal and one external), this schema includes three *mandatory role constraints*. A mandatory constraint on a single role is called a *simple mandatory* constraint, and is displayed as a black dot. A mandatory constraint on a set of two or more roles is called a *disjunctive-*

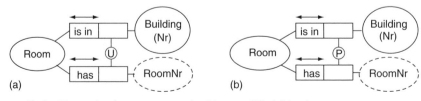

Figure 5–6   External uniqueness constraint (a) unqualified (b) primary.

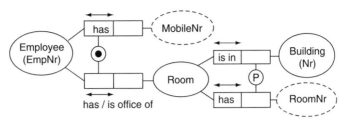

Figure 5–7   Simple and disjunctive mandatory role constraints.

mandatory constraint, or *inclusive-or* constraint and is displayed as a circled dot attached to the constrained roles.

The simple mandatory constraint on the first role of Room is in Building verbalizes as Each Room is in some Building. You already know how to add this constraint using the Fact Editor. You can also *add a simple mandatory* constraint in the Add Constraint dialog as follows. Right-click the predicate, choose Add Constraints from its context menu to invoke the Add Constraint dialog, select, Mandatory from the Constraint type drop-down list, and then select the role, as shown in Figure 5–8. Press Apply to apply the constraint and leave the dialog open, or press OK to apply the constraint and close the dialog.

The disjunctive-mandatory constraint in Figure 5–7 verbalizes as: Each Employee has some MobileNr or has some Room. For example, a contract employee might have a mobile number but not a room, and a permanent employee might have a room (and perhaps a mobile number too).

To *add a disjunctive mandatory constraint,* select its predicates (hold the Shift key down), right-click to open the context menu, select the Add Constraints option to invoke the Add Constraint dialog, select Mandatory from the Constraint type drop-down list, and then select the constrained roles. The selected roles are automatically numbered, as shown in Figure 5–9. Press Apply to apply the constraint and leave the dialog open, or press OK to apply the constraint and close the dialog. The constraint is displayed with a circled dot, as in Figure 5–7. To reposition an external uniqueness constraint on the diagram, simply select it and move it.

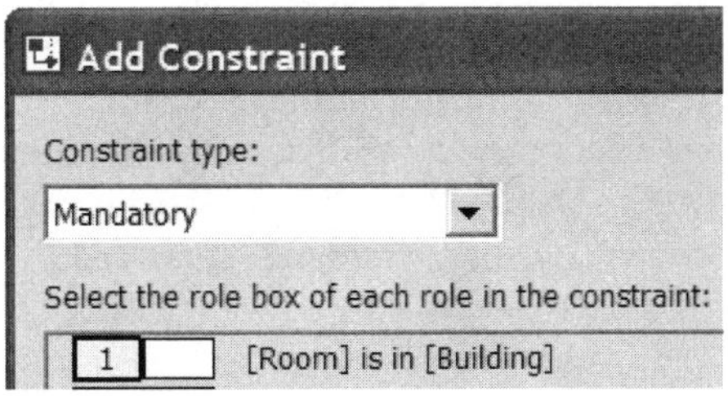

🔲 **Add Constraint**

Constraint type:

| Mandatory ▼ |

Select the role box of each role in the constraint:

| 1 | [Room] is in [Building] |

Figure 5–8   Adding the simple mandatory constraint: Each Room is in some Building.

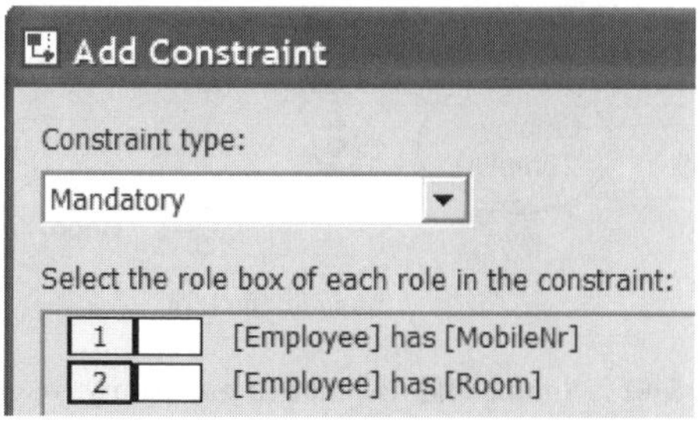

Figure 5–9   Adding a disjunctive-mandatory (inclusive-or) constraint.

> *Caution*: If an object type has many simple mandatory role constraints, the mandatory dots may sometimes appear to connect to more than one role, leading to an ambiguous diagram. If you cannot solve this problem by repositioning the roles, then move the mandatory dot to the role instead of the object type. To do this for a given role, click the predicate twice to select the role, right-click to bring up the role's context menu, then check the Mandatory on role option.

5.4   Constraint Editing and Deletion

Section 5.1 discussed how to edit or delete a value constraint. To *edit or delete a constraint that applies to one or more predicates,* select any of its predicates in the drawing window, open its Database Properties window, and select the Constraints pane. All the constraints that apply to that predicate are now displayed as icons along with the verbalization. For example, Figure 5–10 displays the two constraints that apply to the fact type Employee has Room.

To make minor edits to a constraint listed in the Constraints pane of the Database Properties window, select the constraint in the constraint listing, then press the Edit button to display its Constraint Properties dialog. Use the Notes pane of this dialog to *add notes about the constraint.* For some constraints, the dialog also has a Definition pane for simple edits (e.g., declaring a uniqueness constraint to be primary). For most constraints, you can also access the dialog by right-clicking the constraint shape and choosing Constraint Properties or Database Properties from its context menu.

To make major edits to an internal constraint, you may *edit an internal constraint using the Fact Editor.* To do so, right-click the predicate, select Fact Editor from its context menu, open the Constraints pane, and then make the desired changes. Another option is to delete the constraint and then add another constraint in its place.

To *delete a constraint* other than a value constraint, internal uniqueness constraint, or internal mandatory constraint, select the constraint shape and press the Delete key. You are now prompted "Remove selected item from the underlying model?" Press Yes to remove the constraint from the model and the diagram. Press No to remove it from the diagram only.

To delete a constraint listed in the Constraints pane of the Database Properties window, select the constraint in the constraint listing, then press the Remove button. To add

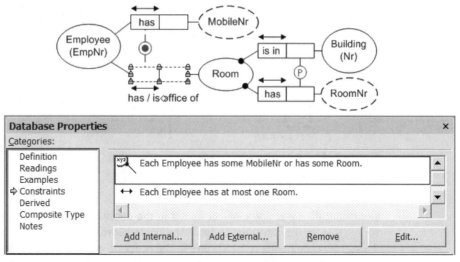

Figure 5–10   You may edit, remove, or add constraints in the database properties window.

an internal constraint to the predicate, press the Add Internal button to invoke the Add Constraint dialog and add the constraint there. To add an external constraint to the predicate, press the Add External button to invoke the Add Constraint dialog, and add the constraint there.

5.5   Set-Comparison Constraints

If two roles are played by the same object type, or their object types share a common supertype, they are said to be *compatible,* and it is meaningful to compare their populations. The same is true for role-sequences (ordered lists of roles). For databases, only three set-comparison operators are relevant: subset ($\subseteq$), equality ($=$) and mutual exclusion ($\otimes$).

Subset Constraints

A *subset constraint* from a source role sequence to a target role sequence asserts that the population of the source role sequence must always be a subset of the population of the target role sequence. The constraint is displayed graphically as a circled "$\subseteq$" connected by a dotted arrow running from the source to the target. The simplest case of a role sequence is just a single role. In Figure 5–11, the subset constraint means that the set of patients with a second given name must be a subset of the set of patients with a first given name. In other words, if a patient has a second given name, then he/she must also have a first given name.

To *add* this *subset constraint,* hold the Shift key down as you select the two predicates, right-click, and choose Add Constraints from the context menu. When the Add

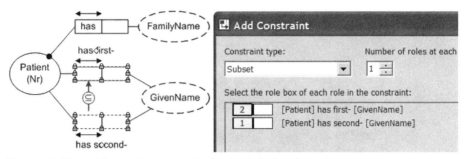

Figure 5–11   Adding a subset constraint between single roles.

Constraint dialog appears, select Subset in the Constraint type field, and then select the source role for the constraint followed by the target role. As you select role boxes in the dialog, they are numbered 1, 2, etc. in the order of selection. If you do this correctly, the dialog box should now appear as in Figure 5–11. The constraint is automatically verbalized in the lower section of the dialog box. To apply the constraint and close the dialog, press OK. The subset constraint should now appear on the diagram as shown in Figure 5–11. To reposition the constraint, select it and move it as desired.

Figure 5–12 illustrates a subset constraint between role-pairs (each role-sequence contains two roles). If, as here, the roles in a pair are contiguous, the constraint connects to the junction of the roles. This constraint means that the population of Employee-Committee pairs instantiating the chairperson association must be a subset of the population of the membership association. That is, each person who chairs a committee must be a member of that very same committee.

To *add* this *subset constraint,* hold the Shift key down as you select the predicates, right-click, and choose Add Constraints from the right-click menu. When the Add Constraint dialog appears, select Subset in the Constraint type field. Notice that the lower section now prompts: If there is more than one role at each end of the constraint, increase the indicated "Number of roles at each end" to show this. By default, the number of roles at each end of the constraint is set to 1. Since there are two roles at each end of this constraint, change this setting to 2 (as in Figure 5–12). The label "Number of roles at each" should actually read "Number of roles at each end."

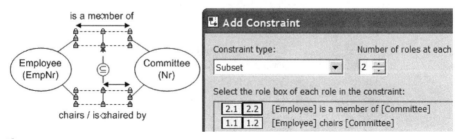

Figure 5–12   Adding a subset constraint between role-pairs.

Now select the source role pair, and then the target role pair, ordering the roles within each pair to match their corresponding role from the other pair. As you select role boxes in the dialog, they are numbered 1.1, 1.2, 2.1, 2.2 in the order of selection. The first part of each number denotes the role sequence, and the second part denotes the position within that sequence. If you do this correctly, the dialog box should now appear as in Figure 5–12. The constraint is automatically verbalized in the lower section of the dialog box. Press OK to have the constraint accepted and added to the diagram.

Equality Constraints

An *equality constraint* between role sequences indicates their populations must always be equal. This is depicted as a circles "=" connected by a dotted line to the role sequences. To *add* this *equality constraint,* hold the Shift key down as you select both predicates, right-click, and choose Add Constraints from the right-click menu. When the Add Constraint dialog appears, select Equality in the Constraint type field, and then select the role sequences (in this example, each sequence has only one role). If you do this correctly, the dialog box should appear as in Figure 5–13.

Actually, the order of the role-sequences in an equality constraint doesn't matter, since equality is symmetric (unlike subset). The constraint is verbalized in the lower section of the dialog box. Equality constraints between longer role sequences may be added in a similar way as for subset constraints.

Exclusion Constraints

An *exclusion constraint* between role sequences indicates their populations must always be disjoint (mutually exclusive). This is depicted as a circled "X" connected by a dotted line to the role sequences. Figure 5–14 includes a pair-exclusion constraint (no person wrote and reviewed and the same book) and a simple exclusion constraint (no book can be both recommended and banned).

To quickly add these exclusion constraints, hold the Shift key down as you select all four predicates, right-click, and choose Add Constraints from the right-click menu. When the Add Constraint dialog appears, select Exclusion in the Constraint type field, and then select the recommended and banned roles (as in Figure 5–14). Now press Apply to have

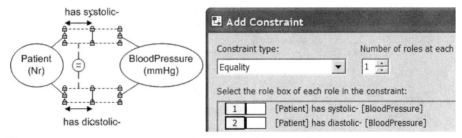

Figure 5–13 Adding a simple equality constraint between roles.

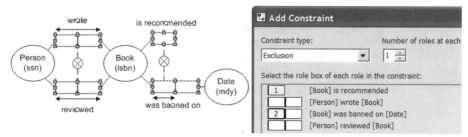

Figure 5–14 Adding a simple exclusion constraint.

the constraint accepted and displayed, while leaving the dialog box open, ready to add the other exclusion constraint.

Now select Exclusion in the Constraint type field, increment the number of roles at each end to 2, and then select the role pairs in the writing and review fact types (as in Figure 5–15). Now press OK to apply the constraint and exit the dialog.

Exclusive-or Constraints

In ORM, an *exclusive-or* constraint is simply an orthogonal combination of an inclusive-or (disjunctive mandatory) constraint and an exclusion constraint. By default, these two constraints are overlaid, as shown in Figure 5–16(a), where superimposing a circled dot (disjunctive mandatory) and circled "X" (exclusion) results in a lifebuoy symbol. To create this example, add the two fact types to the diagram window, select them, right click to bring up the Add Constraint dialog, and add first one constraint and then the other to the same roles (press Apply after adding the first constraint, and OK after the second constraint).

If you wish to visually *separate* the two constraints making up the inclusive-or constraint, right-click on the lifebuoy symbol and chose the option Split X/OR constraint. The constraints will be now displayed separately as in Figure 5–16(b). You can now work with either constraint individually. For example, you could delete just one of them by selecting it and pressing Delete. If the two constraints appear separately, you can *merge* them into the lifebuoy symbol, by selecting one of the constraints and dragging it over the other.

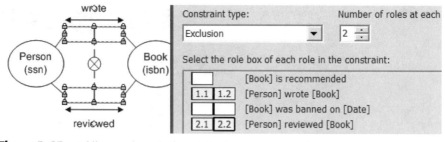

Figure 5–15 Adding a pair-exclusion constraint.

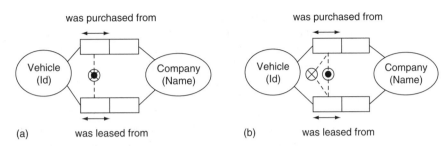

Figure 5–16   Exclusive-or is inclusive-or plus exclusion.

5.6 Subtyping

If the population of an object type *A* must always be a subset of the population of another object type *B*, then *A* is said to be a *subtype* of *B*, and *B* is said to be a *supertype* of *A*. In ORM, this is depicted visually by a solid arrow running from the subtype to the supertype. For example, Figure 5–17 shows a fragment of a model used for a hospital information system. In this model, MalePatient and FemalePatient are each subtypes of Patient.

The main reason for introducing a subtype is to declare that specific roles are played only by that type. For example: prostate status may be recorded only for male patients; pregnancy counts and pap smear results are recorded only for female patients. Hence subtyping provides another kind of *constraint*.

Other reasons for subtyping are to encourage reuse of supertypes, and to display a type taxonomy. Currently, the Visio ORM source model solution does not allow subtypes to be introduced purely for taxonomy reasons (i.e., merely to show a classification scheme). So each subtype must play at least one specific role.

To *add a subtype connection,* first ensure that the object types that are to play as subtype and supertype appear on the same page of the drawing window (e.g., declare them in the Business Rules window, and then drag them onto the drawing window). Now

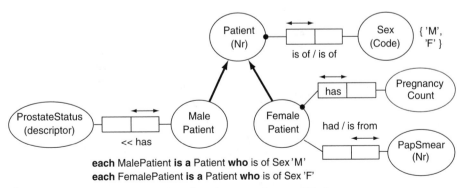

Figure 5–17   MalePatient and FemalePatient are subtypes of Patient.

drag the *Subtype Relationship arrow* from the ORM stencil onto the drawing window. Drag the end of this arrow into the center of the subtype until it is framed by a red rectangle, and then release the mouse button. The end of the arrow should now be glued to the subtype ellipse, as shown by a small red box at its end. Now drag the arrow tip to the center of the supertype until it is framed by a red rectangle, then release the mouse button. The tip of the arrow should now be glued to the subtype ellipse. Figure 5–18 shows the subtype arrow glued to MalePatient and Patient.

By default, a subtype inherits the reference scheme of its supertype, so there is no need to add a reference scheme for the subtype, except in rare cases where the reference scheme varies with different contexts. For a discussion of context-dependent reference, see Chapter 6 of Halpin (2001).

In strict ORM, each subtype must have a formal subtype definition, enabling membership in the subtype to be determined by properties of its supertype(s). For example, Figure 5–17 includes the subtype definitions: each MalePatient is a Patient who is of Sex 'M'; each FemalePatient is a Patient who is of Sex 'F'. Given this definition, and the value constraint {'M', 'F'} on Sex, the subtypes must be collectively exhaustive (their union is equal to their supertype). Given the subtype definition, and the uniqueness constraint (each Patient is of at most one Sex), the subtypes must be mutually exclusive.

So the subtypes form a partition of the supertype. In ORM, this implied partition constraint may be displayed as an xor-constraint between the supertype ends of the subtype connections (see circled X and mandatory dot in Figure 5–19). This notation is used because the xor constraint applies to roles in virtual predicates underlying the subtype connections.

This implied subtyping constraint approach enables far richer subtyping support than other approaches provide. Subtype definitions of arbitrary complexity may be expressed as queries in a formal ORM language such as ConQuer, enabling automatic generation of DDL code to enforce the constraints at the database level. This goes far beyond simple foreign key clauses and completeness and disjointness checks. For more details on this, see sections 6.5, 10.3, and 10.4 of Halpin (2001).

In practice, however, the Visio ORM tool does not yet support formal subtype definitions, or the automated display of implied exhaustion and exclusion constraints

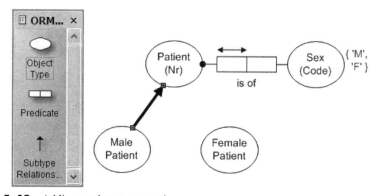

Figure 5–18 Adding a subtype connection.

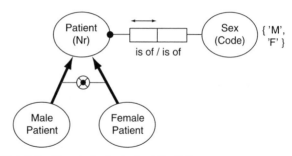

Patient
(Nr)
is of / is of
Sex
(Code)
{ 'M',
'F' }
Male
Patient
Female
Patient
each MalePatient **is a** Patient **who** is of Sex 'M'
each FemalePatient **is a** Patient **who** is of Sex 'F'

Figure 5–19 In principle, the subtype partition constraint is implied.

between subtype connections, or the full DDL code generation capabilities to map formal subtype definitions. Even without this support, it is good practice to *add subtype definitions* as comments in the Database Properties sheet for the subtype. For example, to add a subtype definition for MalePatient, double-click that object type to bring up its properties sheet, select the Subtype category to bring up the Subtype pane, and then enter the definition in the Subtype definition field, as shown in Figure 5–20.

You can phrase the subtype definition in any way you like, because it is treated simply as a comment. If you do not enter a definition for each subtype, the tool issues a warning about this when a model error check is invoked (either directly or during a build). These subtype definitions are included in the automated verbalization, but do not appear on the diagram. To display a subtype definition on the diagram, use Visio's standard Text Tool to open a text box, and then copy the definition into that. This is how the definitions were included them in the figures above.

If you want to display exhaustion and exclusion constraints between subtype connections, as in Figure 5–19, you need to do this manually using other Visio shapes and connectors. You can use the rich diagramming power of Visio to add as many adornments as you to like to the model diagrams. This is very useful for documentation purposes. However any such annotations are ignored when a relational model is built from the underlying ORM source model, or when physical DDL code is generated.

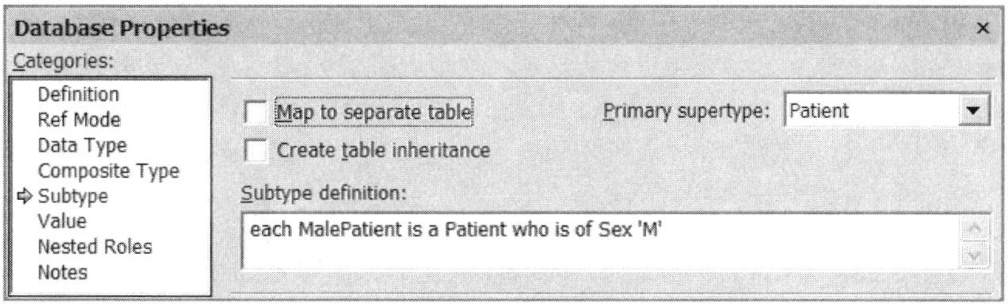

Database Properties
Categories:
Definition
Ref Mode
Data Type
Composite Type
Subtype
Value
Nested Roles
Notes
Map to separate table
Create table inheritance
Primary supertype:
Patient
Subtype definition:
each MalePatient is a Patient who is of Sex 'M'

Figure 5–20 Adding a subtype definition.

The Subtype properties pane includes a list box for the primary supertype (see Figure 5–20). The *primary supertype* provides the default reference scheme for the subtype. If a subtype has only one supertype, this is its primary supertype. If a subtype has more than one supertype, one of these must be chosen as its primary supertype. For example, the ORM schema in Figure 5–21 exhibits multiple inheritance, because FemaleInPatient has two supertypes. To choose the primary supertype, first select the subtype, then choose the relevant option from the Primary supertype drop-down list box. The tool displays the primary supertype connection as a solid arrow, and other supertype connections as a broken arrow. In Figure 5–21, FemalePatient is the primary supertype of FemaleInPatient, and InPatient is its other supertype.

In addition to the subtype definition field and primary supertype list box, the Subtype properties pane includes and check boxes for table mapping and inheritance (see Figure 5–20). The check box options do not relate to the conceptual level at all. Instead they are used to control how subtype specific details are mapped to a relational database schema. These options are discussed in detail in Chapter 7.

To *delete a subtype connection,* select the subtype arrow, then press the Delete key. Answer Yes when prompted to remove it from the underlying model. If you answer No, the arrow is removed from the diagram, but the subtype relationship remains in the model. To redisplay hidden subtype connections, right-click the subtype, then select Show Relationships from its context menu. However, this will display all the relationships in which the subtype plays, not just its subtype relationships.

5.7 Frequency Constraints

In ORM, an *occurrence frequency constraint* declares how many times an entry may occur in the population of a role, or role combination. The number of times may be a simple integer (e.g., 2), a bounded range (e.g., 2.5) or an unbounded range (e.g., >=2).

Consider the ORM model in Figure 5–22. Here each patient is allocated to at most one test group. The ">= 5" frequency constraint next to the role played by TestGroup

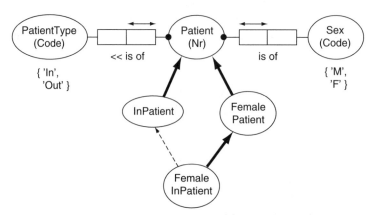

Figure 5–21   FemalePatient is the primary supertype of FemaleInPatient.

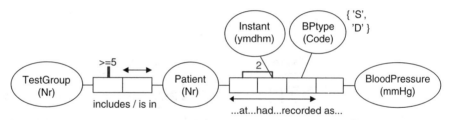

Figure 5–22   Simple and compound frequency constraints.

means that any test group that does play this role must do so at least 5 times. If you populate this fact type, each entry in the TestGroup column must appear there at least 5 times. So, non-empty test groups must include at least five patients. Be careful in choosing the role(s) to which the constraint applies. If in doubt, populate the relevant fact types to clarify the meaning of the constraint.

The quaternary fact type in Figure 5–22 is used to maintain a history of patients' blood pressure readings. BPtype (Blood pressure type) is identified by a code (D = Diastolic, S = Systolic). The "2" frequency constraint besides the role connector linking roles played by Patient and Instant indicates that any given (patient, instant) pair that populates that role pair does so exactly 2 times. In the context of the 3-role uniqueness constraint and the {'D', 'S'} value constraint on BPtype, this ensures that any time a patient has his/her BP recorded, both diastolic and systolic readings must be recorded.

To *add frequency constraints* to predicates, use either the Add Constraint dialog or the Advanced pane of the Fact Editor. The following discussion shows how to use the Add Constraint dialog to enter the two frequency constraints in Figure 5–22.

Hold the shift key down as you select both predicates, then right-click, and choose Add Constraints from the context menu. The Add Constraints dialog appears with both predicates included, as shown in Figure 5–23. To add the first frequency constraint (each test group has at least 5 patients), choose Frequency as the Constraint type, select the TestGroup role, set the Minimum frequency to 5, and delete any entry in the Maximum frequency box (no entry here means no upper limit).

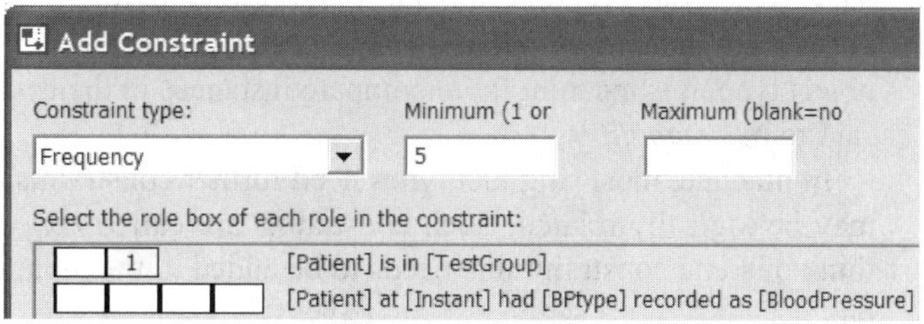

Figure 5–23   Adding the frequency constraint that each test group includes at least 5 patients.

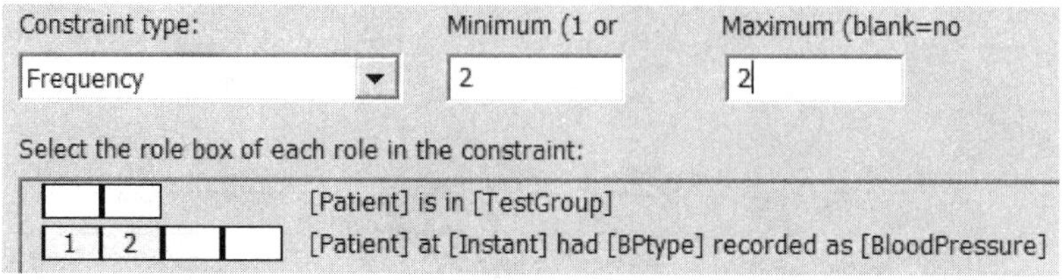

Figure 5–24 Constraint: each Patient-Instant pair in the quaternary fact table is there twice.

Take care to select the correct role—in this example, the predicate is displayed in reverse order to that shown on the diagram. Read the constraint verbalization to ensure this is consistent with your intention, and press the Apply button. The tool now displays ">=5" next to the relevant role on the ORM diagram and resets the entries in the Add Dialog window.

To add the frequency constraint on the quaternary predicate, choose Frequency as the Constraint type, select the Patient and Instant roles, and then set both the Minimum frequency and Maximum frequency to 2, as shown in Figure 5–24. Check the verbalization and then press OK to apply the constraint and exit the dialog. A "2" should now appear next to the Patient-Instant role connector as shown in Figure 5–22. If desired, you can reposition things by using standard Visio controls (e.g., use Flip Vertical on the predicate to move its uniqueness constraint to the other side, and select and drag relevant constraints and predicate text).

5.8   Ring Constraints

In some universities, it is common practice for an academic to be monitored by another academic. Monitoring involved attending a lecture by the other academic, and giving him/her feedback on how to improve it. Although each academic has at most one monitor, it is possible for the same academic to monitor many other academics. This monitoring relationship is modeled as an n:1 binary fact type in the simple ORM model shown in Figure 5–25.

Notice that both roles in the is-monitored-by predicate are played by the same object type, Academic. The fact type path goes from the object type through the role pair and back to the object type, forming a ring. For this reason, the fact type Academic is monitored by Academic is called a *ring fact type*. Since both roles are played by the same object type, it is meaningful to compare instances in their populations, and the roles are said to be *compatible*.

In practice, most ring fact types need further constraints on how their role instances may be logically related. Such constraints are called *ring constraints*. See if you can think of some constraint that needs to be added to the monitor fact type, before reading on.

As you may have guessed, we should at least require that no academic is monitored by himself/herself. Technically this is said to be an *irreflexive* ring constraint, and is

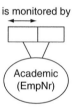

Figure 5–25   The monitoring association is a ring fact type.

denoted by the symbol "°*ir*" besides the two roles involved, as shown in Figure 5–26. The "°" suggests a ring, and the "*ir*" is short for "irreflexive".

To *add a ring constraint* to a predicate, you can use either the Add Constraint dialog or the Constraints pane of the Fact Editor. *Note:* If the constrained roles are played by different but compatible object types (e.g., a subtype and its supertype) then you must use the Add Constraint dialog, not the Fact Editor. The following discussion shows how to add the ring constraint in Figure 5–26 using the Add Constraint dialog, assuming the fact type is already displayed in the drawing window.

Right-click the monitor predicate, and select Add Constraints from the context menu to bring up the Add Constraint dialog. Now choose Ring from the Constraint type field, and click the two roles in the displayed predicate (see Figure 5–27).

As you select the two roles, they are automatically numbered 1 and 2, and the Ring Constraint Properties dialog appears, with the mouse cursor appearing as a cross-hair. Move this cursor to select the ellipse marked ir (irreflexive), which sets the constraint's Ring Type to Irreflexive (see Figure 5–28).

Press the OK button to apply this choice and close the properties dialog. The Add Constraint dialog now displays the constraint verbalization as "No Academic is monitored by itself". If you would rather see the verbalization at the same time as you move the cross-hair cursor over the constraint selector, you can alternatively enter ring constraints directly via the Fact Editor.

Press OK in the Add Constraint dialog to apply the constraint and exit the dialog. The ring constraint now appears on the diagram, as shown in Figure 5–26. You can finesse the diagram by using standard Visio controls (use Flip Vertical on the predicate to move its uniqueness constraint to the other side, then select and drag the predicate text). As

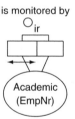

Figure 5–26   The irreflexive constraint declares that no academic monitors himself/herself.

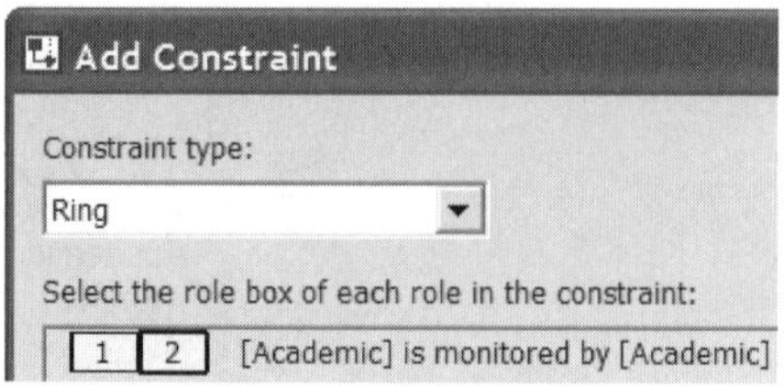

Figure 5–27   Selecting the roles for a ring constraint.

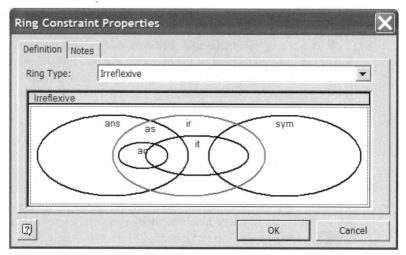

Figure 5–28   Choosing the specific type of ring constraint.

usual, you can see the verbalization of all constraints on the predicate by selecting it and opening the Verbalizer.

A *ring constraint* may apply only to a pair of roles played by the same (or a compatible) object type. The role pair may form a binary predicate or be embedded in a longer predicate. Let R be the relation type comprising the role pair. Using "iff" for "if and only if", "~" for "not" and "→" for "implies," we say that R is *irreflexive* iff for all x, $\sim xRx$. This is denoted by connecting the role pair to the constraint symbol "^{o}ir".

As shown in Figure 5–28, you may specify six kinds of ring constraint. The other five may be summarized as follows. R is *symmetric* iff for all x, y, $xRy \rightarrow yRx$. Symmetry is used more often for derivation, but if used as a constraint, it is denoted by connecting the role pair to "^{o}sym". R is *asymmetric* (^{o}as) iff for all x, y, $xRy \rightarrow \sim yRx$. R is *antisymmetric* (^{o}ans) iff for all x, y, $x \neq y$ & $xRy \rightarrow \sim yRx$. R is *intransitive* (^{o}it) iff for all x, y, z, xRy & $yRz \rightarrow \sim xRz$. Asymmetry and intransitivity each imply irreflexivity. Exclusion implies asymmetry (and irreflexivity). An irreflexive, functional relation must be intransitive. One very expensive ring constraint to enforce is *acyclicity* (^{o}ac), i.e., no cycles are permitted by using the relationship type one or more times. For further explanation of these concepts, see section 7.3 of Halpin (2001).

Although the Euler diagram in Figure 5–28 may appear complex, it actually simplifies things by avoiding incompatible or redundant ring constraints. For example, if you choose Asymmetric, the tool won't let you choose Irreflexive as well because this is implied by asymmetry. For the monitoring relationship discussed earlier, it is possible for two academics to monitor each other, so this is a simple case of irreflexivity, not asymmetry.

More than one atomic ring constraint may apply to the same predicate. For example, the fact type Person is parent of Person in Figure 5–29 is declared to be both asymmetric (as) and intransitive (it). The tool treats this as a single, composite ring constraint, as indicated by bracketing the two components (as,it). To add this constraint, use the Add Constraint dialog as before and position the cross-hair cursor to obtain the "Asymmetric + Intransitive" option.

To facilitate checking of incompatible or duplicate ring constraints, the tool relies on the Euler diagram interface for ring constraints, allowing only one ring constraint (simple or composite) per predicate. So if you previously added one ring constraint to a predicate, and wish to add a second one to it, you need to edit the original constraint, replacing it with the composite constraint. To edit an existing constraint on a single predicate, select the predicate to invoke its Database Properties sheet, choose the Constraints category, select the constraint, and then press the Edit button.

The tool verbalizes the asymmetric and intransitive constraints as shown below. The intransitive constraint assumes that parenthood is restricted to genetic parenthood and that no incest is allowed. In reality, the parenthood relation is not just asymmetric, but acyclic. Acyclicity constraints involve recursion, and may be expensive to enforce. For details of how the tool maps ring constraints to DDL code, see section 7.5.

    If Person p1 is parent of Person p2
       then it cannot be that
       Person p2 is parent of Person p1.

    If Person p1 is parent of Person p2
       and Person p2 is parent of Person p3
       then it cannot be that
       Person p1 is parent of Person p3.

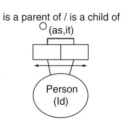

Figure 5–29   The parenthood association is asymmetric and intransitive.

5.9 Indexes

Just as an index to a book enables you to quickly find a topic of interest, indexes on database columns enable the database system to quickly access entries for those columns. Being a performance issue, indexes relate to the physical level rather than the conceptual level. However you may annotate roles in an ORM schema with index markers to declare facts you want efficient access to in the physical implementation.

An *index marker* is displayed as a circled "I" attached to the role(s) it impacts. For example, Figure 5–30 includes indexes to provide efficient access to a patient's family name and birth country. Most DBMSs automatically create unique indexes on primary keys and columns with unique constraints, so there is normally no need to add an index to a role if it has a simple uniqueness constraint.

An index on family name makes sense if you often want to access a patient's details without having to specify their patient number, but rather by entering a family name to list all patients with that name.

To *add an index* to one or more roles, right-click the predicate(s) and choose Add Constraints to open the Add Constraint dialog. Then choose Index as the Constraint type, select the role(s), then press OK to apply the constraint and exit the dialog (or press Apply to apply the constraint without exiting the dialog).

For example, to add an index for a patient's family name, make the selection shown in Figure 5–31. The message field at the bottom of the dialog will advise that a non-unique index will be created over the role played by Familyname. When the model is mapped to a relational schema, a non-unique index will be created over the column(s) to which that role maps. Since many people may have the same family name, the index will be non-unique. Hit the OK button to apply the index and exit the dialog. An index marker now appears as a circled "I" on the ORM model, attached to the family name role, as shown in Figure 5–30. Although stored with the ORM model, this physical annotation is not part of the pure conceptual schema.

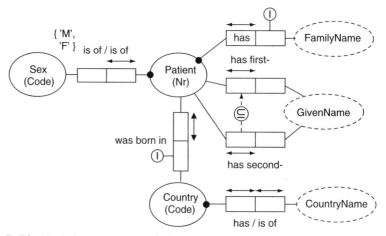

Figure 5–30 An index appears as a circled "I" attached to the role(s) it constraints.

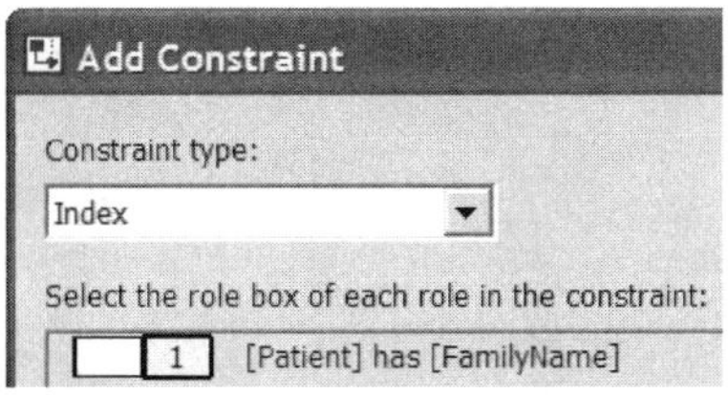

Figure 5–31 Adding an index marker to the role played by FamilyName.

In Figure 5–30, another index is applied to the role played by Country in the association Person was born in Country. If you often want to inquire about where a person was born, and you want the name of the country, not just the country-code, when you make such a query, then this entails a frequent conceptual join operation between the two roles played by Country. These roles map to separate tables, one role mapping to a foreign key and the other to its referenced primary key. At the relational level, this means we have a need to efficiently join the tables by matching the foreign and primary key values. In this case, you can add an index on the birth-country role by clicking on its fact type and using the Add Constraint dialog.

Non-uniqueness indexes are sometimes over-used. In most cases, an index should be applied only after an analysis of the focused transactions for the application reveals a performance need for it.

Indexes can also be specified directly on a logical model. Examples of DDL code generated to enforce indexes are discussed in Chapter 7.

5.10 Constraint Layers

One of ORM's strengths is its richly expressive constraint notation. When specifying detailed requirements, it's often helpful to visualize the relevant business rules graphically. However, there may be times when you wish to ignore the fine details. One way to do this is to use *constraint layers* to control which kinds of constraints are displayed on screen and/or printed. In the ORM Source model solution, constraint layers are implemented using Visio's standard layer properties mechanism.

For example, the ORM model in Figure 5–30 displays five kinds of constraints: simple mandatory, internal uniqueness, value, subset, and index. Simple mandatory and internal uniqueness constraints are stored as part of the predicate shape, so are always displayed. But you can suppress the display of all other kinds of ORM constraints by controlling the layer properties settings for the diagram. To access the Layer Properties dialog, choose View > Layer Properties from the main menu. The dialog for our current model is shown Figure 5–32.

Different kinds of constraint exist on different layers. In addition to the always-shown constraints (simple mandatory and internal uniqueness), this model has constraints on layers 2, 3, and 5. Layer 2 shows disjunctive mandatory (inclusive-or) and set-comparison (subset, equality, exclusion) constraints. Layer 3 shows value constraints. Layer 5 shows index markers.

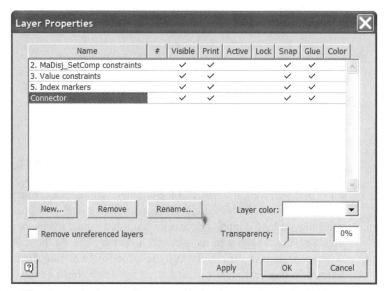

Figure 5–32   Constraint layers allow most kinds of constraints to be hidden.

To *suppress display on screen of a constraint layer,* click the check mark in the Visible column in this dialog (this removes the check mark), then press the Apply button. If you remove all check marks for Visible in this example, Figure 5–30 will be redisplayed without value, subset, and index constraints. The diagram will still print as Figure 5–30 unless you uncheck the entries in the Print column. The column entries are toggles, so you can restore a check mark to a cell simply by clicking it. ORM models may include other kinds of constraint that exist on other layers.

With the exception of simple mandatory and internal uniqueness constraints, ORM constraints are partitioned into five layers, as shown in Figure 5–33. Each layer can be individually controlled.

Layer 1 includes external uniqueness constraints. Layer 2 includes disjunctive-mandatory (inclusive-or) and set comparison (subset, equality, exclusion) constraints. Since exclusive-or constraints are simply combinations of inclusive-or and exclusion constraints, these are included on layer 2. Layer 3 holds value constraints. Layer 4 displays frequency and ring constraints. Finally, layer 5 is used for indexes. By default, all constraints are displayed and printed, unless their display/print setting is unchecked.

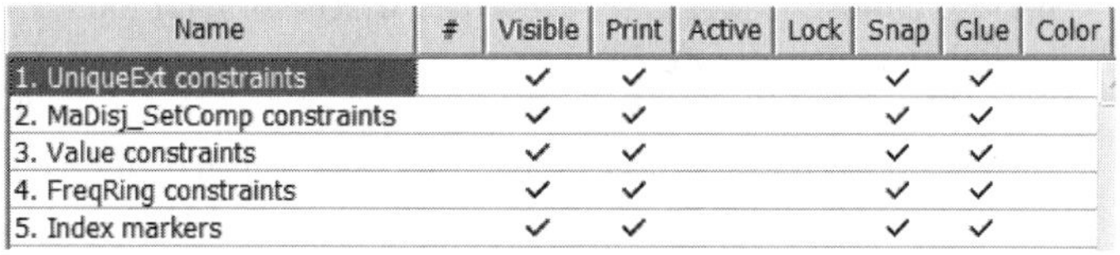

Name	#	Visible	Print	Active	Lock	Snap	Glue	Color
1. UniqueExt constraints		✓	✓			✓	✓	
2. MaDisj_SetComp constraints		✓	✓			✓	✓	
3. Value constraints		✓	✓			✓	✓	
4. FreqRing constraints		✓	✓			✓	✓	
5. Index markers		✓	✓			✓	✓	

Figure 5–33   Five layers of constraints may be suppressed.

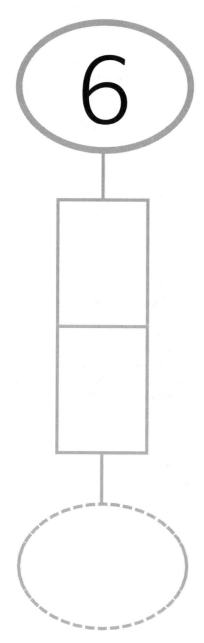

Configuring, Manipulating, and Reusing ORM Models

6.1   Configuring ORM Preferences

When you first work with the ORM modeling solution, the tool applies various default settings to determine how it displays the user interface, and how it reacts to certain user commands. You can change these settings to better suit your personal preferences by entering your choices in the *Database Modeling Preferences* dialog.

To access this dialog, choose Database > Options > Modeling from the main menu. The dialog includes Fact Editor and ORM Diagram panes for setting ORM preferences. The other two panes deal with preferences for the logical modeling solution, and are covered in a later chapter.

Figure 6–1 shows the Fact Editor pane of the dialog with the category set to Input preferences. Use this to choose Guided or Freeform entry, decide whether to combine "at most one" and "some" as "exactly one" in constraints, and use capitals or brackets to distinguish object types. These options were explained in sections 4.2 and 4.3.

Use the Category list-box in the Fact Editor pane to select the Miscellaneous preferences and Syntax Colors options displayed in Figure 6–2. These options should be self-explanatory. For further details on any of these options, select the option, then press the F1 key to display the context-sensitive help.

Select the ORM Diagram tab of the Database Modeling Preferences dialog to display the ORM Diagram pane shown in Figure 6–3. By default, the option for When removing an object from a diagram is set to "Ask user what to do." This ensures that if you press the Delete key when one or more model elements are selected, you are prompted whether to delete them from the diagram only or from the model as well. This prompt can save you from an accidental deletion, so don't change this default setting unless you have good reason to do so.

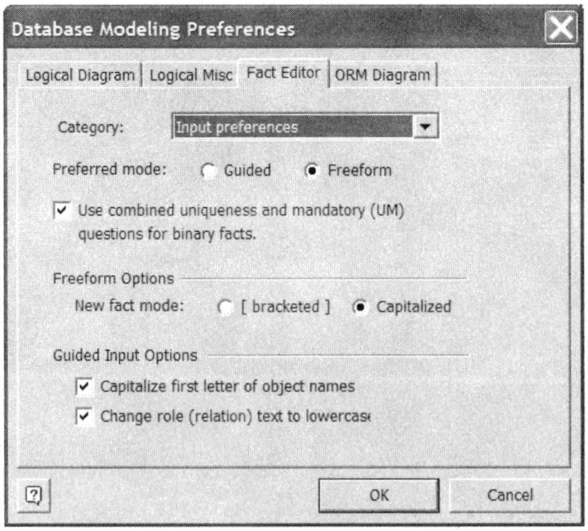

Figure 6–1   Configuring input preferences for the Fact Editor.

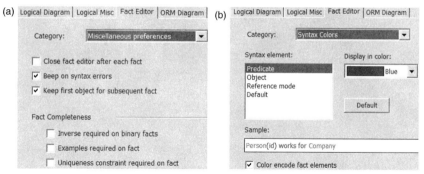

Figure 6–2 Configuring other Fact Editor preferences.

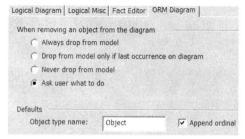

Figure 6–3 Configuring ORM diagram preferences.

The Object type name field allows you to control the base default name for new object types. By default, this is "Object." The Append ordinal check box is used to append numbers 2, 3, etc., to the default names of second and later object types. So unless you choose otherwise, new object types are named "Object," "Object2," etc., until you rename them. To view this behavior, drag the Object Type shape from the ORM stencil multiple times onto the drawing window.

6.2 Showing Relationships for Object Types

In an ORM schema, object types may be connected by predicates and/or subtype relationships. Graphically, a predicate is depicted as a named sequence of one or more role boxes, and a subtype relationship is depicted as an arrow from subtype to supertype. To understand the impact of a given object type within a model, it is extremely useful to view all of its connections to the rest of the schema.

Although you can use the Business Rules window to drag all of an object type's fact types onto the drawing window, this can be tedious since you need to search for all the fact types that include the object type at any position in the predicate (start, middle, or end). Moreover, the Business Rules window does not include the subtype connections for the object type. Fortunately, the context menu of an object type includes a *Show Relationships* operation that let's you display all of its connections in one go. Applying

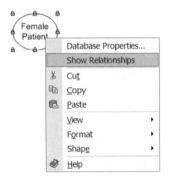

Figure 6–4   Right-click an object type to access its context menu.

this operation to an object type displays all of the fact types and subtype relationships in which it participates.

The best way to understand this operation is to watch it in action. Let's see how it works using the Patient CS model. Open this model, and then insert a new page by selecting Insert > New Page... from the main menu. If the Page Setup dialog appears, press the OK button to accept the default settings. The drawing window now displays a new, blank page. Open the Object Types pane of the Business Rules window, and drag FemalePatient onto the drawing surface. Now right-click this shape to display its context menu, and select Show Relationships, as shown in Figure 6–4.

This results in the display shown in Figure 6–5. In the global schema, FemalePatient participates in the two fact types shown and in a subtype relationship to Patient.

Now right-click the PapSmear object type, and choose Show Relationships from its context menu. This adds to the display all the other connections for PapSmear. This results in two more fact types being displayed, as shown in Figure 6–6.

Using the Show Relationships feature, you can progressively open up a model, expanding the neighborhood displayed for any object type you choose. This is very useful for model browsing, and for deciding what the impact would be of removing

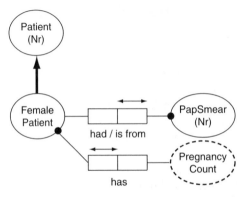

Figure 6–5   The display after applying Show Relationships to FemalePatient.

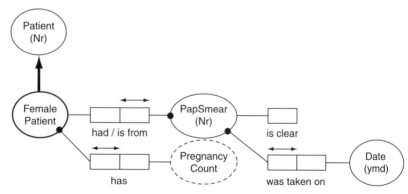

Figure 6–6   The display on applying Show Relationships to PapSmear in Figure 6–5.

an object type from the model. As we'll see in a later chapter, it is also extremely useful for displaying an ORM model that has been reverse-engineered from an existing database.

6.3   Redisplaying Model Elements

Each model element such as an object type or predicate occurs only once in the underlying model. However, you can display as many copies as you like of the same model element on the diagram, on the same page or on different pages.

One reason to display multiple copies of a model element on the same page is to provide a cleaner layout by avoiding line crossings. This is especially true if your model includes object types like Date and MoneyAmount, which often play lots of roles. For example, the diagram for the insurance model fragment shown in Figure 6–7 is untidy because the role connector from Date to the birthdate role crosses over the branch location fact type.

One solution to this problem is to place another copy of the Date object type on the diagram, and connect the birthdate role to it, as shown in Figure 6–8. The easiest way to *copy a diagram instance of a model element* is to *Control-drag it* to another place on the diagram. To do this, select the element shape, then hold the Ctrl key down as you drag a copy of it to the new position using the mouse. In this example, we also need to reposition the role connector. To do this, select the role (two mouse clicks) then drag the end of its connector (displayed as a small, red diamond) and glue it to the desired copy of the object type shape.

Although the diagram displays two different copies of the Date object type, both copies denote the same underlying object type in the model. If you make a change to one (e.g. change its name or data type) this change is immediately reflected in the other copy.

An alternative way to redisplay an object type or a fact type is to *drag it onto the page from the Business Rules window*. This is also the only way to display an object type or fact type on a page where no instance of it is yet displayed.

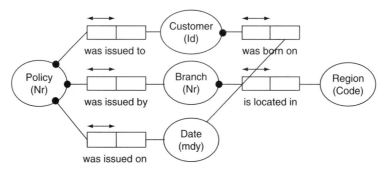

Figure 6–7   This diagram is untidy because of edge crossings.

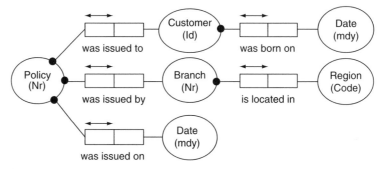

Figure 6–8   An extra copy of Date is used to avoid edge crossings.

If the object types in a subtype-supertype relationship have been redisplayed without the relationship itself, you can now redisplay the relationship as well by selecting the arrow and control-dragging it to connect to the object types.

More than one model element can be redisplayed at once. So long as you stay on the same page, you can select all or part of the model displayed on that page, and redisplay the selection by controlling-dragging it to another position on the page.

6.4 Cloning Model Elements

It is also possible to *clone a model element*. Cloning creates a new model element (not just a shape) based on an existing one. When created, the clone has the same model properties as the original, except for the name. To clone a model element that is displayed on a diagram page, select the element, press Ctrl+C to copy it to the clipboard, then move the mouse cursor to the position (on the same page or a different page) where you wish to display the clone, and press Ctrl+V to paste the clone there. Instead of Ctrl+C, you can use the main menu option Edit > Copy. Instead of Ctrl+V, you can use the menu option Edit > Paste.

Each clone of an object type is assigned the name of its source, appended by a number that indicates the order in which it has been cloned from the original. For example, if you copy the Date object type to the clipboard and paste it, this results in the clone Date1. If you now copy the Date1 object type to the clipboard and paste it, this results in the clone Date11. If instead you copy the Date object type to the clipboard and paste it twice, this results in the clones Date1 and Date2. Any cloned predicate is assigned the name of its original predicate, with no additional number. Within the same model or namespace, each object type must have a different name, but different predicates may have the same name.

A clone initially has the same model properties as the original, except for its name. If you later make a change to the original (e.g., modify its data type), this change is not propagated to the clone. Similarly, if you later make a change to the clone, this change is not propagated to the original. This is because the original and the clone correspond to different underlying model elements.

You can clone all or part of the model displayed on a page by selecting the relevant model elements, copying the selecting to the clipboard (Ctrl+C) and then pasting the cloned selection to the new position (Ctrl+V). For example, if you select the fact type Customer was born on Date, and then copy and paste it, this results in the clone fact type Customer1 was born on Date1, as shown in Figure 6–9. As you can confirm by looking in the Business Rules window, these are two different fact types. Collectively, they include four different object types (Customer, Customer1, Date, Date1) and two different predicates that just happen to have the same name "was born on."

Cloning within the same model can speed up the process of adding new elements that have similar properties to existing ones. However, the most useful application of this copy-paste technique is to *clone all* or *part of a model into another source model*. For example, if you select and copy the model shown in Figure 6–8 to the clipboard, you can then open a new ORM source model and paste the clone into that. In this case, the diagram of the cloned model looks identical to the original model, with the names unchanged. Numbers are not appended to object type names in the new model, because the cloned model is already distinguished from its source by being in a different document. This cloning feature is extremely powerful, allowing you to duplicate whole models very quickly.

For *documentation* purposes, you can also copy and paste any selection from a model diagram into a word-processing document or a slide-presentation document for display there. For example, to copy an ORM diagram into Microsoft Word, select and copy the diagram to the clipboard, open a Word document, choose Edit > Paste Special from its main menu, and then choose the desired Paste option (the Picture option is usually best for copying just the diagram). See Chapter 9 for further details on model reporting and documentation.

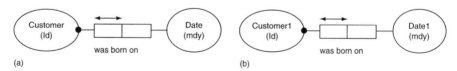

Figure 6–9 Fact type (a) is copied and pasted to produce the clone (b).

6.5 Cutting and Pasting Model Elements

Although it is possible to cut and paste model elements, this procedure has limited use, and needs to be handled with care. To *cut* one or more model elements to the clipboard, first select the relevant model elements on the diagram surface, and then press Ctrl+X or choose Edit > Cut from the main menu. To *paste* this selection from the clipboard onto a drawing page, move the mouse cursor to the desired position and then press Ctrl+V or choose Edit > Paste from the main menu.

Cutting and pasting a model element selection to another position on the same or a different page moves the display of those model elements to the new position. However, *any connections that the model elements had with the rest of the model will be lost*. For example, Figure 6–10 shows the effect of cutting the Patient object type from the first page of the Patient model. The six fact types in which Patient played on this page are now incomplete. Even if you pasted Patient back onto this page, it would have no connection to these fact types. You would need to re-establish the connections yourself by gluing the dangling role connectors to it. Moreover, all the connections that Patient had on other pages of the model would also be lost.

Essentially, the cut operation deletes the selection from the underlying model (not just the diagram). Although the model element selection on the clipboard is kept intact, it no longer has any semantic connection to the model. When you later paste that selection onto the diagram, you must re-declare any connections that you wish it to have with the rest of the model. This can be a lot of work, especially for model elements that were displayed more than once (on the same page or on multiple pages), since all those connections need to be redrawn. For such reasons, you will probably find little use for cutting and pasting model elements.

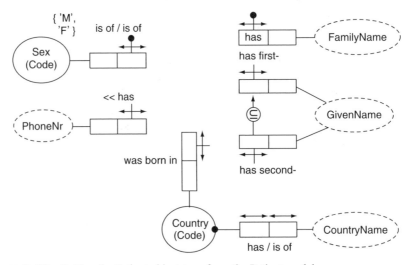

Figure 6–10 Cutting the Patient object type from the Patient model.

If you really want to move an object type or fact type from one page to another, drag a copy of it from the Business Rules window onto the other page, then select it on the original page, press the Delete key and answer No when prompted whether to delete it from the model.

If the whole model is displayed on a single page, and no element is displayed on another page, you can select the whole diagram then cut and paste it safely to a new page. However you can achieve the same effect simply by renaming and reordering pages. Our advice is to ignore the cut operation entirely when working with models.

6.6 Referencing Model Elements

Each object type is either an entity type or a value type, and is defined in exactly one model. Each predicate is also defined in exactly one model. It is possible however to define an object type or predicate in one model, and then reference it from one or more other models. In this case, the object type or predicate is said to be *external* to the referencing model(s).

For example, suppose the schema in Figure 6–11 is our preferred way to model states and countries. Here a country is primarily identified by a code (e.g., 'US') but also has a unique name (e.g., 'United States of America'). A state is primarily identified by combining its country with its state code, but also has a unique name within its country. For example, Washington State is identified by the country code, state code combination 'US', 'WA', and West Australia is identified using the code combination 'AU', 'WA'. Suppose we save this model using the name StateCountry_CS.

Now suppose the simple schema at the top of Figure 6–12 is another ORM source model named Invoice_CS. This schema *references an object type* named State, which has been declared external by checking the External check box in the definition pane of its Database Properties window, as shown. Object types that are external to a model are displayed in that model with a shaded fill pattern, and with no identification scheme.

In the model where they are defined, external object types are displayed as normal object types, along with their identification scheme, since they are internal to that

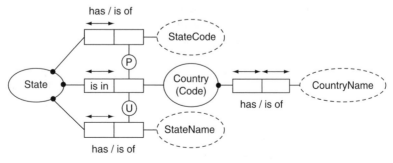

Figure 6–11 A standard model for States and Countries.

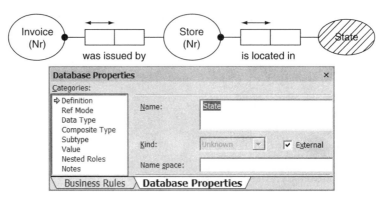

Figure 6–12   State is declared to be an external object type for the Invoice model.

model. Although the Invoice schema in Figure 6–12 declares State as an external object type, there is so far no connection between this and the State object type defined in the schema of Figure 6–11. It is possible that we might define a State object type in many models, and the system has no way of knowing at this stage which definition is intended for the Invoice schema.

To make the connection, both models must be included in the same *database model project*. Chapter 3 provided an introduction to project building, and Chapter 7 discusses this process in more detail. If you create a project that includes both the StateCountry_CS and Invoice_CS source models, the system automatically *merges* these models into a single, global model, matching the name of each object type that has been declared external to one model with the name of an object type defined in another model.

Once this resolution has taken place, each external object type is effectively replaced by a pointer to its definition in the other source model. Hence, if at any time later the definition of the external object type is changed in the model that defines it, this change is immediately reflected in the source model that references it. To propagate this change to a logical database model already built from the source model, you still need to rebuild the project.

When you try to build a project, if no match is found for an external object type, an error message notes that the object type is undefined. Right-click the error message to highlight the undefined external object type, and then take appropriate action to ensure it is defined in another source model for that project.

If more than one match is found for an external object type, an error message reports that the object type has more than one definition. You can then rename all but one of the candidate defining object types to ensure only one match is made. If you really do want more than one object type with the same name in the global model, you can add a different namespace for each candidate defining object type except the one you want to match up with.

Adding multiple ORM source models to the same project effectively forms the union of these source models, matching external and internal object types by name. When you build the project, this union is then mapped to a logical database schema.

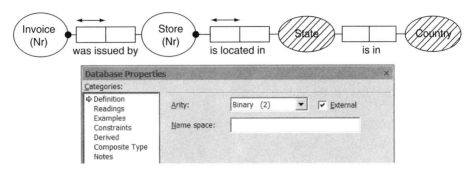

Figure 6–13 The predicate in State is in Country is declared as external.

For example, a project formed by adding StateCountry_CS and Invoice_CS includes all the fact types from both.

To reuse just part of StateCountry_CS (e.g., just the primary reference scheme for State), you could include that subschema in Invoice_CS by cloning (copy-pasting) it from StateCountry_CS, rather than using an external object type. Of course, if you ever change the definition later in the StateCountry_CS model, this won't propagate automatically to your Invoice_CS model.

Predicates may be referenced in a similar way to object types. For example, the expanded Invoice model in Figure 6–13 references two external object types (State and Country) as well as the external predicate contained in the fact type State is in Country. This predicate has been declared external by checking the External check box in the definition pane of its Database Properties window, as shown. Predicates that *are* external to a model are displayed in that model without any constraints (since these are declared in their defining model). Unlike external object types, external predicates are displayed with no special fill pattern.

A predicate reference is resolved when its model is merged with its defining model during a project build. Note that predicates are not distinguished simply by their name (e.g., "is in"). For example, the defining model could have many predicates with the local reading "is in," but it will have only one sentence type with the reading "State is in Country," and the references for State and Country are already disambiguated as discussed earlier. Because a predicate's sentence type provides its context, you should never need to make a name space entry to disambiguate a predicate reference.

As you can see, there are a number of ways in which you can *reuse* model components within other models. If you are building many models for a particular domain, it is often worthwhile to identify model fragments that are likely to be reused in different models, and save these fragments either as separate models that can be added into other projects, or as parts of a standard reference model where they can be selectively cloned into other models. In deciding which technique to apply, consider the impact of later changes to the original definition. Merging takes care of such changes automatically at the source model level, but cloning does not.

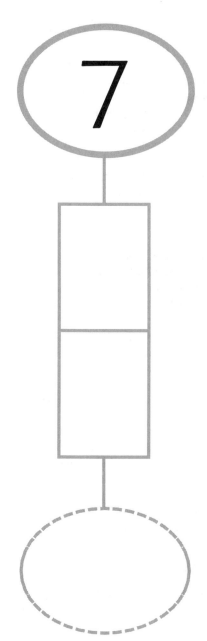

7 Mapping ORM Models to Logical Database Models

7.1   Forward Engineering ORM Source Models

Forward engineering is the process of transforming higher level models to lower level models. Figure 7–1 displays an overview of this process, starting at the conceptual level (ORM), mapping to the logical level (ER or relational), and then generating the physical database model. The first stage, mapping ORM models to logical database models, is called the *build* process and is the main focus of this chapter.

The second stage, transforming a logical database model to a physical database schema, is called the *generate* process. It is usually best to first generate the data definition language (DDL) script containing the SQL statements for creating the relational schema, so you can check it over. Once you are happy with the DDL script, you can execute it in your chosen DBMS to create the actual database schema. With some DBMSs, you may also generate the database schema directly if connected to the DBMS.

If you later make changes to the logical database model, you can propagate those changes to the existing database by using the *update* process. The generate and update processes are covered in detail in later chapters and are not discussed further here.

Chapter 3 included a simple example to illustrate the basic process of building a single logical model from a single ORM model. As illustrated in Figure 7–1, it is also possible to build a logical model from two or more ORM source models. In this case, the tool will automatically merge the source models into a single, global model before building the logical model. If it finds any name clashes, it will prompt you to resolve these before completing the build. As Figure 7–1 also shows, the same source model may be used for building more than one logical model. As discussed in section 6.6, this provides one way to reuse existing source models.

When a logical database model is built from one or more ORM source models, the tool creates a *project* to house the relevant documents. In addition to the logical database model, the project may contain non-source documents, such as a text file you might add to the project for further documentation. In this case, when you build the project a harmless warning is issued that that file is not recognized as a source model. When you open a project file, each of its component files (source or non-source) is displayed, and you can open each file by double-clicking its icon.

Building a Logical Database Model from ORM

To transform a set of one or more ORM models to a logical database model, first add the ORM model(s) to a database model project, and then build the project. The following steps summarize the procedure.

1. For each saved ORM model that you wish to include as a source, perform an error check by choosing Database > Model Error Check, and make any corrections needed.
2. From the File menu, open the logical modeling solution by choosing File > New > Database > Database Model Diagram.
3. To create a database model project, choose Database > Project > Add existing document from the Database menu.

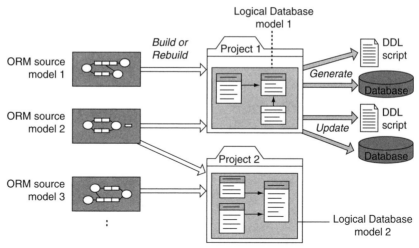

Figure 7-1 Forward engineering models: conceptual → logical → physical.

4. The Add Document to Project dialog box appears. For each ORM model you wish to add, use the Look in: field to navigate to the model, then press the Open button. The ORM model(s) should now be listed in the project window. To add non-model files to the project, change the dialog setting for the Files of Type: field to All Files (*.*), before pressing the Open button.

5. Save the project file by pressing the Save icon on the main menu and giving it a filename. The project file automatically has the extension ".vsd." The name and page of your current model is always listed in the title bar at the top of the screen.

6. Now *build* the logical model by choosing Database > Project > Build from the Database menu.

The relational database schema is now automatically built. The Output window records the progress of the build process. If the build fails, error messages are generated. If the build succeeds, the resulting table schemes appear in the Tables and Views window. By default, if the ORM models are correct, the build process generates a relational schema in fifth normal form.

Although the table structures have been created, they do not yet appear on a diagram. To see the logical database model in graphical form, drag the table schemes you wish to see onto one or more drawing pages of the project window. To select one table scheme, simply click it before dragging. To select a group of adjacent table schemes, hold the Shift key down as you click the first and last member. To select a group of non-adjacent table schemes, hold the Ctrl key down as you click each member. To add a new drawing page, select Insert > New Page from the main menu.

For example, suppose the conceptual schema in Figure 7–2, which is a variation of our Patient model, is saved as the file P_CS. Now suppose that this is used as the only source model to build a logical database schema named P_LS.

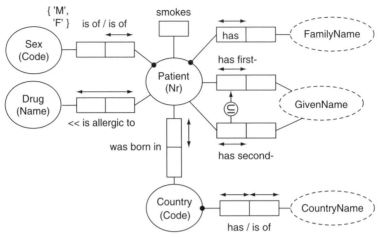

Figure 7–2   A sample ORM model.

When the project is saved, an icon for the ORM source model appears in the Project window, as shown in Figure 7–3. When the project is built, the fact types are grouped into three table schemes, as shown in the Tables and Views window of Figure 7–3. This window shows only the names of the base tables and views. In this example, there are just three base tables and no views. A more detailed depiction of the logical model results from dragging the table schemes onto the drawing window, as shown in Figure 7–3. This displays the names of each table and column, as well as the foreign key connections between them.

Each table has its name in the shaded header, with its columns listed below. Primary keys are underlined, marked "PK" and appear in the top compartment for the columns. Mandatory (not null) columns are displayed in bold. Foreign key columns are marked FK*n* where *n* is the number of the foreign key within the table. Each foreign key connection is depicted as an arrow from the foreign key table to the target table. Uniqueness constraints on columns other than primary keys are marked U*n* where *n* is the number of the uniqueness constraint within the table.

ORM constraints that map to check clauses, triggers, or stored procedures are not displayed on the logical diagram, but may be viewed separately in code windows, as discussed later in the chapter. In this example, the constraints missing from the logical diagram are the value constraint for SexCode and the subset constraint involving given names. If desired, the column data types may be displayed on the diagram by choosing the menu option Database > Options > Document, opening the Table Pane, and then picking the Data Types radio button Show physical. It's best to set the data types on the ORM model, where object types correspond to conceptual domains. The correct data types then automatically propagate to all the attributes based on these domains.

It is good practice to keep the ORM source model open when you build a project. You can then toggle between the conceptual and logical models by choosing the relevant model from the Window option of the main menu. If the ORM model is closed, you can open it by clicking its icon in the Project widow.

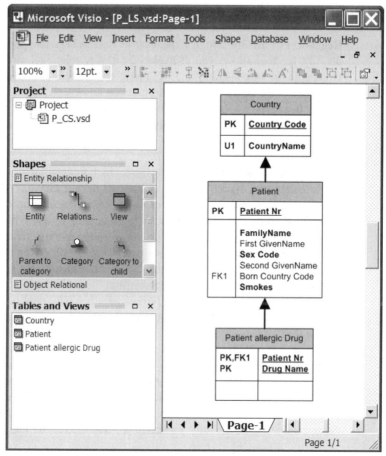

Figure 7–3   Default mapping of the sample ORM source model.

If the tool's original default settings are used, the table and column names shown in Figure 7–3 are generated automatically. The order in which the columns are listed may vary from that shown, depending on the order in which the fact types were entered into the original ORM source model. In the example, some of the names generated, as well as the order of some of the columns, are less than ideal. We now discuss how to overcome these deficiencies.

The next section reviews how to manually refine a logical model by reordering columns and renaming relational model elements. We then discuss how to migrate such changes back to the ORM source model, and why it is generally best to avoid renaming at the logical level. The following section discusses how to avoid the need to rename relational model elements, by specifying options on the ORM source model to automatically generate the desired logical names when mapping. Later sections review options for mapping subtypes, and discuss how to view constraint code.

7.2   Refining the Logical Model

Regardless of whether a logical database model has been mapped from ORM or entered directly, the tool allows you to freely edit it. Any relational model element, such as a table, column, or constraint, may be modified, deleted, or added, and you can reorder columns within tables as desired. In practice however, direct refinements to a logical model that was mapped from ORM should normally be restricted to *reordering columns and renaming tables*. As discussed later, other changes should be made by configuring the ORM model(s) to automatically map to a logical model with the desired refinements.

Any given table may be refined by selecting it in the drawing window to bring up its Database Properties dialog, and then making the desired changes. To *move a column* to a new position, choose the Columns category, select the column to be moved, and then press the Move Up or Move Down button to move it up or down respectively. Figure 7–4 shows the result of using the Move Up button to move the Second GivenName column up one place from its former position shown in Figure 7–3. To rename a column, you may simply edit the name displayed in the Physical Name field of the dialog, but as explained later it's better to control column names from the ORM level.

In addition to columns, you may rename other relational model elements such as tables, primary key constraints, indexes and foreign key constraints. To *rename a table,* choose the Definition category in its Database Properties dialog and edit the Physical Name field. For example, the "Patient allergic Drug" table has an awkward name, and would be better named "Allergy," Figure 7–5 illustrates how to perform this renaming. The Allergy table is mapped from the ORM fact type Patient is allergic to Drug.

In cases like this, where the table corresponds to an ORM fact type with a composite key, the ORM source model solution provides no flexible way to control the table name generation, so the table renaming is performed at the logical level. The Country

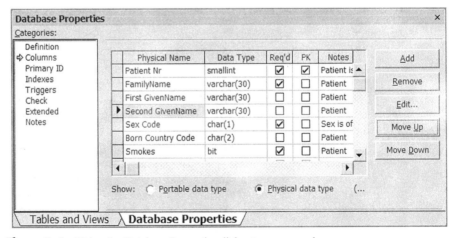

Figure 7–4   Using the Database Properties dialog to move a column.

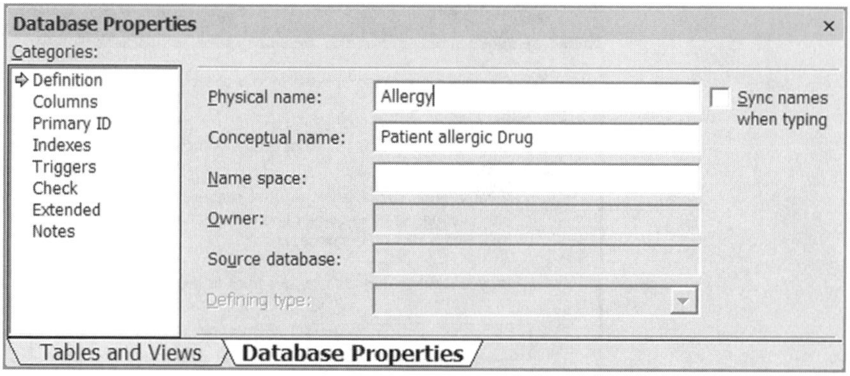

Figure 7–5   Using the Database Properties dialog to rename a table.

and Patient tables however house fact types with simple keys, based on the object types Country and Patient respectively. As discussed later, you can control these table names at the ORM level by setting options on the Country and Patient object types.

Names changes for other kinds of model element may also be controlled at the ORM level, so we discuss them only briefly here. To rename a primary key constraint (e.g., Patient_PK), select the Primary ID category and edit the Physical Name field. To rename indexes, choose the Indexes category, and edit the index name. To rename a foreign key constraint (e.g., Patient_Allergy_FK1), select the foreign key arrow on the diagram, choose the Name category, and edit the Physical Name field of its Database Properties dialog. As discussed in a later chapter, this dialog may also be used to change the referential actions (e.g., on update of Parent, no action) for foreign key constraints.

7.3 Migrating Changes Back to ORM Source Models

On saving changes to a logical model built from ORM, you are prompted whether to migrate these changes to the ORM source model(s) used to generate the logical model. The migration prompt is displayed in Figure 7–6.

If the only changes you made to the logical model are non-structural (renaming columns, or reordering columns other than primary key columns) and you do not intend to reuse the ORM source model(s) to build a separate logical model, you may answer No to migrate, since the non-structural modifications will be stored with the current project. So if you rebuild the project at a later time, these non-structural changes will be applied during mapping. Since migration can take a long time with large models, migrating changes only when needed can save you some time.

If the logical model was built from a single ORM model, and the only changes you made to the logical model are non-structural, and you intend to reuse the same ORM model to build a different logical model, answer Yes to migrate. Otherwise these changes will be lost the next time you build or rebuild a separate logical model from the ORM source model.

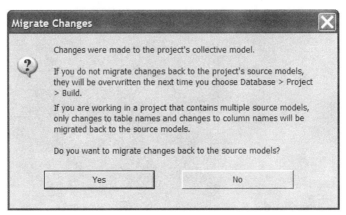

Figure 7–6   Choosing whether to migrate logical changes to the source model(s).

If the logical model was built from a single ORM model, and you made some structural changes to the logical model (e.g., adding or deleting tables, columns or constraints, or changing the primary key), answer Yes to migrate. Otherwise these changes will be lost the next time you build or rebuild this or any other logical model from the ORM source model.

If the logical model was built from more than one source model, migration has no effect, so answer No to the prompt. So with the current version of the tool, migration is only useful if the logical model is built from a single ORM source model. In this case, you may build and migrate as often as you like. This looping possibility is depicted in Figure 7–7. When you migrate, all structural and non-structural changes are communicated to the ORM model.

A structural change to the logical model migrates to a structural change in the ORM model. For example, if you add a FaxNr column to the Patient table, and then migrate this change, the fact type Patient has FaxNr will be added to the ORM model. Additional fact types arising from migration appear in the Fact Types pane of the Business Rules window. To add a migrated fact type to the ORM diagram, drag it onto the drawing window.

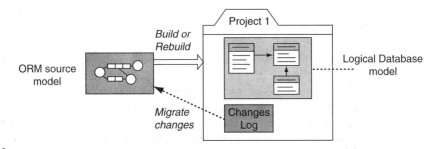

Figure 7–7   Migration of logical model changes to an ORM source model.

Although you can make all kinds of logical model changes and migrate them to a single ORM source model, we strongly encourage you to *avoid making any structural changes at the logical level*. As far as possible, you should also *avoid making any non-structural changes at the logical level, with the exception of column reordering and, table renaming* as discussed earlier. Instead, configure the ORM model to automatically generate the required names in the logical model.

There are good reasons for controlling all naming decisions from the conceptual model. The conceptual model is easier to validate with the domain expert, so changes made at this level are typically best understood. Annotating the conceptual model with required naming options for target implementations facilitates the desirable approach of driving the execution directly from the conceptual model.

Another pragmatic reason is that the Visio tool currently exhibits the following undesirable behavior: *if name changes made at the logical level are migrated to ORM, any changes made later to names of the corresponding ORM model elements are ignored in subsequent builds of the logical model*. Hence renaming at the logical level can make it much harder to synchronize conceptual and logical models. To illustrate this problem, consider the following scenario. Suppose we create the ORM model in Figure 7–8(a), map it to the logical model in Figure 7–8(b), and then rename the columns as shown in Figure 7–8(c).

Suppose we now save the changes to the logical model, and answer Yes when prompted to migrate those changes to the ORM source model. This is fine if we never want to make changes to the relevant aspects of the ORM model. But suppose we later decide that social security numbers are not a good way to identify all persons in our universe of discourse, so we change the reference scheme to Person(Id). Also we decide that Sex is better renamed as Gender. The ORM model now appears as shown in Figure 7–9(a). On rebuilding the logical model, we would expect those changes to be reflected in the column names generated. Instead these changes are ignored, and the logical model still appears as shown in Figure 7–9(b).

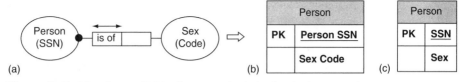

Figure 7–8 Mapping an ORM schema to a logical schema, then renaming.

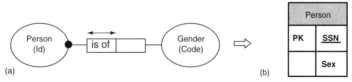

Figure 7–9 Later ORM name changes are overridden by the migrated renaming.

To avoid this undesirable behavior, either press the No button when prompted to migrate logical name changes of this kind, or better still, configure the mapping options on the ORM model to automatically obtain the desired logical names so you can avoid this kind of renaming at the logical level. The next section explores the second alternative. If you ever find yourself in a situation like that of Figure 7–9, you can fix the problem by renaming the logical columns and then migrating these changes back to the ORM model. For example, rename "SSN" to "Person ID" and "Sex" to "Gender" and then migrate. However, it's better to avoid getting such a situation in the first place.

7.4   Controlling Logical Name Generation

Visio for Enterprise Architects includes several options for controlling how the names of logical model elements are generated from an ORM source model. In the pure ORM model itself, the names of model elements have a large bearing on the logical names generated. Most important in this regard are the names of object types, predicates, reference modes and roles. In addition, various mapping settings may be stored with the ORM model to control name generation.

Settings made at the document level apply to the whole model unless overridden by local settings on individual object types and predicates. Most of the document level options are specified in the ORM Document Options dialog, while preferences for keys, indexes, and foreign key constraint names may be set in the Database Modeling Preferences dialog. We discuss these two dialogs first before moving onto the use of local settings and roles names to control name generation.

Document Level Options for Name Generation

To set mapping options that apply by default to the whole ORM model, open the *ORM Document Options dialog* by choosing Database > Options > Document from the main menu of the ORM model. This dialog has six panes: General, Abbreviation, Prefix, Suffix, Capitalization, and Miscellaneous. The General pane has a check box for showing physical constraints: you should normally leave this checked (the default). The Prefix and Suffix panes allow you to automatically insert prefixes or append suffixes to column and/or table names in the logical model. You will normally want to accept the default settings (No prefix, No suffix), as shown in Figure 7–10.

Some companies enforce naming standards that require tables or columns to be prefixed or suffixed. For example, to prefix each table name by "DEMO_", choose the Custom Prefixes option for Table Prefix and enter "DEMO_" in the field. Custom column prefixes and suffixes are sometimes used help delineate context or sub-areas, but in the version used at the time of writing, there appear to be bugs with the generation of custom column prefixes/suffixes.

The Capitalization pane allows you to control upper and lower case settings for column and table names. Different companies adopt different standards in this regard. The settings shown in Figure 7–11 are recommended if you prefer camel casing for column

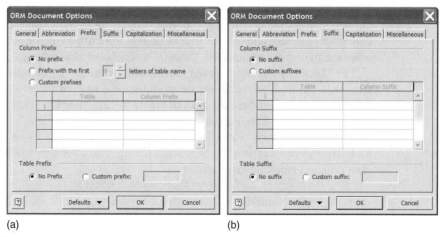

(a)   (b)

Figure 7–10   Setting prefix and suffix options at the ORM document level.

names (e.g., countryCode) and Pascal casing for table names (e.g., LineItem). Here the case used in the conceptual names is preserved, except for the first letter, which is forced lower case for columns, and forced upper case for tables. To generate table names in all upper case (e.g., LINEITEM) choose the "Force upper" setting for Table Names.

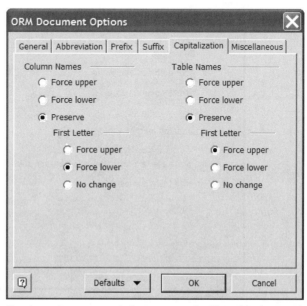

Figure 7–11   Starting column names in lowercase and table names in uppercase.

The Defaults button has a drop-down list with three options: choose Set As to make the new settings the default; choose Restore to return to the settings in place when the dialog was opened; and choose Restore Original to return to the original default setting when the tool was first installed. Press OK to apply the new settings.

The Miscellaneous pane is even more useful. Although conceptual names may contain spaces, embedded spaces are often undesirable or even illegal at the logical level, unless delimited identifiers are used. In Figure 7–12, setting the Spacing Character to None removes all spaces from generated names for relational elements. For example, "First GivenName" becomes "FirstGivenName". To replace a space by an underscore (e.g., First_GivenName), choose the Underscore setting. The Other setting allows you to specify a different replacement character.

The default setting for Reference Mode is Add to object type name. For example, the reference scheme Country(Code) generates the name "CountryCode." This is usually best as a document wide setting. You can override this for individual object types, as discussed earlier. The Do not use for naming setting ignores the reference mode, instead using just the object type name, e.g., "Country." The Use as column name setting ignores the object type name and uses just the reference mode name, e.g., "Code."

The maximum name length setting specifies the maximum number of characters allowed in generated names. This defaults to 128, which is the maximum length for an identifier in the SQL-92 and SQL:1999 standards. Although a number of DBMSs, including Microsoft SQL Server, allow 128 character names, some DBMSs do not (e.g.,

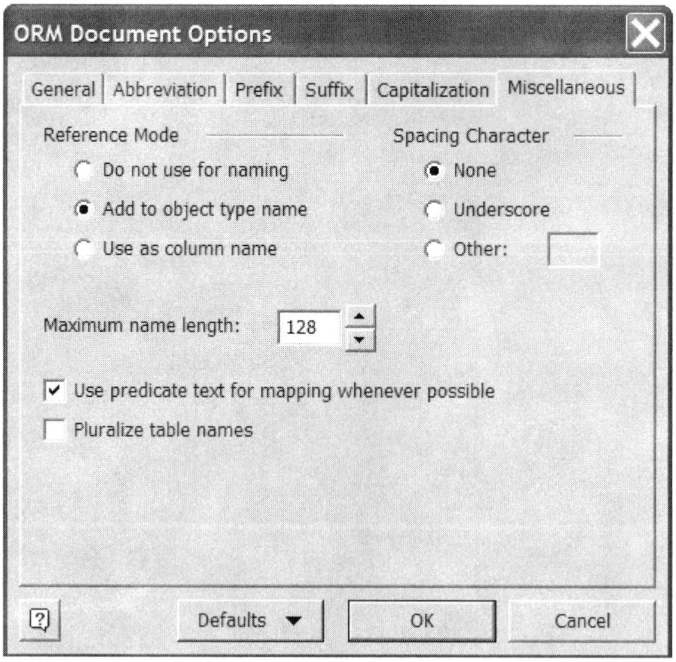

Figure 7–12   Setting miscellaneous naming options.

Oracle identifiers are restricted to 30 characters). It is not uncommon to generate names that are longer than 30 characters, especially for foreign key constraints or tables that correspond to an n-ary predicate.

One way to avoid names that are too long for the target DBMS is to enter a smaller value (e.g., 30) for the maximum name length in this dialog. The tool then does its best to produce a shorter name that is still meaningful, mainly by eliminating vowels starting at the right-hand end. For example, if you specify an independent object type with the conceptual name "Person_or_Organization_or_Company" and set a thirty character limit on logical names, then this object type maps to a relational table named "Person_or_Organization_r_Cmpny".

The Use predicate text for mapping whenever possible check box should normally be checked, as this helps to provide more meaningful names. The Pluralize table names check box should be unchecked, unless the naming standards in your company require plural table names. Singular table names are preferable, especially for referencing columns (e.g., "Patient.familyName" is more natural than "Patients.familyName"). If you do specific plural names, the tool does a reasonable job of rendering these naturally. For example, "Country" is pluralized as "Countries," and "Mouse" is pluralized as "Mice."

The Abbreviation pane enables finer control over name generation, by enabling you to specify standard abbreviations for various words. This is especially helpful if your company naming standards require such standard abbreviations. The tool comes with a list of predefined abbreviations that are displayed when you open the Abbreviations pane (see Figure 7–13).

Each predefined entry in the Name column ("a," "an," ..., "would") is abbreviated to the null string, as shown by the absence of an entry in the Abbreviation column. This causes those words to be removed from any generated names. You can add your own entries to the abbreviation list, as shown in Figure 7–13(b). Here the words "country," and "code" are to be abbreviated as "CNTRY", and "CD," respectively. Although such

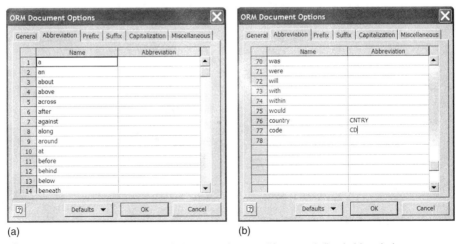

(a)   (b)

Figure 7–13 Predefined abbreviations supplemented by user-defined abbreviations.

abbreviations like these may lose clarity, they may be imposed on you by company naming standards.

For example, Figure 7–14 shows the result of mapping the ORM schema in Figure 7–2, using the column reordering, table renaming, and ORM document settings discussed earlier (including the abbreviations "CNTRY" and "CD" for "Country" and "Code"). The Country table is now named "CNTRY," and its primary key is named "cNTRYCD" instead of countryCode—the setting to start column names with lower case works poorly with words that are all upper case. The column "countryName" is not named "CTRYName" because abbreviations work only on whole words, not parts of words. However, you can automatically generate the name "CNTRYName" in this case simply by including a space to separate the words in the conceptual name (i.e., name the ORM object type "Country Name" instead of "CountryName").

The foreign key of the Patient table is now named "bornCNTRYCD." This uses the user-defined abbreviations for Country and Code, as well as the predefined abbreviation of "was" to the empty string. Although the effect is not illustrated here, it is best to use "Code" instead of "code" for the reference mode of Country because the tool does not provide a capitalization option to start each successive word in a name with a capital letter.

The other document level dialog relevant to name generation is the *Database Modeling Preferences dialog*. To invoke this dialog from either an ORM source model or a logical database model use the main menu option: Database > Options > Modeling. Now select the miscellaneous pane (Logical Misc). For naming purposes, the relevant aspects of this pane are the Default names suffixes for keys and indexes, and the FK name generation option. Unless your company's naming standards differ, we suggest you use the predefined default suffixes (e.g., primary key constraint names are appended with "_PK").

The predefined default for foreign key constraint names appends the base suffix (e.g., "_FK") and a distinguishing numeral (e.g., "1" or "2" to cater for multiple foreign keys) to the concatenation of the names of the parent (referenced) table and child (referencing) tables. For example, for the model in Figure 7–14, the foreign key connection from Patient to Country is named "CNTRY_Patient_FK1." If your target DBMS allows only short identifiers, you may wish to choose a shorter option from the drop-

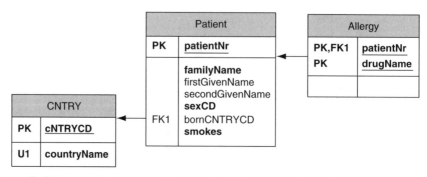

Figure 7–14   A second mapping of the sample ORM model in Figure 7–2.

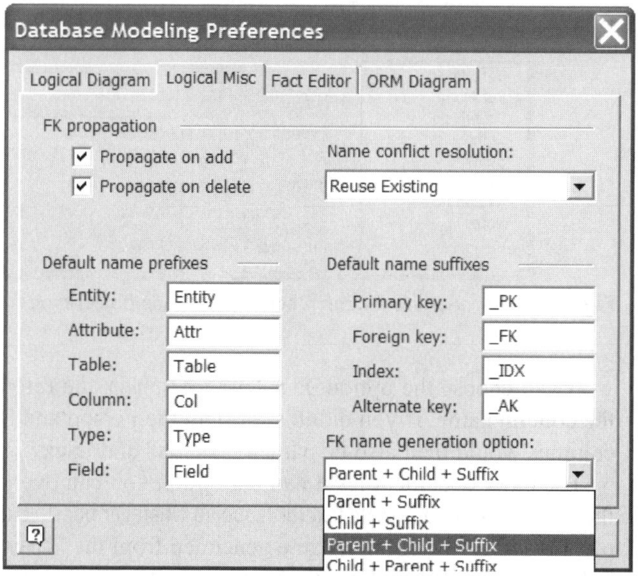

Figure 7–15 Setting preferences for key and index suffixes, and FK constraint names.

down list, as shown in Figure 7–15. You may also choose to start the constraint name with the name of the child table instead of the parent table.

As you may have noticed, some of the names in Figure 7–14 are still not ideal. The abbreviations for Country and Code are not really advisable, so we will remove those from now on. The other naming problems can be overcome by using local options and role names for name generation, as we now discuss.

Local Options for Name Generation

Some naming options set at the document level can be overridden on an individual basis for ORM model elements by choosing a different setting for them in their *Database Properties dialog*. For example, refer back to the simple ORM schema mapping in Figure 7–8(b). By default, the column names generated are "Person SSN" and "Sex Code" because the default document level setting for reference modes is to add them to the name of the object type (see Figure 7–12).

To generate the column name "SSN" instead of "Person SSN," select the Person object type, and in the Ref Mode pane of its Database Properties dialog, change the radio button option from "Use document's setting" to "Use as column name," as shown in Figure 7–16. This overrides the reference mode document level setting for the Person object type only. When you save this change and rebuild the logical model, the primary key of Person is named "SSN." If you use the "Do not use for naming" setting for the Sex object type, then the "Sex Code" column would be renamed "Sex," so you can achieve the result shown in Figure 7–8(c) without needing to do any renaming at the logical level.

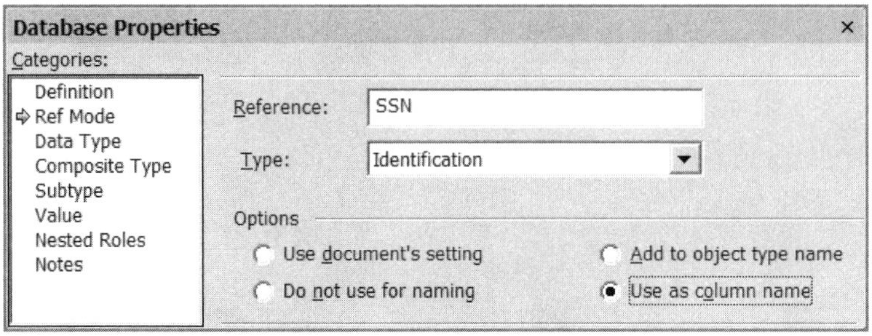

Figure 7-16   Setting the reference mode of one object type for use in column naming.

If you choose the option Do not use for naming, the reference mode is removed from the column name. If you did this for both the Person and Sex object types, the mapped columns would then also be named "Person" and "Sex."

The other document level naming option you can override on an individual basis is the setting to Use predicate text for mapping wherever possible (see Figure 7–12). For example, by default the column name generated from the Patient was born in Country fact type in Figure 7–2 is "Born Country Code." The "was" and "in" from the predicate are omitted from the column name because their abbreviations are predefined to the null string.

If for some reason you wanted to remove the whole predicate from the column name, you could open the Database Properties dialog for Patient was born in Country and choose the Do not use option for Text use for naming, as shown in Figure 7–17. If you then rebuild the logical model, the column name appears as "Country Code." This option is rarely used because it typically makes it harder to determine the precise meaning of the column names. If you apply this setting to more than one Country predicate that mapped to the same table, the tool appends numbers to the column names to distinguish them.

Note that *naming option changes for an ORM object type or predicate are ignored if you previously migrated a logical name change back to that model element.* For example, suppose you changed "Person SSN" to "personSSN" in the logical model,

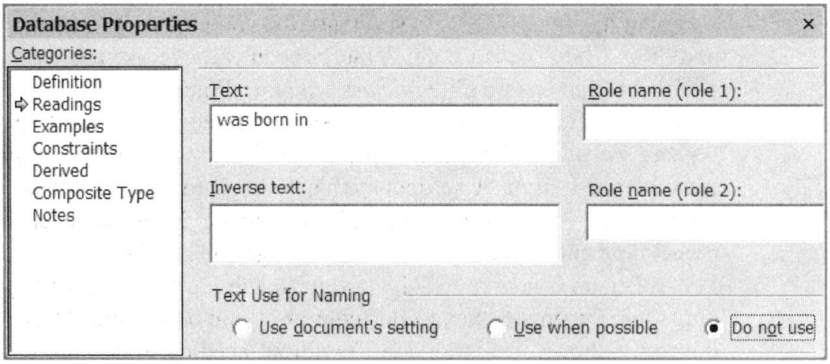

Figure 7-17   Setting the text of an individual predicate for use in name generation.

migrated that change back to the ORM model, then chose the "Use as column name" setting for Person's reference mode. If you now rebuild the logical model, you will still get "personSSN," not "SSN" as the column name. This is yet another reason to *avoid renaming at the logical level wherever possible.*

Using Role Names to Generate Column Names

In an ORM model, each predicate must have at least one reading, but it is optional whether any role in a predicate is named. Although not displayed automatically on the diagram, role names are useful for controlling how column names are generated in logical models (and for specifying attribute-style derivation rules). For example, suppose we add the name "birthCountry" for the second role of Patient was born in Country by entering it in the Readings pane of the predicate's Database Properties dialog, as shown in Figure 7–18.

This role name "birthCountry" will now be used in place of the predicate name "was born in" when generating the relevant column name. For example, instead of "BornCountryCode" the column will be named "birthCountryCode." If you also set the reference mode naming option for Country to Do not use, the column will be named "birthCountry". However the countryCode column for the Country table would then also be renamed "country," which is not advisable.

The ORM schema in Figure 7–19 reproduces our sample ORM model, to which we have now added two role names using the Database Properties dialog. Here, bracketed role names are displayed in text boxes on the diagram for visualization purposes. The role named "isSmoker" is added to the single role in the Person smokes fact type, and the role name "birthCountry" is added to the second role of Patient was born in Country. The ORM document options have been set to start column names with a lower case letter and to ignore space characters (as shown in Figure 7–11 and Figure 7–12).

Figure 7–20 shows the resulting logical schema. Except for renaming the Allergy table, and reordering columns in the Patient table, all the logical names were determined by choosing appropriate names and settings in the ORM source model.

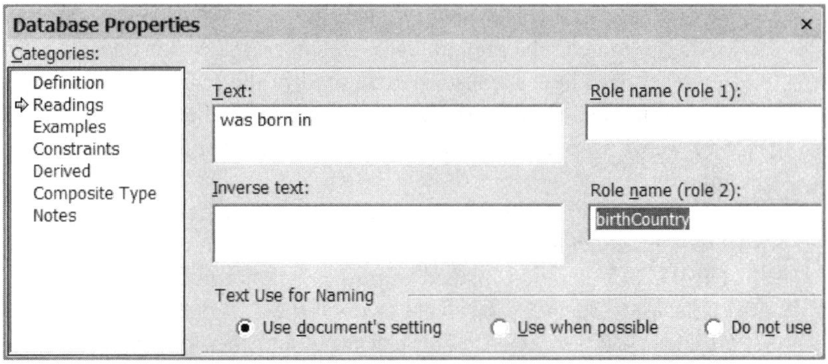

Figure 7–18   Using a role name to generate a column name.

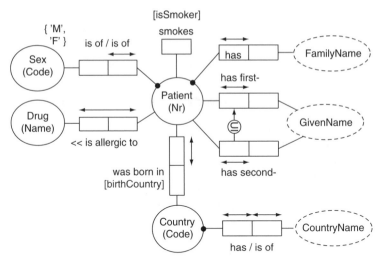

Figure 7–19   Using role names to control name generation.

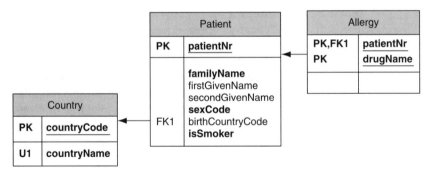

Figure 7–20   The final mapping for the ORM sample model in Figure 7–19.

The tool uses role names to generate column names but not table names. If a predicate is either many: many or n-ary, it maps to a table all by itself, and role names are ignored in name generation. This is why it was necessary to rename the Allergy table at the logical level. However, the options discussed give you almost total control over how names are generated in the logical model. Try to avoid as much as possible making any name changes directly to the logical model, because this makes it very awkward to make later changes to the corresponding elements in the conceptual model.

In addition to naming options, the tool provides several options for the *presentation style* in which the logical model is displayed. For example, to display the logical model in IDEFIX notation instead of pure relational notation, choose the main menu option Database > Options > Document to open the *Database Document Options dialog* for the logical solution, open its General pane, and then choose IDEFIX for Symbol set. This setting causes the model shown in Figure 7–20 to be redisplayed in IDEFIX notation,

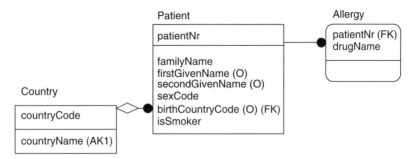

Figure 7–21 Displaying a logical model in IDEFIX notation.

as shown in Figure 7–21. Many other display preference settings are available through this dialog, as discussed later in the book.

7.5 Constraint Code

A logical database model diagram can display primary key, foreign key, uniqueness, and mandatory column constraints, as well as indexes. Any other constraints in the logical model can be viewed only textually in a *code window*. If an ORM constraint maps to a *check clause*, *trigger*, or *stored procedure*, you can open a code window to view the constraint code generated. In those few cases where the tool does not generate the code for an ORM constraint, you can use a code window to manually add the relevant code to the logical model.

To view *or edit a check clause on a single column*, proceed as follows.

1. Select the relevant table on the diagram, and open its Database Properties dialog.
2. Open the Columns pane, and select the relevant column. For example, Figure 7–22 highlights the sexCode column of the Patient table in Figure 7–20.

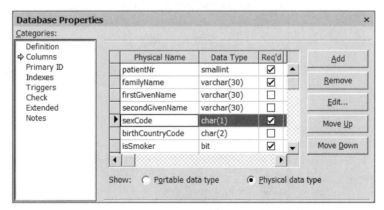

Figure 7–22 Columns pane of the Database Properties dialog for Patient.

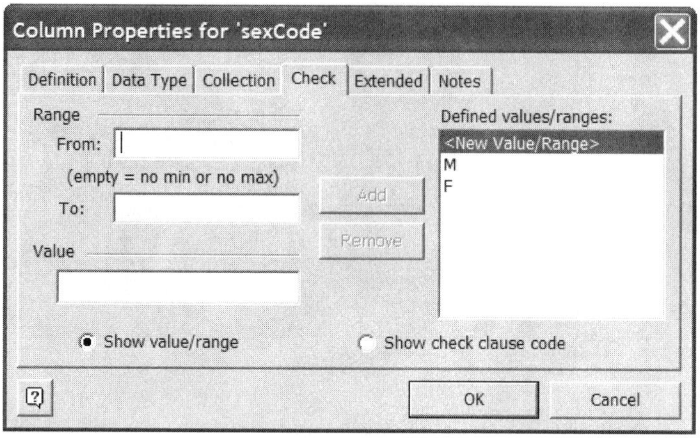

Figure 7–23   Check pane of the Column Properties dialog for sexCode.

3. Press the Edit button to open the Column Properties dialog for that column and choose the Check pane. If the column has a value constraint, this is displayed by default using the ORM value constraint dialog (see Figure 7–23).

4. Select the radio button: Show check clause code. To edit or delete the code, press the Customize button, which then becomes a Delete button (Figure 7–24).

   If you do not press the Customize button, the name and body of the check clause are displayed in read-only format (grayed-out). The Physical name field displays the name that is automatically generated for the check clause (e.g., PatientsexCode_Chk). The Check clause field shows just the body of the clause. For our sexCode example, the actual check clause that will appear when the DDL is generated is:

constraint "PatientsexCode_Chk" check ("sexCode" in ('M','F'))

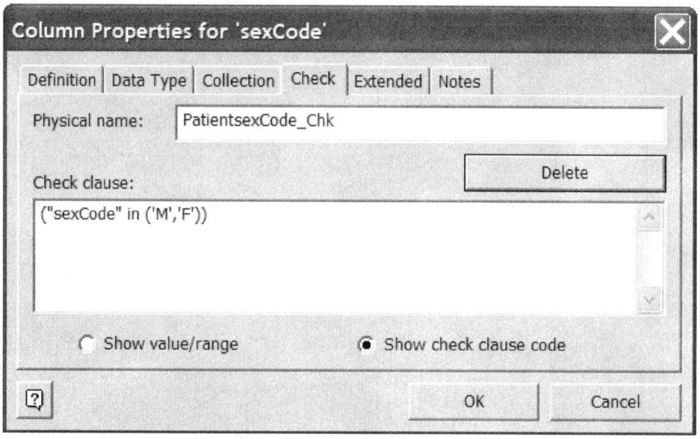

Figure 7–24   Viewing the body of the check clause code for sexCode.

To *view or edit a multi-column check clause*, proceed as follows.

1. Select the relevant table on the diagram, and open its Database Properties dialog.
2. Open the Check pane. The ORM verbalization of the constraint appears in the Check clauses field, and the code body for the check clause appears in the Preview field. Figure 7–25 shows this for the Patient table in Figure 7–20. This code enforces the ORM subset constraint that each patient with a second given name must also have a first given name.
3. To edit the check clause, either press the Edit button or double-click in the Check clauses field. The body of the check clause is now displayed in the Code Editor, ready for editing (see Figure 7–26).

   For our example, the actual check clause that will appear when the DDL is generated is:

alter table "Patient" add constraint Patient_subset check ((("firstGivenName" is not null) or ("secondGivenName" is null))

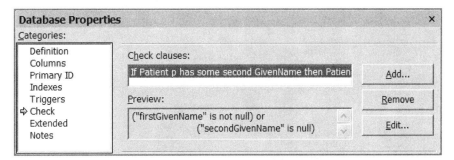

Figure 7–25   Table-level Database Properties Check pane for the Patient table.

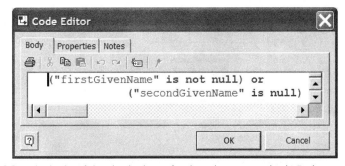

Figure 7–26   The body of the check clause for the subset constraint in Patient.

As Figure 7–25 shows, the Check pane of the Database Properties dialog also includes an Add button for adding a check clause in the Code Editor and a Remove button for deleting a check clause. The Triggers pane of the Database Properties dialog may be used to view or edit triggers on the table.

If a logical model includes stored procedures, these can only be viewed via the *Code window*. This window also provides access to check clause and trigger code associated with the model. To open the Code window, choose Database > View > Code from the main menu. To open the Code Editor for any listed entry, simply double-click it. You can also use the code window to add new code and delete existing code.

The code window for our Patient example is shown in Figure 7–27. This contains one single-column check clause and one multi-column check clause. Single-column check clauses are depicted with a CC icon. Other rules are depicted with the Ru icon. If a check clause does not appear in the code window, you may need to first generate the physical DDL from the model to make it appear.

A more comprehensive example is shown in Figure 7–28, which displays the code window for the sample Employee Database model that ships with the product. To access this model, choose the following options from Visio's main menu: File > New > Browse Sample Drawings > Database > Employee Database.vsd. If the DBMS is SQL Server, the Global Code section includes a stored procedure to enforce an exclusion constraint that spans two tables. The Local Code section includes several single-column and multi-column check clauses. You may double-click any item to view or edit its code in the Code Editor.

If an ORM constraint cannot be enforced in the target DBMS as a simple declarative constraint (e.g., primary key, foreign key, not null, unique, or simple check clause), the tool usually attempts to enforce the constraint by generating triggers or stored pro-

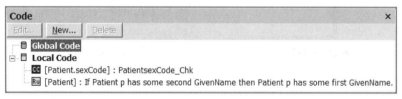

Figure 7–27   The Code window allows all code for the model to be viewed and edited.

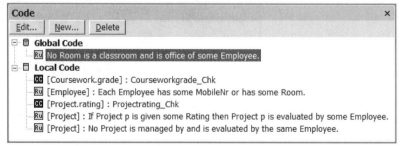

Figure 7–28   The code window for the Employee sample database model.

cedures, depending on the DBMS. Although generated code for a stored procedure contains the logic to enforce the constraint, you still need to manually write code to execute the procedure or transform it into appropriate triggers.

For those DBMSs that do not support stored procedures (e.g., Microsoft Access), stored procedures are documented in the DDL as comments, which you can use to help develop an alternative way to enforce the constraints.

ORM constraints that generate trigger or stored procedure code include constraints that span tables (e.g., external uniqueness and inclusive-or constraints spanning roles that map to separate tables), frequency constraints, some ring constraints, and some set-comparison (subset, equality, exclusion) constraints.

Ring constraints were discussed in section 5.8. An *irreflexive* ring constraint whose roles map to columns in the same table is enforced as a simple check constraint. For example, the mapping in Figure 7–29 shows the ORM constraint no Academic monitors itself mapping to a check clause with the condition academicEmpNr <> monitorEmpr. For visualization purposes, the relevant role names and check condition are displayed in text boxes, using superscripts to cross-reference the rule to its referents.

But now consider the mapping of the parenthood fact type shown in Figure 7–30, which is an extension of an example discussed in Chapter 5. Again, roles names are added in text to aid visualization. The *frequency* constraint indicates that a child may have at most two parents, and the ring constraints declare that parenthood is both *asymmetric* and *intransitive*. None of these constraints are mapped to check clauses.

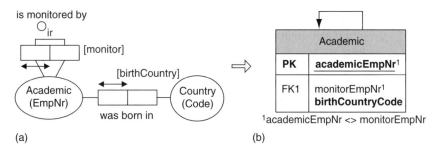

Figure 7–29   The irreflexive ring constraint maps to a simple check clause.

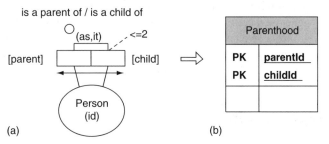

Figure 7–30   The ring and frequency constraints do not map to check clauses.

If SQL Server is the target DBMS, each of these constraints is mapped to a stored procedure, which you can view in the Code Editor. The constraint code generated (minus comments) is as follows.

```
Create Procedure sp_Parenthood_freq1 as
if (not exists (select* from "Parenthood"
    group by "Parenthood"."childId"
    having count(*) > 2))

return 1
else return 2

Create Procedure sp_Parenthood_ring2 as
if (not exists (select* from "Parenthood" X, "Parenthood" Y
    where X."parentId" = Y."childId" and X."childId" = Y."parentId")

    and

    not exists (select* from "Parenthood" X, "Parenthood" Y, "Parenthood" Z
    where X."childId" = Y."parentId" and Y."childId" = Z."childId"
    and X."parentId" = Z."parentId"))

return 1
else return 2
```

The irreflexive constraint discussed earlier was enforced as a simple check clause, since its condition for any given row could be checked by looking at that row alone. This is not true for the frequency constraint and the asymmetric and intransitive ring constraints. Instead of a check clause, the tool generates stored procedures for these more complex constraints. If a procedure returns 1, then the constraint is satisfied; if it returns 2, the constraint is violated. These procedures could be expensive, so are not run automatically. It is your responsibility to decide how to use them. For example, you might write code to run the procedures, or you might replace the procedures by equivalent triggers.

Notice that the composite (as, it) ring constraint maps to a single stored procedure, with the first existential subquery checking asymmetry, and the second existential subquery checking intransitivity.

In reality, the parenthood relation is not just asymmetric but *acyclic*. Acyclicity is different from the other ring constraints because it involves recursion, so might be quite expensive to enforce. Some modern DBMSs, such as DB2 and the Yukon release of SQL Server, include the capability of performing recursive queries but not all DBMSs do so. Moreover, the SQL syntax used to support recursion may differ among DBMSs. If you wish to declare an acyclic ring constraint, the tool currently does no more than generate a comment for it, so you have to look after coding this yourself. Moreover, if you choose a composite ring constraint that includes acyclicity, the whole code for the composite constraint is simply a comment. You can view the comment in the Code Editor and edit it like any other code.

7.6   Subtype Mapping

Section 5.6 discussed how to specify subtyping in an ORM source model. We now consider subtype mapping and coding options to enforce subtype constraints within a log-

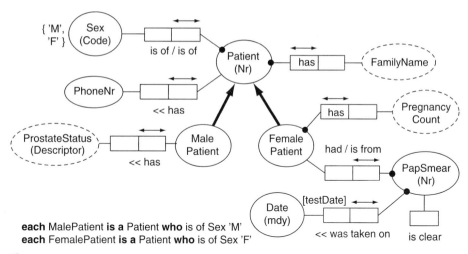

each MalePatient **is a** Patient **who** is of Sex 'M'
each FemalePatient **is a** Patient **who** is of Sex 'F'

Figure 7–31   MalePatient and FemalePatient are subtypes of Patient.

ical database model. To illustrate these ideas, an extension of the ORM Patient model discussed in chapter 5 is used as the source to the mapping (see Figure 7–31). Here, the Patient object type directly plays three functional roles. A *functional role* is a role with a simple uniqueness constraint (and hence it functionally determines the other role). Indirectly, Patient also plays the roles of its subtypes MalePatient and FemalePatient.

MalePatient plays only one role, and this is functional and optional: **each** MalePatient has **at most one** ProstateStatus. For example, one male patient might have his prostate status recorded as 'BE' (benign enlargement), while another male patient has never had his prostate checked.

FemalePatient plays two roles. One of these is functional (**each** FemalePatient has **at most one** PregnancyCount) and mandatory (**each** FemalePatient has **some** PregnancyCount). If a female patient has never been pregnant, this is recorded as a pregnancy count of 0. The other role played by FemalePatient is non-functional (it does not have a simple uniqueness constraint on it): **it is possible that the same** FemalePatient had **more than one** PapSmear. The other role in this fact type is functional (**each** PapSmear is from **at most one** FemalePatient) and mandatory (**each** PapSmear is from **some** FemalePatient).

As discussed in Chapter 5, subtyping details are entered in the Subtype pane of the subtype's Database Properties dialog. In addition to the subtype definition field, there are check boxes for table mapping and inheritance and a list box for selecting the primary supertype (see Figure 7–32). The check box titled "Map to separate table" does not relate to the conceptual level at all. Instead it is used to control how subtype specific details are mapped to a logical database schema. If this box is unchecked (the default), any functional roles attached to the subtype will be absorbed back into the supertype when the model is mapped to a relational database schema.

By default, the ORM schema in Figure 7–31 maps to the relational schema shown in Figure 7–33 (with some column reordering, and name control, and ignoring the value constraint on sexCode). This is the structure you get by default if you leave the Map-

Database Properties   ✕

Categories:

| Definition |
| Ref Mode |
| Data Type |
| Composite Type |
| ⇨ Subtype |
| Value |
| Nested Roles |
| Notes |

☐ Map to separate table   Primary supertype: Patient ▼

☐ Create table inheritance

Subtype definition:

each MalePatient is a Patient who is of Sex 'M'

Figure 7–32   The Subtype pane of the Database Properties dialog for MalePatient.

to-separate-table options unchecked for the two subtypes. The prostate and pregnancy fact types are functionally dependent on their subtype, so are absorbed into the super-type table Patient. Hence the Patient table includes prostateStatus and pregnancyCount as optional columns. Recall that mandatory (not null) columns are displayed in bold, unlike optional (nullable) columns, and that "PK" denotes "primary key" and "FK" denotes "foreign key."

The three pap smear fact types in Figure 7–32 are functionally dependent on the object type PapSmear, so they maps to a table for that object type. The arrow between the tables is a foreign key reference or subset constraint (each patient number in the PapSmear table must also occur within the primary key of the Patient table).

If you compare the ORM model in Figure 7–31 with the relational model in Figure 7–33, it is obvious that much of the subtyping semantics have been lost in the translation. The Patient table has three optional columns: phoneNr, prostateStatus, and pregnancyCount. The phoneNr column is simply optional (there is no formal way of deciding which patients have their phone number recorded). But the prostateStatus and preganancyCount columns are not simply optional. Nor is the foreign key constraint a simple subset constraint.

To preserve the additional semantics in the ORM source model, we need to add *qual-ifications* to any optional columns or subset constraints that result from subtyping. We could denote these qualifications by annotating the relational diagram with superscripts and text as shown in Figure 7–34.

Here the annotations were added in simple text boxes, using the relational constraint syntax discussed in Halpin (2001). Qualification 1 means that prostateStatus is

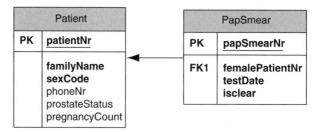

Figure 7–33   By default, functional subtype roles are absorbed into the supertable.

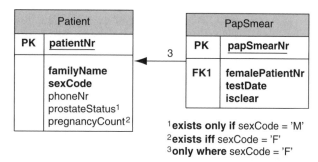

Figure 7–34   Subtyping yields qualifications on optional columns or subset constraints.

recorded only if the patient is male (sexCode = 'M'). Qualification 2 means that pregnancyCount is recorded iff (if and only if) the patient is female (sexCode = 'F'). Qualification 3 means that each patient number in the PapSmear table must equal the patient number of a female patient recorded in the Patient table (sexCode = 'F'). Note that simply naming the foreign key column as "femalePatientNr" does not enforce the constraint that the patient number must be that of a female patient. Formally, this column may just as well have been named "patientNr." The informal semantics in the name is for the benefit of the human reader only and carries no formal weight.

Because the ORM tool does not yet support formal subtype definitions, it cannot generate the code to enforce these qualifications. So for now, you need to write this code for yourself. You can do this by editing the table properties of the logical model before generation (or less preferably, by editing the DDL that is generated from the logical model). For example, qualification 1 may be implemented by the following check clause on the Patient table: **check** (prostateStatus is null or sexCode = 'M').

This involves more than one column, so requires a table-check clause rather than a column-check clause. To add the check clause, proceed as follows. Click the Patient table to bring up its Database Properties dialog, select the Check pane, and press the Add button to bring up the code editor. Select its Properties pane and enter a meaningful name for the check constraint, e.g., "ProstateStatusOnlyIfMale" (see Figure 7–35).

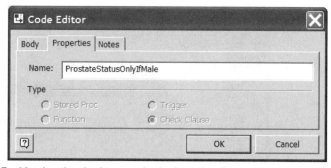

Figure 7–35   Naming the check constraint in the code editor.

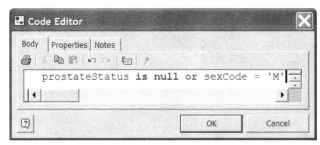

Figure 7–36   Adding the body of a check-clause.

Now select the Body pane and enter the body of the check-clause, as in Figure 7–36. Do not enter the "check ( )" wrapper for this code, since the tool does this automatically when generating the DDL. If you do include this wrapper, it will be treated as part of the code body, and hence generate an error.

Press OK to enter the check-clause. This returns you to the properties dialog, with the check-clause listed as shown in Figure 7–37.

You may now remove or edit the check-clause, or add more check clauses in a similar way. To implement qualification 2, you should add the following two check clauses. Try this for yourself. Suggested names for these constraints are appended as comments.

```
check(pregnancyCount is null or sexCode = 'F')      --PregnancyCountOnlyIfFemale
check(sexCode <> 'F' or pregnancyCount is not null) --PregnancyCountIfFemale
```

If you add the three check-clauses as discussed, the following code is included in the generated DDL after the create-table clause for the Patient table:

```
alter table "Patient" add constraint ProstateStatusOnlyIfMale
    check (prostateStatus is null or sexCode = 'M')

alter table "Patient" add constraint PregnancyCountOnlyIfFemale
    check (pregnancyCount is null or sexCode = 'F')

alter table "Patient" add constraint PregnancyCountIfFemale
    check (sexCode <> 'F' or pregnancyCount is not null)
```

Database Properties   ×

Categories:

Definition	Check clauses:	
Columns	ProstateStatusOnlyIfMale	Add...
Primary ID		
Indexes		
Triggers	Preview:	Remove
⇨ Check	prostateStatus is null or sexCode = 'M'	
Extended		Edit...
Notes		

Figure 7–37   The check clause has been added.

Qualification 3 (restricting the foreign key reference to female patients) can be implemented by using the Database Properties dialog to add appropriate triggers to the Patient and PapSmear tables.

Mapping Subtypes to Separate Tables

To summarize our earlier discussion, the ORM schema in Figure 7–31 maps to the logical schema shown in Figure 7–34, if we use the default mapping procedure, where subtypes roles that are functional (with a simple uniqueness constraint) are effectively absorbed back to the supertype before mapping. The prostate and pregnancy fact types are functionally dependent on their subtype, so are absorbed into the supertype table Patient. Hence the Patient table includes prostateStatus and pregnancyCount as optional columns. The actual subtype constraints (indicating the conditions under which subtype facts may be recorded) are now captured by qualifications on the optional prostateStatus and pregnancyCount columns, and on the subset constraint depicted as a foreign key relationship from PapSmear.patientNr to Patient.patientNr. These qualifications need to be coded as check clauses or triggers.

As a non-conceptual issue, the tool also allows you to specify options on the ORM model to provide alternative logical mappings for subtypes. If you double-click a subtype to bring up its Database Properties dialog, select the Subtype pane, and then check the "Map to separate table" option, this causes fact types that functionally depend on the subtype to map to a separate table, with the primary identifier of the subtye as the primary key. For example, to specify a separate table for the MalePatient subtype, mark the check box as shown in Figure 7–38.

Choosing the separate table mapping option for both the MalePatient and FemalePatient subtypes results in the logical schema shown in Figure 7–39. Prostate status is now stored in the MalePatient subtable, and pregnancy count is stored in the FemalePatient subtable. Pap smear facts are still stored in a separate PapSmear table, because these are a function of PapSmear rather than FemalePatient (a patient may have many pap smears). The numbered qualifications on the foreign key references have been manually added, and are explained later.

When you choose the separate subtable mapping option, the tool uses a different notation for displaying foreign key relationships from subtables to supertable. Instead

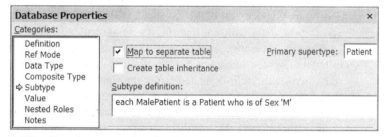

Figure 7–38   Choosing to map functional details of MalePatient to a separate table.

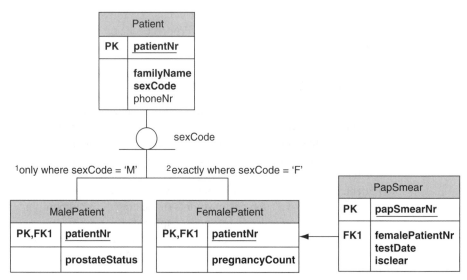

Figure 7–39   Functional subtype details are now mapped to separate tables.

of arrows, a circle-bar notation is used, as shown. The circle is connected by a line to the supertable and has one or two bars underneath, connected by lines to the subtables.

If desired, you may specify a supertable attribute as a *discriminator* for the subtable hierarchy, by clicking the circle-bar icon to bring up its Database Properties dialog and selecting the discriminator from the attribute list displayed, as shown in Figure 7–40. The tool displays the discriminator (in this case "sexCode") besides the circle-bar icon. If desired, you can drag the control handle for this shape to reposition the discriminator on the diagram.

A single bar beneath the circle indicates that the categorization of a supertable into subtables is *incomplete*. In other words, it is possible that the union of the subtable primary key populations is a proper subset of the supertable primary key population. This is true for our example because recording of prostate status is optional for males, so there may be male patients recorded in the Patient table that are absent from both the subtables. Constraints are on populations, rather than types.

If we had made it mandatory for males to have their prostate status recorded, the categorization would be *complete,* and this could be declared by checking the "Category is complete" check-box in the properties dialog. The tool displays completeness of categorization as a double bar instead of a single bar.

The use of discriminators and completeness indicators covers only a fragment of ORM's subtyping semantics, which allows subtype definitions of arbitrary complexity (e.g., involving multi-branched paths through ORM space). However, since the tool does not yet support formal ORM subtype definitions, it will not generate a discriminator, or guarantee the correct completeness setting when you map to the logical level. So if you want these aspects displayed properly you need to look after them manually yourself.

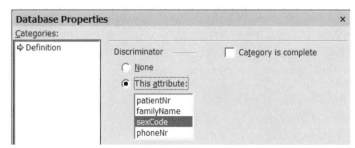

Figure 7–40 Specifying a subtyping discriminator and completeness status.

Even for the simple example in Figure 7–39, the discriminator and incompleteness settings do not convey the full ORM subtyping semantics captured in Figure 7–31. To preserve the additional ORM semantics, we need to qualify the subtable foreign key references as shown in Figure 7–39. Here the annotations have been manually added in text boxes, using the relational constraint syntax discussed in Halpin (2001). Qualification 1 means that the set of patient numbers in the MalePatient table must be a subset of the set of patient numbers of male patients in the Patient table. So prostateStatus is recorded only where the patient is male (sexCode = 'M'). Qualification 2 means the set of patient numbers in the FemalePatient table must equal the set of patient numbers of female patients recorded in the Patient table. So pregnancyCount is recorded exactly where the patient is female (sexCode = 'F').

Since pap smear tests are optional for female patients, there is no need to qualify the foreign key reference from the PapSmear table to the FemalePatient table. This foreign key connection is just an unqualified subset constraint, so will be enforced as a simple foreign key declaration generated in the DDL.

Because the ORM tool does not yet support formal subtype definitions, it cannot generate the code to enforce the two qualifications on the subtable foreign key references. So for now, you need to write this code for yourself. You can do this by editing the table properties of the logical database model before generation (or less preferably, by editing the DDL that is generated from the relational model). As neither of these qualifications can be implemented as a check-clause, you will need to enforce them by means of triggers or stored procedures.

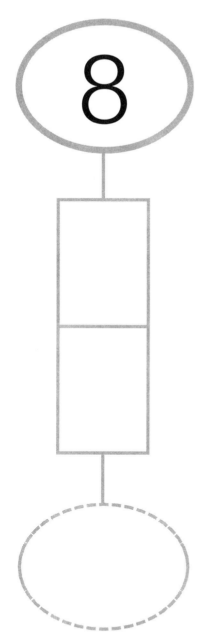

Reverse Engineering and Importing to ORM

8.1   Reverse Engineering to ORM

Ideally, you should always develop a database by forward engineering from ORM to a logical model and then to a physical database schema. This is feasible if you are developing a new database from scratch. In practice, however, you might also need to modify existing databases that might not have been forward engineered from ORM. These databases might also be populated with large volumes of data.

If the database was originally forward engineered from ORM, but changes were later made directly to the physical database, you can reverse engineer those changes to the logical model by refreshing it (see Chapter 16), and then migrate those changes to the ORM source model. If the database was not generated from ORM, you may reverse engineer the database schema directly to a draft ORM schema, and then make any needed changes to clean it up conceptually.

Once you have a correct ORM schema for the existing database, you may add the desired functional modifications, and then forward engineer the changes back to the database by building the logical model and using it to update the database automatically. Details on refreshing, updating, and synchronizing models are provided in Chapter 16. Alternatively, you can forward engineer the ORM model to a logical model and generate a fresh physical database; if the original database was populated with data, you may manually migrate the data to the new database.

The tool can reverse engineer an existing physical database schema to a fresh ORM schema or a fresh logical database schema (see Figure 8–1). However it cannot further reverse engineer a logical database model created in this way to an ORM schema. This chapter discusses reverse engineering to a new ORM schema. Reverse engineering to a logical database schema is discussed in chapter 14.

To reverse engineer an existing database, an Open Database Connectivity (ODBC) *data source* is needed to enable access to that database. Visio refers to a data source by a data source name (DSN). If the data source does not exist, you can create it using either the Windows ODBC Data Source Administrator dialog or Visio's Reverse Engineering Wizard.

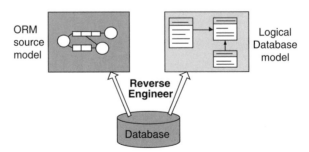

Figure 8–1   Two options for reverse engineering a physical database schema.

Creating an ODBC Data Source

To *create a new data source using the Windows ODBC Data Source Administrator dialog,* proceed as follows. The ODBC Data Source Administrator dialog is accessible from the Windows Control Panel. For example, to open this dialog in Windows XP, click Start > Control Panel > Performance and Maintenance > Administrative Tools and then double-click Data Sources (ODBC). On the User DSN pane, press the Add button to open the Create New Data Source dialog. Select the relevant ODBC driver (e.g., Microsoft Access Driver, or SQL Server) and press the Finish button. In the driver-specific dialog box that opens, type a name and description for the data source, browse to select the relevant database, and then press OK. Press OK to close the ODBC Data Source Administrator dialog.

For example, the Visio product includes a sample Microsoft Access database named Championzone. This is stored in the database samples folder (typically c:\Program Files\Microsoft Office\Visio 10\1033\Samples\Database). If you select Microsoft Access as the driver, you can add a data source for this database by adding a data source name (e.g., ChampionzoneDB) and description in the ODBC Microsoft Access setup dialog, and pressing the Select button to browse and select this database file (see Figure 8–2). For illustration purposes, the example used in the following discussion of reverse engineering assumes that you have created this data source.

Reverse Engineer a Database to ORM

To *reverse engineer a database to ORM,* open Visio's ORM Source Model solution (e.g., File > New > Database > ORM Source Model), and then open the Reverse Engineering Wizard by choosing Database > Reverse Engineer from the main menu. Now select the database driver for the database you wish to reverse engineer (see Figure 8–3).

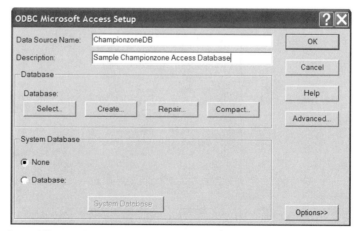

Figure 8–2   Adding a new data source for a Microsoft Access database.

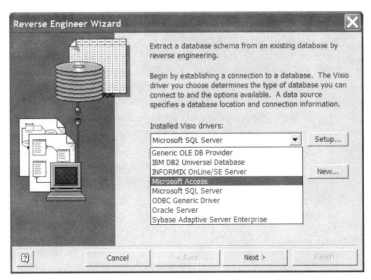

Figure 8–3   Choosing a database driver in the Reverse Engineering wizard.

Press the Setup button to associate the Visio driver with the relevant ODBC driver and set any desired preferences and default data source. For example, if you chose Microsoft Access as the installed Visio driver, you could use the settings in Figure 8–4 to associate this with the Microsoft Access ODBC driver and choose the Championzone database as your default data source for this driver (assuming you had created this data source earlier as discussed).

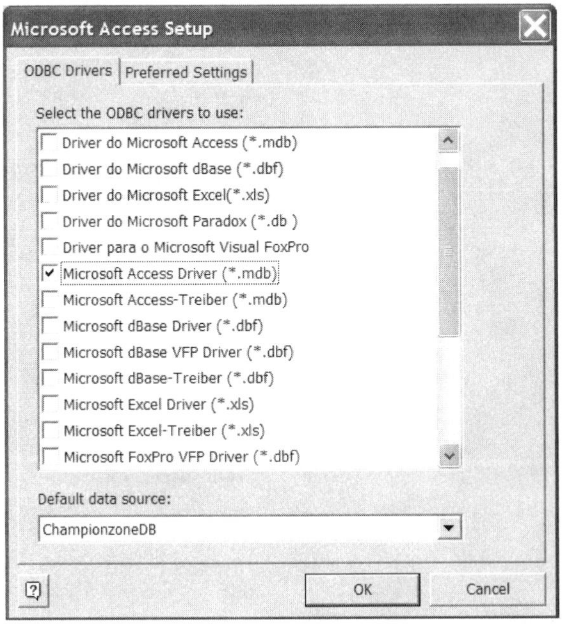

Figure 8–4   Setting up the database driver and default data source.

Press OK to close this dialog, then select the relevant data source from the data sources field of the Reverse Engineering wizard (see Figure 8–5).

If you had not previously created the data source, you may do so now by pressing the New button, choosing User Data Source from the next dialog, selecting the driver from the next dialog, pressing Finish, then adding a data source name and description and choosing the relevant database, as described earlier (e.g., see Figure 8–2).

Press the Next button to open the Connect Data Source dialog, enter any user name and password details required, and press OK (see Figure 8–6). If you changed the driver, a notice appears indicating that the new driver will be used by default until you change it again.

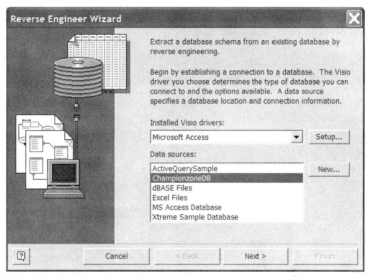

Figure 8–5   Selecting the relevant data source.

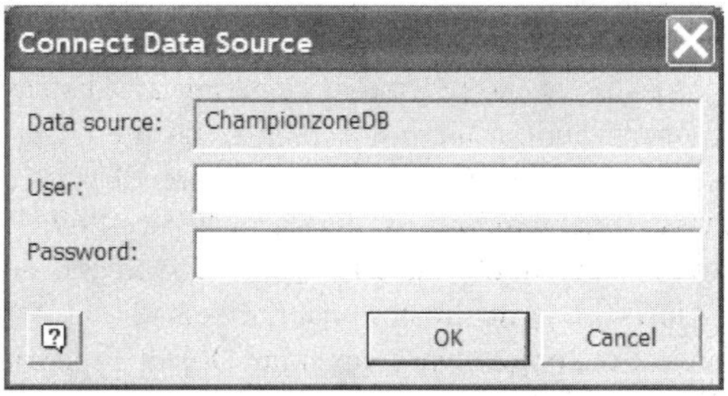

Figure 8–6   Connecting to a data source.

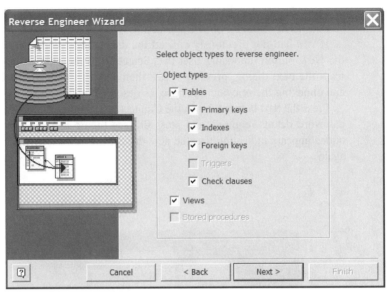

Figure 8–7   Selecting which kinds of model element to reverse engineer.

The Reverse Engineer wizard now displays a dialog that allows you to choose which types of relational database element to reverse engineer (see Figure 8–7). By default, all element types are selected. Microsoft Access does not support triggers or stored procedures, so those options are disabled when reverse engineering from an Access database. Make your selection, then press Next to continue.

The next dialog allows you to select which individual model elements to reverse engineer. Base table names are prepended by "T" and view names are prepended by "V" (see Figure 8–8). To select all of them, press the Select All button. To select only some, select the relevant check boxes. If triggers or stored procedures are available, these also appear for selection. After making your selection, press Next if you wish to review your selections, otherwise press Finish.

The results of the reverse engineering are displayed in the Output window. If any errors occur, correct these and then rerun the wizard. If the reverse engineering succeeds, the resulting ORM fact types are displayed in the Fact Types pane of the Business Rules window, as shown in Figure 8–9. Fact types derived from views are displayed with a double asterisk "**" (derived and stored), which is not strictly correct, since views are typically not materialized.

To view the object types, open the Object Types pane of the Business Rules window (see Figure 8–10).

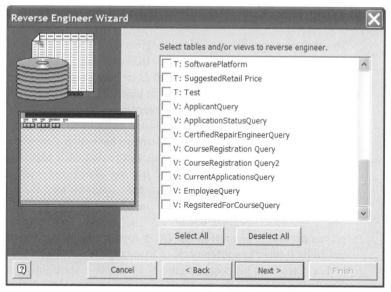

Figure 8–8   Selecting which individual elements to reverse engineer.

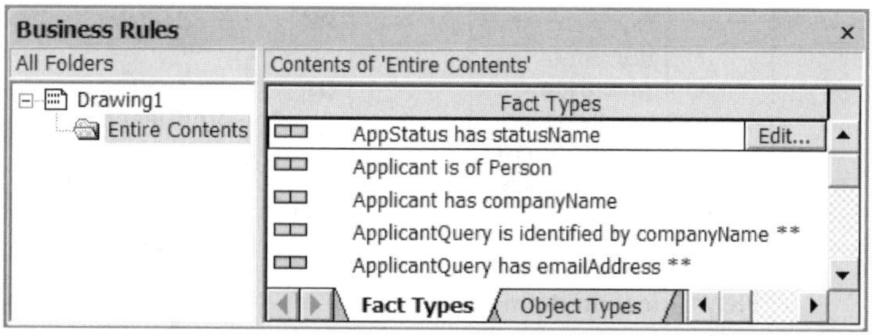

Figure 8–9   Reverse engineered fact types.

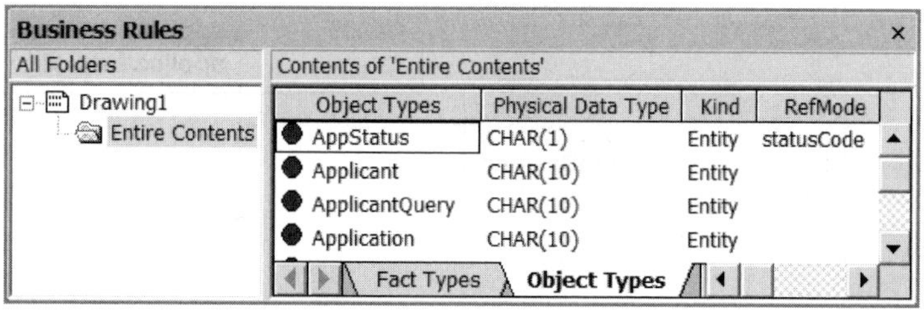

Figure 8–10   Reverse engineered object types.

8.2 Displaying the ORM Model Graphically

To obtain a diagram for a reverse engineered ORM model, it is better to drag object types onto the drawing window rather than dragging fact types out. In the business rules window, each object type is depicted as an entity type (solid circle with dark blue fill) or a value type (dotted circle with light blue fill). *After reverse engineering, each object type depicted as an entity type corresponds to a base table or view.* If the reverse-engineered schema is large, it should normally be displayed on many pages, each of which displays a submodel whose elements have high semantic cohesion.

After reverse engineering, you can ensure that each page displays strongly related elements by *dragging onto that page just one object type, then use ShowRelationships* to display its fact types. Unless the diagram already fills the page, *apply ShowRelationships again to one or more object types that are connected to the original object type by a relationship with "FK" in its name.* This ensures that the fact types displayed on that page correspond either to fact types stored in tables that are directly linked by foreign key references, or to subtype relationships between the tables.

For discussion purposes, Figure 8–11 displays six tightly coupled tables from the sample logical model for the Championzone database. Recall that ORM fact types cap-

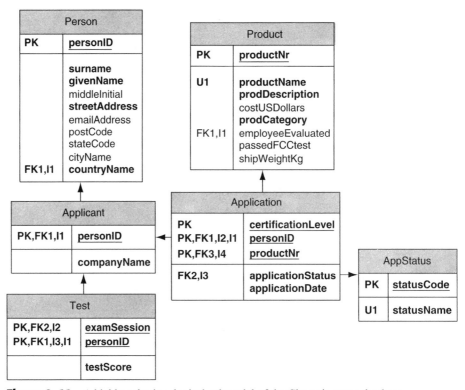

Figure 8–11   A highly cohesive, logical submodel of the Championzone database.

ture the semantic connections between primary key and nonkey columns and that some ORM subtype-supertype connections may appear as foreign key references.

Figure 8–12 shows the result of dragging the Applicant and Application object types onto the drawing page, then choosing ShowRelationships from their context menus. This displays all the fact types in the Applicant and Application tables as well as some related foreign key connections. For tidiness, display of indexes has been turned off (using View > Layer Properties). Here, each entity type corresponds to a table in the database. If a table has a simple primary key, this displays as the reference mode of the entity type (e.g., Person, Product and AppStatus).

If a table has a composite key, and all the key fact types are displayed, then the composite key constraint appears as a primary, external uniqueness constraint (circled "P"), as shown in the reference scheme for Application. The identification scheme for Test is not displayed because one of its reference types is not displayed (you could display this by applying ShowRelationships to Test).

If a column is neither a simple primary key nor a foreign key, its underlying fact type is displayed as a relationship from the table entity type to a value type of that name (e.g., companyName, applicationDate, certificationLevel).

Any fact type underlying a foreign key is displayed with a relationship name that has "FK*n*" appended to its name, where *n* is a positive integer.

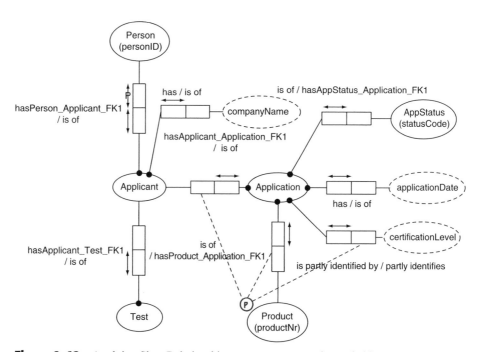

Figure 8–12 Applying ShowRelationships to two reverse engineered object types.

8.3   Refining the ORM Schema

In practice, any draft ORM schema obtained by reverse engineering usually needs many refinements. For example, Figure 8–13 shows the result of applying several improvements to the schema fragment in Figure 8–12. All these changes can be made using techniques already discussed.

Several changes have been made to the names of predicates, object types, and reference modes, in order to make the semantics easier to understand. Some value types have also been changed to entity types. Reverse engineered role names may be retained if the same column name mapping is required. To ensure the logical model names are unaltered when you forward engineer the new ORM schema you will often need to configure various naming options as explained in the previous chapter.

The change from "applicationDate" to "Date" requires more discussion. In the reverse-engineered global schema, there are several date object types (applicationDate, examDate, birthDate, registrationDate, etc.). These should all be replaced by the object type Date, with the reverse-engineered name retained as a role name. Apart from simplifying the schema, this merging of object types ensures that if ever we make any changes to the data type for Date, this will apply universally.

Where relevant, reverse-engineered injective (1:1 into) identifying relationships should be replaced by subtyping (e.g., the relationship between Applicant and Person). The tool does not generate nesting as an alternative to co-referencing when it reverse engineers. When it makes the schema easier to understand, awkward co-referenced

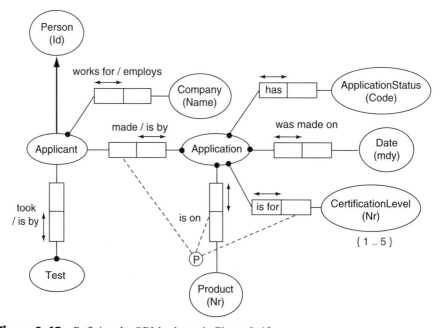

Figure 8–13   Refining the ORM schema in Figure 8–12.

object types should be replaced by nested object types. If the original database involved views, you need to make any needed adjustments to prevent the reverse-engineered constructs leading to base tables when the schema is forward engineered.

Once the semantics of the as-is database schema have been clarified, you should look to see if some additional constraints need to be added to provide a more complete to-be model. As a trivial example, the value constraint {1..5} has been added to CertificationLevel in Figure 8–13.

Often, you may find that the database was badly designed in the first place, with problems such as uncontrolled denormalization and incompatible data types. Working in ORM, you will find it much easier to expose and correct these problems.

Once you are satisfied with the new ORM schema, and it passes model error checks, you may forward engineer it to the DBMS of choice by building a fresh logical model and then generating a new physical database schema from it. If the reverse engineered database included code such as view definitions, triggers or stored procedures you can transfer these across as discussed in Chapter 16. Chapter 16 also discusses how to update an existing database with changes made to a model.

If the original database was already populated with data, you may perform data migration to the new physical database once it is generated. This process can be tedious but is usually not very challenging to do manually. Various DBMSs include facilities to assist in this process (e.g., SQL Server's Data Transformation Services).

Once the new database is generated and populated, you should not need to perform reverse engineering on it again. As far as possible, make any subsequent changes at the ORM level and propagate them downwards. If it is necessary to make changes at lower levels, the tool allows you propagate the changes to the other levels to keep your models in sync. This topic is discussed in Chapter 16.

8.4   Importing VisioModeler and ERX Files

In addition to reverse engineering physical databases, the tool can import ORM models and logical models that were built using VisioModeler or InfoModeler (version 1.5 onwards). You may also import logical models built using Computer Associates ERwin tool, if they have been saved as ERX files (up to version 3.5.2).

To import such a model, open the ORM Source Model solution, choose the menu option Database > Import/Export and then select the relevant import option (see Figure 8–14). For VisioModeler files, options for ORM models, logical models, and dictionary files are distinguished by the relevant suffix (.IMO, .IML, .IMD, respectively).

When the import dialog appears, either type the path and file name for the desired model, or press the Browse button to browse for and select the relevant file. Then press OK to import the file.

The progress of the import is displayed in the Output window. Once the import is complete, open the Business Rules window, and drag the relevant object types or fact types onto the drawing window. As for reverse engineering, it is usually better to drag the relevant object types onto the desired drawing page, then right-click the object types and apply ShowRelationships. The tool is not capable of importing the original layout

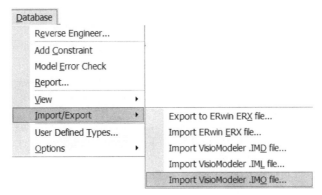

Figure 8–14   Importing VisioModeler or ERwin ERX models.

of the model elements, but by using ShowRelationships, you can usually layout the model yourself fairly quickly.

You can also import a logical model directly into an ER Source Model document using the same menu option. In this case, after the import you can drag the relevant tables onto the drawing surface, and use ShowRelationships on tables to display their foreign key connections.

As indicated in Figure 8–14, the tool also allows you to export to ERX models. However recent versions of ERwin no longer use the ERX format, so this may be of limited use.

If you need to construct an ORM model from an ERwin model that is stored in a newer format than ERX, you should first use ERwin to generate a physical database from the model, then open the ORM Source Model solution and use its reverse engineering facility to extract the model from the physical database.

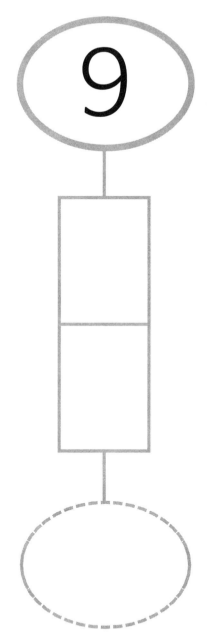

9 Conceptual Model Reports

9.1   Overview

This chapter shows you how to prepare ORM reports by printing model diagrams directly and by using the New Report Wizard for ORM to prepare reports on constraints, fact types, object types, and supertypes. This chapter describes four reports, each of which extracts a different set of properties from your model using customizable filters and attributes.

You can prepare ORM reports from within an ORM source model or from within a Database Model Diagram. There are three additional reports for logical models: Statistics, Table, and Data type. These are described in Chapter 15.

You can create, print, preview, and export comprehensive reports based on the properties stored in an ORM source model. For example, you can create a report that fully documents your conceptual design, or you can prepare a selective report for review with a domain expert. You can preview your report to ensure that you have chosen the right filters, attributes, and formatting options to create a report that precisely meets your needs. You can export your report to an .RTF file for further editing with a word processing application.

In the Database Model Diagram, you can merge several models into a single project and use the reports described in this chapter to report on the merged project file. The "merge and report" is facility is useful for tasks such as creating organization wide data dictionaries.

From within an ORM source model, you can preview or print your model's diagrams directly. You can choose to print all the pages, the current page, or a range of pages.

You can choose from 29 filters and 61 attributes (Table 9–1), and after sorting the contents, you can customize the title, subtitle, and group headers.

Many features in each report type are similar to those in other report types. Some features are identical. Some of the features described in this chapter also apply to the logical model reports described in Chapter 15. For example, the pagination window shown in Figure 9–7 is the same in all reports. All the other report options have some unique features that are explained in each report.

New Report Wizard–How to Prepare ORM Reports

When you want to create reports from an ORM Source Model, you must first open the ORM source model and display it on the Visio drawing surface.

Table 9–1   Summary of filters and attributes.

Tabs	Reports			
	Object Types	Constraints	Fact Types	Supertypes
Filters	10	12	7	
Attributes	23	6	16	16

Figure 9–1   Start New Report Wizard.

Hint: In the ORM Source Model solution, you may have several models open at once. However, the New Report Wizard operates only on the model displayed in the active window. To use ORM reports on merged models, you must use the reports with a project in the Database Model Diagram.

To start the *New Report Wizard* choose Database > Report from the main menu, and click on the Report option shown in Figure 9–1.

The New Report Wizard dialog then appears as shown in Figure 9–2. The next four sections describe what you can do with each of the four options.

9.2 Object Type Reports

Choose the Object Type report when you want to report on ORM object types and their definitions. For example, you can use this report to help domain experts to agree on the names and meaning of ORM object types, or to find synonyms and homonyms. You can issue Object Type reports from an ORM source model or from a Data Model Diagram.

To run an *Object Type report*, ensure that the model on which you want to report is the active window, then choose Database > Report to open the New Report Wizard selection list shown in Figure 9–2. "Highlight Object Type Report" in the list, and then

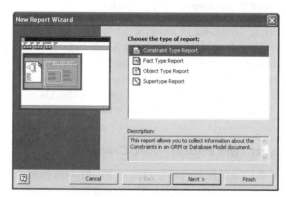

Figure 9–2   New Report Wizard dialog.

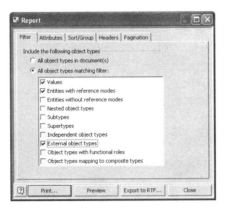

Figure 9–3   Object Type Report—Filters.

click the "Finish" button. The Object Type Report dialog shown in Figure 9–3 now appears.

Object Type Report–Filter Tab

To select the object types on which you want to report: click the Filter tab shown in Figure 9–3. To restrict the object types that appear in the report, click the radio button All object types matching filter and then check the object types of interest. For example, to report on entity object types that don't have a reference mode, choose the check box for that option. You can choose any combination of filters by clicking one or more of the check boxes. Figure 9–3 shows the ten available filters, with three of them checked.

If all your filter options are grayed out, the radio button All object types in document(s) may be selected. This option causes all filter check boxes to be selected but grayed out. Table 9–2 gives some examples of when you might use each filter.

Object Type Report–Attributes

You can select one or more of the fifteen selectable attributes shown in Figure 9–4. To report on all attributes, click the Select All button, and all check boxes will be ticked as shown in Figure 9–4. To report on fewer attributes, click the Deselect All button and click those checkboxes of interest. You can also choose Select All and then deselect the attributes you don't want by clicking on each checkbox

Table 9–3 gives examples of when you might want to report on each attribute.

Object Type Report–Sort/Group

Use the Sort/Group tab shown in Figure 9–5 to choose a sorting sequence and to format the result into groups. The Group sorted records by drop-down menu displays only

Table 9–2 Sample filter usage for an Object Type Report.

Filter	Usage example
Values	Review consolidation of Value Object Types. Generally, ORM models have relatively few Value Object Types.
Entities with reference modes	Review appropriateness of reference modes.
Entities without reference modes	Review externally identified objects with the aim of introducing standard identification schemes.
Nested object types	Review definitions and candidates for flattening or co-referencing.
Subtypes	Review "is a" relationships (e.g., Car is a Vehicle) with subject matter experts. Review subtype definitions.
Supertypes	Review "is a" (e.g., Car is a Vehicle) relationships. Review roles attached to supertypes and ensure they are shared by all subtypes. Agree on classification rules with domain experts.
Independent object types	Unless an object type is an objectified association, it is rare for it to be independent. Reporting only Independent object types makes it easy to review these cases.
External object types	Use this option when to review Object Types that are used in your displayed model but which are defined in a different model.
Object types with functional roles	Functional roles have simple uniqueness constraints. Selecting only this filter reports on object types that are often involved in keys.
Object types mapping to composite types	To compare candidates for flattening, co-referencing, and nesting. Composite types are object/relational types as defined in SQL:1999.

those items that you have added to the Selected sort keys: list. Table 9–4 provides details on using sort keys.

You can choose one of three grouping options from a drop-down list as shown in Figure 9–5. For example, to identify homonyms (same name, different meaning), you use the Attribute tab shown in Figure 9–4 to select Name space, Notes, Object Kind and Object Name. Then you add Object Name to the selected sort keys, choose sort by Object Name and Group by Object Name. This generates a report in alphabetic sequence of Object Name with duplicate objects grouped together. An ideal report for homonym trapping!

Figure 9–4   Object Type Report—Attributes.

Object Type Report–Headers

You use the headers dialog box shown in Figure 9–6 to set the values for the three parts of your report's header. The grayed sub-window headed Sample report title shows the contents of the text that appears in the active sub-window. Clicking a sub-window makes it the active sub-window and changes the content accordingly.

The Default button at the bottom resets the three sub-windows: Report title, Report subtitle, and Group header. The default values are shown in Figure 9–6(a). You can type your own text into each window, and you can use the Insert button to add macros from the drop down list. Click the sub-window into which you want to insert a macro, then click the insert button and choose one or more fields from the drop down list.

When you click on the Report title or Report subtitle sub-windows, the Insert button shows the four options in Figure 9–6(a). Clicking on the Group header sub-window and then on the Insert button shows the four extra options in Figure 9–6(b).

> *Hint:* The Insert button shows a different list for the Group header sub-window.

Report title: The default is "Object Type Report." You can change the title by typing any text that you want. There is no practical limit to the size of your title. You can add a title that covers several pages and you can cut and paste symbols from Microsoft Word such as those for currency or mathematical formulae. The sub-windows do not accept diagrams.

Report subtitle: The default is the model file name, for example, "Patient_CS.vsd." You can add free text, symbols, or one of the insert menu options.

Group header: The fields that initially appear in the group header sub-window are those that you chose for your group header in the Sort/Group tab (see Figure 9–5). If you chose to group sorted records by "none," then this sub-window is grayed out. If you want to add some text, you must return to the Sort/Group tab and choose any selection other than "none." You can then add free text and one or more of the eight macros from the insert menu in Figure 9–6(b).

Table 9–3 Sample attribute usage for an Object Type Report.

Filter	*Usage Example*
ID	ID is a system assigned number that VEA uses to uniquely identify each object type.
Object kind	Check that you have chosen the correct kind of object type (Entity or Value)
Name space	When you need to uniquely identify objects with the same conceptual name but a different meaning (homonyms.) For example, the word "Right" can be used to mean "correct" or it can be used to mean "the opposite to left."
Notes	Review object type definitions with one or more domain experts. You put object definitions in the "Notes" field by right clicking an object type and choosing Database Properties > Definition > Notes.
Mapping option	*Does not result in a composite type:* The most common case. *Named row type:* Can be used with some Object-Relational databases. *Unnamed row type:* Can be used with some Object-Relational databases. *Domain:* Domain mapping prevents two object types that have similar data types from being compared (e.g., =). For example, even though you can use a numeric data type for both Blood Pressure and Atmospheric Pressure, the domains have different units so should not be compared. *Distinct type:* Can be used with some Object-Relational databases.
Composite-type name	Use this to review composite object names with domain experts.
Value/Range	Review allowed ranges with domain expert.
Independent	Review entity types that are used to create separate tables.
Numeric	Compare all numeric data types to see if any can be combined.
Portable data type	Review the database independent data types that you have chosen. Portable data types are mapped to a physical data type in a DBMS.
Physical data type	Check that a target physical data type can accept the range of values you have set as a domain constraint on an ORM object type.
Referencing facts	Domain expert review.
Fact count	Review the number of roles played by each object type.
Pages	Review subject areas with a domain expert. Paginating a model adds structure and makes it easier for domain experts to understand.
Personal pronoun	Review the verbalization options to check that you have correctly applied "his/her" or "its" in the verbalization.

Figure 9–5   Object Type Reports—Sort/Group tab.

Table 9–4   Object Type Report—Sort/Group usage.

Sort Key	Usage example
Object Kind	Sorts by the three object kinds (Entity, Value, External)
Object Name	Sorts by the conceptual name of the object type.
Type Name	Review data types.
Type Mapping Option	Reports on the mapping option selected for each object type.

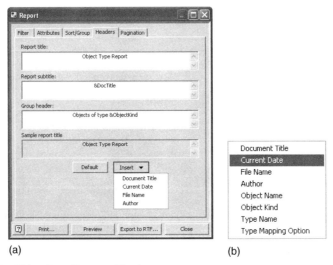

(a)   (b)

Figure 9–6   Object Type Report—Headers.

Object Type Report—Pagination Tab

The pagination tab has identical features in all reports. The pagination tab features are described once here. All other report descriptions, including the reports described in Chapter 15, refer back to this section.

Each report type has three levels: Document, Group, and Record.

- *Document level* is for reports based on multiple documents.
- *Group level* refers to those parts of your report that you have chosen as groups in the Sort/Group dialog box.
- *Record level* refers to a part of your report. For example, in a report showing many ORM object types a record is the information for one object type. In an ORM Fact Type report, a record holds the information for one fact type.

Document separator: The word "document" refers to the separate subsections of the report that include (for example) ORM entity types and ORM value types. The ORM entity types are collected into one "document" and the ORM value types appear in a connected but separate "document." The document separator specifies what will appear between the subsections of your report. The drop-down menu has four options: New Page; Single Line, Double Line, and None.

You can apply a separator between each Document, Group, and Record by selecting from the drop-down list shown in Figure 9–8. The meaning of each separator is shown below.

None: You don't get a separator between each section of your report.
Single Line: Inserts a single horizontal line from margin to margin.

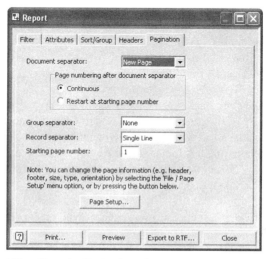

Figure 9–7   Object Type Report—Pagination tab.

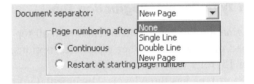

Figure 9–8   Document separator drop-down list (see Figure 9–7).

Double Line: Inserts two horizontal lines from margin to margin.
New Page: Starts each section of your report on a new page.

Page numbering after document separator

Continuous (Radio button). Select this option to number your report pages consecutively from front to back. If you deselect this option, your page numbers start at 1 for each subsection of your document.

Restart at starting page number (Radio button). This option starts the page numbering with 1 for each new source document in a report based on multiple source documents. If you don't select this option, each report page is numbered consecutively from front to back. This will also apply to multiple documents.

Group separator. Specifies the formatting to use to separate groups in the report. You choose groups with the Sort/Group tab.

Record separator. Specifies the formatting to use to separate records in the report. In this report, a "record" refers to all the information about one object type.

Starting page number. Sets the starting page number for the report.

Report Pagination tab—Page Setup button

Clicking on the Page Setup button shown at the bottom of Figure 9–7 opens a Page Setup dialog box with three tabs. You use this dialog box to control page size, type, margins, headers and footers.

Header/Footer tab. Figure 9–9 shows the Header/Footer tab that you use to change the contents of the page header and footer. Click on the page image at the right to change the headings and values of the two windows on the left. Figure 9–9 shows the result of clicking on the left footer region of the page image. The top scroll window shows the macro code and the bottom window shows the result of the macro so you can see when this example was created.

Size/Type tab. You can use the Size/Type tab to adjust page sizes with the controls shown in Figure 9–10.

Margin tab. You can use the margin tab to adjust page margins with the controls shown in Figure 9–11.

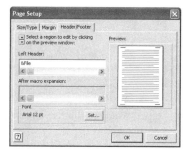

Figure 9-9 Page Setup Window—Header/Footer tab.

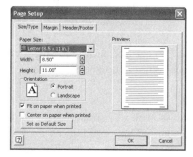

Figure 9-10 Page Setup Window—Size/Type tab.

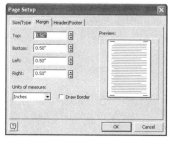

Figure 9-11 Page Setup Window—Margin tab.

Report Window bottom row of buttons

Along the bottom of every report dialog, you will see the four buttons shown in Figure 9–12. The following paragraphs discuss the functions of each button.

Print button

Clicking on the print button at the bottom left of the report window (Figure 9–12) reveals the print button dialog as shown in Figure 9–13. The succeeding paragraphs explain the options in this dialog.

Copies. Use the print dialog box to set print options and printer properties. If you select more than one copy the collate checkbox appears. When you check this box, your

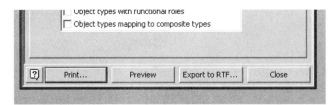

Figure 9–12   Report window—bottom row of buttons.

printer will print each copy as a separate document. If you don't check this box then the pages will print in the sequence. For example, three copies will be printed in the sequence 1, 1, 1, 2, 2, 2, and so on.

Page range.   You can select individual pagers or groups of pages. For example, clicking the "Pages" radio button and entering 2, 5, 7–9 will print page 2, page 5, and pages 7,8, and 9.

Print to file.   To print to a file, click the Print to File radio button, and enter a filename, for example, "MyORMreport." If you click the Browse... button you will see a file location window that helps you to choose where to store your report.

Setup button (printer)

You can directly change your printer settings by clicking the Setup... button at the bottom of the print button dialog shown in Figure 9–13. This button opens the Print Setup dialog shown in Figure 9–14 which allows you to change your printer settings. The Network button allows you to locate a shared printer on your network.

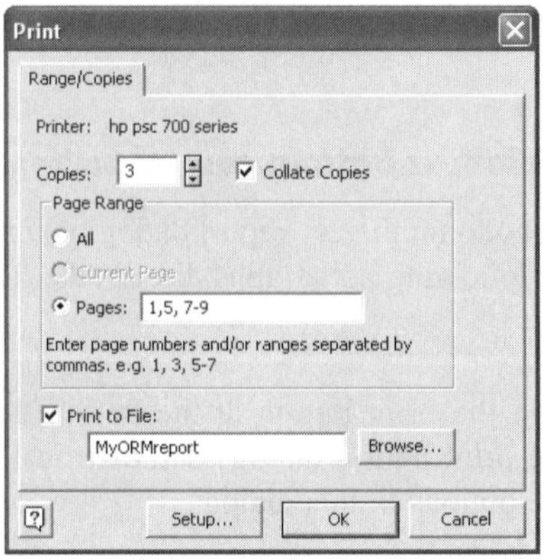

Figure 9–13   The print button dialog.

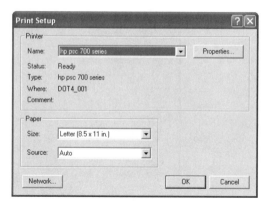

Figure 9–14   Print Setup dialog.

Preview button

Clicking the Preview button displays a preview of your report. This feature works only if you have a printer driver installed. The following paragraphs explain the functions of each button in the preview window (see Figure 9–15).

Print. Clicking the Print button in the preview dialog box reveals the Print dialog shown in Figure 9–9.

Next Page. When you click the Next Page button, you will see the next page of your previewed report in the preview window.

Prev Page. This button takes you to the previous page in your previewed report.

Two Page. When you click the Two Page button, you will see two consecutive pages of your report in the preview window.

Zoom In. When you click the Zoom in button you can less of your report on screen but what you can see is magnified.

Zoom Out. This button displays more of the report on screen but at a smaller scale.

Close. When you click the Close button you are returned to the Report window shown in Figure 9–12. *Note:* If you close this window using the X control, you also close the

Figure 9–15   Preview dialog.

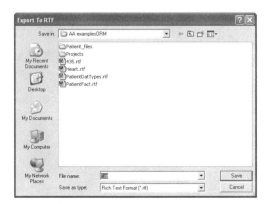

Figure 9–16   Export to RTF... button.

New Report Wizard and your earlier selections are lost. This can be annoying if you wanted to return to the New Report Wizard to continue to work with the report that you were preparing. Always use the Close button!

Export to RTF button

Clicking on the Export to RTF... button at the bottom of Figure 9–12 opens the Export to RTF dialog box shown in Figure 9–16, which asks you for a file name and location. If you are connected to a network, you can save the file in any accessible folder on the network. There is a "save as type" option with a single *.rtf option. After you have saved your report in rich text format, you can edit it with a word-processing program.

Save in.   Choose the windows folder in which you want to save your file.

File name.   Type in a filename then click on the *Save* button.

Close button

Clicking the *Close* button ends New Report Wizard and returns you to the drawing page.

9.3 Constraint Type Reports

Constraint type reports describe the business rules in an ORM Source Model or in a project in the Database Model Diagram. A constraint type report helps you to navigate through a large model by including information about the location of the constraint with the constraint description that appears in the Verbalizer window.

Constraint Type Report–Filter

You use the filter tab to choose which constraint types that you want in your report. The Constraint Type report Filter tab has twelve constraint checkboxes as shown in

Figure 9–17 Constraint Type Report—Filters.

Figure 9–17. To add a constraint to your report, just click the appropriate checkbox. You may select all, one or a just a few. You can learn about constraints in Chapters 4 and 5.

Constraint Type Report–Attributes

Use the attribute tab shown in Figure 9–18 to choose the attributes that you want in your constraints report. The record counter number is used to give a sequence number to the constraints in your report and it has no other significance. The constraint type appears as "constraint kind" on the report and you normally use this property to group the records in your report. "ID" is an internal VEA number and you will rarely use it.

Constraint notes are entered during the ORM modeling process and are not processed by VEA. The Statistical summary shows how relationships and roles are affected by a constraint. Definition information shows which domains are affected by each constraint.

Figure 9–18 Constraint type report—Attributes.

The last attribute shows the constraints verbalization. Your report includes verbalization whether you want it or not, so it does not appear as an optional attribute.

Constraint Type Report–Sort/Group

The Constraint type report Sort/Group is similar to that of the Object Type report explained in the text associated with Figure 9–5. The difference being that here you have a take it or leave it option. You can choose to sort and group by Constraint kind or choose not to sort at all. You would normally use the default and sort by Constraint kind.

Constraint Type Report–Headers

The header tab is similar to the Object Type report header shown in Figure 9–6 and you have the same four basic options: Document Title, Current Date, File Name, and Author. The only difference being that in the Group header sub-window you have an option to insert Constraint kind. For an explanation of the other header windows you can refer to the text associated with Figure 9–6.

Constraint Type Report–Pagination

This works in exactly the same way as the Object Type report pagination described in the text associated with Figure 9–7.

9.4   Fact Type Reports

Fact Type reports show information about the fact types in an ORM source model or in a project containing an ORM source model. When you want to review all or just a selection of the fact types in a single ORM model you can choose the Fact Type report from within an ORM Source Model. If you want to report on the fact types across merged models in a project, you must open your merged model from within the Database Design Diagram and use the Fact Type report from there.

You can use the Fact Type report to bridge the gap between a domain expert's perception of the application domain and the keys in a derived logical model. The Fact Type report is also helpful in finding out which ORM are used in groups of Fact Types.

To run a Fact Type report, make sure that the model on which you want to report is the active window, then choose Database > Report to open the New Report Wizard selection list (see Figure 9–2). Then highlight Fact Type Report in the list and click the Finish button. The Fact Type Report dialog shown in Figure 9–19 will then appear.

Fact Type Report–Filter Tab

The filter tab shown in Figure 9–19 allows you to choose which facts to include in your report. You can use the radio buttons to choose one of the following three options:

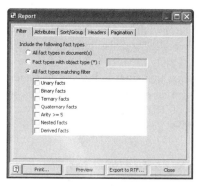

Figure 9–19   Fact Type Report—filter tab.

All fact types in the document(s). This is useful for completely documenting all the assertions made in your model(s).

Fact types with object type(*). Allows you to select just those facts that contain the Object Type whose name you put into the option box. Figure 9–20 shows this option selected with "Patient" as the Object Type name. This feature helps you to keep track of all statements that are made about a domain or set of domains.

All fact types matching filter. Refer to Figure 9–19. With this option, you can choose any combination from the seven options: Unary, Binary, Ternary, Quaternary, Arity >=5, Nested, and Derived.

Recall that the arity of a fact type is the number of roles in it. Sometimes, you can use a single role to uniquely identify an object type. For example, social security number can be used to uniquely identify a person. However, in some cases you need to use two or more roles to uniquely identify a fact instance. For example, the code "DL 058" is the Delta Airlines code for the flight from Atlanta (USA) to Gatwick (UK). However, if you try to reserve a seat on DL 058, you will be asked to choose the date on which

Figure 9–20   Facts with object type(*).

you want to fly. Flight number is really a code for a route flown by a particular airline on specific days such as Monday, Wednesday, and Friday. To uniquely identify a specific flight instance, you also have to specify a date. So, the minimum number of roles needed to uniquely identify a flight instance is two: flight number and date of flight.

In summary, this filter helps you to review your fact types to make sure that they contain the lowest possible number of roles but no fewer than that! In other words, this filter helps you to answer the question "Are all my facts as simple as they should be, and not simpler?"

Fact Type Report—Attributes Tab

You can choose any combination of the sixteen options shown in Figure 9–21 by clicking the appropriate checkbox. The window size is fixed so you can only see twelve of the available sixteen attributes. To see the other four attributes, use the vertical scroll bar on the right of the window. The hidden attributes are for derivation, mapping option, composite type name, and collection types.

The Select All and Deselect All buttons do exactly what they say. The default button selects eleven of the check boxes and deselects the remaining five (ID, Arity, Verbalize external constraints, Notes, and Name Space). Figure 9–15 shows the default selection.

Fact Type Report—Sort/Group tab

Figure 9–22 shows the Fact Type report's Sort/Group tab. This tab works in the same way as the Object Type's Sort/Group tab shown in Figure 9–5.

You can sort by Fact arity, First Object Name, or First fact character. Whatever sort key you add to the Selected sort keys window appears in the Group sorted records by drop-down list.

Figure 9–21   Fact Type Report—Attributes tab.

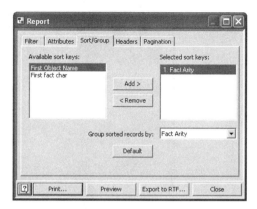

Figure 9–22   Fact Type Report—Sort/Group tab.

The option "First fact char" sorts your report in alphabetic order of Fact Type name. For example consider the four fact types Country has CountryName, Country has Population, Country has President, and Country has Area. The "First fact char" option would sort them in strict alphabetical sequence thus: Country has Area, Country has CountryName, Country has Population, Country has President. These facts would appear together under a group header entitled: Facts starting with "C."

Using a good domain naming convention will help you to get best value from this feature.

Fact Type Report–Headers tab

As you might expect, the Fact Type report headers tab works in the same way as the Object Type header tab shown in Figure 9–6. As with the other reports, you can add the fields for Document Title, Current Date, File name, and Author. When the Group header window is active, you can also add First Object Name, Fact Arity, First fact char, and Fact Verbalization as shown in the drop down insert menu in Figure 9–23.

If you want a detailed explanation of the other header windows, you will find one in the text associated with Figure 9–6.

Fact Type Report–Pagination

This works in exactly the same way as the Object Type report pagination described in the text associated with Figure 9–7.

9.5   Supertype Reports

As the title implies, supertype reports provide information about the subtype and supertype definitions in your ORM source model or in a project in a Database Model Diagram.

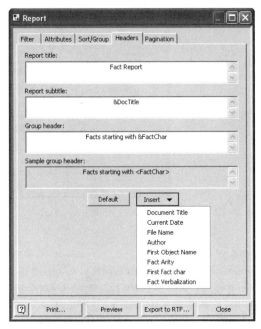

Figure 9-23   Fact Type Report—Headers tab.

Supertype Report–Attributes Tab

You can choose any combination of the sixteen attribute options by clicking on the appropriate checkbox. The window has a fixed size which shows twelve attributes when you open it so this prevents you from viewing all of the attributes at one time. If you want to see the other four attributes you have to use the vertical scroll bar on the right of the window. Figure 9–24 shows the lower part of the window with the default drop down list extended.

The Select All and Deselect All buttons do what they say. The default button gives you the two option sets shown by the bullets listed in Table 9–5.

Supertype Report–Headers Tab

This tab is similar to the tab shown in Figure 9–6. The Report title and Report subtitle windows have macro options for Document Title, Current Date, File name, and Author. Unlike the other report headers tab, the Supertype header tab does not have a Group header, and there are no sorting options.

Supertype Report–Pagination Tab

This works in exactly the same way as the Object Type report pagination described in the text associated with Figure 9–7.

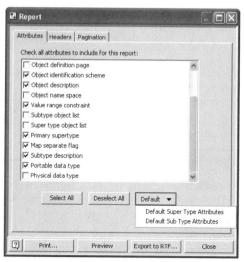

Figure 9–24   Supertype Report—Attributes.

9.6   Copying Diagrams and Text

Copying an Object from Another Program to a Visio Drawing

Start in the source program. Select the object you want to copy and choose Edit > Copy. In Visio, make sure that the Visio document in which you want to paste the object is the active Visio document. Choose Edit > Paste Special. The Paste Special function allows you to choose the format of the pasted object. A dialog box similar to Figure 9–25 will appear. The options in this dialog depend on the properties of the object you want to paste. Choose the format you want from the list in the Paste as window then click OK.

If you paste a bitmap into Visio, it may arrive in Visio as an image that is ten or more times bigger than your model. If this happens, your Visio window will be filled with the pasted image. If you have a scroll mouse, rotate the mouse wheel to rescale the drawing surface until the pasted image is a small object. Then click the image to make it the active object with its handles displayed. Click on a corner handle, hold the left mouse button down and drag the corner handle to proportionally resize the image to meet your needs. If you don't want proportional resizing, use a handle that is not at a corner of the object.

> *Caution: Using Visio Diagrams in Reports:* Images and other objects that you paste onto the drawing surface will not appear in an *.rtf file generated by the New Report Wizard. If you want a report that includes diagrams from your model then you must first generate an *.rtf file, open it in Word and then copy your Visio diagrams into the Word document. You can then open your Visio diagrams directly from within Word using "Edit Visio Object."

Table 9–5   Supertype report—Attribute defaults.

Attribute	Supertype default	Subtype default
Draw graphical supertype tree	●	●
Subtype line definition page		●
ID	●	●
Object verbalization	●	●
Object definition page		
Object identification scheme	●	●
Object description	●	●
Object name space		
Value range constraint	●	●
Subtype object list	●	
Super type object list	●	
Primary supertype		●
Map separate flag		●
Subtype description		●
Portable data type	●	●
Physical data type		

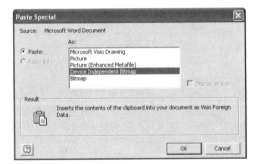

Figure 9–25   Paste Special dialog.

Copying or Moving a Single Item from Visio to Visio or to Another Program

Select the Visio object(s) that you want to move or copy by clicking to make control handles appear. Then right-click, and a menu similar to Figure 9–26 will appear. Figure 9–26 is the result of right-clicking an object type in an ORM source model. Some objects have different menus.

The next step is to do one of the following:
To move the item, click Cut on the menu
To copy the item, click Copy on the menu

If you want to move or copy the item to another document, switch to the other document and click where you want the item to appear. Then choose Edit > Paste Special, and choose the relevant format for pasting.

Figure 9–26   Visio right click menu.

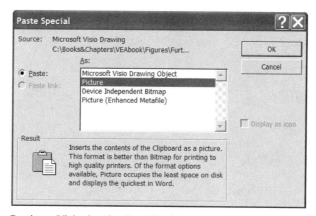

Figure 9–27   Pasting a Visio drawing into Word.

Copying from Visio to Word

It is easy to copy all or part of a Visio diagram to Microsoft Word. First select the relevant part of the diagram to copy by dragging the mouse over the relevant diagram area. Then copy the selection to the clipboard, either by typing Ctrl+C or choosing Edit > Copy from the main menu.

Then place the cursor in the relevant place in the Word document where you wish to place the copy. Then choose Edit > Paste Special from Word's main menu. The Paste Special dialog shown in Figure 9–27 then appears.

To paste an image of the copied drawing, you have four options. For most purposes, we recommend the Picture option. This adds only a little to the size of your Word document, but still gives a good quality image.

If the model fragment you want to copy is spread over more than one page in Visio, you can insert a new page in Visio and drag the relevant model elements onto that page so that you can copy just the model fragment you want.

Part 3

The Logical Modeling Solution (ER and Relational)

Parts 1 and 2 provided an overview of the database modeling features in Visio for Enterprise Architects, and discussed the ORM conceptual modeling solution in depth.

Part 3 focuses on the logical modeling solution. It shows how to create and edit a logical database model and how to generate a physical database schema from it. It also explains how to reverse engineer a physical database schema to a logical data model, and how to generate reports that document the logical model.

Chapter 10 shows you how to use the Database Model Diagram and ER Source Model solutions to create a logical database model directly, using either pure relational notation, or an ER-like notation such as IDEF1X. You learn how to add attributes to relation schemes, and specify primary, alternate, and foreign key constraints. You also learn the basics of managing logical models, and how to add ER source models to database projects.

Chapter 11 shows you how to generate a physical model from a logical model. You learn how to setup database drivers, choose generation options, and generate DDL scripts.

Chapter 12 provides detailed instructions about editing and managing a logical model. You learn to rename and move columns, edit foreign key and category relationships, and find closely related tables. You learn about views and the SQL code editor.

You learn to paginate and verbalize a logical model. You learn how to set the options for drivers, documents, and models.

Chapter 13 shows you how to copy and clone parts of a logical model. You learn how to add notes and manage indexes. You learn how to edit triggers and stored procedures, and make use of user defined data types and extended properties.

Chapter 14 shows you how to reverse engineer an existing database into a logical model. You learn how to refine a logical model and how to view related SQL code.

Chapter 15 shows you how to generate logical model reports for statistics, tables, and data types.

Part 4 discusses advanced topics such as round-trip engineering and model management.

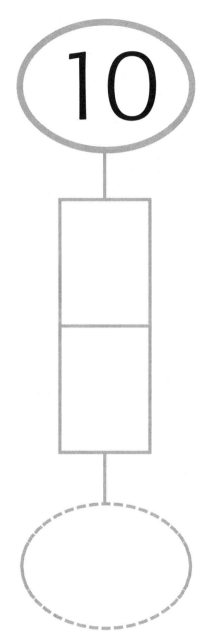

Creating a Basic Logical Database Model

10.1 The Database Model Diagram Solution

Most people who have used both Object Role Modeling (ORM) and Entity Relationship (ER) modeling prefer to use ORM for conceptual analysis, because of its expressiveness, completeness, and flexibility. An added benefit of ORM is the automatic normalization that occurs during the mapping process. However, if you prefer working with entity relationship models, VEA allows you to bypass ORM and create data models using ER techniques.

VEA provides two ways to create a logical database model using ER techniques. You can create an ER (Entity Relationship) source model, or you can directly draw a logical database diagram using the database model diagram solution. We'll cover the database model diagram in sections 10.3 to 10.7 of the chapter, and discuss ER source models at the end. Building a database model diagram and building an ER source model are *very* similar, so nearly all the material in sections 10.3 to 10.7 of this chapter applies to ER source models as well.

Unlike ORM and ER source models, database model diagrams cannot be part of larger projects. The database model diagram is well suited for simple or one time tasks. If you intend to model a complex or large universe of discourse that could benefit from being developed as a set of sub models, then you should consider using source models instead of just the database model diagram solution.

In pure ER modeling, entity types and attributes are conceptual constructs, and relationships between entity types may be expressed directly. In the VEA database model diagram and ER source model solutions, the correspondence between entity types and tables is 1:1, as is the correspondence between attributes and columns. VEA supports separate conceptual and physical naming for these constructs, which allows the modeler to present users with familiar business names for objects, while maintaining physical naming standards at the database level.

For ease of reference, the remainder of this chapter will use the term "entity" loosely to mean either a conceptual entity type or a relational table scheme, and the term "attribute" to mean either a conceptual attribute or relational column.

10.2 Notation Options

A logical data model can be expressed in different notations. VEA supports a generic relational notation, IDEF1X notation, and some other variations. The choice of notations and display options does not affect the underlying model. Before discussing how to create models using the database model diagram solution, let's take a quick look at some the different logical notations available in VEA.

Relational Notation

With relational notation, each entity is shown as rectangular box. The name of the entity is in the gray shaded portion of each box. The entities represented by the model in Figure 10–1 are *Country, Patient, BloodPressureTest* and *PapSmear*.

Each entity's primary key is underlined and is also identified by the letters *PK* on the left hand side of the entity. The primary key is shown just below the name of the entity, and is separated from the other attributes by a horizontal line. For instance, the primary key of *Patient* is *PatientNr*. All of the non primary key attributes are listed below the horizontal line. Required attributes are shown in boldface type, and migrated attributes (i.e., attributes that are part of a foreign key) are marked with the letters *FK<ordinal>* on the left hand side of the entity. Attributes like Country.CountryName that represent an alternate identifier for an entity are marked with the uniqueness symbol *U<ordinal>* on the left hand side of the entity.

Relationships (foreign key references) are shown as solid arrows. With VEA's relational notation, all relationship lines look the same, as do all entity outlines. As you will discover in the next section, this is not the case with IDEF1X notation. The arrowhead always points to the "parent" (e.g., the "one" side of a 1:m) entity in the relationship. For instance, in the relationship between Country and Patient, many patients may be born in one country, but each patient is born in at most one country.

If you are used to notations that reverse the arrowheads, it can be confusing to remember which way the arrow points in VEA. Thinking in terms of logical implication may help. In the Country/Patient example, the constraint symbolized by the relationship line can be verbalized thus: "*If* a country code is listed in the *Patient* entity,

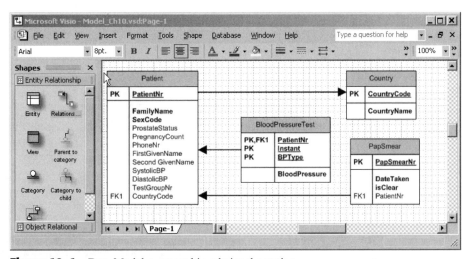

Figure 10–1   Data Model expressed in relational notation.

then that country code MUST be listed in the *Country* entity." Substituting the variable *P* for the antecedent ("a country code is listed in the Patient entity") and the variable *C* for the consequent ("that country code must be listed in the Country entity") yields the argument from *If P then Q*. By longstanding convention, such argument forms are graphically denoted with an arrow pointing from the antecedent to the consequent like this: $P \rightarrow Q$. If one thinks of the entities as the variables in the statement, the direction of the arrow in VEA is consistent with the conventional direction of the arrow in logical statements.

As an option, VEA's relational notation can display cardinality indicators next to each relationship line. Cardinality is the number of instances of each entity that can participate in the relationship. The cardinality display option is turned off by default, and is not enabled for Figure 10–1, so the symbols are not visible in the figure. However, Table 10–1 shows the full set of cardinality indicators that could be displayed if you enabled the cardinality display option. In addition to this UML-style notation, you can choose the popular crowsfoot notation used in approaches such as Information Engineering (see the Glossary for examples).

IDEF1X Notation

This notation has become quite popular in certain sectors, especially for military contractors, because of its adoption as a FIPS (Federal Information Processing Standard), as outlined in FIPS 184.

With IDEF1X notation, each entity is shown as a rectangular box, but the shape of the rectangle depends on the kind of relationships in which the entity participates. An entity whose primary key does not contain any foreign keys is said to be "independent." An entity whose primary key contains at least one foreign key is termed "dependent." IDEF1X uses rectangles with square corners to represent independent entities, and rectangles with rounded corners to depict dependent entities. In Figure 10–2, the *Country, Patient,* and *PapSmear* entities are independent, while *BloodPressureTest* is a dependent entity.

Table 10–1   Relational Notation Cardinality Indicators.

Indicator	Relationship Cardinality
*	One to zero or more
1..*	One to one or more
0..1	One to zero or one
1	One to exactly one
x..y	One to (range between x and y inclusive where x and y are positive whole numbers)

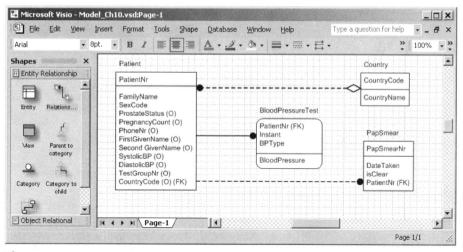

Figure 10–2   Data model expressed in IDEF1X notation.

Relationships appear as lines between that terminate in a solid dot on the "child" entity of the relationship. The line itself is either dashed or solid, depending on the type of relationship depicted. If the migrated attribute becomes part of the primary key of the "child" entity the relationship is called "identifying." Relationships where the migrated attribute does *not* become part of the child's primary key are termed "non-identifying." IDEF1X shows identifying relationships as solid lines, and non-identifying relationships as dashed lines. In Figure 10–2, the relationship between "Patient" and "BloodPressureTest" is identifying. The other relationships in the diagram are non-identifying.

In contrast to relational notation, IDEF1X uses special symbols to indicate if a relationship is optional. A hollow diamond on the "parent" side (e.g., the side opposite the dot) of the relationship indicates that the relationship, and thus the associated migrated attribute, is optional. In Figure 10–2, the hollow diamond on the relationship line touching the *Country* entity means that a given instance of *Patient* (the entity at the other end of the line) may or may not be related to an instance of *Country*. On a relational level, the optional nature of this relationship causes the attribute Patient.CountryCode to be optional. Contrast this with the relationship between "PapSmear" and "Patient" where the lack of a hollow diamond shows that the relationship is mandatory. Thus, it is impossible to record an instance of *PapSmear* that is *not* related to some instance of *Patient*.

As in relational notation, IDEF1X separates the primary key of the entity from the non key attributes with a horizontal line. However, the primary key itself is not underlined, nor are there any additional letters denoting the key. Boldface type is not used for any attribute, regardless of whether the attribute is optional or mandatory. A display option (which has been enabled for Figure 10–2) allows VEA to use the standard IDEF1X method for indicating optional attributes—letter 'O' enclosed in parentheses after the attribute name. Migrated attributes are indicated by the letters *FK* enclosed in parentheses after the attribute name.

Table 10–2 IDEF1X Notation Cardinality Indicators.

Indicator	Relationship Cardinality
<none>	One to zero or more
P	One to one or more
Z	One to zero or one
I	One to exactly one
x .. y	One to (range between x and y inclusive where x and y are positive whole numbers)

As with relational notation, IDEF1X can optionally display relationship cardinality. Table 10–2 shows the full set of cardinality indicators that that VEA can display if you enable the cardinality option when using IDEF1X notation.

VEA's use of notation and other display options are controlled through a number of menus and dialog boxes. It is easier to see the effect of these display options in a simple diagram. In the next few sections, you will learn how create a simple diagram. Chapter 12 explains how to control the appearance of your diagram through the use of document display options.

10.3   Creating a Database Model Diagram

From the main menu, choose File > New > Database > Database Model Diagram to create a blank database model diagram. Your screen should look similar to Figure 10–3.

Because of VEA's anchored windows and dockable toolbars, your screen may look somewhat different. However, you should see at least three major areas: the shape stencils (shown here on the left side of the screen), the drawing pane (upper portion of screen), and the Tables and Views anchored window in the bottom portion of the screen.

If you cannot see the Tables and Views window, choose Database > View > Tables and Views from the menu. You may or may not have an Output tab. Anytime you perform an action that causes the tool to generate status messages, the Output window will automatically be displayed. Because the tab will automatically show up when you need it, there is no need to specifically enable the Output tab from the Database > View menu, though you can if you wish.

It will be easier to follow the examples in this chapter if you ensure that your display options are set to the original factory defaults. From the main menu, choose Database > Options > Document. A tabbed dialog box like the one in Figure 10–4 will appear. Click on the Defaults button and choose Restore Original from the sub menu. Click the OK button to return to the diagram.

In the next chapter, you will learn how to set up the database drivers that come with VEA. Database drivers translate your model into platform specific DDL (data

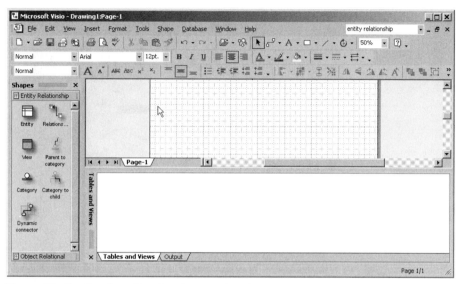

Figure 10–3   Creating a New Database Model Diagram.

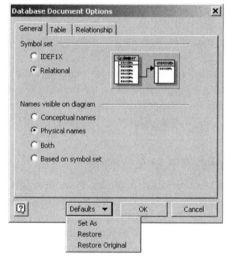

Figure 10–4   Database Document Options, General pane.

definition language) code with platform specific data types. You will find it easier to follow the examples in this chapter if you set the Microsoft SQL Server driver as your default driver. To set the default driver, choose Database > Options > Drivers from the main menu. Your screen should look like Figure 10–5. Highlight Microsoft SQL Server if it is not already selected and click the OK button. The other tabs in the dialog box and the Setup button are described in the next chapter, so don't worry about them for now.

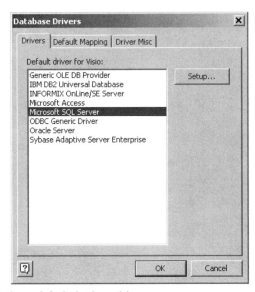

Figure 10–5   Selecting a default database driver.

In contrast to the ORM solution, the database model diagram does not provide a sentence driven tool like the Fact Editor to help you build the data model. Instead, you build the model by dragging and dropping shapes. Before going onto the next section, make sure that the Entity Relationship stencil is open. If you cannot see the Entity Relationship stencil, open it with the command File > Stencils > Database > Entity relationship. VEA also provides an Object-Relational stencil that you can use to create models for servers that support object-relational constructs. The Object-Relational stencil is described in Chapter 13.

Adding Entities to a Diagram

To add an entity to the diagram, drag the entity shape from upper left portion of the stencil, and drop it on the drawing surface. While you are dragging the shape, you will notice that the object is named *Table*. As soon as you drop the entity on the drawing surface, it will receive a default physical name of *Table1*. The ordinal appended to the word *Table* will increase with each new entity added, so the next entity added would be called *Table2,* the third would be called *Table3* and so on . . . The entity will show up as box on the drawing surface, and it will be listed in the Tables and Views window, shown at the bottom of Figure 10–6.

To give the entity a meaningful name, double click on the new entity to bring up the Database Properties window in the anchored window portion of the screen.

Click on the Definition category if it is not already selected. Your screen should now look like Figure 10–7. The default physical name for the newly created entity is *Table1,* and the default conceptual name is *Entity1*. You can change either the physical or conceptual name of the entity by typing into the appropriate field. For this example, type

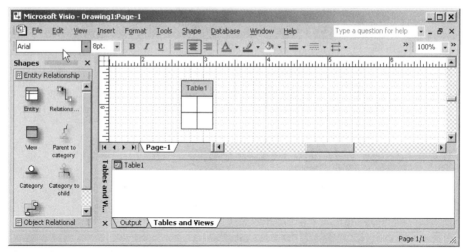

Figure 10–6 Just added a new entity.

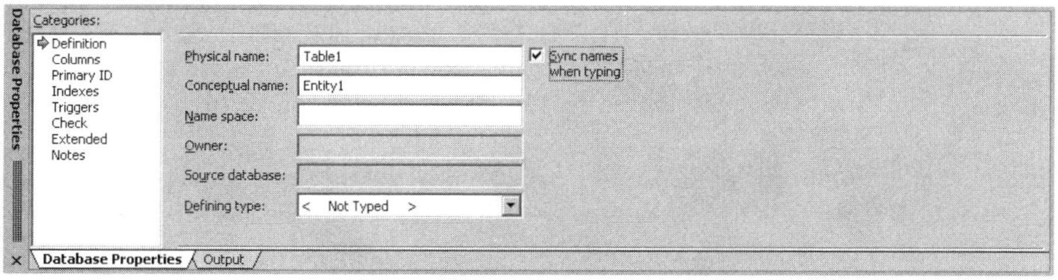

Figure 10–7 The Database Properties Window; Definition category.

the word "Patient" into the Physical name field. You will notice that the conceptual name automatically changes to match the Physical name. Because of the default display options, only the physical name of the entity will show on the diagram. In this case, the physical and conceptual names are the same, so the display option chosen doesn't make much difference. Chapter 12 will discuss controlling the display of physical or conceptual names on the diagram.

> ***Hint:*** To assign different physical and conceptual names to an entity, clear the checkbox labeled Sync names when typing. If this checkbox is selected, the Physical name and Conceptual name will be forced to match as soon as you type into either field. This checkbox is selected by default. The discussion of Modeling Options at the end of chapter 12 explains how to change the default behavior.

The Name Space property should rarely, be used. Name spaces are designed for differentiating entities that are actually different in nature, but share the same name (e.g. the "homonym problem"). If you find homonyms in the Universe of Discourse that you are modeling, it is vastly preferable to facilitate a change of terms among users than to perpetuate the confusion in a data model. However, in very large environments, it may be impossible to resolve all homonyms, so the namespace option provides a way for the model to accommodate the issue.

The Owner and Source database properties are specific to reverse engineering and will be discussed in the chapter on reverse engineering. The Defining type property is only used in Object-Relational models, which are discussed in chapter 13.

10.4   Adding Attributes to an Entity

To add attributes to the Patient entity, double click on the entity and select the Columns category of the Database Properties window to view the Columns pane. The fastest way to add attributes is to enter text directly into the various fields of the Columns table as shown in Figure 10–8.

As you fill out the fields of the table in the Database Properties window, VEA creates the attributes for the selected entity. This window makes it easy to add multiple attributes to an entity very quickly. Table 10–3 explains the purpose of each field in the Columns table of the Database Properties window.

Adding attributes through in-place editing of the table in the Database Properties window is very fast, but it does not address *every* property that an attribute can have. The

> *Note:* In the VEA tool itself, the Notes for an entity or attribute are essentially unlimited in length. However, certain database engines impose length limitations on comments that are generated into the data dictionary. For instance, Oracle 8.x and above allows comments of 4,000 characters, while Microsoft Access only allows comments of 256 characters, and MS SQL Server doesn't store any comments in the database dictionary. When you generate DDL (explained in the next chapter), your comments may be truncated or suppressed based on your target database server.

Conceptual name of an attribute can only be set through the Column Properties dialog which is invoked via the Edit button. To set the conceptual name of an attribute, highlight the attribute in the Database Properties table and click the Edit button on the right side of the window. Performing these actions on the screen in Figure 10–8 would invoke the dialog box shown in Figure 10–9.

By default, the conceptual name of the attribute will be the same as the physical name. To make the conceptual name different from the physical name, clear the Sync names when typing checkbox, and type "Patient Number" in the Conceptual Name field.

Many organizations have strict physical naming conventions that dictate the use of class words (for instance, "Nr" for all numbers) and forbid embedded spaces in the database. By setting physical and conceptual names independently, the modeler conforms to physical naming standards while retaining the more readable conceptual name for user reviews.

The Allow NULL values checkbox in Figure 10–9 is in effect a "mirror image" of the Req'd checkbox in Figure 10–8. Checking the Allow NULL values checkbox in Figure 10–9

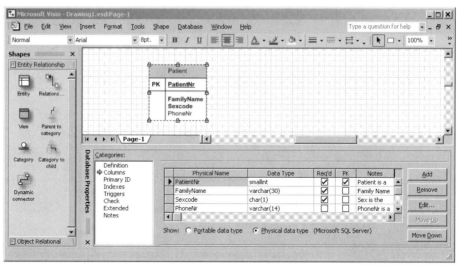

Figure 10–8   Adding an attributes to an entity.

Table 10–3   Database Properties Columns Table.

Field Name	Purpose
Physical Name	The name the attribute should have when it is generated as a column in the physical database.
Data Type	The data type the attribute should use. The radio button at the bottom of the window switches between *portable* and *physical* data types. Portable data types are platform independent data types, while physical data types are specific to particular database engine products. This field has a drop down list of available data types.
Req'd	The field name is an abbreviation for "Required." If the attribute is mandatory, check this box. Checking the PK box (see below) will cause the Req'd box to be automatically checked.
PK	The field name is an abbreviation for "Primary Key." If the attribute is part of the primary key (or the entire primary key) of the entity, check this box.
Notes	A descriptive comment about the attribute. This note can be generated into the physical database as a comment for those servers that support the feature.

has the effect of making the attribute optional, while checking the Req'd checkbox in the Database Properties (Figure 10–8) makes the attribute mandatory.

The Data Type pane of the Column Properties dialog allows the user to edit the data type for an attribute. Data Types are dealt with extensively in section 4.10 of chapter four

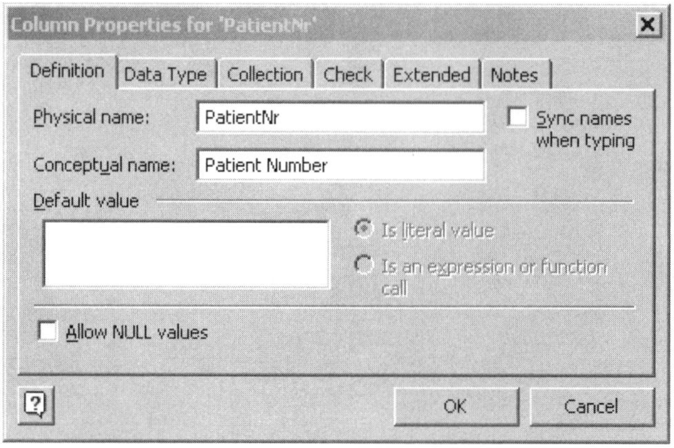

Figure 10–9   Column Properties Dialog.

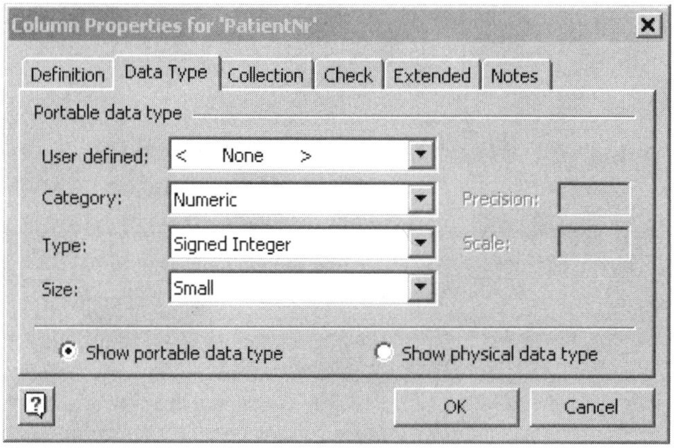

Figure 10–10   Data Type Pane (Portable Data Types).

and thus only receive a short explanation here. The radio button at the bottom of the pane switches the mode of the pane between portable and physical data types. In Figure 10–10, the radio button has been set for portable data types.

Portable data types are generic, while physical data types are specific to a particular DBMS product. The mapping from portable to physical data types is determined by your choice of database driver. For instance, the Numeric, Signed integer, Small portable data type shown in Figure 10–10 will generate a SMALLINT column when using the Microsoft SQL Server driver. The same portable data type will generate a NUMBER column when using the Oracle driver.

Many modelers know their target database, and prefer to work directly with physical data types. Figure 10–11 illustrates the results of changing the radio button selection for the Data Type pane of the Column Properties window.

You cannot use this pane to edit a physical data type. If you want to change a data type, click on the Edit button and use the pop up dialog box, as shown in Figure 10–12.

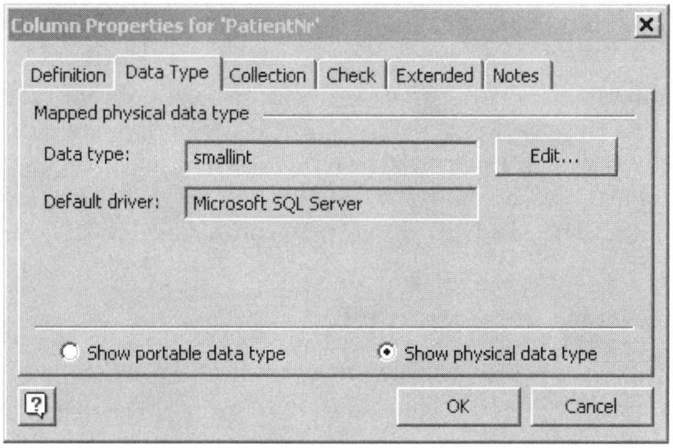

Figure 10–11   Data Type Pane (Physical Data Types).

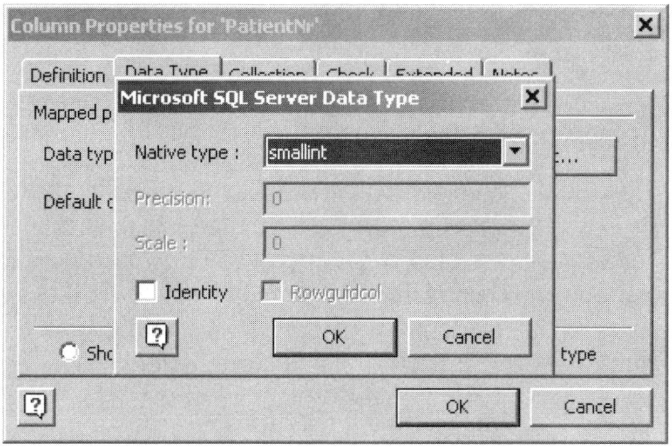

Figure 10–12   Editing physical data types.

The drop down list is populated with all the data types that are supported by the DBMS driver you have chosen. This window also allows one to select the Identity and Rowguidcol properties for data types that support these features.

> ***Hint:*** Invoking the window in Figure 10–12 can be time consuming if done one step at a time. Fortunately, there is a much quicker way to reach this window. Simply type a non-recognized data type (the letter "x" works well) into the Data Type field of the Database Properties window (see Figure 10–8), and hit <Return>. VEA will immediately invoke the window in Figure 10–12. Clicking the Okay or Cancel button returns you directly to the Database Properties window.

10.5   Adding Basic Constraints

Constraints are rules that restrict the population of the schema to allowable sets of data. Previous chapters covered the ORM constraints, which are more comprehensive than the constraints supported by Entity Relationship diagrams and source models. This section addresses only four constraints, the *Primary Key, Alternate Uniqueness,* the *Mandatory* (also called *Not Null*) constraint, and the *Foreign Key* constraint.

Primary Key Constraint

The most fundamental constraint is the *Primary Key* constraint, which ensures that each row in an entity is uniquely identifiable. Section 10.4 showed how to apply a primary key constraint by checking the PK checkbox in the Database Properties window (see Figure 10–8). You can also add (or edit) the primary key of an entity in the Primary ID pane of the Database Properties window, as shown in Figure 10–13

The Primary ID pane allows you to choose from the available attributes to construct a Primary key. VEA has special generation and physical naming options that are described in chapter 12.

Alternate Unique Constraint

Sometimes there is more than one way to uniquely identify a particular row of data in an entity. The *Country* entity is a good example. The ISO (international standards organization) assigns a two letter code to each country. Because these codes are unique, and *Country_code* is the most common way to refer to a country (at least for the purposes of this model), the *Country_code* attribute is the primary key of the *Country* entity. However, it is important to keep Country Names from being repeated within the

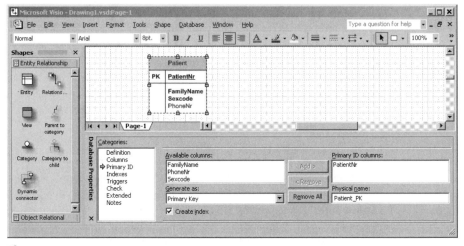

Figure 10–13   Database Properties window, Primary ID pane.

Table 10–4 Illegal population of the
Country entity.

Country_code	CountryName
CA	Canada
GB	Canada
FR	France
US	United States

entity. Table 10–4 shows an example of the *Country* entity improperly populated with repeating country names.

Rows one and two cannot both be true, because two countries with different codes should not use the same name. The data modeler should apply a rule so that the value of the attribute *CountryName* cannot repeat within the entity *Country,* even though *CountryName* is not the primary key of the entity. The Alternate unique constraint is designed for these exact situations.

The alternate unique constraint is enforced through a unique database index. VEA's database model diagram does not actually use the words "Alternate Unique Constraint." To apply the constraint in VEA, you must apply a unique index. Follow these steps to apply a unique index:

1. Click on the *Country* entity to invoke the Database Properties window.
2. Choose the Index category on the left side of the window.
3. Click on the New button in the Index pane and type a name for your new index in the popup dialog box, as shown in Figure 10–14.
4. After you click the OK button to close the popup dialog box, the Available columns box will be populated with the names of the columns in the entity. Double click on the column *CountryName* to move the column to the Indexed columns box.
5. By default, the index type is non unique. Make the index unique by choosing from the Index Type list box one of the three choices that contains the word "unique," as shown in Figure 10–15. The three different choices for uniqueness are: Unique Index with constraint, Unique index only, and Unique constraint only. Depending on your database implementation, you may wish to avoid catalog constraints, but still have the unique index, or vice versa.

Not Null Constraints

The not null constraint roughly corresponds to the ORM simple mandatory constraint that is discussed in section 5.3, and has the effect of requiring a value to be supplied for the attribute to which it is applied. To create a not null constraint, use either the Req'd field of the Database Properties window, shown in Figure 10–8, or the Allow NULL values checkbox shown in Figure 10–9.

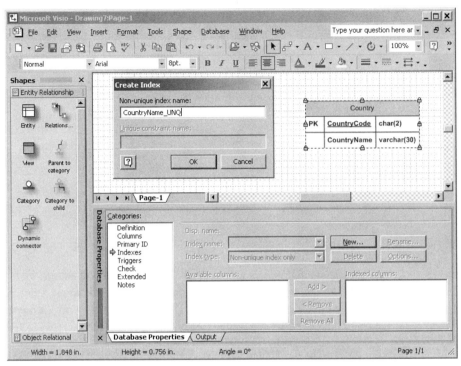

Figure 10–14   Creating a new index.

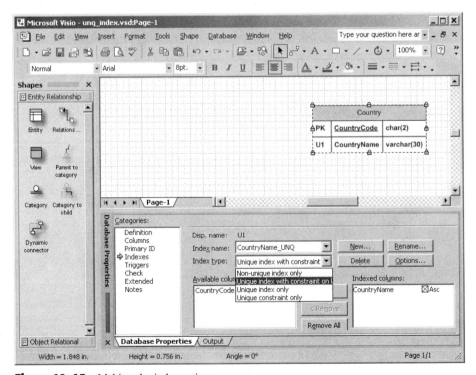

Figure 10–15   Making the index unique.

Section 5.3 also discussed disjunctive mandatory constraints, which involve multiple roles and cannot be enforced by declaring an individual attribute to be required (not null). Enforcement of a mandatory disjunctive constraint involves the creation of database code. If you use the ORM solution, VEA will write the code for you. If you create the logical model directly you will have to write the code yourself. In certain cases, the enforcement of even simple mandatory constraints can require database code. Regardless of the source of your database code, editing and managing database code is covered in chapter 13.

Foreign Key Constraints

A foreign key constraint is a relational implementation of a conceptual subset constraint. Consider the relationship line between *Country* and *Patient* shown in Figure 10–1. The relationship line is a graphical notation for the fact type "*Patient was born in Country.*" The information in the schema will be inconsistent if a user is allowed to record a non-existent country as the birthplace of patient, or to delete country information for a country that is recorded in the *Patient* entity. The explanation that follows makes use of the sample populations in Table 10–5 and Table 10–6.

The set of valid country codes recorded in the *Country* entity shown in Table 10–5 is {'CA', 'GB', 'FR', 'US'}. The set of country codes associated with patients 101–104 in the *Patient* entity (Table 10–6) is {'CA', 'GB', 'US'}. Every element in the second set is contained in the first, set, so patients 101–104 present no constraint violations. However, patient 105 was born in Zambia, and the code for that country (ZM), does not

Table 10–5 Population of Country Entity.

Country_code	CountryName
CA	Canada
GB	United Kingdom
FR	France
US	United States

Table 10–6 Patient Entity (selected attributes) with illegal row shaded.

PatientNr	FamilyName	FirstGivenName	Country_code
101	Sara	Jones	CA
102	Dan	Smith	US
103	Rex	Green	US
104	Joseph	Jones	GB
105	Mary	Fischer	ZM

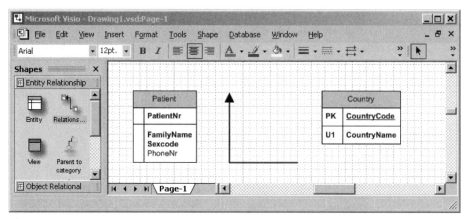

Figure 10–16   Dropping a relationship shape onto the drawing surface.

exist in the set recorded in the *Country* entity. To maintain data integrity, the row for patient 105 cannot be inserted into the *Patient* entity unless a row for Zambia is first added to the *Country* entity.

Conversely, deleting a row of data from the *Country* entity may also violate the subset constraint. For example, deleting the row for the United States in the *Country* entity will have the effect of "orphaning" the rows for patients 102 and 103. A foreign key constraint protects against both insert and deletes that would violate the subset rule.

Adding a relationship between two entities will automatically create a foreign key constraint when VEA generates DDL for your model. If you want to follow along with the upcoming example, first add a *Country* entity to your sample model. To add a relationship in VEA, do the following:

1. Position the involved entities so that at least a portion of both entities are visible on the screen. If necessary, zoom the display to make room.
2. Drag a relationship shape from the stencil, and drop it onto the drawing surface, as shown in Figure 10–6. Do not worry about the orientation of the relationship shape. The shape will automatically orient itself in the next step.
3. Click on the arrowhead of the relationship, and drag it to the *Country* entity. When the cursor approaches the middle of the *Country* entity, the entity will be automatically outlined in red, as shown in Figure 10–17.

Release the mouse button, and the relationship will be attached to Country as shown in Figure 10–18.

Perform the same steps to attach the other end of the relationship to the *Patient* entity. Successful attachment of the second end of the relationship will yield a screen similar to the one in Figure 10–19.

The attribute Country_code has been automatically migrated to the *Patient* entity and marked as a foreign key. Note that the migrated attribute is marked with the symbol FK<ordinal>. The second foreign key in a table would be marked FK2, the third, FK3 and so on.

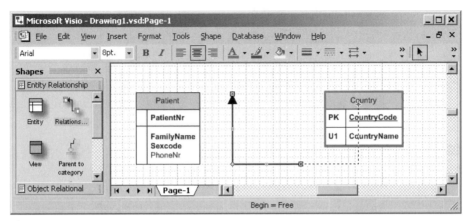

Figure 10–17   Attaching the relationship to the *Country* entity.

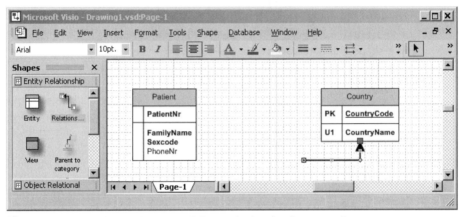

Figure 10–18   Relationship successfully attached to the *Country* entity.

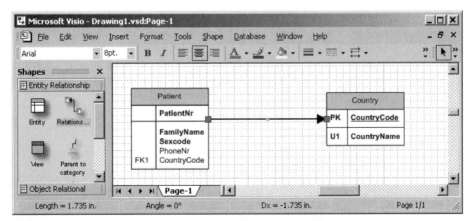

Figure 10–19   Relationship successfully attached to both entities.

Hint: VEA does not rely on the order in which the relationship is attached to determine "parent" (superset) and "child" (subset) entities. VEA relies on *which end* of the relationship is attached to an entity. When using relational notation, the arrowhead always attaches to the parent, and the plain end of the relationship attaches to the child. When using IDEF1X notation, the plain end of the relationship attaches to the parent, and the "dot" end of the relationship attaches to the child.

10.6   Basic Model Housekeeping

Deleting and Displaying Entities

An entity may exist in a model without being displayed on a diagram. The same entity may be displayed in many places on the diagram, on the same or different pages. You can *delete* an entity from the drawing window by selecting it, and then pressing the Delete key. This invokes a message box with the prompt "Remove selected item from the underlying model?" If you answer Yes the entity is removed from the model, so every shape depicting it on the diagram is also removed. If you answer No the selected shape is only removed from the diagram you are viewing. Because the entity still exists in the model, any shapes depicting the entity elsewhere on the diagram remain unchanged.

The Tables and Views window contains a list of *all* entities in a model, regardless of whether they are displayed. To display an entity, drag its icon from the Tables and Views window to the drawing surface. Right clicking on any entity in this window allows you to sort the entities alphabetically. To ensure that an entity you intended to delete is truly gone, sort the list in the Tables and View window, and check for the entity in this list.

Deleting Attributes

Invoke the Database Properties window by clicking on the entity containing the attributes you wish to delete, and select the Columns category on the left side of the window. Highlight the attribute you wish to delete, and click the Remove button, as shown in Figure 10–20.

Unlike entities, removal of an attribute is immediate and complete, with no confirming dialog box. If you accidentally remove an attribute, use the *undo* command to restore it.

Saving Models

To save your model, choose File > Save from the File menu, or click the Save (diskette) icon. If the model has not been saved before, this opens the Save As dialog box. Choose the folder where you want to save the model, add a filename for the model, press the Save button in the dialog, then press OK in the properties dialog. The file will be saved with the extension ".vsd" (Visio document). If you previously saved the file, then the

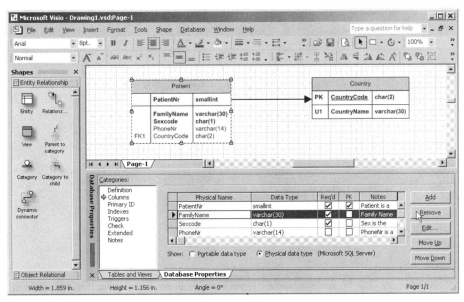

Figure 10–20   Ready to delete the attribute *FamilyName*.

Save operation simply replaces the old copy with the latest version of the model without opening any dialog boxes.

10.7   Projects and ER Source Models

Chapter 7 discussed VEA's use of the *Project* construct for mapping ORM models to logical models. Projects also allow the modeler to merge multiple *source models* into a single logical schema, as part of the build process. The source models contained in a project are not restricted to ORM models. In fact, you can mix ER and ORM source models in the same project and still build a single logical schema.

Earlier in this chapter, you created a database model diagram without a source model. When using source models, the modeler does not directly create a database model diagram. Instead, VEA builds the database model diagram from the source model(s). The process of building the database model diagram is known as a project build.

The biggest functional difference between an ER source model and a database model diagram revolves around projects. An ER source model can (in fact must) be built as part of a project, while the database model diagram cannot be part of a project. If a project contains more than one source model, those models can use *external* objects.

An external object is a pointer to a natively defined object in another source model. For the external reference to be successfully resolved, both the model referencing the object and the model with the definition of the object must be included in the same project. Using external objects allows the modeler to separate the Universe of Discourse into smaller units that can be modeled individually, and then merged back into a single logical schema.

> *Caution:* In theory, ER source models can contain external objects (pointers to objects in other models), as well as exposing their natively defined objects to other source models. However, a bug in the VEA beta used to develop this book prevents ER source models from properly using external objects. You should check with Microsoft to see if this bug has been fixed in your release. The bug in the beta version does *not* prevent an ER source model from exposing its natively defined objects to ORM source models. The example that follows shows how to create a project that has two source models, one ER model and one ORM model. The ER source model will expose its natively defined objects, which will be used by an external object in the ORM source model.

Creating an ER Source Model

The same stencils, shapes and windows you used to create a database model diagram are used to create an ER source model. To avoid repetition, this section will only give detailed explanations for operations that are unique to source models. Operations that have already been covered will be referred to but not be explained in this section. For this example, you will need one ER source model and one ORM source model.

Create the first source model by choosing File > New > Database > ER Source Model from the main menu. Add *Patient* and *Country* entities to the new model. To save time, you do not have to add lots of attributes to each entity. However, make sure that each entity includes at least the primary key attribute. Also add the relationship between *Patient* and *Country*. Save the new model to a file called Patient_ER_Source.vsd, and then remove it from memory by closing the document.

Create the second model by choosing File > New > Database > ORM Source Model from the main menu. In this second model, you will create facts about the *PapSmear* object and relate it to the *Patient* object that is already defined in Patient_ER_Source.vsd. Add the facts and constraints shown in Table 10–7 to your ORM source Model. The first column in the table shows the fact as you should type it into the Fact Editor. The second column tells you how to answer Constraint Question #1 on the Constraints tab of the Fact Editor (don't answer Constraint Question #2, the default is fine). The third column shows the constraint verbalization. Compare the text in this column with the output of the VEA verbalizer to confirm that you have entered the proper constraints.

Use the following reference modes for the objects in your model: Patient(nr), PapSmear (nr), and Date (mdy). Assign the MS SQL server physical data type "datetime" to the Date object. Assigning the other data types is not important for this example. At this point, your ORM source model should look like the model in Figure 10–21.

Your ORM model makes use of a *Patient* object, but the entity *Patient* has already been defined in the model Patient_ER_Source.vsd. Both the ER and ORM source models are going to be included in the same project, so one of the models must have the

Table 10–7   Add these facts and constraints to the ORM Source Model.

Fact Type	Fact Editor Constraint	Constraint Verbalization
PapSmear was taken on Date	Exactly One	Each PapSmear was taken on Some Date Each PapSmear was taken on at most one Date
PapSmear is clear	\<None\>	\<None\> Unaries don't have explicit constraints.
PapSmear is from Patient	Exactly One	Each PapSmear is from Some Patient Each PapSmear is from at most one Patient

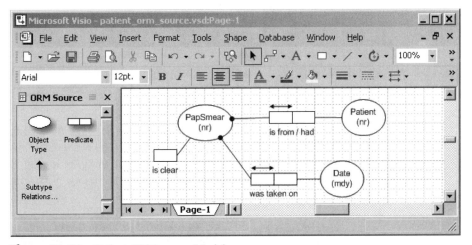

Figure 10–21   Patient ORM source Model.

natively defined *Patient* object, and the other model must use a pointer to the natively defined *Patient* object. This pointer is called an external object. In this example, you will make *Patient* an external object in the ORM source model. Click on the *Patient* entity to invoke the Database Properties window, as shown in Figure 10–22 and select the External checkbox.

Selecting the External checkbox tells VEA that the object is a pointer to the fully defined object in another model. As a visual cue, the oval that represents the object will be shaded with gray diagonal lines. It may be useful to think of the object as being "grayed out" because the actual definition of the object *Patient* resides in another model.

The reference mode is automatically removed from external objects. Since the object is defined in another model, there is no way for this ORM source model to be aware of

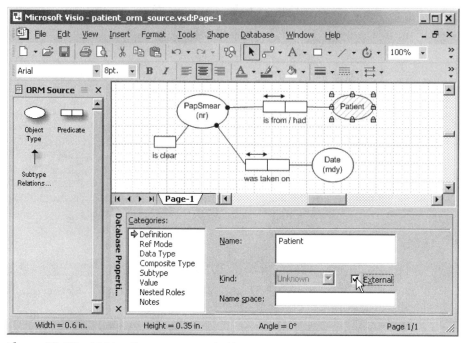

Figure 10–22 Making *Patient* an external object.

the reference mode before the project is built. Also note that the Kind list box immediately to the left of the External checkbox has been grayed out. The Kind list box normally stores information denoting whether the object is an entity or a value. However, since this object is defined externally, the Kind (entity or value) is unknown until the project is built.

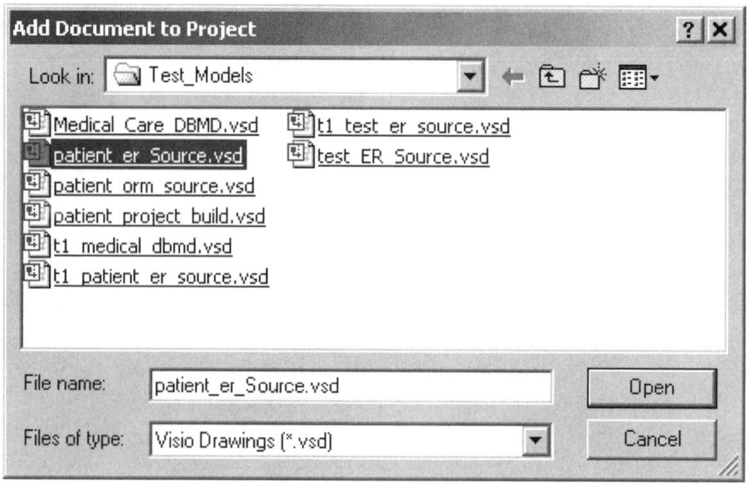

Figure 10–23 Adding a document to a project.

Hint: For an external reference to resolve successfully within a project, the conceptual name of the natively defined object in one source model and the conceptual name of the external object in the other source model(s) must be exactly the same. For a given object name, only one source model in a project can contain the natively defined object. If other source models have objects of the same name, those objects must be external.

Save your ORM source model to a file named Patient_ORM_source.vsd, and close the document to remove it from memory. You are now ready to create and build a database project. To build a project, do the following:

1. Create an empty database model diagram by choosing File > New > Database > Database Model from the main menu.
2. Save the new diagram to a file called Patient_Project_Build.vsd This file will contain your database project, and will be referred to as "the project" in the rest of this example.
3. Add the ER source model to the project:
   a. Choose Database > Project > Add Existing Document. A browse window like the one in Figure 10–23 will be shown.
   b. Highlight the ER source model, and click the Open button (or double simply double click on the file name).
   c. A new pane called "Project" will automatically open at the bottom of the model. This pane shows which models are included in the current project. Your screen should now look similar to Figure 10–24.
4. Add the patient ORM source model to the project. As an alternate to choosing using the Database > Project > Add Existing Document in step 3a, you can highlight the root node in the Project pane, right click to bring up the context menu and choose Add Existing Document.
5. Choose Database > Project > Build from the main menu. VEA will now merge the two source models into a single logical schema and create a database model diagram from the result of the project build. The database model diagram should

Caution: If you change any column names or table names in your project model, you will be prompted (see the dialog box in Figure 10–26) to migrate your changes back to the source model(s). If you click on the Yes button, VEA will "push" the column and table name changes into the source model(s) of your project, so that on the next build, the table and column name changes will be preserved. A bug in the VEA beta used to develop this book prevents VEA from migrating column name changes back to ORM source models for projects that have multiple source models. There is no problem migrating these names back to a single source model. You should check with Microsoft to see if this bug has been fixed in your release.

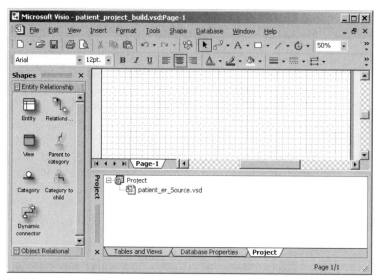

Figure 10–24   Patient ER source model successfully added to project.

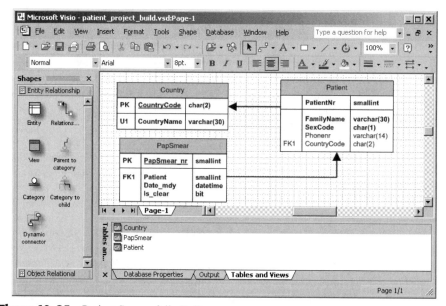

Figure 10–25   Project Successfully Built.

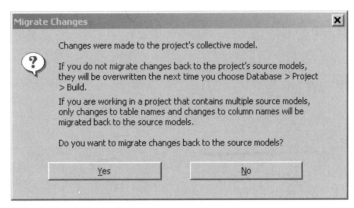

Figure 10–26   Project Migrate Prompt.

show the three entities *Patient, Country* and *PapSmear* in the Tables and Views pane. Dragging the entities onto the drawing surface will reveal the foreign key relationships as shown in Figure 10–25.

6. Save your project model.

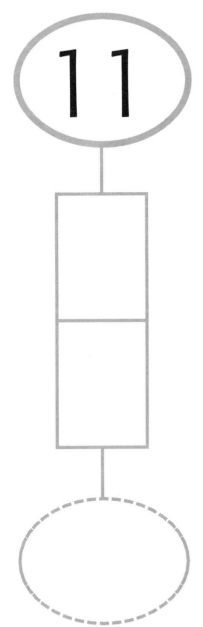

Generating a Physical Database Schema

11.1   Physical Schemas and Database Drivers

To create a physical database schema from your model, you can either create a DDL (data definition language) script, or connect directly to a database server via an ODBC driver. The fundamental issues with both methods are the same, although there are additional considerations when using an ODBC connection. This chapter will first explain how to create a DDL script using basic driver settings, and then describe driver setup options, and finally explain how to use ODBC connections.

DDL for different database platforms generally looks quite similar. All platforms provide syntax for creating tables and constraints, and some allow for stored and procedures and triggers. However, the differences in DDL syntax by platform are pronounced enough that DDL written for one database product will generally not run unmodified on another platform. Thus, VEA must be able to translate models into platform specific DDL.

VEA database drivers translate data models into platform specific DDL the same way that printer drivers translate between word processors and various printer control languages.

11.2   Creating a Basic DDL Script

Physical schemas, whether created via ODBC connections or DDL scripts, can only be generated from a database model diagram. It doesn't matter whether you create the diagram directly, or build a project from source models. For the following example you need a simple database model diagram that looks like Figure 11–1. To save space, the graphic shows only the database model diagram and not a full screen shot.

If you build the database model diagram directly or use an ER source diagram, refer to Table 11–1 for a list of the entities, attributes and keys that you should include in your model. In this table, the primary key of each entity is double underlined, unique attributes are single underlined, and mandatory non-key attributes are shown in

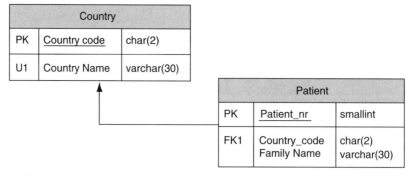

Figure 11–1   Database model diagram for testing physical schema generation.

boldface. Also, make sure to add a relationship from the *Patient* entity (child) to the *Country* entity (parent), and make the *Country_code* attribute optional in the *Patient* entity.

An ORM source model with the correct facts and constraints will automatically generate a database model diagram like the one in Figure 11–1. If you choose to create an ORM model, the first part of section 16.1 in this book lists the facts and constraints that you would need to include in the ORM source model. Regardless of how you created the database model diagram, save it to a file called Patient_ch11.vsd.

To generate a DDL script:

1. Set the Visio default driver to match your target database. To set the default driver:

    a. Choose Database > Options > Drivers from the main menu. Your screen should look like Figure 11–2.

Table 11–1   Entities and Attributes for test database model diagram.

Entity	Attributes
Country	Country code, **CountryName**
Patient	Patient Nr, **FamilyName,**
	Country_code (automatically migrated as a result of the foreign key from Patient (child) to Country (parent))

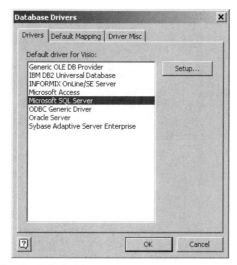

Figure 11–2   Selecting the default driver.

    b. Highlight Microsoft SQL Server if it is not already selected and click the OK button. The Setup button and the other tabs will be described later in the chapter.

> **Caution:** In the VEA beta used to for this book, the drivers for INFORMIX Online/SE Sever and Sybase Adaptive Server appear in the Database Drivers window, but are non functional. These drivers will neither generate nor reverse engineer a physical schema. Check with Microsoft to see if these drivers have been changed in the production release.

2. Invoke the Generate Wizard by choosing Database > Generate from the main menu. Your screen should now look like Figure 11–3.

    By default, your DDL script will be generated to a file with the following path and file name: <Path of Model File> <Model File Name>.DDL. If you wish to change the path or name of the DDL file, you can use the File name text box and the Browse button shown in Figure 11–3. If you were to select the Generate new database box, VEA would try to establish an ODBC connection with a database server. For this example, accept the default choices and click on the Next button.

3. The Installed Visio Drivers list box on page two of the generate wizard (Figure 11–4), allows you to choose the VEA database driver for generating your DDL.

    The list box will default to the driver you chose in step one. The Setup button will be explained later in the chapter. At the bottom of the page, supply a name for the database that you will generate. Do not select the Extract Server Information box. Click the Next button.

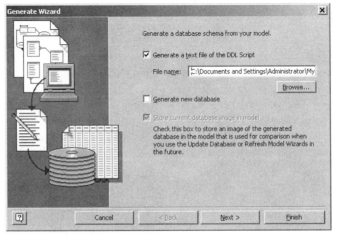

Figure 11–3   Generate Wizard page one.

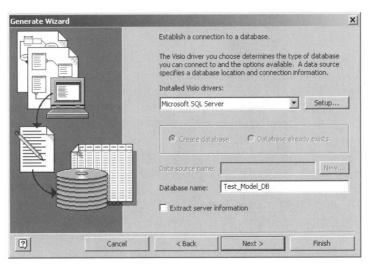

Figure 11–4   Generate Wizard, page two.

Note: Because you can choose a Visio database driver from page two of the Generate Wizard (Figure 11–4), you are not technically not required to set the correct default driver (step one of this example) prior to generating DDL. However, setting the default driver ahead of time makes it much easier to assign the proper physical data types to objects in your model. The default database driver setting is persistent, so you only have to set it once.

4. Page three of the wizard (Figure 11–5) shows a graphical representation of the tables that will be created when the schema is generated. If the table list isn't correct, you can cancel out of the wizard. Click the Next button.
5. The fourth and final page of the generate wizard (Figure 11–6) reports the results of VEA's physical validation of your model. During this validation, VEA checks to ensure that your model does not violate any platform specific rules. For instance, Oracle only allows 30 character object names, while MS SQL Server allows much longer names. The rules that VEA enforces are based on the diver you chose in step three.

Click the Finish button to start the actual DDL generation.

Hint: The physical validation page of the Generate Wizard is the most likely place for errors to occur during DDL generation. Platform specific rules, such as object name length, reserved words, and characters, etc, are not enforced during the modeling phase prior to DDL generation. It is thus possible for a model with no conceptual or logical errors to fail physical validation. Figure 11–7 shows a Generate Wizard page for a model that has failed physical validation.

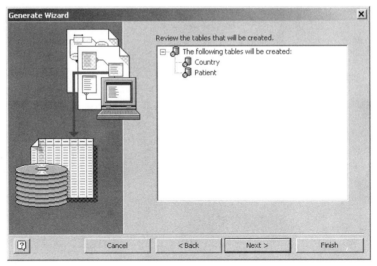

Figure 11–5   Generate Wizard page three.

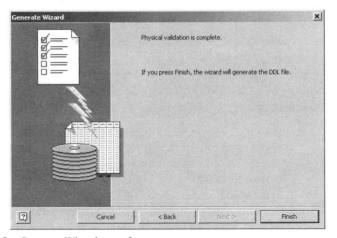

Figure 11–6   Generate Wizard page four.

The errors that occur during physical validation are *not* listed on the Generate Wizard page. Instead the errors are listed in the Output window (Figure 11–8). Warnings, which are recommendations but not fatal errors, *are* listed in a text box on the Generation Wizard page.

In most cases when physical validation fails there are no warnings, only errors. Thus, it is common to see the message "There are no warnings" in the text box when validation fails. The absence of warnings does not mean the absence of errors. When physical validation fails, always check the Output window.

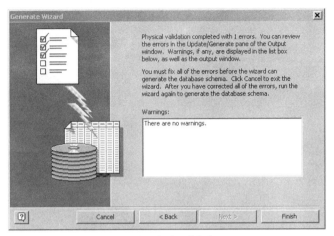

Figure 11–7 Generate Wizard, failed physical validation.

Figure 11–8 Output window with physical validation errors.

6. The next screen allows you to specify physical parameters that are specific to your chosen database server. This window is not part of the Generate Wizard, and is different depending on the database driver you chose in step three. If you are generating MS SQL Server DDL, as in this example, the screen will look like Figure 11–9.

   The analogous screen for Oracle (Figure 11–10) is more complex because of the additional physical parameters that apply to Oracle databases. You will not see the Oracle window if you are following along with this example. Figure 11–10 is included here for information only.

   If you fill out the screen, the result of your input will be generated into your DDL file using the proper syntax. If you leave the screen blank, your DDL will not contain these parameters. Leave the screen blank and click the Close button

7. You will be asked if you wish to view the generated DDL, as in Figure 11–11.

   Click the Yes button to invoke the VEA code editor and automatically load the DDL file, as shown in Figure 11–12.

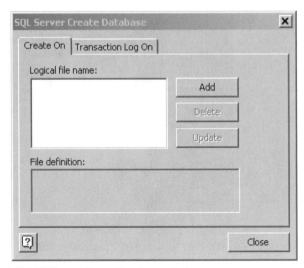

Figure 11–9   MS SQL Server Create Database window.

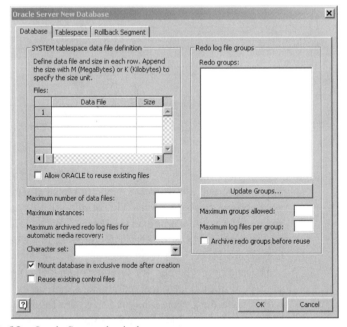

Figure 11–10   Oracle Server physical parameters.

11.3 Database Driver Options

The preceding example showed how to create a DDL script, but ignored database driver options. The options fall into two categories, driver specific options, and options that apply to all drivers.

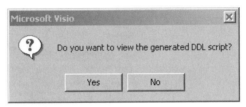

Figure 11–11   View DDL prompt.

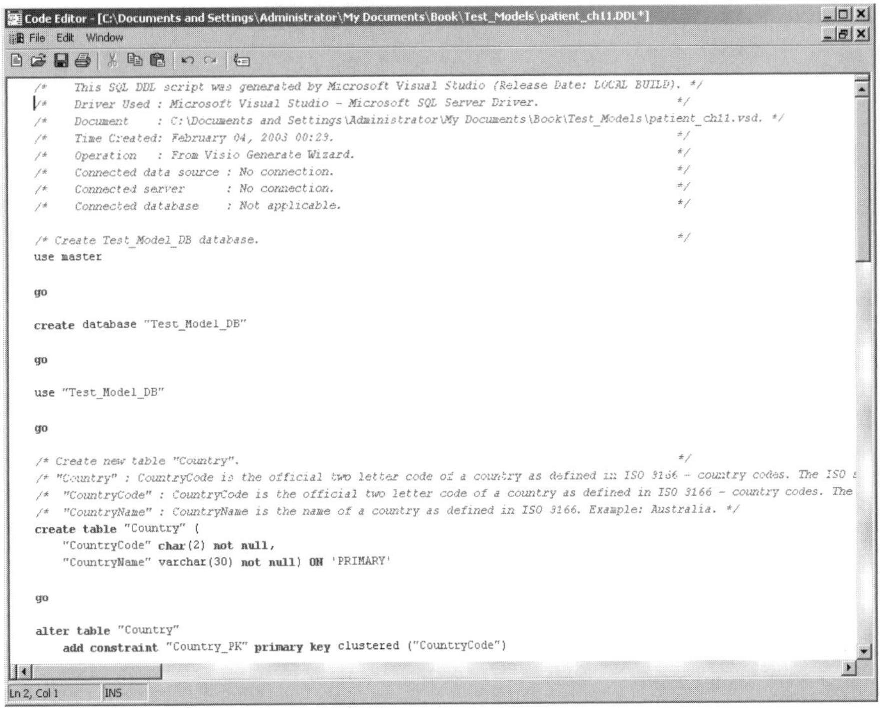

Figure 11–12   Generated DDL script.

Driver Specific Options

Discussion of the Setup button on the Database Drivers window was deferred in step one of the DDL script generation example (Figure 11–2). Re-Invoke the Database Drivers window by choosing Database > Options > Drivers from the main menu. Your screen should once again look like Figure 11–2. Click the Setup button to invoke the VEA driver setup dialog box. The first tab is labeled ODBC Drivers, and the second is labeled Preferred Settings. The ODBC Drivers pane is discussed in section 11.5. For now, click the Preferred Settings tab to make your screen look like Figure 11–13.

The choices available on the Preferred Settings pane are specific to the driver being configured, in this case MS SQL Server. The top portion of the pane is devoted to

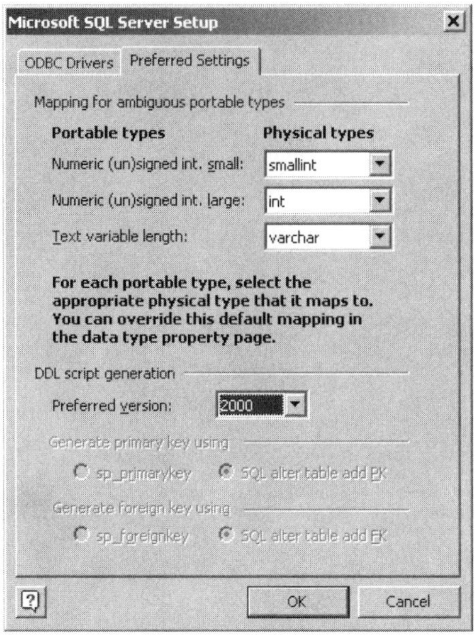

Figure 11–13 VEA driver setup, Preferred Settings pane.

resolving data type mapping ambiguity. Portable data types are mapped to a single physical data type for each supported database product. MS SQL Server has three physical data types that deal with integers: tinyint, smallint, and int. Each portable data type must map to just one physical type, which can be specified on this pane.

In the list box on the bottom of the Preferred Settings pane, choose the version of MS SQL Server for generating DDL or making an ODBC connection. In versions subsequent to 6.0, primary and foreign keys are generated with SQL statements, which is why the radio buttons at the bottom of the pane are disabled. In version 6.0, primary and foreign keys can optionally be defined by stored procedures instead of SQL statements.

If you have set MS SQL server as your default driver, you will not see the Oracle Server Setup dialog box (Figure 11–14), but it is shown here for informational purposes.

The radio buttons along the top of the pane specify which version of Oracle to use when generating DDL or making an ODBC connection. The text box in the middle of the pane is for specifying the default array size for the Oracle VARRAY collection type, an object relational data type.

The "Create uppercase . . ." checkbox forces all column names and table names to full upper case. Many Oracle developers prefer uppercase object names because of case sensitivity issues that arise otherwise.

The final checkbox causes VEA to create an Oracle sequence for any single column primary key that is an Auto Counter portable data type. In addition to the sequence object, VEA will write an INSERT trigger for the column to automatically populate the primary key with the next value in the sequence.

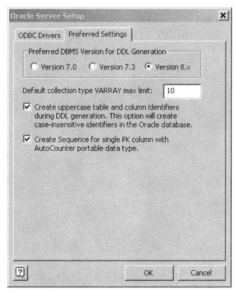

Figure 11–14   Oracle Setup, Preferred Settings pane.

Caution: Oracle does not use an "identity" property nor does it use a special physical data type to create an auto incrementing key. Instead, Oracle relies on a data type to create an auto incrementing key. Instead, Oracle relies on a separate database object called a "sequence" to provide auto incremented numbers. A table INSERT trigger calls the next value in the sequence and inserts it into the appropriate column. If you select the "Create sequence..." checkbox in Figure 11–14, VEA will not only create the sequence, but write the required trigger as well.

Use this feature carefully. The sequence that is created will always be called <Table Name>_SEQ, and the trigger will be called <Column Name>_TRIG. If your table name is 30 characters long (the Oracle maximum), the last four letters of the table name will be replaced with the characters "_SEQ." Thus, if your database has more than one table where the first 26 characters of the table name are the same and you declare the keys of both tables to be the portable data type Auto Counter, you will generate a name collision with the two sequence objects. A similar problem can arise with the trigger.

Once you have filled out the Preferred Settings for your driver, click the OK button to be returned to the Database Drivers window (see Figure 11–2).

Options that Apply to All Drivers

The options discussed in this section apply to all database drivers. Click on the Default Mapping tab to open the next configuration pane, as shown in Figure 11–15.

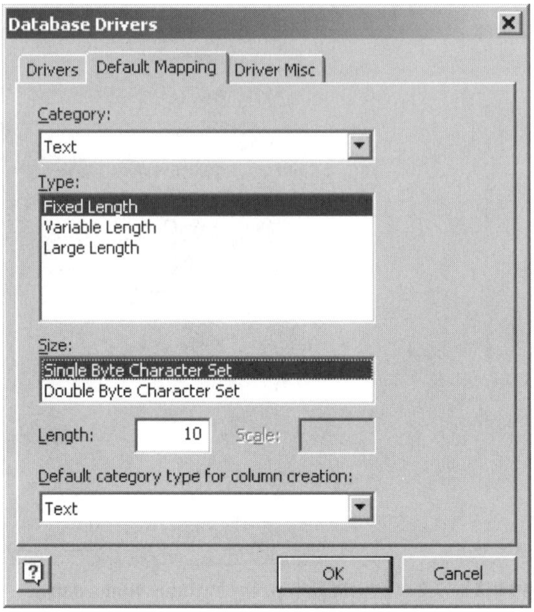

Figure 11–15   Setting Default Mapping for portable data types.

In this pane you can make minor customizations to your database driver.

> ***Hint:*** VEA will work perfectly for you even if you never touch the Default Mapping pane. Some modelers find this pane useful, but many are only vaguely aware of its existence. Most people find the out-of-the box settings for Default Mapping to be fine.

The Category list box in Figure 11–15 contains the major kinds of portable data types which are Text, Numeric, Raw Data, Temporal, Logical, and Other. The Type text box contains further subdivisions of the selected major category. As Figure 11–15 shows, the portable data type of the major category Text can be Fixed Length, Variable Length, or Large Length.

The Size text box allows you to specify the default character set for portable data types that belong to the Text category. For portable that data types that belong to the Numeric category, use the Size box to indicate magnitude (e.g., "small" or "large"). In the Length text box, you set the default data length that should be used for the chosen Category / Type combination.

In Figure 11–15, the default length for a Text, Fixed Length portable data type will be 10 characters. The Scale text box is disabled, because scale only applies to certain numeric portable data types. These adjustments only affect the default length of a portable data type.

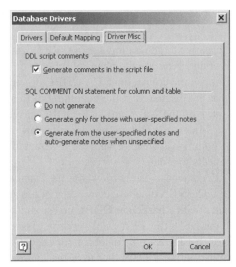

Figure 11–16   Setting Miscellaneous preferences.

The final list box in Figure 11–15 is labeled Default category type for column creation. This list box tells VEA what portable data type to assign to ORM objects and logical columns for which data types have not been specifically declared.

Click on the Driver Misc tab to invoke the next configuration pane, shown in Figure 11–16. This pane is confusing, because it appears that all the options it are applicable to all drivers, when in fact one of the options is driver specific.

The first checkbox on the Driver Misc pane controls whether VEA will put comments about each database object into the generated DDL script file. These comments can be derived from user entered notes only, or they can include notes that VEA automatically generates during database project builds. The comments inserted into the script will not execute, because they will be marked as comments /* like this */. If you want "bare bones" DDL, deselect this box.

Choose among the three radio buttons in the middle of the pane to control VEA's generation of SQL COMMENT ON statements, which actually store comments in the server data dictionary. Generating SQL statements to store comments in the database server dictionary *is not the same* as simply generating comments into the DDL script. Not all database engines support the COMMENT ON feature. In the generated script, VEA will truncate any comments that exceed the server's maximum comment length.

> *Note:* The SQL COMMENT ON feature is actually driver specific, and probably belongs in a different window. However, if you enable SQL COMMENT ON statements, and then generate DDL for a database that does not support this feature, no harm will be done. VEA will recognize that the target database does not support COMMENT ON statements and suppress their generation, regardless of the settings you have chosen.

11.4 Generating Schemas Via an ODBC Connection

As an alternative to generating a script, VEA can establish a connection with your database server and generate the physical schema directly. VEA makes use of ODBC drivers to establish the connection. The ODBC drivers are different from the VEA database drivers that are discussed in the beginning of this chapter. VEA database drivers are an integral part of the VEA product. ODBC drivers are supplied by various vendors (including Microsoft) and are not actually part of the VEA product, although some of the more common ODBC drivers are distributed with VEA. Figure 11–17 shows how VEA connects to a database server.

The VEA database driver translates the Database Model Diagram into platform specific DDL. The VEA database driver attaches to an ODBC DSN (data source name) that is associated with a particular ODBC driver and points to a particular database instance. Through the DSN, the VEA database driver issues DDL to the ODBC driver, which in turn passes that DDL to the database for execution.

You must define a DSN that uses the appropriate ODBC driver and points to the proper physical database instance. DSNs are defined through the ODBC Data Source Administrator, which is an administrative tool of the Windows operating system.

The VEA Generate Wizard gives you two choices when generating a physical schema to a physical database. You can have VEA create a new database, or you can have VEA connect to an existing database.

Creating A New Database Using the Generate Wizard

1. Invoke the Generate Wizard by choosing Database > Generate from the main menu. Select the Generate new database checkbox. A lightning bolt symbol will be added to the Generate Wizard (Figure 11–18) to confirm that you have chosen to generate your database via a direct connection to the server. By default, the other two checkboxes on the page are selected. The box labeled Generate a text file of the DDL script tells VEA to create a text file of the DDL in addition to generating the database directly. The box labeled Store current database image in model tells VEA to store a copy of the physical schema image once the generation is complete. Storage of this image is important for later updates and synchronizations. Click the Next button.

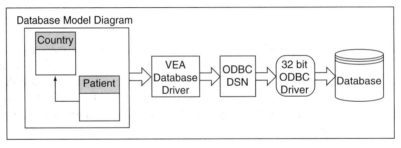

Figure 11–17   VEA connects to the database.

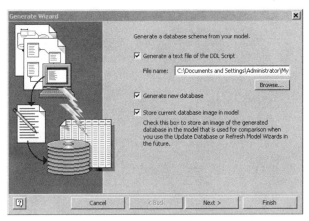

Figure 11–18 Database generation, page one.

2. On the next page of the Generate Wizard (Figure 11–19), make sure that the Installed Visio Driver is set to MS SQL Server Retain the default radio button choice Create database.
3. Click the New button next to the Data source name text box. This action invokes the Windows ODBC Data Source Administrator from within VEA. You will work through two wizards before returning to VEA. Use the first wizard to choose the type of DSN and the associated ODBC driver. Use the second wizard to actually create the DSN based on the specific features of the ODBC driver you have chosen.
4. On the first page of the Create New Data Source wizard (Figure 11–20), choose User Data Source (the middle radio button) and click Next.
5. The second page of the wizard (Figure 11–21) presents a list of all the ODBC drivers installed on your system. Scroll to the SQL Server ODBC driver, select it, and click the Next button.

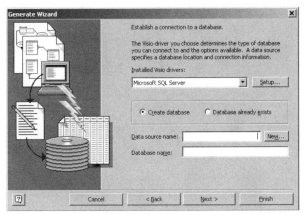

Figure 11–19 Database generation, page two.

Figure 11–20   Create New Data Source, page one.

6. The third page of the Create New Data Source Wizard (image not shown to save space) merely confirms your choice of ODBC driver. Clicking on the Finish button invokes the second wizard, where you actually create the DSN and supply options based on the ODBC driver you have chosen.

7. On the first page of the database specific ODBC Wizard (Figure 11–22), supply a name for your DSN and choose the server to which you wish to connect. The Description field is optional. Click the Next button.

8. The second page of the wizard (Figure 11–23) allows you to configure logon options for your database. Choose the appropriate authentication method for your environment, and click the Next button.

9. Accept the default choices on page three of the wizard (Figure 11–24), and click Next.

10. Accept the default choices for page four of the wizard (Figure 11–25) and click Finish.

> *Hint:* The "Connect to SQL Server..." checkbox is selected by default. If the checkbox is selected and the Server that you specified on the first page of the wizard (Figure 11–22) is unreachable, you will receive an ODBC connection failure message when you click on the Next button. If you wish to configure a DSN for a temporarily unavailable server, deselect the checkbox.

11. Test your DSN by clicking the Test Data Source button (Figure 11–26). When the test completes successfully, click OK.

12. After testing your DSN, you will be returned page two of VEA's Generate Wizard (Figure 11–27), which is exactly where you left the program when you invoked the ODBC Data Source Administrator in step three of this example. VEA will automatically fill the Data source name text box with the name of the DSN you just created. You must manually type in the name that you want to use for your new database in the Database name textbox. Click the Next button.

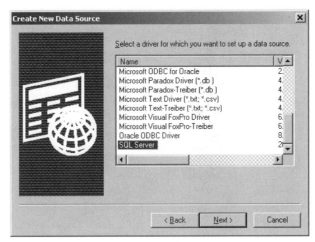

Figure 11–21   Create New Data Source, page two.

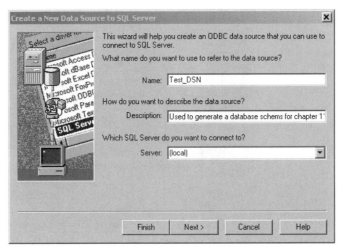

Figure 11–22   Driver specific ODBC Wizard, page one.

Note: If you already have an existing DSN that points to the correct instance of SQL Server, you do not have to perform steps 4–12 of this example. Instead, type the DSN name into the Data Source Name box (Figure 11–27), and type the desired name of your new database into the Database name. Once you generate the schema, the database that you typed into the text box will become the default database for the DSN that you used.

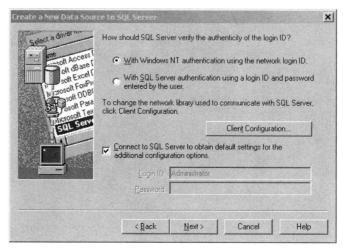

Figure 11–23   Driver Specific ODBC Wizard, page two.

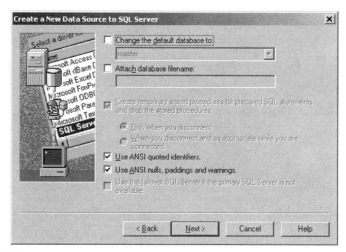

Figure 11–24   Driver Specific ODBC Wizard, page three.

13. You will be prompted to provide logon information (Figure 11–28), even if you chose Windows authentication in the setup of your DSN (Figure 11–23). If your are using Windows authentication, leave the fields empty and click on OK. If you set up your DSN with SQL server authentication, you must provide a user name and password.

The next steps are almost exactly like the final steps in generating a DDL script, and will refer to those screen images. The difference is that model objects (tables, keys, etc) will be generated directly into the database server.

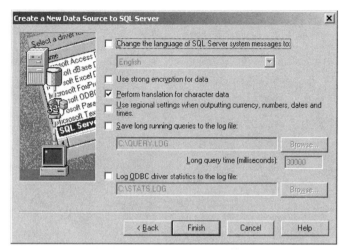

Figure 11–25 Driver Specific ODBC Wizard, page four.

Figure 11–26 DSN test screen.

14. After connecting to the database server, you will be shown a graphical list of the tables that are to be created. This screen should be the same as Figure 11–5. Click Next to physically validate your model.

15. Upon successful validation of your model (see Figure 11–6), click the Finish button.

16. The next screen will be the MS SQL Server Create Database window (Figure 11–9). Click Close to continue.

17. VEA will generate your database schema directly into the server. The Output window (Figure 11–29) shows the results of this generation.

18. If you close to generate a DDL script, you will be prompted to view the scirpt (see Figure 11–11).

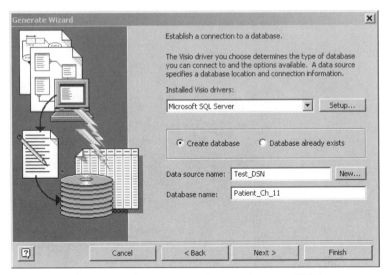

Figure 11–27   Database generation, page two after creating a new DSN.

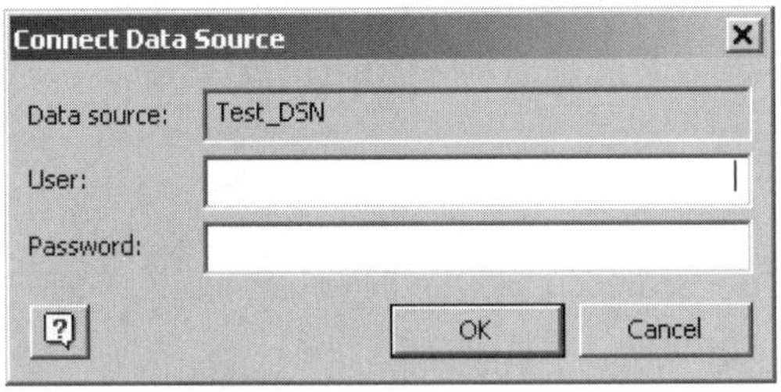

Figure 11–28   Connection prompt.

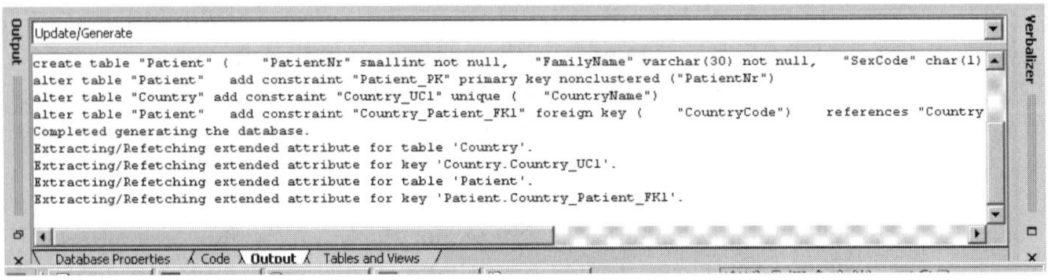

Figure 11–29   Output Pane after database generation.

Hint: It is always wise to generate a DDL script when using and ODBC connection to generate a schema directly to a database server. Select the checkbox on the first page of the generate wizard (see Figure 11–18).

If the database generation fails, you will see a server error message in the Output window. After the first error, no other commands will be executed on the server. Right click in the Output window and select Copy All Messages from the context menu. Paste the messages into a text editor. Compare the error messages to the generated DDL script to determine the cause of the database generation failure. If you don't have the DDL script, determining and correcting the cause of the failure can be very difficult.

Connecting to an Existing Database Using the Generate Wizard

Instead of creating a new database from within VEA, can generate your schema into an existing database. To generate into an existing databse:

1. Create a DSN for an existing database using the Windows administrative tools.

Note: The database you use does not have to be empty, but make sure that none of the existing database objects (i.e., tables, constraints, views, triggers, etc) share a name with the objects in the model you intend to generate. For instance, if you are going to generate the Patient_Ch_11.vsd model into an existing database, that database must not contain a table named *Patient*.

2. Invoke the Generate Wizard and make the same choices on the first page as you did in the previous examples (see Figure 11–18). Click the Next button.
3. On page two of the Generate Wizard (Figure 11–30), choose the radio button labeled Database already exists. The Data source name field, Setup button, and Database name field will all be disabled. Click the Next button.
4. In the text box labeled Data Sources (Figure 11–31), the generate wizard shows a list of DSNs that are defined on your machine.
   Highlight the correct DSN and click the Next button.
5. From this point forward, the generation process is the same as steps 13 through 18 of the previous example.

11.5 The ODBC Driver Setup Pane

As shown in Figure 11–17, models ard translated by VEA database drivers, which connect to databases via a DSN. Each DSN is associated with an ODBC driver. For database generation to function properly, the ODBC driver of a DSN must be designed for the same target database engine as the selected VEA driver.

Ideally, the list of available DSNs in Figure 11–31 should be limited based upon the ODBC driver associated with each DSN. For instance, if you are using the VEA MS SQL Server database driver, then the list in Figure 11–31 should only include DSNs that use

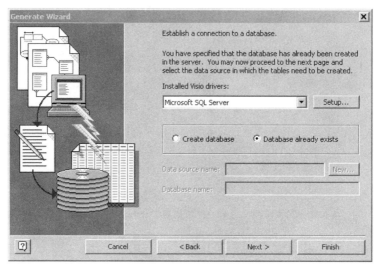

Figure 11–30   Generating to an Existing Database, page two.

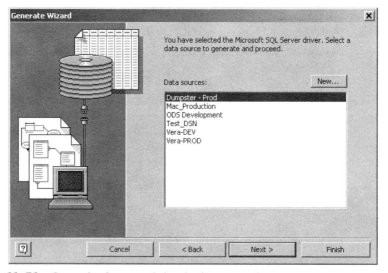

Figure 11–31   Generating into an existing database, page three.

the SQL server ODBC driver. Similarly, if they are using the VEA Oracle Server driver, the list of DSNs should only include those DSNs that use the Oracle ODBC drive.

By default *all* DSNs are included in the list of available data sources, regardless of the associated ODBC driver. To change this default behavior:

1. Choose Database > Options > Drivers from the main menu. Your screen should look like Figure 11–2. Highlight the Microsoft SQL Server driver and click the Setup button.

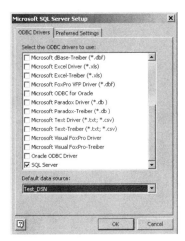

Figure 11–32   VEA Driver setup ODBC Drivers pane.

2. Select the ODBC Drivers tab (Figure 11–32) from the new window. Depending on the number of ODBC drivers installed on your computer, your list may be longer or shorter than the one shown in the figure. Scroll to the bottom of the list and select the SQL Server entry.

3. Click OK to return to the Database Drivers window (see Figure 11–2), and then click OK again to return to the main window.

The VEA MS SQL Server driver is now associated with the SQL Server ODBC driver. From now on, the list of available DSNs will be limited to only those DSNs using the SQL Server ODBC driver. You can repeat this procedure for each VEA driver that you use, though it is not necessary for the proper functioning of the tool.

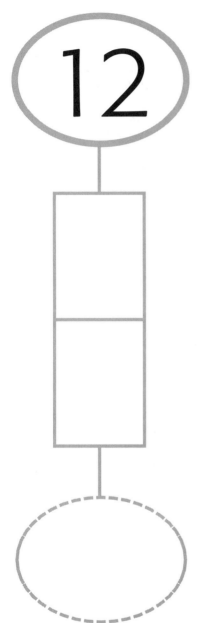

Editing Logical Models: Intermediate Aspects

12.1   The Database Properties Dialog

The ORM Source Model, ER Source Model, and Database Model Diagram solutions all allow you to work with data models. Within any of these solutions, you can use the *Database Properties Dialog* to set the properties of the model element that is currently selected in the drawing window.

The Database Model Diagram solution allows you to work on a logical database model, and its project feature allows you to optionally include ORM models or ER Source Models as additional source documents. This chapter focuses on logical database models displayed in the Database Model Diagram solution, and ignores source models. If you are including an ORM model or an ER source as source documents, then be aware that migrating changes in the database model back to the ORM or ER models is required. Failure to manage this properly will result in the loss of these changes when the database model is next built. Synchronization of models is discussed in Chapter 16.

When working in the Database Model Diagram solution, the database properties window may be closed, open, or hidden. If you do not see the database properties window, then double click some object in the drawing window to open its properties window. The list of categories displayed varies according to the kind of model element selected. There is one category list for tables and another category list for relationships.

Figure 12–1 shows the Categories Database Properties when nothing is selected in the diagram. The Information Category does not respond to any action.

12.2   Table Properties

The categories list in Figure 12–2 is displayed when a table is selected.

The Definition category assigns the table name and an optional name space. There is a physical and a conceptual name. The conceptual name is the name meant for human communication, while the physical name is the name in the physical database.

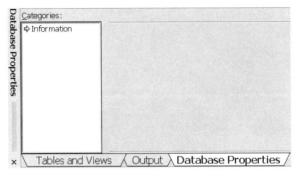

Figure 12–1   Initial Database Properties Window.

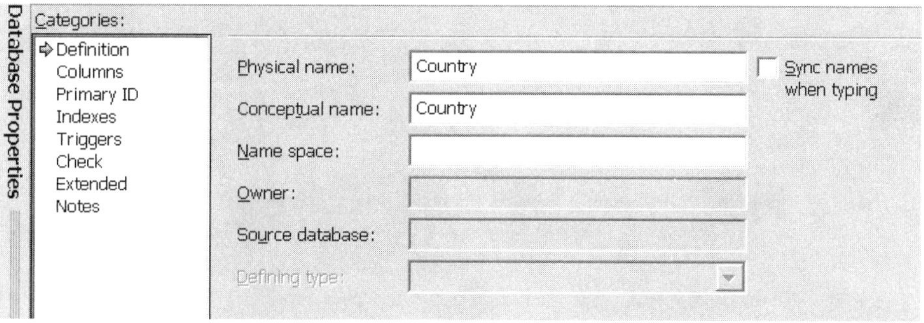

Figure 12–2   Table definition.

Note: The "sync names when typing" assures the two names are always the same. Do not use this option if you want to record both the conceptual and the physical name. For example, the conceptual name "Instant Blood Pressure" is different from the physical name "InstantBP". The logical and physical names are subject to the naming options defined when ORM is a source document.

Caution: When using an ORM source model, be careful about renaming any object in the logical model.

If you change a name in the logical model, that new name overrides the ORM to logical name mapping. This sounds like a reasonable action. However, if you change the ORM object name to something completely different, the logical model will still override the new ORM name. It may now be the case that the logical name makes no sense as a proper override name. You are forced to change the logical model name on your own yet again. As far as possible, it is best to do all naming only on the ORM side when including an ORM model as the source document.

Name space is used to assign uniqueness to the definition. This permits the same fact to exist more than once in the model where the name space indicates the specific context.

12.3   Column Properties

There are five column properties: Physical Name, Data Type, Required, Primary Key, and Notes. Refer to the grid in Figure 12–3.

The data types are shown as physical data types in this example, with the target DBMS set to Microsoft SQL Server. By changing the "Show" option, you can display the portable data types. Using portable data types postpones your view of the data types for a specific DBMS. The DBMS specific data types are always used when generating the Data Definition Language (DDL) script. Portable data types are also useful when the model may be mapped to more than one target DBMS.

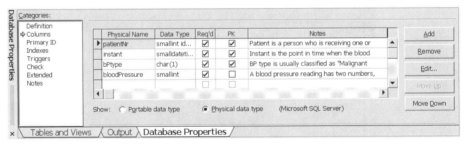

Figure 12–3   Selected table column properties.

The Required option is checked if the column is mandatory (not null). Primary key fields are always required. The Primary Key option is checked if the column is, or is part of, the primary identification scheme for the table.

Enter appropriate notes for the reviews, and for future reference. It is best to do this initially, so you don't forget what the column names really meant. If the model was created from an ORM source model, note is automatically entered based on the fact type source for the table/column mapping.

Rename and Edit Column Properties

There are two methods to edit a column. The first is to directly change the properties shown on the property grid (Figure 12–3). This is fast but has limited editing capability, as not all options are shown in the grid. The second is to *select the column of interest and then select Edit* (Figure 12–4). Options such as check clauses, collections, and extended properties are now available. This provides a more robust version of column editing. The Allow NULL values option means the opposite of the Required (no nulls allowed) option in the grid version. The collection option is described in Chapter 13.

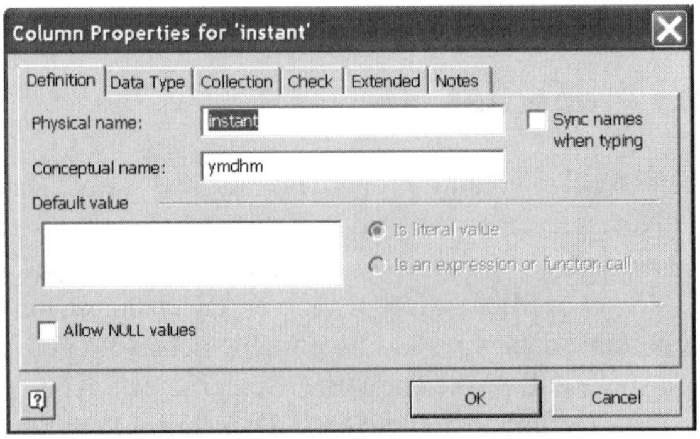

Figure 12–4   Alternate windows for managing column properties.

The Sync names option is available as described in the introduction to this chapter. In this example, the physical name and the conceptual name are not the same, and the "Sync name when typing" is not checked.

A default value may be either a specific value, or a call to a database function. Select the appropriate radio button. The default value text is included in the DDL script. If this is a function name, the function must exist prior to creating the table in the DDL script.

> *Note:* Be sure to review the DDL script and possibly reorganizing the DDL script to position the function prior to the table definition.

The Data Type table shown in Figure 12–5 is shown as a physical data type. It can also be shown as a portable type by selecting the other radio button. To change the data type from the column default type select Edit > Native Type. If the native data type requires Precision and Scale, the fields will be active.

The collection type settings are examined in Chapter 13. This feature is used when defining object-relational database structures. The target DBMS must support this option, otherwise the results are merely relational tables. The current versions of Oracle and IBM DB2 Universal Server support these constructs.

The default is a single valued column, which is expected in a normalized relational database.

The Check tab allows you to constrain the column values to specific values or ranges or values. To *add a value,* enter the value in the Value field and select Add (Figure 12–7). To *add a range of values,* enter both the From and To range values and select Add. Just as you can add many values, you can add several ranges. The ranges do not need to be adjacent. For example: ranges of 1..10 and 20..50 may be included in

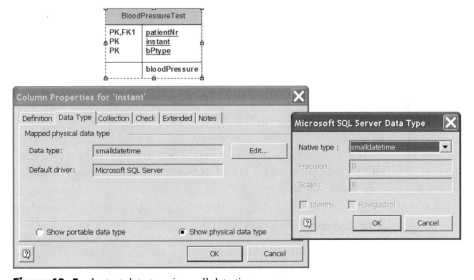

Figure 12–5   Instant data type is small date time.

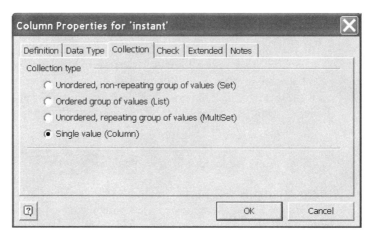

Figure 12–6   Collection tab (rarely used).

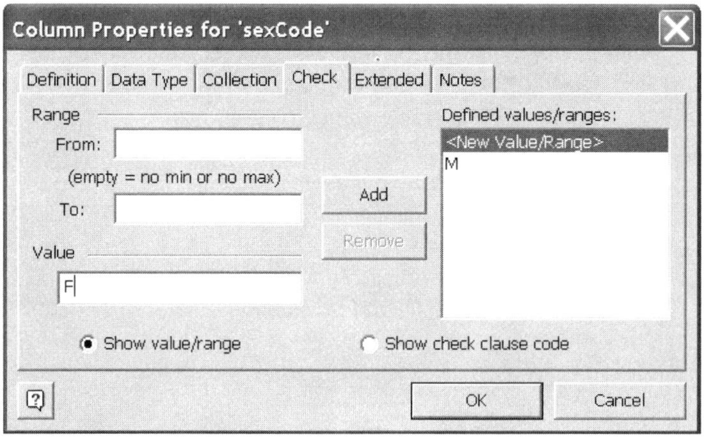

Figure 12–7   Adding a check constraint to specify allowed values.

the same constraint. To *remove a defined value or range,* select it and then press Remove.

You can also view, or edit the value constraint by selecting the Show check clause code radio button, pressing the Customize button in the next dialog to work directly with the SQL check clause.

Add Column

There are two ways to add a new column: *create the column in the first open row in the grid or click the Add button* (Figure 12–3). If you are not using check clauses or collection options, the fastest method is to enter the new column directly in the grid.

Remove Column

There are two ways to remove column, *select the column and press the delete key or click on the remove button* (Figure 12–3)

Move Up and Move Down

Reorder the columns *by selecting a column and then click Move Up or Move Down* until the column is in the desired position. (Figure 12–3)

12.4   Foreign Key Relationships

Create foreign key relationships between tables using the logical model stencil "Relationship" shape. In Figure 12–8(a) the tables, State and Region, have no defined relationship. Note that the State table has only the state code defined. In Figure 12–8(b), the relationship shape was used to drag and drop a relationship connection to the diagram. Then in Figure 12–8(c), the relationship has been established. This was done by dragging each end of the relationship line onto the appropriate table.

> *Caution:* The table border will turn red when it detects the relationship. It is a common mistake to drag the end into the table while thinking that merely being inside the table is adequate. If the border does not change to the color red, the connection is not made.

After the connection is made, the key from the parent table is automatically inserted into the child table in the relationship. See the end of this chapter for alternatives to this default behavior. If you had already entered the region code into the State table, you would now have a duplicate region code column. In the relational notation below, the child points to the parent. For other notations, refer to the glossary.

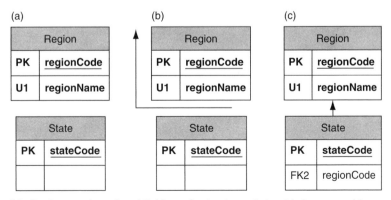

Figure 12–8   Progression of establishing a foreign key relationship between tables.

Figure 12–9   Viewing the relationship—table column connection.

Once the connection is established, clicking on the relationship line displays the list of categories for relationships. First is the definition category, which is shown in Figure 12–9.

If you select the associated columns in the parent table and in the child table, the Associate button changes to Disconnect Clicking on Disconnect removes the relationship. You are prompted to either remove the relationship line from the drawing or from the model (Figure 12–10). Answer Yes to remove it from the model. Answer No to remove it from the diagram, but retain it in the underlying model.

Selecting the Name category allows you to create meaningful forward and inverse readings for the relationship. If an ORM source document is used, the readings are taken from the predicate readings of the associated fact type. The physical name is either generated from the ORM source document or is entered at this time.

The Miscellaneous category is used to define the cardinality, relationship type and a range definition (Figure 12–12). Again, if using an ORM source model these will be set as part of the logical model mapping. Cardinality indicates how the parent and child participate in the relationship. There can be zero or more children, one or more children, zero or only one child, one child and the child must be present.

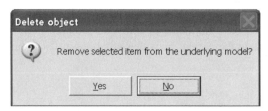

Figure 12–10   Prompt dialog for deleting a model element.

Figure 12–11   Relationship reading.

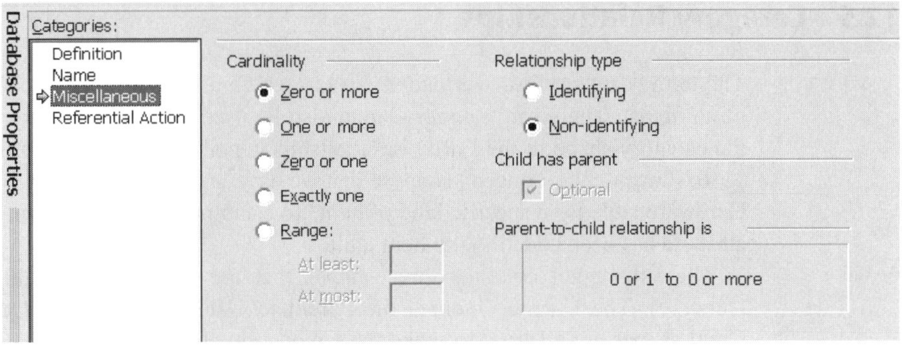

Figure 12–12 Cardinality and Relationship type.

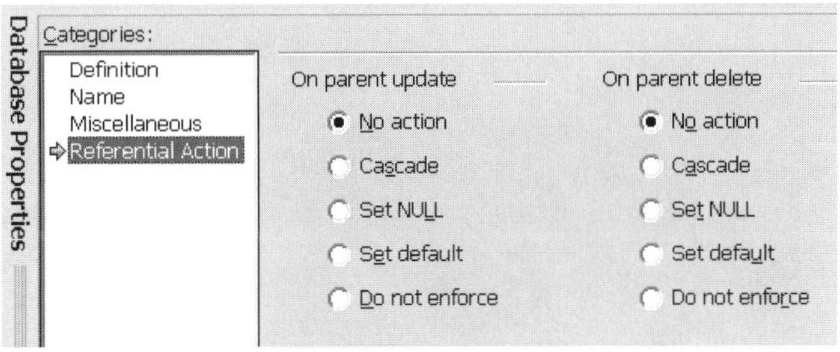

Figure 12–13 Referential Action options.

Range is a special case that allows the setting of a specific number of children. For example, there must be at least 2 children and no more than 5 children. The relationship type "Identifying" means the column in the child is part of the child's key, whereas "Non-identifying" is merely a column—not part of the child key The text "Parent-to-child relationship" is a generated explanation of the relationship.

The *Referential Action* category (Figure 12–13) defines what action is to be taken if an attempt is made to violate the referential integrity constraint that requires the child values to also exist in the parent. This choice has a large impact on the supporting code, either in the database or the application. The default is "No Action," meaning if the constraint is violated by an attempted update, the update is simply rejected. The Cascade setting means a compensating action will be taken on the child. For example, if you delete the parent, the children are also deleted. Set NULL means the associated column in the child is set to NULL if the parent is deleted. The Set default option is allowed only if the column has been defined with a default. "Do not enforce" means that referential integrity will not be enforced.

Note: These options can impact the integrity of the data. Be careful, and understand what may have to happen in the application or other database functions. It may be the case that you instead need trigger code to handle complex situations.

12.5 Category Relationships

The term "category" is overloaded. So far, we've used it to refer to class of properties of an object. The term "category" may also be used to denote a subtype. This is what the category shape in the Entity Relationship stencil is used for (Figure 12–14).

To illustrate this concept, suppose that we have an Item table, and wish to introduce a Hardware table for a specific kind of item. To establish the kind of item, a categoryCode attribute has been added to the Item table.

The ER stencil contains three shapes that are required to establish a Category (subtype). The Category shape, the Parent to Category shape, and the Category to Child shapes are all used to make the connection. To complete the example shown in Figure 12–15, the Category shape is placed between the Item and Hardware tables. The

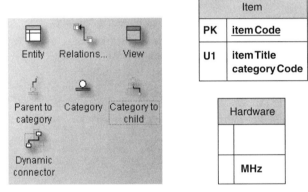

Figure 12–14 Logical model template and super/subtype tables.

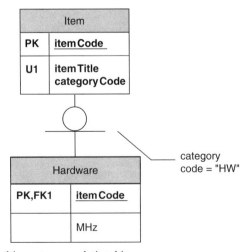

Figure 12–15 Resulting category relationship.

Figure 12–16 Selecting discriminator for the categorization.

Parent to Child shape connects the Item to the Category. Then the Category to Child shape is used to connect the Category to the child table. When making the connections, ensure that the table borders flash red to indicate the connection.

The Item table (super-type) includes the discriminator column categoryCode. In this example, we've annotated the category with the specific discriminator value 'HW' that determines membership in the Hardware table. (Figure 12–15). This annotation was made using Visio's callout stencil. It is handy during a review to add such comments on the drawing. The annotations can also be assigned to layers to enable their display to be turned on or off.

Click the category relationship to bring up its properties dialog. You can now record the categoryCode attribute as the discriminator (Figure 12–16). The "Category is Complete" check box is checked by default. In our case, not all Items are Hardware, so the check has been removed.

> ***Hint:*** It is possible that a Category has no discriminator, but this is not the recommended practice.

12.6 Show Related Tables

A large logical model may be spread over many drawing pages. Hence on any given page, some tables may be hidden from view. Suppose that for some given table, you want to see all the other tables to which it is connected by foreign key relationships. Here is an easy way to do this.

1. Insert a new drawing page by choosing Insert > New Page from the main menu.
2. Drag a copy of the relevant table from the Tables and Views window onto the new drawing page.
3. Right-click the table to display its context menu, and select Show Related Tables option.

This adds the related tables and the foreign key relationships to the drawing. This feature is very handy when doing a review, and questions arise about what is related to the table currently under discussion.

12.7   Views

There is more than one way to create a view. If you are an SQL programmer you can open the code window and enter the SQL statement. This provides code for the DDL script. This does not create a view symbol on the diagram. The other option is dragging a view shape from the ER stencil onto the drawing. You can then create the view and the SQL statement using the view definition window.

The first option is easier if you code SQL and care to do so directly. The code window is opened by selecting from the main menu bar Database > View > Code. Select Global Code (Figure 12–17) to open an instance of the code window. When using the code window, there is no resulting symbol on the logical model diagram. The code is authored and kept for the DDL generation.

Note: The drawback to this option is that your coding is not immediately checked. It will be checked when you do a model error check (Database > Model > Error Check) or when you attempt to generate the DDL script.

Figure 12–17   Select global code for authoring a view.

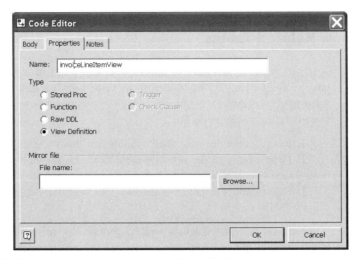

Figure 12–18   Indicating that the code is a view definition.

Although the Body is the first tab, it is more useful to first provide the properties. Here you name the code set and indicate the type of code, in this case the View Definition (Figure 12–18)

> *Note:* Code maybe global or local. Local code is local to a table and may be a check clause or trigger code. SQL procedures and views are part of the global code collection.

The properties tab is where the type of code is indicated, in this case a view definition. The name is therefore the name of your view. This name should be created following your naming conventions.

If a mirror file is selected, then the code is loaded from the file. You can also save the code to a mirror file by providing a name when a new code set is created.

> *Hint:* Even if your source model was an ORM model, which has naming rules, these rules do not apply to view names.

Next, select the Body tab and enter your code. It is normal to also include comments and other information pertaining to the view. Most IT shops have a template for this purpose.

In this code block, you are entering the SQL statement that defines the View. This code is checked for errors when you attempt to create the generate DDL script or when performing an error check. Shown below is the script for the view defined in Figure 12–19.

```
/*Create procedure/function invoiceView.*/
Select
    invoice.invoicenr,
    invoice.issuedate,
```

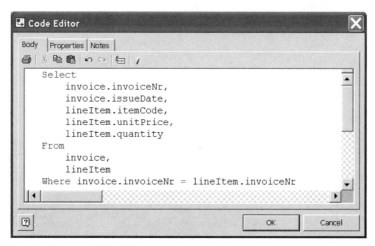

Figure 12–19   Enter the SQL Select for the view.

```
itemline.itemcode,
itemline.unitprice,
itemline.quantity
from invoice,
    itemline
where invoice.invoicenr = itemline.invoicenr
```

> ***Caution:*** The SQL code must be suitable for the target DBMS. If you change the target DBMS and you used DBMS specific SQL code options, they may fail to compile.

The second method for creating views is to use the view shape from the stencil. This creates a gray shaded table on the drawing. Select the Definition field to change the default view name from "Table 1" (Figure 12–20).

If more than one table is involved in the view, select Join Criteria, then select the first table in the join and the appropriate column; then select the second table and appropriate column. Figure 12–21 shows the join between Invoice and Line Item using the Invoice Number from both tables. Select Add to complete the join.

You must enter the physical name. Also indicate if the column may be null. The datatype is correctly assigned from the source column.

Select columns from the Category list. To select the columns from the associated tables, there is a three step sequence for each column. First select Add, which automatically inserts a default column into the column grid as shown in Figure 12–22. This activates the Edit button. Select Edit.

Change the selection from "Unknown column in another table or view" to "Known column in another table or view" Then select Change, since you are changing from the default name to a real column name (Figure 12–23).

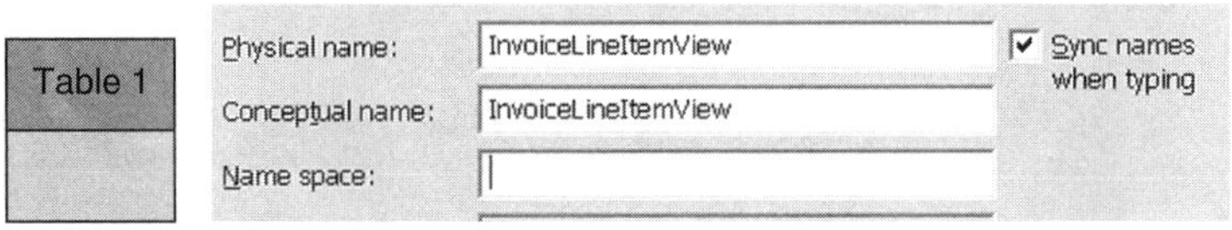

Figure 12–20   Using the View icon from the logical model stencil.

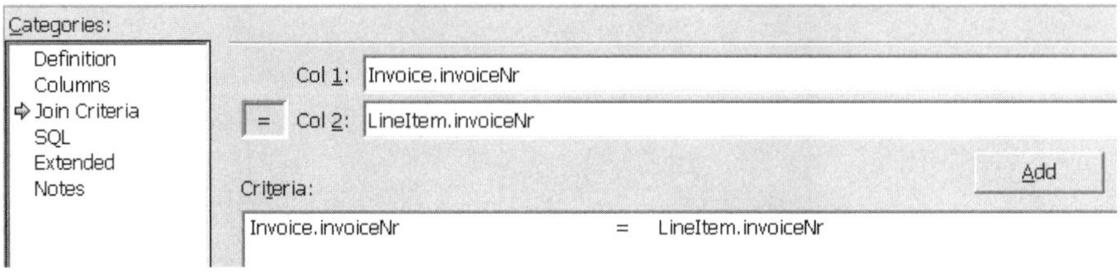

Figure 12–21   Adding columns to the view.

Figure 12–22   Using the grid to populate the view.

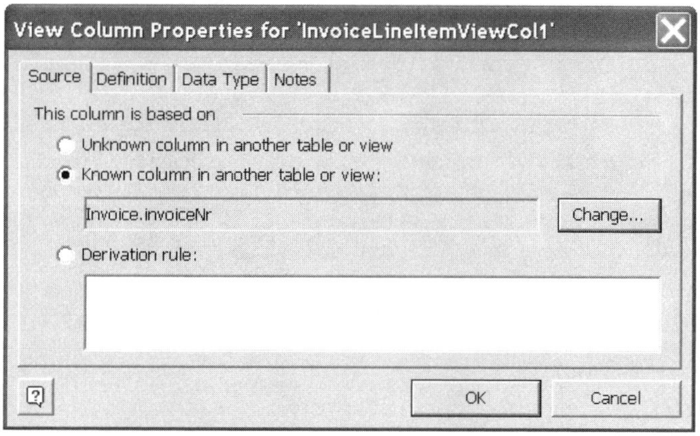

Figure 12–23   Selecting a known column name.

Select the column from the list presented after selecting Change. Your column then appears in the Change Row.

If you select Derivation rule, you must enter valid SQL code to perform the derivation, for example, "quantity * unitPrice AS Line Total."

> *Note:* Even though you have selected a known column name from the table, the name has not changed from the default. You must select the Definition Tab and manually change the view column name.

Continue to repeat the sequence of "Add," "Edit," "Change," and "Definition" for each required column until you have completed your view columns. Figure 12–25 shows a view based on the LineItem base table, to which a derived LineTotal column has been added.

> *Hint:* This cycle is neither fast nor friendly. If you know SQL, use that option.

Selecting the SQL category of the properties dialog displays the generated code. Do not alter this code, as changing anything in the columns or join criteria will recreate the code eliminating your additions. The code shown below is for SQL Server 2000, since that was the active driver option.

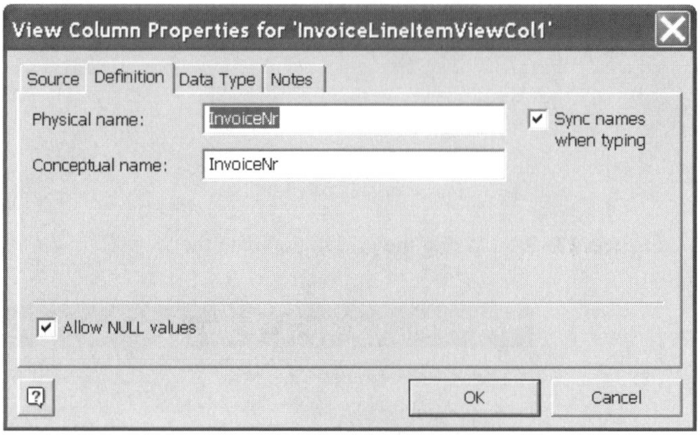

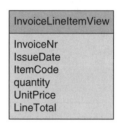

Figure 12–24 Changing the column name manually from the default name.

Figure 12–25 View after selecting and editing desired columns.

```
create view "InvoiceLineItemView"
("InvoiceNr", "IssueDate", "ItemCode", "quantity", "UnitPrice", "LineTotal") as select
c1."invoiceNr",
c1."issueDate",
c2."itemCode",
c2."quantity",
c2."unitPrice",
c2."lineTotal"
    from "Invoice" c1, "LineItem" c2
    where c1."invoiceNr" = c2."invoiceNr" with check option;
```

This is a bit awkward to repeat for each column. Hence, if you know SQL the first option is a lot faster. However, the first option has the disadvantage of not displaying the view on the drawing page.

12.8   Pagination

The logical model may be very large, making it difficult to review. Visio provides many sizes for a page, but all pages in the model are the same size. You may want to place some selected tables on each page. You may create any number of pages for the drawing. Each page focuses on a smaller subject area. Give each page a distinct page name for easier navigation. A table may be placed on more than one page without causing definition duplication in the DDL script. All of this helps to reduce relationship line confusion and review sized pages. Controlling relationship lines is discussed in Chapter 13.

> *Caution:* Be very careful when attempting to move relationship lines. They have a tendency to disconnect. If that happens, immediately use the undo feature. Another way to redirect lines and the layout is to choose Shape > Layout Shapes. There are several layout options native to Visio. You should investigate them for various alignments.

Creating several pages also provides extra space for adding other information on the page with less clutter. To insert a page, choose Insert > Page from the main menu. Name the page based on its content. Naming pages is especially useful if you create hyperlinks from an external document into the Visio model. You can reference the file and the drawing page within this link.

12.9 Verbalization

The major objects in a logical model can be verbalized by selecting Database >View > Verbalizer from the main menu bar. The verbalizer describes the selected object in natural language. Three examples are shown in Figure 12–26, Figure 12–27, and Figure 12–28.

12.10 Model Error Check

A logical model can be checked at any time for consistency or omission errors. It is best to check the model frequently. It is easier to fix errors when there are fewer to resolve. Double clicking on the error message places you at the point of the error. It is best to resolve not only errors, but also all warnings.

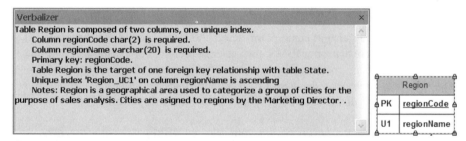

Figure 12–26 Table verbalization.

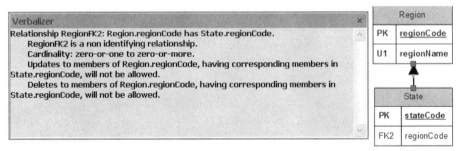

Figure 12–27   Relationship verbalization.

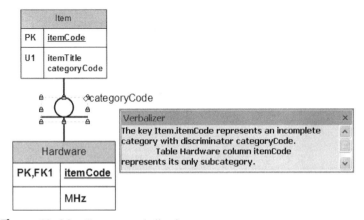

Figure 12–28   Category verbalization.

Coding done within the model is also checked. A double click on the error will position the cursor diagram where the error is occurring. This is performed automatically when doing a Generate.

Hint: Do an error check with each unit of code.

12.11   Driver, Document, and Modeling Options

Driver Options

You must, at some point, select the target DBMS for the model. If you are targeting more than one DBMS, then select a preferred driver initially and select the actual driver when generating the database. This is a case where using portable data types is useful. To select a database driver, choose Database > Options > Drivers from the main menu. The dialog shown in Figure 12–29 is now displayed.

Note: You may change your selected DBMS at the time you generate the DDL script. This may impact your custom SQL code, as it might not compile in every DBMS.

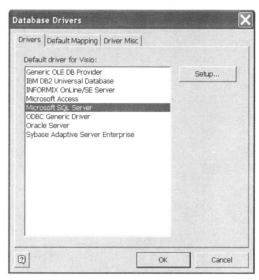

Figure 12–29   Select your preferred driver.

Clicking the Set Up button displays the available ODBC drivers (Figure 12–30). Select the appropriate driver for your DBMS. Once connected, you can review the databases associated with that driver. Select the default database for your model and proceed to the Preferred Settings.

You can establish several defaults by selecting the Preferred Settings tab. (Figure 12–31) The upper section allows you to map ambiguous portable data types to physical data types. In this example, a small numeric either signed or unsigned will be mapped to the SQL Server smallint data type.

The lower portion allows you to select the version of default DBMS. Continue to establish your other defaults for large integers and for variable length text. The default variable text length is 10.

Sp_primarykey   SQL Alter table add PK
Sp_foreignkey   SQL alter table add FK

These options may or may not be active. If they are active, then select the method by which you wish to create primary and foreign keys. Choose whether to use a stored procedure or to use the Alter Table statements in the DDL.

Default mappings are assigned to each new column in a table. (Figure 12–32) You can override the default on a column by column basis. There are defaults for: Test, Numeric, Raw Data, Temporal, Logical, and Other. In the example, the default for Text is variable length, using a single byte character set and a maximum length of 10.

The default portable data type for a column is currently Text. This can also be set to any member in the category drop-down list box.

Finally, you can set a few options for the generation of the DDL script. (Figure 12–33) Do your want comments in the script? This is usually advisable. The

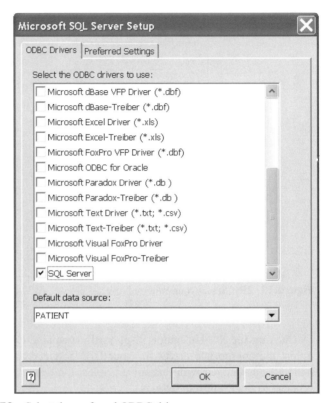

Figure 12–30   Select the preferred ODBC driver.

SQL Comment On feature creates comments in the physical database. The last option uses all the notes fields in the logical model, and uses verbalization for those that do not have user provided notes.

Document Options

The document is the current model. If you create yet another model, these options will be the defaults. Keeping the document options the same for each model is usually a good idea.

Altering the options on-the-fly is handy when reviewing a model. For example, the symbol set choice shown in Figure 12–34 is relational. If your audience is more familiar with the IDEFIX notation, open this form, change the option to IDEFIX and the model diagram changes to that presentation notation. The same is true for the names. Physical names may not be friendly for non-technical audiences. Select the Conceptual Name option to display the conceptual names. This is a reasonable case for not using merely physical names. *Note:* This all relates back to "sync when typing" options. If you chose not to sync the names, you can provide two sets of meaningful names.

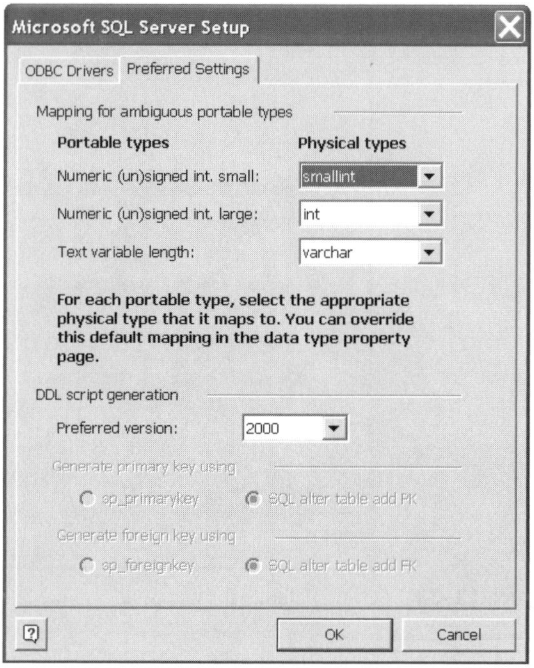

Figure 12–31   Setup default data type mapping.

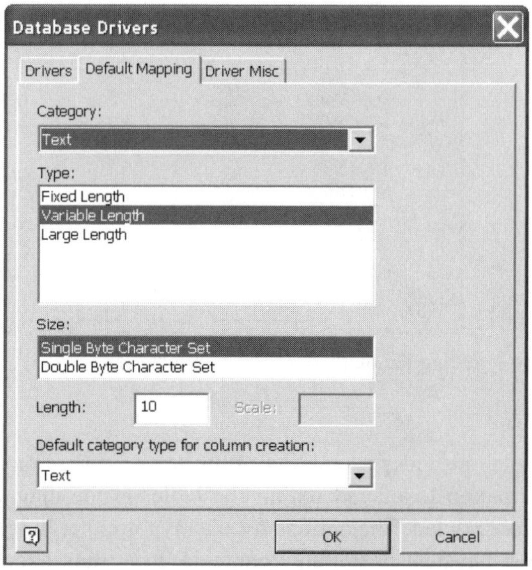

Figure 12–32   Setting the defaults for text type data.

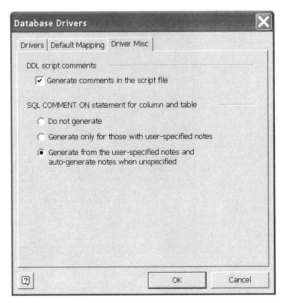

Figure 12–33   Setting defaults for mapping comments to DDL.

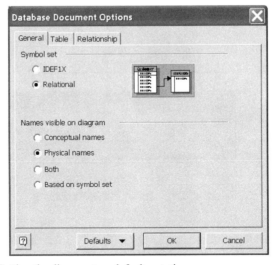

Figure 12–34   Setting the diagram to a default notation.

The Table tab provides a long list of display options. For each checked item, there will be information displayed within the table on the diagram (Figure 12–35). The defaults are all selected. The options for data types either hide or show the column data types in either physical or portable contexts. It is often handy to hide the data types when addressing non technical audiences.

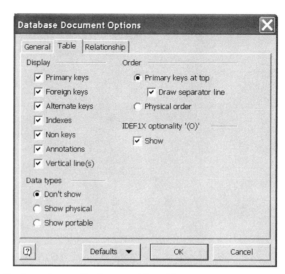

Figure 12–35   Setting what to display on tables objects.

For column order, the Primary keys at top option forces the presentation sequence to place the primary key columns first. An optional line can be included to help in the visual separation. Displaying the primary key columns at the top may hide the actual sequence of columns. If you need to rearrange the column's physical order, then select Physical order You can then arrange the columns in a preferred order. If you are using the IDEXIX notation, you can decide whether to show or hide the optionality symbol "(O)" for the table columns.

The Relationship tab allows you to alter the presentation of the foreign key relationship lines. After you have selected relational or IDEFIX as a notation in general, you can then include other options (Figure 12–36).

The option to show relationships is on by default. It hardly makes sense to present a logical model without any relationship lines. If you wish to have crow's feet (the trident symbol on the child side of the relation), then select that option as well. The cardinality places multiplicity numbers at each end of the relationships.

The referential actions may be displayed as well. Although this often leads to a messy diagram, it can be helpful temporarily for review purposes. The relationship lines may or may not display a verb phrase. If the source model is an ORM model, the verb phrase will be the predicate from the associated fact type. You can also select to see forward, inverse, or both readings. The inverse reading can be included in the ORM model, and you can also provide it in a logical mode when editing relationships.

Modeling Options

To access the Database Modeling Preferences dialog, choose Database > Options > Modeling from the main menu (Figure 12–37). These options control what happens when you delete an object from the diagram, as well as some other behavior.

Figure 12–36   Setting relationship line options for notation.

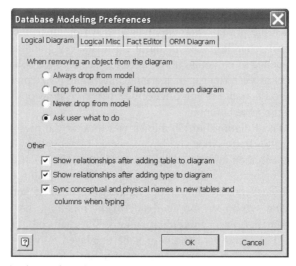

Figure 12–37   Setting options for removing object and when to show relationships.

Hint: The "Ask user what to do" choice is a very important option. If you want some protection when deleting, choose this option.

Showing relationships after adding a table to a diagram automatically inserts the relationship lines immediately after a table is dragged to the page. This is a good option to select. Synchronization of conceptual and physical names is usually set on. However, if you want to keep a set of conceptual names, turn this option off. For example, a col-

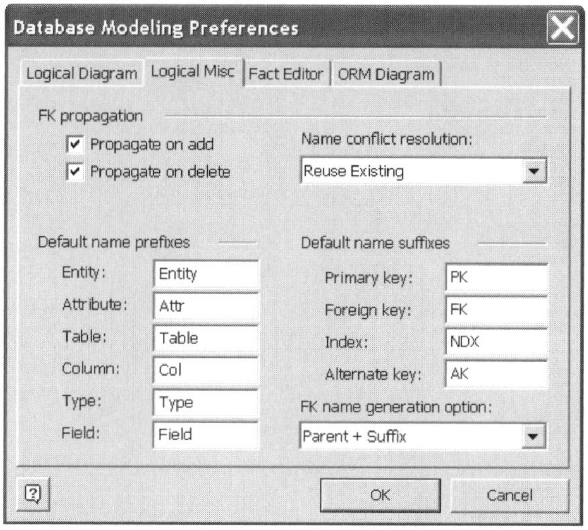

Figure 12–38 Setting Logical Naming Options.

umn physical name may be "LineItem" and you may want a more readable conceptual name of "Line Item".

The Logical Misc tab (Figure 12–38) permits the definition of several model defaults. The FK Propagation has three settings.

If checked, the Propagate on add option adds a column in the child table that is the same as the parent column when a relationship line is drawn. If this is not selected, then the line is drawn, but the child column is not created. You must then select a valid column to complete the relationship.

If checked, the Propagate on delete option causes the child column to be deleted from the table if the relationship is removed. If not selected, the child column remains in the table, but the relationship is removed.

The last option is Name conflict Resolution. The list of options is: Allow, Reuse Existing, Do Not Allow, Auto-Rename and Ask. These are the possible actions taken when creating a column in the child that causes a duplicate column name.

The Default name prefixes and the suffixes are defined here, but they are only used if prefix and suffixes are selected for use. To change the default, enter the new value.

The Foreign Key name generation includes the following options: (Parent + Suffix, Child + Suffix, Parent + Child + Suffix, Child + Parent + Suffix).

Note: DBMS vendors define the maximum name length for model elements. Select an option to keep the names within the set limit without a lot of manual renaming.

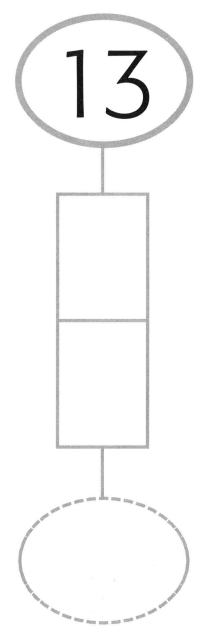

13 Editing Logical Models: Advanced Aspects

13.1 Copying Model Elements

Each logical model element such as a table scheme or foreign key relationship occurs only once in the underlying model. However, you can display as many copies as you like of the same model element on the diagram, on the same page or on different pages.

One reason to display multiple copies of a model element on the same page is to provide a cleaner layout of foreign key relationships. An easy way to *copy a diagram instance of a table* on the same page is to *Control-drag it* to another place on the diagram. To do this, select the table shape on the diagram, then hold the Ctrl key down as you drag a copy of it to the new position using the mouse.

Although the diagram displays two different copies of the table, both copies denote the same underlying table in the model. If you make a change to one (e.g. change its name) this change is immediately reflected in the other copy. When you copy table shapes this way, the foreign key relationships on that table are not redisplayed. If you want to display those relationships on the copy, right-click the table copy and choose Show Related Tables from the context menu.

An alternative way to redisplay a table is to *drag it onto the page from the Table and Views window*. If this window is not open, you can open it by choosing Database > View > Tables and Views from the main menu. This is also the only way to display a table shape on a page where no instance of it is yet displayed. When you copy table shapes in this way, all the foreign key relationships on it are redisplayed as well. You can hide any duplicated relationship lines by deleting them from the diagram (not the model).

If you drag and drop a table on a different page, you can then add other tables to that page and the tool will draw the appropriate relationships between them. In this way, you can have different drawing pages that repeat tables as needed.

> *Caution:* If you want to remove a table from a page, do not use the "cut" option. Instead make sure your option for delete is set to "ask the user what to do." Select the table and press the delete key. You will be asked if you want to delete the table from the drawing. Choose NO. This has no impact on other pages, nor does it remove the table from the model. If you performed a "cut" it will be removed from all pages and the model.

In Figure 13–1, the Store table was dragged onto the drawing page as a duplicate. The foreign key relationship lines are duplicated between Store and State, and between Store and Invoice. We manually applied a fill color of yellow (this appears shaded in monochrome prints) to the duplicated table to indicate it is a duplicate on the drawing. To *apply a fill color to a shape,* right-click it, choose Format > Fill from the context menu, and then select the desired fill color. If the formatting toolbar is displayed, you can also apply the fill by clicking the Fill Color icon. This is a normal Visio feature.

Color is useful in many cases to indicate information about a table. For example, you can use different colors to indicate major tables, reference data tables, intersection tables for many-to-many relationships, or duplicate tables.

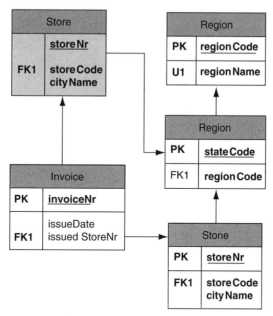

Figure 13–1 An extra copy of the Store table has been dragged onto the page.

If you select a duplicated foreign key relationship and press the delete key, the Delete prompt dialog appears as shown in Figure 13–2.

Choose No. If you say "Yes," then the relationship is removed from the model, not the merely the drawing. Do the same for the other connection. The diagram will now appear as shown in Figure 13–3. Often, on a drawing page, it is difficult to prevent line entanglements. By placing a duplicate copy of the table on the page and by hiding selected relationships you can untangle the mess.

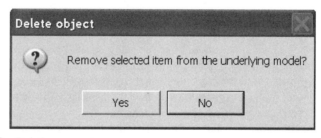

Figure 13–2 Deletion prompt.

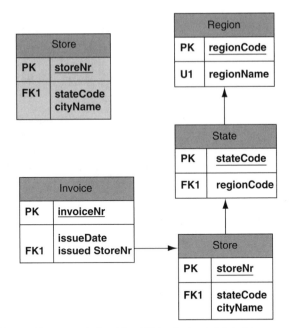

Figure 13–3 Page with some relationships hidden but not deleted.

13.2 Cloning Model Elements

It is also possible to *clone a model element*. Cloning creates a new model element (not just a shape) based on an existing one. When created, the clone has the same model properties as the original, except for the name. To clone a model element that is displayed on a diagram page, select the element, press Ctrl+C to copy it to the clipboard, then move the mouse cursor to the position (on the same page or a different page) where you wish to display the clone, and press Ctrl+V to paste the clone there. Instead of Ctrl+C, you can use the main menu option Edit > Copy. Instead of Ctrl+V, you can use the menu option Edit > Paste.

Each clone of a table is assigned the name of the original table, appended by a number that indicates the order in which it has been cloned from the original. For example, if you copy the Store table to the clipboard and paste it, this results in the clone table Store1. If you now copy the Store1 table to the clipboard and paste it, this results in the clone Store11. If instead you copy Store to the clipboard and paste it twice, this results in the clones Store1 and Store2.

A clone table initially has the same model properties as the original, except for its name. If you later make a change to the original (e.g., add a column), this change is not propagated to the clone. Similarly, if you later make a change to the clone, this change is not propagated to the original. This is because the original and the clone correspond to different underlying model elements.

If you select objects from one model, open a new or existing model, and paste the selection into that model, all the selected tables, relationships and associated code will be copied into that model. This is useful for model reuse. Although database projects may include multiple ORM source models, the version of VEA used at the time of writing has only limited support for the inclusion of multiple ER source models in the same project.

13.3   Database Properties: Definition and Notes

To open the Database Properties dialog for a shape, simply select the shape. In the case of a foreign key relationship, the *Definition* category displays the names of the related table columns. The names should comply with your standard naming conventions. If you are using naming from an ORM model, most of these names will be defined using your defined naming convention available in ORM models (see Chapter 8).

The Database Properties dialog for tables includes a *Notes* category. Notes are very important for understanding the model. If you use an ORM drawing as a source to the model, the notes from the ORM model are copied as comments to the logical model. Notes are printed in model reports and provide context for reviews of the model. It is useful to create a template that you can copy into the notes area and then add the specific information. Some suggested notes sections are: Owner, Date Recorded, Steward, Source Document, Source System, and Description. The more consistent you make the template for the different element types, the more useful is your documentation. You can also hyperlink from objects to other documentation (see Chapter 17).

13.4   Check Clauses

In Chapter 12, we defined check clauses using the value constraints window. Here we create check clauses using the code editor. Check clauses are assigned either to a column or to a table. If the check clause involves more than one column, it must be specified at the table level. To create a check clause on a table, select the table then select Check Clauses from the database properties. To create a check clause on a column, you may select the Edit option for the column and then open the Check pane. When the Code Editor dialog appears, give the check clause a name under the Properties tab and then select the Body tab (Figure 13–4).

Within the body, enter the check clause code using the syntax appropriate for your DBMS. Figure 13–5 shows a simple example for declaring a list of possible values for the regionCode column.

In the following generated SQL Server code fragment, the check clause is applied to the appropriate column within the table. There are two distinct check clauses for this table.

```
create table "Region" (
"regionCode" char(2) not null constraint "RegionregionCode_Chk" check ("regionCode" in
   ('N','S','E','W','C')),
"regionName" varchar(20) not null constraint "RegionregionName_Chk" check ("regionName"
   in ('North','South','East','West','Central')))
go
```

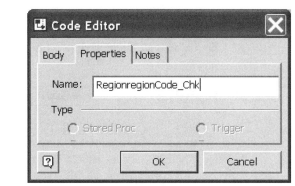

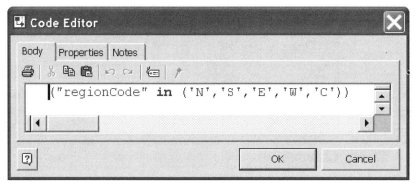

Figure 13–4   Code Editor Code Name—Type Check Clause.

Figure 13–5   Enter the Check Clause Code.

13.5   Indexes

The Database Category Index is used to define unique or non-unique indexes on table columns. *First, select the table to receive the index, then select New*. The Create Index window is then displayed. It always appears as a non-unique index that can be changed later in the process. *Enter the index name, and then select OK*. The example creates a non-unique index on the Invoice Issue Date.

The next window allows you to select the column(s) for the index. Highlight the column on the left and select "Add" until you have selected all the required columns for the index. You can also rename or delete the index. The options button is for extended properties that only apply to SQL Server.

Designate the index type from the index Type drop-down box.

The Extended Index Attributes (Figure 13–9) define several index management parameters. If the index is clustered then the rows in the physical database match the primary key order. The STATS_NORECOMPUTE option prevents outdated index statistics from being recomputed. The Drop Existing option causes the index to be dropped

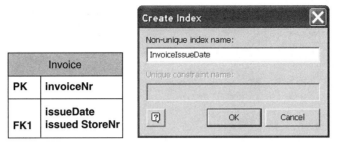

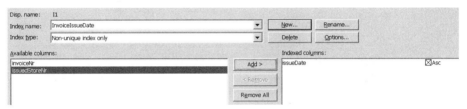

Figure 13–6   Creating an index on the Invoice Table named "InvoiceIssueDate."

Figure 13–7   Index column selection.

Figure 13–8   Index types.

and rebuilt. The Fill factor controls the how full an index page can be. The PAD_INDEX determines how full intermediate levels can become. The combination of the FILL_FACTOR and the PAD_INDEX affects index performance. Refer to SQL Server tuning documentation to determine the best setting for specific indexes (this topic is not covered in this text).

13.6   Triggers

The code window permits the creation and editing of several code types. These include Stored Procedure, Trigger, Check, Raw DDL, and View. Views were discussed in Chapter 12.

To open the code window for any type of code, select Database > View > Code from the main menu. For all the code examples that follow, the same code window is displayed. The difference is in the type of code. These options are not shown with each code

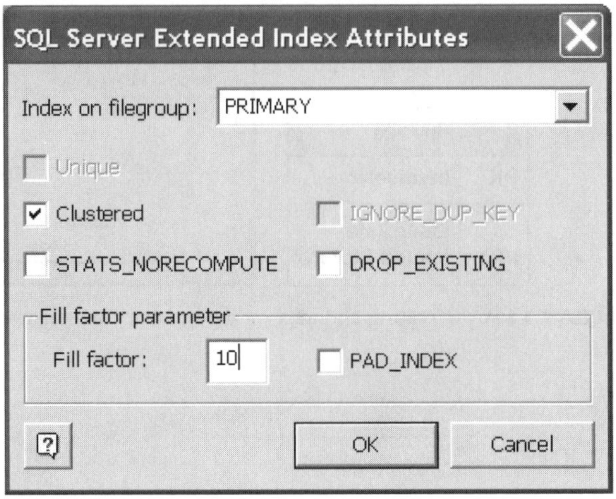

Figure 13–9   Index extended properties.

example. However as you can see in Figure 13–10, the code type is determined by selecting the appropriate radio button. Select the Trigger option in the Database Category list and then select "Add." The code editor window opens with the Trigger Option selected. Enter a name for trigger and then select the "Body" tab.

> ***Caution:*** When defining these options you must give the code block a name. However, this name is not included in the CREATE statement. For example, you must include the "*CREATE PROCEDURE LineTotal sp*" as part of your code when in the Body pane of the Code Editor, even though you named the code "LineTotal_sp."

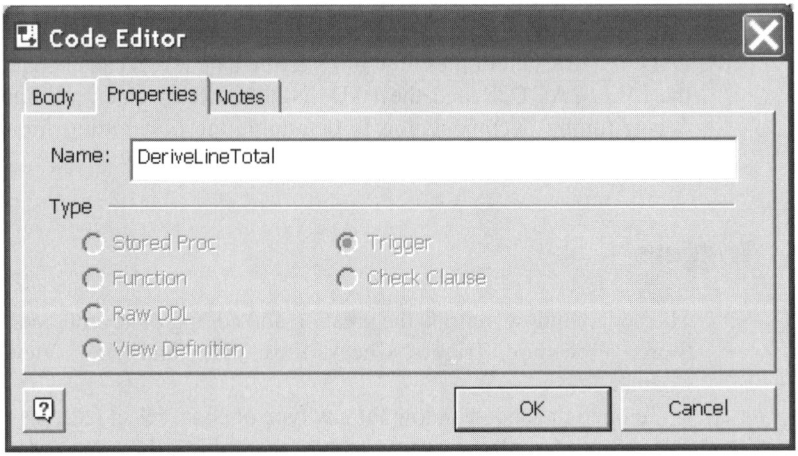

Figure 13–10   Setting the Trigger Name.

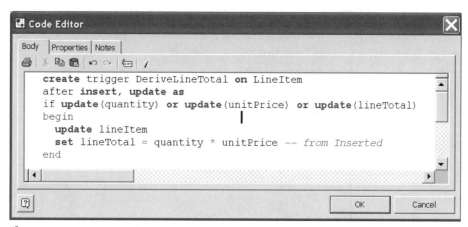

Figure 13–11   Trigger Code to compute the line Total.

Enter the trigger code. In this example, the lineTotal is to be recomputed if the quantity or unitPrice has been updated. Notice that trigger name "DeriveLineTotal." This name is not automatically inserted into the code. Therefore, you must enter the create trigger line in the code block.

13.7   Stored Procedures

Stored procedures are often DBMS specific. From the code editor, indicate the type of code is Stored Procedure and enter the procedure name. Figure 13–12 shows an example.

The body of the stored procedure code is shown in Figure 13–13. Notice the Create Procedure "name" was entered. It is not derived from the name automatically.

13.8   Raw DDL

Select the Raw DDL code type to author any DDL syntax to include in the generate script. For example, you may include user permission syntax, user definitions and user roles. The following is a simple example of using raw DDL to create a default value. This code example establishes a default region code. The region code is also part of a check clause, therefore the value must also be a member in the set of legal values. The code window is not shown here, but it is the same code window as for any code type.

```
USE Sales
GO
CREATE DEFAULT RegionCodeDefault AS 'N'
```

The syntax must be valid for the target DBMS. If you select a different DBMS during a generate operation, the code may become invalid.

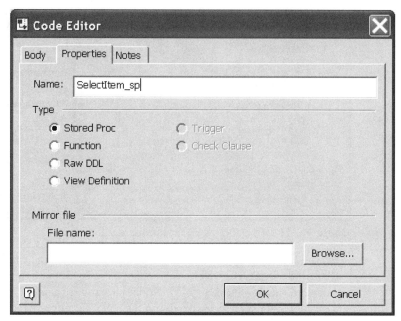

Figure 13–12 Starting a Stored Procedure.

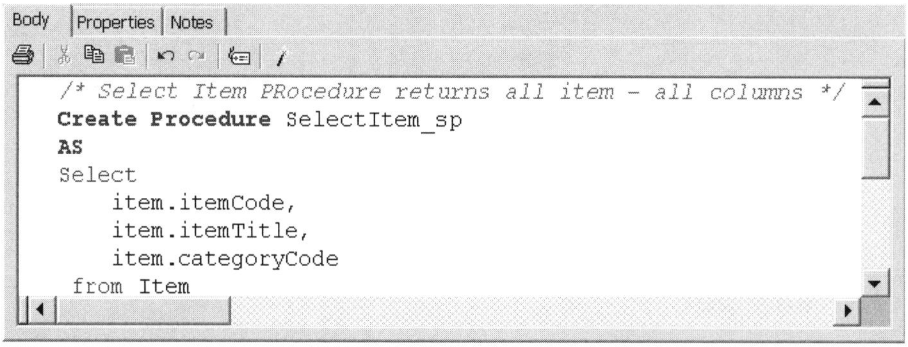

```
/* Select Item PRocedure returns all item - all columns */
Create Procedure SelectItem_sp
AS
Select
    item.itemCode,
    item.itemTitle,
    item.categoryCode
from Item
```

Figure 13–13 Stored Procedure.

13.9 User Defined Functions

The following is a sample of the function to compute Line Total. This is another option for creating the value. This example was shown elsewhere as trigger code.

```
CREATE FUNCTION Line Total (@quantity int, @unitPrice money)
RETURNS Money AS
BEGIN
  RETURN (@quantity * @unitPrice)
END
```

Here is the definition of a test table to demonstrate the defined function usage:

```
Create table Test (
quantity int,
UnitPrice money,
lineTotal As dbo.LineTotal(quantity, unitPrice))
```

The following test of the function produces the results: quantity = 2, unit price = 3.00, line total = 6.00.

```
insert into Test (quantity, unitPrice) values (2,3.00)
select * from Test
```

13.10   User Defined Types

User defined data types are based on the DBMS's built-in data types. A user defined data type has its own specific name. This name may be used to provide consistency for column data types in different tables. For example, the data type InvoiceNumber may be defined as small integer. Then when assigning the data type to the column InvoiceNr the data type can be declared as InvoiceNumber rather than smallint.

You can display the basic data types for the selected DBMS of the model by selecting Types from the main menu (Database > View > Types). All user defined types are built upon these basic types (Figure 13–14).

To add a user defined type, choose Database > User Defined Types from the main menu. Select Add to begin the definition. Enter a name for your new data type (Figure 13–15). The Copy From option permits you to copy one user defined type from another user defined type. Since there are no other defined data types at this time, the list is empty. It would seem natural that you could copy from the DBMS defined data types, but that is not the case. After entering the name, select "OK".

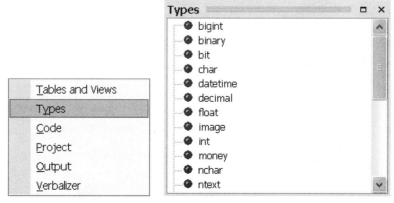

Figure 13–14   Menu selection and a partial list of SQL 2000 data types.

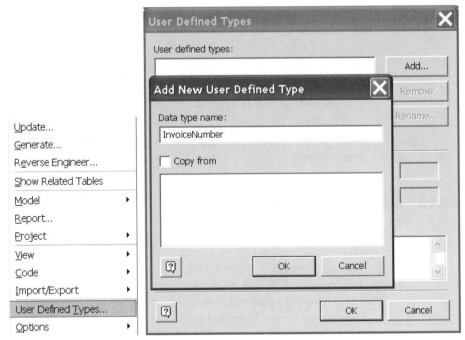

Figure 13–15   Defining the Invoice Number data type.

Now define the type based on the natural DBMS data types. Here InvoiceNumber is defined as numeric, small, signed integer (Figure 13–16). Once defined, this data type can be assigned to any InvoiceNr columns as a valid data type.

For this example, the following code will be added to the top of the generated DDL script. This must be loaded into the script prior to using the user defined data type. The DDL generation automatically places user defined data types prior to create table statements.

```
/* Add, update user defined datatype. */
sp_addtype "InvoiceNumber", "smallint"
```

13.11   Extended Properties

Extended properties may be used to define where tables or images are stored. To add an extended property to a table, select the Extended category in its Database Properties sheet, and press the Edit button. If you are using SQL Server, the extended attributes dialog now appears (Figure 13–17).

Primary is the default group, which indicates the tables are stored in the Primary space definition. The DBA may assign several spaces for the database. It is here you can make the assignment. The Text Images can also be stored in a defined space in this example.

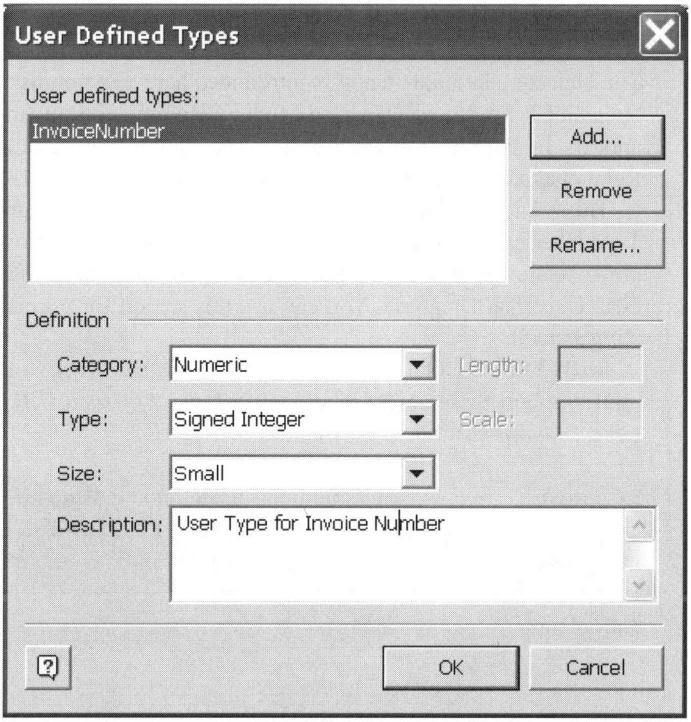

Figure 13–16   Setting User defined data type.

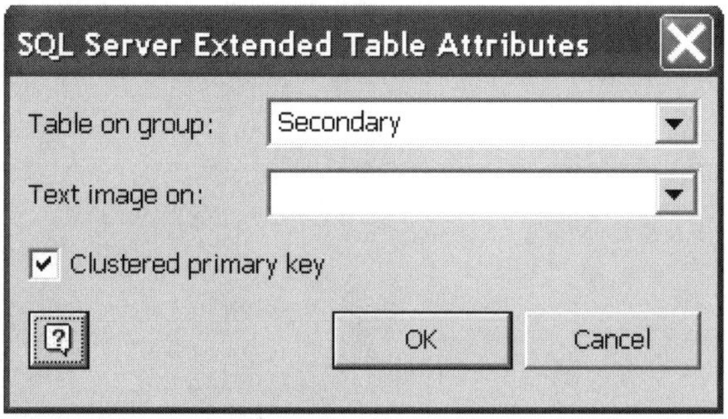

Figure 13–17   Extended properties option for SQL server.

In this example (Figure 13–17), the LineItem table was selected and placed in the Secondary group. The generated DDL code for this example is shown below.

```
create table "LineItem" (
    "invoiceNr" smallint not null,
    "lineNr" tinyint not null,
    "quantity" tinyint not null,
    "itemCode" varchar(10) not null,
    "unitPrice" money not null,
    "lineTotal" money null) ON 'Secondary'
```

13.12   The Object-Relational Stencil

The Object-Relational stencil is introduced here, but not discussed in detail. When you open an ER Source or Database Model Diagram solution, an Object-Relational stencil appears in the shapes window along with the ER stencil. To display the Object-Relational stencil shapes, simply click its title bar (Figure 13–18).

This stencil includes three new icons for modeling: Table inheritance, Type, and Type inheritance (Figure 13–19). The three special icons provide additional support for object relational features supported in a few DBMSs such as Oracle 8 or higher, or IBM DB2 Universal Database. You can use this stencil for normal entity relationship modeling as well.

Many DBMSs, including Microsoft Access and Microsoft SQL Server, do not currently support these object relational features. *For such DBMSs, you should ignore the Object-Relational stencil completely.*

> ***Caution:*** Do *not* use the table inheritance feature as an alternative to the Parent-to-Child category relationship feature supported in the ER stencil. These features have completely different semantics, and should not be confused. *Never* use table inheritance in Microsoft SQL Server or Microsoft Access, as such usage may cause severe problems.

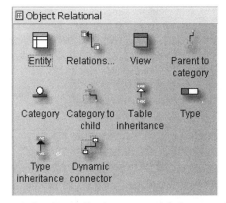

Figure 13–18   Object-Relational stencil. Also opens with the normal ER stencil.

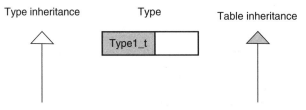

Figure 13–19   Type inheritance, Type, and Table inheritance icons.

Even if your DBMS does support object-relational features, *we recommend that you ignore the Object-Relational stencil* unless you have a compelling reason to use object-relational features. Currently, the object-relational solution in VEA is far less robust than the ER solution, mainly because it has rarely been used in practice, so comparatively little attention has been given to its support issues.

If you are familiar with object-relational features, the Type icon is used to create a set of columns that can be implemented within a single column of the associated table-column. The Type inheritance connection is used to form this association. The Table inheritance connector is used for the same purpose, except a table is used in the association. Use these features only with an object-relational database, and only as a last resort.

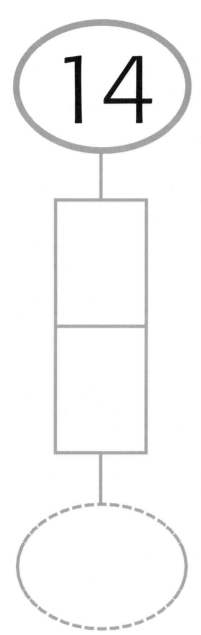

14 Reverse Engineering Physical Schemas to Logical Models

14.1 Using the Reverse Engineer Wizard

A physical database may be reverse engineered to either an ORM model or to a logical model. Reverse engineering to ORM was covered in Chapter 8 and enforces stricter model checking rules than are required for reverse engineering to a logical model. If the ORM reverse engineering process fails, you may still be able to reverse engineer the database to a logical model.

We now discuss reverse engineering to a logical database model. This process requires an ODBC connection, which may already exist or can be created from within the reverse engineering wizard. Creating this connection is not discussed in depth here, because it has been covered in detail in Sections 8.1 and 11.4. A wizard guides you through the reverse engineering process. If the process succeeds, the result is a logical ER model corresponding either to the whole of the physical database schema, or that portion of it that was selected to reverse engineer.

To reverse engineer an existing database, open a new instance of the Database Model Diagram solution and choose Database > Reverse Engineer from its main menu (Figure 14–1). This opens the Reverse Engineering Wizard.

If you are reverse engineering into an ER Source Model, the Reverse Engineering Option is located in the same menu, but it is the first selection, and there are fewer options in that list.

Create the Database Connection

The opening window of the Reverse Engineer Wizard lists the available data sources for you to reverse engineer. In our worked example, two SQL Server data sources already exist (see Figure 14–2). Here PATIENT EXAMPLE is a data source for an SQL Server database generated from a logical model similar to the Patient_LS model considered in earlier chapters.

If a data source for your database is not in the list, you will have to create the connection definition at this time. Select New and follow the ODBC Connection wizard.

Figure 14–1 Drop-down menu for database-related actions.

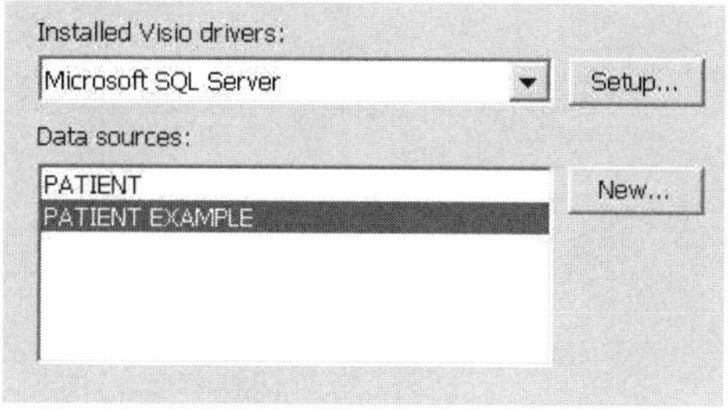

Figure 14–2 List of ODBC data sources.

This ODBC wizard is used in many products and is the same here. See Sections 8.1 and 11.4 for detailed instructions on how to do this. Within the ODBC definition the setup option is used to select the appropriate driver. For example, if you are connecting a SQL Server 2000 database, select SQL Server as the driver. Because there are several drivers in the list, be sure to check the type of connection and the version. There is more than one driver version for SQL Server, Oracle, and several others. The selection of the version is important for the proper transformation in either forward or reverse engineering where the DDL script syntax may differ. After creating the connection you are returned to this form to select the connection, with your new data source added to the list.

To make the ODBC connection to the physical database, select the relevant data source, then click Next. In the Connect Data Source dialog, provide the appropriate database logon to establish the connection (Figure 14–3). If you do not know the login, or your logon does not permit reverse engineering capability, see your database administrator. Click OK.

Select Model Elements to Reverse Engineer

The wizard now presents a dialog in which you can choose which model elements to reverse engineer (Figure 14–4). By default, all available objects are selected. Deselect the objects you do not require. Reverse engineering options include Tables, Views and Stored Procedures. You can choose to reverse engineer only the Stored

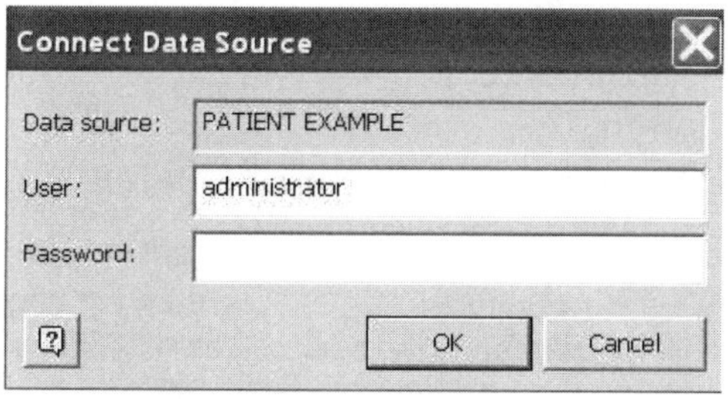

Figure 14–3 Database Logon.

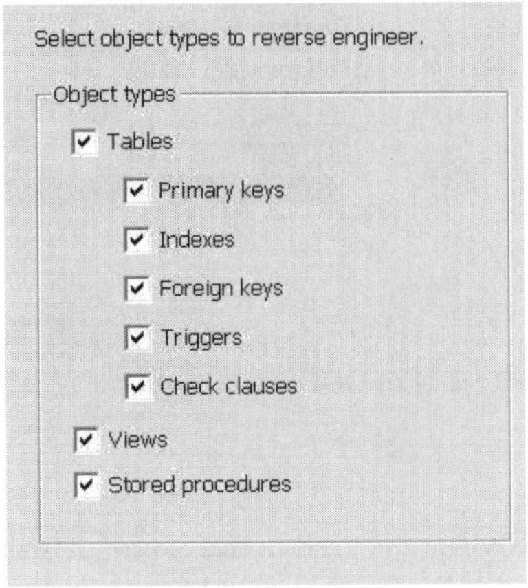

Figure 14–4   Selection of Object Types to Reverse Engineer.

Procedures or any combination of the three. When selecting Tables to reverse engineer, the primary keys, indexes, foreign keys, triggers, and check clauses are all included by default. Again, deselect any object your do not wish to reverse engineer. Click Next to proceed.

Select Base Tables and/or Views to Reverse Engineer

The next screen prompts you to select which base tables and/or views to reverse engineer. (Figure 14–5). Base tables are marked "T" and views are marked "V." In our example, there are four base tables and no views. By default, none are selected. If only some are needed, select the individual items by clicking the appropriate check box. If all are desired, then click Select All. To reset the selections, click Deselect All.

A similar screen is displayed for selecting stored procedures (Figure 14–5). Note that no naming choices were used in the ORM model from which this database model was generated, so one of the stored procedures has a really long name. See Section 7.4 for ways to improve the names of logical model elements that are generated from an ORM model.

Place Shapes on the Drawing Window

The next screen allows you to choose whether to have shapes for the reverse engineered elements placed automatically on the drawing page (Figure 14–7). In general, if you have only a few tables, then select Yes. If you have many tables, it may be easier to arrange the layout manually. You can also use pagination when you lay it out manually, as discussed in section 12.8. Select your option, and click Next.

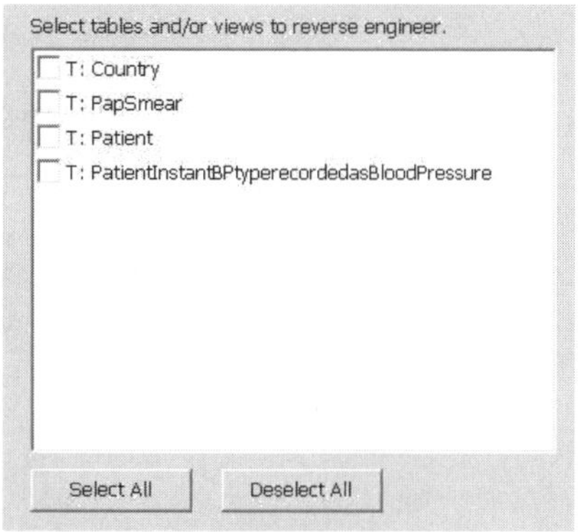

Select tables and/or views to reverse engineer.

☐ T: Country
☐ T: PapSmear
☐ T: Patient
☐ T: PatientInstantBPtyperecordedasBloodPressure

Select All   Deselect All

Figure 14–5   Choosing tables to reverse engineer.

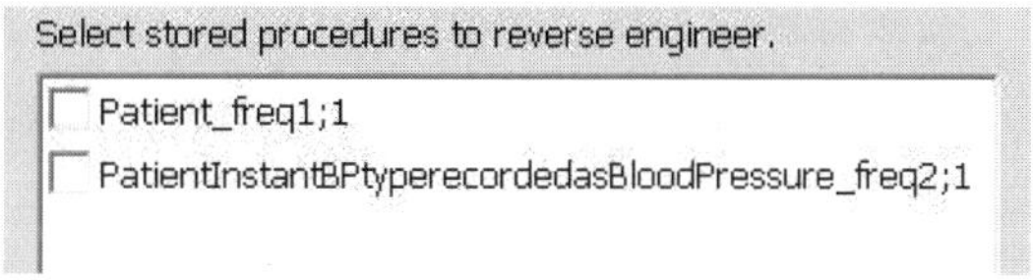

Select stored procedures to reverse engineer.

☐ Patient_freq1;1
☐ PatientInstantBPtyperecordedasBloodPressure_freq2;1

Figure 14–6   Choosing which stored procedures to reverse engineer.

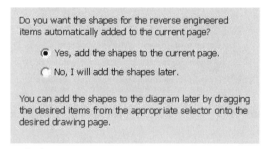

Do you want the shapes for the reverse engineered
items automatically added to the current page?

⦿ Yes, add the shapes to the current page.
○ No, I will add the shapes later.

You can add the shapes to the diagram later by dragging
the desired items from the appropriate selector onto the
desired drawing page.

Figure 14–7   Layout Options.

Preview the Selection

The next screen provides a preview of the tables and catalog information to be reverse engineered (Figure 14–8). If the selections are correct, then click Finish otherwise click Back to change your selections, and then finish.

14.2   Reviewing the Result

The results of the reverse engineering are displayed in the output window (Figure 14–9). Make sure to review the contents for errors and warnings. If you encounter

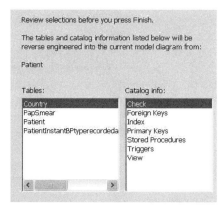

Figure 14–8   Reviewing the Selections for Reverse Engineering.

```
Output

Import/Export

Reverse engineering from database 'Patient' on server 'MINEPAT'...
Extracting columns of table 'Country'.
Extracting columns of table 'PapSmear'.
Extracting columns of table 'Patient'.
Extracting columns of table 'PatientInstantBPtyperecordedasBloodPressure'.
Extracting check of table 'Country'.
Extracting check of table 'PapSmear'.
Extracting check of table 'Patient'.
Extracting check of table 'PatientInstantBPtyperecordedasBloodPressure'.
Extracting primary key of table 'Country'.
Extracting primary key of table 'PapSmear'.
Extracting primary key of table 'Patient'.
Extracting primary key of table 'PatientInstantBPtyperecordedasBloodPressure'.
Extracting indexes of table 'Country'.
Extracting indexes of table 'PapSmear'.
Extracting indexes of table 'Patient'.
Extracting indexes of table 'PatientInstantBPtyperecordedasBloodPressure'.
Extracting foreign keys of table 'Country'.
Extracting foreign keys of table 'PapSmear'.
Extracting foreign keys of table 'Patient'.
Extracting foreign keys of table 'PatientInstantBPtyperecordedasBloodPressure'.
```

Figure 14–9   Beginning of Output Results of the Reverse Engineering.

errors or serious warnings, you should correct these in the physical database prior to redoing the reverse engineering. Alternatively, you may deselect the object types creating the errors, and run the wizard again.

If the reverse engineering succeeds, and you choose Yes for the automatic layout option, the model will now be laid out for you in the drawing window. Figure 14–10 shows the result for our worked example.

If you answered No, you may manually drag the relevant shapes from the Tables and Views window onto the drawing surface. If you drag one table onto the drawing window you can automatically add its related tables by right clicking on the table and selecting Show Related Tables from its context menu. Using this option gives you pagination control. You can create subject area pages, and place selected tables on each page.

If needed, you may now edit the logical model in the normal way to make any desired changes.

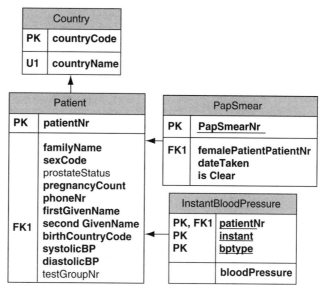

Figure 14–10   Logical Model Layout.

For our example, in addition to the tables shown on the diagram, stored procedures and check clauses were reverse engineered from the physical model. The code window contains two code types: Global Code and Local Code. Global Code includes stored procedures [SP] or code that is in a self-contained code block. The Local Code is contained in some other model element, in this case a table. The Code window is opened by the reverse engineering wizard (Figure 14–11).

Examples of the stored procedure code are displayed in Figures 14–12 and 14–13.

Figure 14–11   Code window.

```
Body  | Properties | Notes |

/* Create procedure/function InstantBloodPressure_freq2.      */
/* The constraint:                                            */
/* Each Patient, Instant combination that occurs in           */
/*  Patient at Instant had BPtype recorded as BloodPressure   */
/*  occurs there exactly 2 times.                             */
/* is enforced by the following DDL.                          */
Create Procedure InstantBloodPressure_freq2 as
/*  Microsoft Visual Studio generated procedure code. */
if (
    not exists (select * from InstantBloodPressure
                group by InstantBloodPressure.patientNr, InstantBloodPressure.instant
                having count(*) < 2 or count(*) > 2)
)
  return 1
else
  return 2
/* End PatientInstantBloodPressure_freq2        */
```

Figure 14–12   Procedure to enforce patient group frequency constraint.

```
Body  | Properties | Notes |

/* Create procedure/function Patient_freq1.      */
/* The constraint:                               */
/* Each TestGroup that occurs in                 */
/*  Patient is in TestGroup                      */
/*   occurs there at least 5 times.              */
/* is enforced by the following DDL.             */
CREATE Procedure Patient_freq1 as
/*  Microsoft Visual Studio generated procedure code. */
if (
    not exists (select * from Patient
                where Patient.testGroupNr is not null
                group by Patient.testGroupNr
                having count(*) < 5)
)
  return 1
else
  return 2
/* End Patient_freq1                    */
```

Figure 14–13   Procedure to enforce instant blood pressure frequency constraint.

The following check clause code was also reversed engineered.

Reverse Engineered Check Clauses
InstantBloodPressure.bPtype : PatientInstantBPTyperecordedas
([bPtype] = 'D' or [bPtype] = 'S')

PatientsexCode : PatientsexCode_Chk
([sexCode] = 'F' or [sexCode] = 'M')

Reversed Engineer Equality Constraint
Patient : Patient_equal
([diastolicBP] is null and [systolicBP] is null or [diastolicBP] is not null and [systolicBP] is not null)

Reversed Engineered Subset Constraint
Patient : Patient_subset
([firstGivenName] is not null or [secondGivenName] is null)

14.3   Handling Errors and Warnings

The reverse engineering process may encounter errors and fail to create the logical model. Each error is shown in the output window. Each error must be resolved in the physical model. In some situations, you may have to eliminate an object type instance from your selection list. If you choose to correct the physical database, it is a good idea to get a schema (DDL script) from your current database, and then create an empty version of the database. Make the corrections in this new version. Usually you do not have the luxury to change the production database. If you create a new empty database to solve these problems, you will need to establish a new ODBC connection or modify an existing one.

14.4   Other Reverse Engineering Options

You can also import ERwin models and older VisioModeler ORM models or logical models using the Import/Export option. To do this, choose Database > Import/Export from the main menu, and then select the desired option. For further details on this functionality, see Section 8.4.

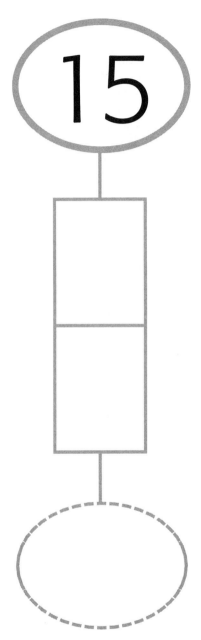

15 Logical Database Model Reports

15.1 New Report Wizard

This chapter shows you how to prepare reports from logical database models. You can print model diagrams directly, and you can use the New Report Wizard to prepare detailed reports on databases, tables and data types. There are three kinds of reports available for logical models: Statistical Report; Table Report; and Types Report.

The *Statistical Report* provides a brief summary of overall model. For example, it lists the total number of tables, columns, foreign keys, and indexes. The *statistical report is available only from the Database Model Diagram solution*. So if you want a statistical report for an ER Source model, you need to first add it to database model project. To do this from the Database Model Diagram solution, choose Database > Project > Add Existing Document from the main menu, and then add the relevant ER source model file into the project. For a detailed discussion of this process, see Section 10.7.

The *Table Report* provides detailed information about all aspects of your logical model, and is the most useful of the three reports. The *Types Report* lists details about the logical data types in your model. You can run table and type reports from either the ER Source Model solution or the Database Model Diagram solution.

You can choose the level of detail in each report by selecting from customizable options to create summary reports or reports with comprehensive detail. The dialog boxes in each report use different input but many have a common structure. To avoid repetition, this chapter describes features that are unique to logical model reports. The Object Type report in Chapter 9 gives a detailed explanation of the common dialog box functions.

The procedures in this chapter refer to models that are open in the Database Model Diagram. You must begin by ensuring that your preferred logical model is open and is the active Visio model. If you have several models open, just click on the model you want in order to make it the active model.

To start the *New Report Wizard* from the Database Model Diagram solution, choose Database > Report from the main menu. The New Report Wizard will open as shown in Figure 15–1. When you are working in the Database Model Diagram solution, the New Report Wizard window shows seven report options in alphabetical order. If you do this from within an ER Source Model, only two options are in the list (Table Report and Types Report).

Four of the reports in the list (Constraint, Fact, Object, and Supertype) are the same reports as those described in Chapter 9. If you run the four ORM reports from the Database Model Diagram, you get the same results as when you run them from the ORM Source Model. Please refer to Chapter 9 for a complete description of the four ORM reports.

The next sections show you how to prepare the Statistical Report, the Table Report, and the Types Report from within the Database Model Diagram solution.

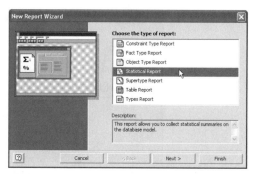

Figure 15–1   New Report Wizard for Database Model Diagrams.

15.2   Statistical Report

The statistical report summarizes a logical model's content by doing the following things:

- Counting the number and type of constraints, foreign keys, and attributes
- Extracting your model's source file information.

You start the Statistical Report by double clicking on "Statistical Report" in the New Report Wizard list shown in Figure 15–1. Double clicking is much faster than using the "Next" and "Finish" buttons. Even if you get it wrong, it is still faster to double click the report name, realize your error, and double click the correct report title to start again.

If you do single click Statistical Report and then click the Next button, you will see the confirmation panel shown in Figure 15–2. You can check that you have selected the correct report and then click either *Back* to correct your selection or *Finish* to confirm and continue.

Clicking *Finish* will reveal the Statistical Report dialog box shown in Figure 15–3. The Statistical report Dialog Box has three tabs: Preferences, Headers, and Pagination. Click on the Preferences tab to ensure that your screen looks like Figure 15–3.

Statistical Report–Bottom Row Buttons

The four buttons along the bottom of the windows shown in Figure 15–3, Figure 15–4, and Figure 15–5 (Print..., Preview, Export to RTF...and Close) work in exactly the same way as in all other reports. Please refer to the description of the bottom row buttons in the Object Type report in Chapter 9.

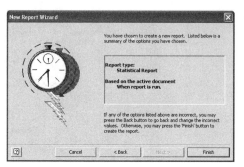

Figure 15–2 New Report Wizard for Logical Models—Confirmation panel.

Table 15–1 Statistical Report tabs.

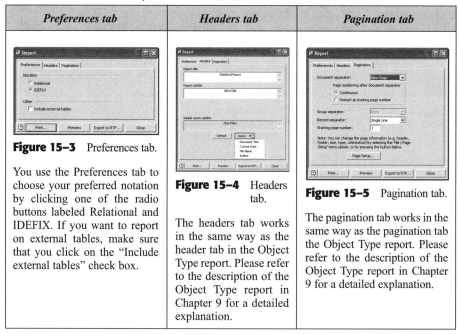

Preferences tab	Headers tab	Pagination tab
Figure 15–3 Preferences tab. You use the Preferences tab to choose your preferred notation by clicking one of the radio buttons labeled Relational and IDEFIX. If you want to report on external tables, make sure that you click on the "Include external tables" check box.	**Figure 15–4** Headers tab. The headers tab works in the same way as the header tab in the Object Type report. Please refer to the description of the Object Type report in Chapter 9 for a detailed explanation.	**Figure 15–5** Pagination tab. The pagination tab works in the same way as the pagination tab the Object Type report. Please refer to the description of the Object Type report in Chapter 9 for a detailed explanation.

15.3 Table Reports

You can start the Table Report by double clicking on "Table Report" in the New Report Wizard list shown in Figure 15–1. Visio will then reveal a tabbed dialog box similar to Figure 15–6. The following paragraphs describe each of the functions in the table report.

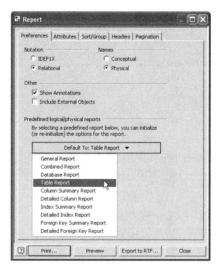

Figure 15–6   Table Report Preferences tab.

Table Report–Preferences Tab

Click on the Preferences tab to make sure that your screen looks similar to Figure 15–6.

Notation: You must choose one of the Notation radio buttons for your report. Even if you defined your logical model using relational notation, you can still switch to IDEFIX here.

Names: You must choose either conceptual or physical. If you want to review a logical schema, choose conceptual. If you want to review a physical schema, choose physical.

Show Annotations: Check this if you wish to include annotations.

Include External Objects: This checkbox will add objects that your model references but that are defined in a different model.

Predefined logical/physical reports—Default To: Button. When you open the Preferences tab shown in Figure 15–6, the Default To: button label, will display the name of one of the predefined reports. For example, it may read "Default To: General Report." You can change the default report by clicking the Default To: button and selecting a report from the drop down list.

Figure 15–6 and Figure 15–7, show the states of the Default To button before and after a report selection. The text label on the Default To button in Figure 15–6 reads "Detailed Column Report." After clicking the button to reveal the drop-down list and then clicking "Table Report," the label on the "Default to:" button changes to "Table Report" as shown in Figure 15–7. When you choose a default report, you are choosing

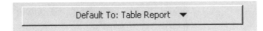

Figure 15–7   Default To: button label.

a predefined subset of the 61 attributes in the attribute tab (see Table 15–5 through Table 15–9).

You can use the default reports as they are. Table 15–2 gives a summary of the contents of each of the ten default reports. The numbers in parentheses after each report name in the column headed "Predefined Report name" indicates the number of pages

Table 15–2   Predefined Report content.

Report Number	Predefined Report Name	What You Get with Each Report
1	General(8)	The first section of this report gives a summary of your model. Each of the remaining sections gives a detailed report on each table.
2	Combined(11)	This report combines the database summary report with the table report.
3	Database(1)	Summarizes the model. Notes are generated for each table. The Notes are derived from the primary key notes.
4	Table(2)	Gives a short summary of each table including Notes and Foreign keys.
5	Column Summary(1)	Gives a list of columns grouped by table number. Shows data type, nulls, and value/range.
6	Detailed Column(5)	For each table shows the column name, physical data type, allowable nulls, and Notes. Prints a group header for each table.
7	Index Summary(1)	Lists each index showing its column name and sort order. Groups by table name.
8	Detailed Index(4)	Expands the index details. Groups by table name with each table beginning on a new page.
9	Foreign Key Summary(1)	Shows foreign key with child column name and parent column name. Groups by table name.
10	Detailed Foreign Key(4)	Shows foreign key name, definition, relationship type, cardinality, nullability, verb phrase, inverse verb phrase, and referential integrity on update and referential integrity on delete. Each table grouped to start on a new page.

Table 15–3 Predefined reports—attribute content.

Report Number	Predefined Report Name	*9* Data base	*22* Table	*12* Column	*5* Index	*13* Foreign Key
1	General	9	11	7	3	11
2	Combined	9	15	10	4	12
3	Database	9				
4	Table		11			
5	Column Summary		1			
6	Detailed Column			7		
7	Index Summary		2			
8	Detailed Index				3	
9	Foreign Key Summary		2			
10	Detailed Foreign Key					11

generated from the sample model Patient_LS.vsd. For example: Combined(11) against report number 2, means that eleven pages are generated when you run the Combined report against the sample model Patient_LS.vsd.

You can use the default reports as an initial attribute selection and then change any combination of the checkboxes in the attribute tabs shown in Table 15–5 through Table 15–9. Each default report uses different attributes. Table 15–3 shows you *how many* attributes each default report uses for input. The numbers above the column names in the five columns on the right indicate the number of attribute checkboxes there are in each table attribute category. The numbers in each report row show how may of the *possible* attributes are used by each report. For example, the Foreign Key Summary (report 9) uses only two attributes out of a possible 22 table attributes and 61 total database attributes.

Table Report—Attributes Tab

You use the attributes tab to set checkboxes for up to 61 attributes. The attributes are classified into five mutually exclusive categories: Database, Table, Column, Index and Foreign Key. You can use the Category: drop down list shown in Figure 15–8, to review the state of each checkbox in each attribute category. You can see the five attribute checkboxes for the index category on the left of Figure 15–8.

You can choose to report some or all of the attributes by selecting each category in turn and selecting or deselecting each attribute checkbox within that category. Table 15–4 shows the scope of each category and the number of attributes it controls.

Table 15-4   Table report attributes category scope.

Category	Category Scope	Number of Attributes
Database	The physical target RDBMS, for example Microsoft SQL Server)	9
Table	each table in the schema	22
Column	every column in the schema	12
Index	every index in the schema	5
Foreign Key	every relation in the schema	13

Caution: Do not hunt and peck among the 61 checkboxes in the five attributes tabs, or you might miss lunch. The number of possible sets of four attributes selected from 61 possible attributes gives you over 5 million options. (Tip: try COMBIN(61,4) in an Excel spreadsheet).

You will find it best to develop and follow a structured attribute selection procedure. Your first step is to make sure that you understand what each attribute can give to you. You could start by trying the following procedure to help you to understand VEA's awesome reporting power.

1. Make sure that you understand the meaning of each attribute (see Table 15–5 through Table 15–9).
2. Load the sample model Patient_LS.vsd
3. Choose "General Report" from the "Default to" list shown in Figure 15–6
4. Open each attribute category in turn and check *all* the checkboxes. (Tip: Use the Select All buttons).
5. Export the twelve-page report as an RTF file.
6. Load the RTF file into your word processor.
7. Add footers to show at least file name and page number.
8. Print the report.
9. Take the report and this book to a quiet place.
10. Study the report.
11. As you study the report, write down every report related question that occurs to you.
12. Return to your PC and explore VEA to find the answers to your questions.

Database attributes category

You can use the database attributes tab to select or deselect any of nine attributes shown in Figure 15–9. Table 15–5 shows the meaning of each database attribute.

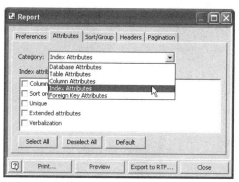

Figure 15–8 Table Report–Attributes tab categories.

Table 15–5 Database attributes meaning.

Database Attribute Name	Attribute Meaning
Target DBMS	Shows the type of RDBMS driver you have selected, (e.g., Oracle).
Number of tables	Gives the total number of tables in your model.
Number of columns	The total number of columns across all tables in your model.
Number of indexes	The total number of indexes across all columns in your model.
Number of foreign keys	The total number of foreign keys across columns in your model.
Last build date	The date of the most recent physical database build.
Extended attributes	Extended database attributes.
Table stats summary	Gives each table name with Notes from the primary key plus, for each table, the number of columns, indexes, and foreign keys.
Include view details	Shows the SQL code used to generate a view that is included in your model.

Table attributes category

You can use the table attributes tab to select or deselect any of the 22 attributes shown in Figure 15–10. Table 15–6 shows the meaning of each table attribute.

Column attributes category

You can use the column attributes tab to select or deselect any of the twelve attributes shown in Figure 15–11. The meaning of each column attribute is shown in Table 15–7.

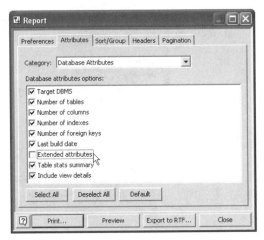

Figure 15–9   Database Attributes.

Figure 15–10   Table Report–Attributes tab.

Index attributes category

You can use the index attributes tab to select or deselect any of the five attributes shown in Figure 15–12. Table 15–8 shows the meaning of each index attribute.

Foreign key attributes category

You can use the checkboxes in the tab header to choose to include Child foreign keys, Parent foreign keys, or both. If you leave both checkboxes unchecked, your foreign key report will be blank.

Table 15–6 Table attributes–attributes category meaning.

Table Attribute Name	Attribute Meaning
Record	The number of each data record in your report.
Physical name	The physical name of each table plus table constraints and code.
Conceptual name	The conceptual name of each table plus table constraints and code.
ID	The internal Visio number for each table plus constraints and code.
Name space	The unique name that you have chosen for this table.
External	Tables that are not external show "No." External tables show "Yes."
Notes	Shows the Notes associated with the tables' primary key. If the primary key is a composite key then no Notes are shown.
Owner	Table owner.
Target DB name	The filename that you have chosen for your target physical database. See Chapters 7 and 11.
Independent	Tables that do not have foreign keys.
Number of columns	The total number of columns in a table.
Number of indexes	The total number of indexes in a table.
Number of foreign keys	The total number of foreign keys in a table.
Primary key	Shows the table's primary key. If the primary key is a composite key, all the columns in the composite key are listed. Code is also shown.
Extended attributes	Extended table attributes.
User defined types	User defined data types.
Summary of columns	Shows the following information about each column in each table: Column named, data type, nullability, value/range.
Code details	Shows the constraint verbalization, type of code, and the SQL code.

You can use the foreign key attributes tab to select or deselect any combination from the thirteen attributes shown in Figure 15–13. Table 15–9 shows the meaning of each foreign key attribute.

Figure 15–11   Column Attributes.

Table 15–6   Table attributes–attributes category meaning–cont'd

Table Attribute name	Attribute meaning
Summary of alternate keys	Shows one line for each alternate key in each table.
Summary of non-unique indexes	Shows one line for each non-unique key in each table.
Summary of foreign keys (Child)	Shows: Foreign key name (table pair), child key and parent key.
Summary of foreign keys (Parent)	Shows Foreign key name (table pair), parent key and child key.

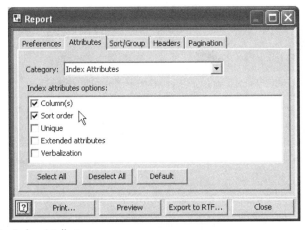

Figure 15–12   Index Attributes.

Table 15-7 Column attributes meaning.

Column Attribute Name	Attribute Meaning
Physical name	Physical column name (to be used in the physical database).
Conceptual name	Conceptual column name (derived from the domain name).
Physical data type	Product specific data type (e.g., Oracle).
Portable data type	One of the 24 built in data types.
Allow NULLs	Defines the nullability of a column.
Value/Range	Shows the permissible values that have been set for each column.
External	Shows if a column that has been defined in a different schema.
Notes	Shows the Notes for each column. (derived from domain notes)
Foreign key role name	Shows all columns with annotations (e.g., index or foreign key).
Extended attributes	Shows all columns plus any extended attributes.
Default value	Shows all columns with any default values that have been assigned.
Check clause	Check clause.

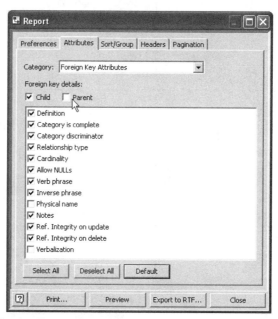

Figure 15-13   Foreign Key Attributes tab.

Table 15–8   Index attributes meaning.

Index Attribute Name	Attribute Meaning
Columns	Shows all columns plus indexes.
Sort order	Shows if the index is ascending or descending.
Unique	Shows all columns, with a summary of the indexes in each table.
Extended attributes	Extended index attributes.
Verbalization	Shows all columns, plus an index summary, verbalization and sort direction.

Table 15–9   Foreign key attributes meaning.

Foreign Key Attribute	Attribute Meaning
Definition	Shows each foreign key name by table, with child column name and parent column name.
Category is complete	Shows foreign key names by table.
Category discriminator	Shows foreign key names by table.
Relationship type	Shows foreign key names by table and whether the foreign key is "identifying" or "non-identifying." (These are IDEF1X terms.)
Cardinality	Shows the foreign keys by table and the verbalized cardinality.
Allow NULLs	Shows nullability of each foreign key.
Verb phrase	Shows the verb phrase that links the parent and child keys.
Inverse phrase	Shows the inverse verb phrase that links the parent and child keys.
Physical name	Shows all foreign keys by table with their physical names.
Notes	Shows notes in the foreign keys' database properties.
Referential Integrity on update	Shows the action to be taken when the foreign key is updated.
Referential Integrity on delete	Shows the action to be taken when the foreign key is deleted.
Verbalization	Gives a full description of all foreign keys.

Table Report–Sort/Group tab

The Sort/Group tab works in exactly the same way as the Sort/Group tab described in the Object Type report in Chapter 9. You can choose to group your report by one of the three options shown in the drop down menu in Figure 15–14. The default sort key is Physical table name.

Physical table names are often short and cryptic. Conceptual names tend to be longer and more descriptive. You can sort by conceptual table name to help you to review database semantics, homonyms, and synonyms. Sorting by physical table name will help you to review your physical naming convention to ensure support for good system performance and ease of use by database performance specialists.

Table Report–Header Tab

The header tab works in exactly the same way as the other headers. Please refer to the Object Type report in Chapter 9 for a complete description of the header tab.

Table Report–Pagination Tab

The pagination tab works in exactly the same way as the other pagination tabs. Please refer to the Object Type report in Chapter 9 for a complete description of the pagination tab.

Table Report–Bottom Row Buttons

The four buttons along the bottom of the window (Print...,Preview, Export to RTF... and Close) work in exactly the same way as in all other reports. Please refer to the Object Type report description in Chapter 9 for a detailed explanation of the function of each button.

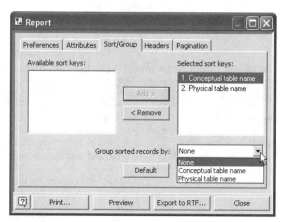

Figure 15–14   Sort/Group.

15.4 Data Types Report

You can use the Types report to report on all aspects of the data types in your database model diagram.

Data Types Report–Selection Tab

You can choose from three data type categories: composite, user-defined, and built-in, as shown in Figure 15–15. If relevant, you can also include any referenced external types that are defined elsewhere. By default, your report sorts by the class of data type and then by type name. You can easily change this.

Table 15–10 summarizes the meaning of these options.

Data Types Report–Attributes Tab

You can select attribute information, such as data type names, base data types, and derived data types, by using the Attributes tab shown in Figure 15–16.

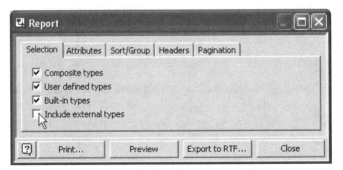

Figure 15–15 Data Types Report–Selection tab.

Table 15–10 Data types report–selection tab meaning.

Selection	Meaning
Composite types	Types with a composite structure.
User defined types	Shows any user defined data types. With physical data type, Notes, and a summary of any related method.
Built in types	Predefined data types for the specific DBMS.
Include external types	External types are data types that you have referenced in your model, but that are defined in a different model.

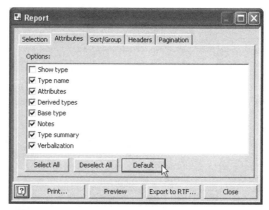

Figure 15–16 Data Types Report–Attributes tab.

Data Types Report–Sort/Group Tab

The Sort/Group tab works similarly to the Sort/Group tab described in the Object Type report in Chapter 9. Please refer to the detailed description of the Sort/Group tab in the Object Type report in Chapter 9.

Data Types Report–Header Tab

The header tab works in exactly the same way as the other headers. Please refer to the detailed description of the header tab in the Object Type report in Chapter 9.

Data Types Report–Pagination Tab

The pagination tab works in exactly the same way as the other pagination tabs. Please refer to the detailed description of the pagination tab in the Object Type report in Chapter 9.

Data Types Report–Bottom Row Buttons

The four buttons along the bottom of the window (Print..., Preview, Export to RTF..., and Close) work in exactly the same way as in all other reports. Please refer to the detailed description of the bottom row buttons in the Object Type report in Chapter 9.

Table 15–11   Data types report types attribute.

Attribute	Meaning
Show type	Creates a placeholder for each individual data type instance. Not for use on its own.
Type name	The data types reported here are the DBMS-specific physical data types.
Attributes	Shows the data type names and their physical types. You must also select at least "Show type" and "Type name" checkboxes to get anything on your report.
Derived types	Derived types.
Base type	Base type.
Notes	Notes for user defined types.
Type summary	Type summary.
Verbalization	Verbalization.

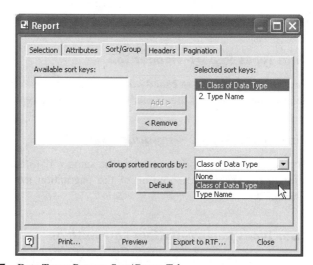

Figure 15–17   Data Types Report–Sort/Group Tab.

Table 15–12   Data types report sort group.

Sort Key	Meaning
Class of Data Type	Sorts your report into the four classes shown on the selection tab in Figure 15–15.
Type Name	Sorts your report into alphabetical order of data type name.

Table 15–13   Data Types report-grouping.

Sort Key	Meaning
Class of Data Type	Groups your data types into the four classes shown in Figure 15–15. (e.g., If you sort by data type name and group by class of data type, your report will have four subsections with data types sorted alphabetically within each subsection).
Type Name	If you group by this sort key, then you will get one report page for each type of data type in your report. For example, if you select only built in types, you will get at least 24 pages in your report–one page for each of the 24 built in data types.

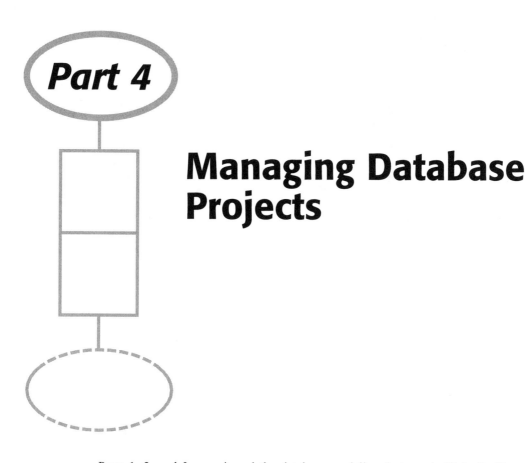

Part 4

Managing Database Projects

Parts 1, 2, and 3 overviewed the database modeling features in Visio for Enterprise Architects and discussed the conceptual and logical modeling solutions in depth.

Part 4 explains how you can manage database changes to keep your models in agreement with each other and with the changes required by domain experts. It also provides practical advice and tips on how to manage and present your database projects.

Chapter 16 shows you how to manage changes to data requirements and how to perform round-trip engineering to synchronize changes across physical, logical, and conceptual models. It also provides details on how to migrate database applications from one platform to another.

Chapter 17 is loaded with practical advice on managing database projects. You learn about best practices in model documentation, model development, and database project management, including tips on presenting and reviewing your models with domain experts or technical specialists.

You learn how to partition a model into pages and how to package a model as part of a database specification document. You learn to use the Visio Viewer to distribute your models to those who do not have Visio installed. This chapter also contains tips on annotating diagrams, using Visio custom properties, and third party add-ins, hyperlinks, and related Visio stencils.

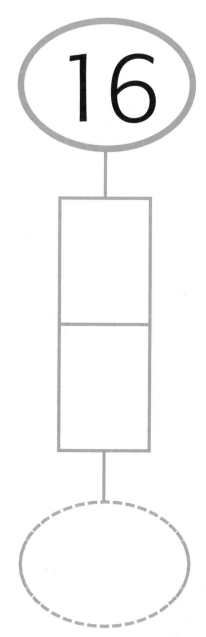

16 Change Propagation and Round Trip Engineering

16.1   Overview

When the ancient Greek philosopher Heraclitus said that "everything is in a state of flux," he was not thinking of data models, but he might as well have been. No matter how good the initial data model and the resulting physical schema, it is almost inevitable you will need to make at least some changes during the life of the database. Good initial modeling will minimize the overall need for changes, and lessen the severity of those changes, but you should still expect to make changes along the way.

Changes to data structures are disruptive, and can have a far reaching impact on existing applications, and the members of a software development team. To minimize this disruption, you need tools that allow you to manage change smoothly and reliably. VEA has some very good facilities for managing database changes.

Making changes at the conceptual level in your ORM source model(s), and then propagating those changes through the logical model and to the physical database schema is the most effective method. The next best alternative is to make changes directly in the logical model and generate them into the physical schema.

The worst alternative is to make changes in the physical database itself, and then update the logical and conceptual models. The toolset in VEA supports all these alternatives, and they'll all be discussed in this chapter. First, we'll discuss managing changes in the modeling environment, and then changes in the physical schema.

> *Note:* Years of observation as a consultant have shown that even the most experienced designers are capable of making truly bone-headed decisions if they bypass the conceptual model when changing existing data structures. ORM conceptual models excel at exposing assumptions, and are easy to validate with users. Because changes usually come about as a result of newly discovered business requirements, changing the ORM model first makes a lot of sense.

16.2   Mapping ORM Changes to Logical Models

Use the facts and constraints listed in Table 16–1 to create a small ORM source model that will be used for the example. The first column shows the fact type as you should type it into the fact editor. The second column shows how to answer the question on the Constraints tab of the Fact Editor. Except where specified, only answer Constraint Question #1 on the tab. The third column shows the verbalization of the constraint. Compare the text in the third column to the output of the Verbalizer window to ensure that you have applied the proper constraints.

The graphical representation of your ORM model should look like Figure 16–1.

Assign the data types and lengths shown in Table 16–2 to the objects in your model. Save your model to a file called Patient_Simple_ORM.

Table 16–1 Fact types and constraints.

Fact Type	Fact Editor Constraint	Constraint Verbalization
Patient has Family Name	Exactly One	Each Patient has some FamilyName. Each Patient has at most one FamilyName.
Patient has PhoneNr	Zero or One	Each Patient has at most one PhoneNr.
Patient was born in Country	Zero or One	Each Patient was born in at most one Country.
Country has Country Name / Country Name belongs to Country	Exactly One (question #1), Zero or One (question #2)	Each Country has some CountryName. Each Country has at most one. CountryName. Each CountryName belongs to at most one Country.

Create an empty database model diagram and add Patient_Simple_ORM to the database project list. If necessary, refer to Chapter 7 for detailed instructions on building database projects with ORM source models. After building the database project you should have a small database model diagram that looks like Figure 16–2.

Your column names may have slightly different names or be in a different order to that shown in Figure 16–2. Chapter 7 discusses controlling automatic column name generation from the ORM level, and Chapter 12 discusses renaming and re-ordering columns in the database model diagram. Save your database diagram model to a file called Patient_Simple_Build.

Caution: If you change a table or column name, or reorder any columns in the database model diagram, you will be prompted to migrate the changes back to the ORM source model. See Figure 10–26 at the end of Chapter 10 for a screen shot of the migration prompt and a more detailed explanation.

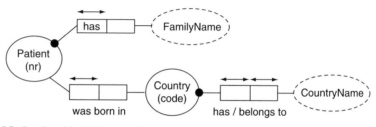

Figure 16–1 Graphical ORM model.

Table 16–2 Object types and data types.

Model Object Type	MS SQL Server Physical Data Type
Country	char(2)
CountryName	varchar(30)
FamilyName	varchar(30)
Patient	smallint
PhoneNr	varchar(14)

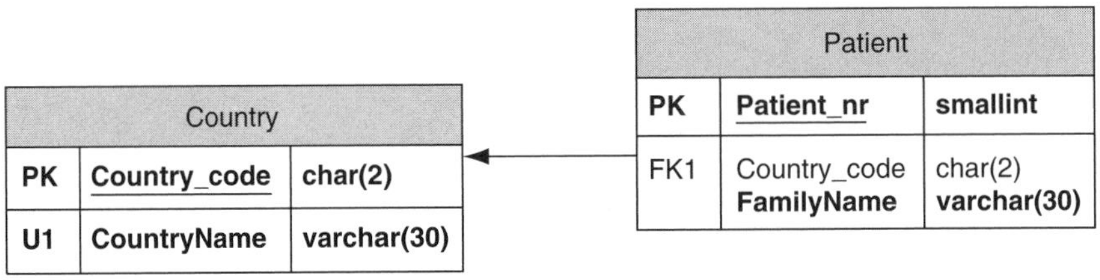

Country

PK	Country_code	char(2)
U1	CountryName	varchar(30)

Patient

PK	Patient_nr	smallint
FK1	Country_code	char(2)
	FamilyName	varchar(30)

Figure 16–2 Logical Model.

Generate a physical database schema from the database model diagram Patient_Simple_Build. Generating physical schemas is explained in Chapter 11. For this exercise, do not create the schema through a DDL script, but instead use an ODBC connection. This physical schema will be used later in the chapter to demonstrate change management, so create the physical schema before proceeding with the following example.

1. Save a backup copy of your models to an alternate subdirectory. This backup will preclude the need to start from scratch if you make a mistake that causes unexpected results.
2. Assume you are creating the "Patient_Simple" data model for a hospital's information system. Some of the users just came forward with a new piece of information and a new requirement.
   a. (New Information) Thirty characters is not long enough for CountryName. A check of the ISO website shows that for the current list, the longest country name is 44 characters.
   b. (New requirement) The system must store a list of the patient's self reported drug allergies. Many patients don't report any allergies, while other patients report allergies to many drugs.
3. To accommodate the information in item (2a) simply click on the CountryName object in your ORM model and edit the data type. Change the length from 30 to 44. Chapter 4 explains how to change data types in an ORM model.

Table 16–3   Drug allergy fact type.

Fact Type	Fact Editor Constraint	Constraint Verbalization
Patient is allergic to Drug	Zero or More (question #1); Zero or More (question #2)	It is possible that some Patient is allergic to more than one Drug and that more than one Patient is allergic to some Drug.

4. To accommodate the new requirement in item (2b), you must add a new fact type to the ORM source model that will allow the system to store information about patient drug allergies. The fact type and constraints are listed in Table 16–3.
5. Adding the drug allergy fact type in the previous step automatically created a new object type called "Drug". Give this object type a reference mode of "Name", and assign it a physical data type of varchar(5). Clearly, five characters is too short for a drug name, but we'll fix this mistake later as part of the three-way synchronization process. Your modified ORM model should look like Figure 16–3.
6. Save the updated ORM source model and open the file Patient_Simple_Build.
7. Choose Database > Project > Build from the main menu. If prompted to migrate changes back to the source, answer No.

> *Caution:* Under certain conditions, you may be prompted to migrate changes from the logical model to the ORM source model. As a general rule, answer No if this prompt appears while you are attempting to build a project.

Migrating changes from a database model diagram to an ORM source model means altering the ORM source model to the consistent with the database model diagram.

Usually, you are building a project because you just made changes to the ORM source model, thus temporarily causing the ORM model to be inconsistent with

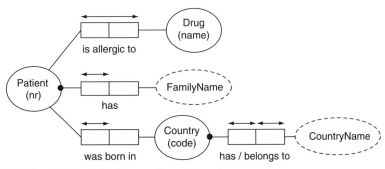

Figure 16–3   ORM model with new drug allergy fact.

the existing database model diagram. If you answer Yes to the migrate question, VEA will push information from the old database model diagram back into the ORM source model, thus undoing the ORM changes that you just made.

The general rule of answering No only applies while building a project. For instance, when saving a logical database model diagram that you have just modified by renaming columns or tables, or adding trigger code, it makes sense to migrate changes back to the source model.

8. The project build updated the length of the CountryName column from 30 to 44. The project build also created a new table, though it is not yet visible on the drawing surface.

9. From the Tables and Views window, drag the new table out onto the drawing surface. Your database model diagram should now look like Figure 16–4. The names in your diagram may be different because of the name generation options you have chosen in the ORM model. CountryName is now 44 characters long, and the new table has the proper key structure to record a list of allergies for patients who report them.

10. Rename the "Patient_allergic_Drug" table to "Patient_Drug_Allergy." Save the file Patient_Simple_Build. When prompted to migrate changes, answer Yes.

16.3 Migrating Logical Model Changes to ORM Models

Until now, the only changes you have migrated back from a database model diagram to an ORM source model have been name changes. However, you can also make actual structural changes in the database model diagram and migrate them back to the ORM model.

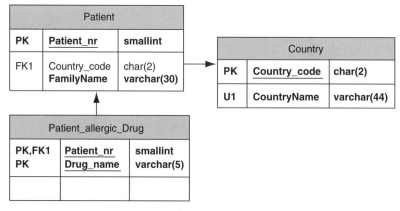

Figure 16–4   Result of a project build after changing the ORM model.

Note: Making structural changes in the database model diagram and migrating them back to the ORM source model is like eating soup with a fork. You can do it, but it's messy. It is much better to make the changes at the conceptual ORM level and push them down into the database model diagram through a project build. Try to limit your changes in the database model diagram to things that can be done *only* at the logical level, like writing triggers and procedures, creating views, renaming tables etc. Even most column names can be controlled from the ORM name generation rules, although some columns must be explicitly renamed at the logical level.

Generally, the bigger the change at the logical level, the uglier the migrated result will be in the conceptual model. The conceptual ORM level contains more semantic information than the logical level of the database model diagram. You can always go from a state of greater information to lesser information, as occurs during a project build. When going from the logical to the conceptual level, some of the information is simply not available.

For instance, ORM supports a verbalized predicate for *every* relationship, regardless of whether the objects involved will become tables or columns at the logical level. However, at the logical level, predicate information is available *only* for relationships between tables. Logical information that does not originate at the ORM level is thus tagged with ugly "placeholder" predicates.

ORM also provides more than one way to model certain situations, even though the end logical result is the same. This is a great advantage in creating understandable data models that can be validated with users. However, when pushing logical information up into ORM, Visio has to arbitrarily choose an ORM modeling technique, whether or not it is well suited to the particular situation.

The simplest way to understand these issues is to go through an example. Make a *copy* of the backup ORM source model that you created at the beginning of section 16.2. Do not use the model that you used in section 16.2, and do not use your actual backup model. Call the copy Copy_Patient_Simple_ORM.

1. Create an empty database model diagram. Add the ORM model Copy_Patient_Simple to the project list and build the project. When prompted to save the database model diagram, name the file Copy_Patient _Simple_Build.
2. The database model diagram that you just built should look like Figure 16–2.
3. In the database model diagram, use the editing tools to build the Patient_Drug_Allergy table. Make sure to add the foreign key. Your database model diagram should look like.
4. Figure 16–4 with the exception of the table name.
5. Save the database model diagram and answer Yes when prompted to migrate changes back to the source model.
6. Open up the ORM model (Copy_Patient_Simple_ORM). The drawing pane will look exactly as it did before. However, you will notice two new fact types in the

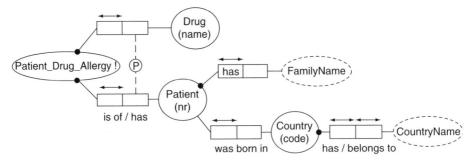

Figure 16–5   ORM model after migrating a table from the logical level.

Fact Types pane of the Business Rules window. If you don't see the Business Rules window, choose Database > View > Business Rules from the main menu.

7. Drag the new fact types (they both contain the word "Patient_Drug_Allergy) onto the drawing surface. The result is shown in Figure 16–5.

The new object type Patient_Drug_Allergy corresponds to the table you created in step three. The object type uses an external primary reference constraint, which is explained in section 5.2 of Chapter 5. Figure 16–5 and Figure 16–3 are conceptually equivalent, but Figure 16–3 is a more natural expression of the facts, and easier to interpret. You can make Figure 16–5 easier to read by putting meaningful words in the predicates of the new fact types.

16.4   Updating Physical Schemas with Logical Model Changes

Regardless of how you make changes to your logical database model diagram, those changes must be propagated into the physical database schema. For this example, we'll use the ORM source model and the generated database model diagram from section 16.2

You generated a physical in Section 16.2 prior to changing the length of the CountryName object, and prior to adding the drug allergy fact type. In this example, you'll use VEA's Update Wizard to update the physical schema with the changes you made to your model.

1. Open the file Patient_Simple_Build.
2. From the main menu choose Database > Update to invoke the Update Wizard (Figure 16–6). By default the Generate a text ... and Detect Changes ... check boxes are selected. Select the Update Database checkbox as well. Click the Next button.
3. On the second page (Figure 16–7), highlight the DSN that you used to first create the physical schema in section 16.2, and click Next. You'll be asked to furnish logon credentials for your database (Figure 16–8). Depending on how your

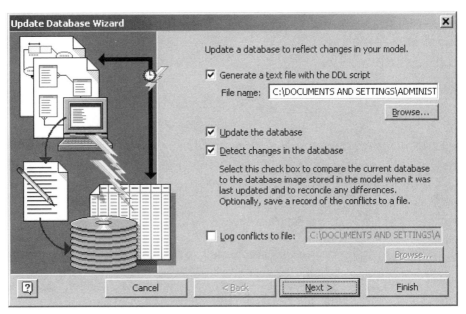

Figure 16–6 Update Wizard, page one.

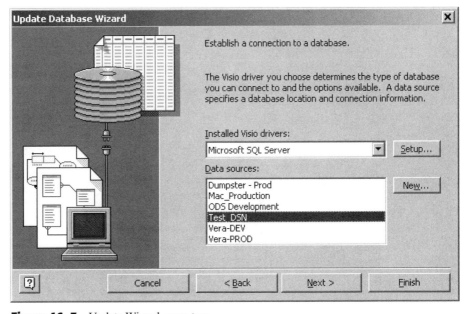

Figure 16–7 Update Wizard, page two.

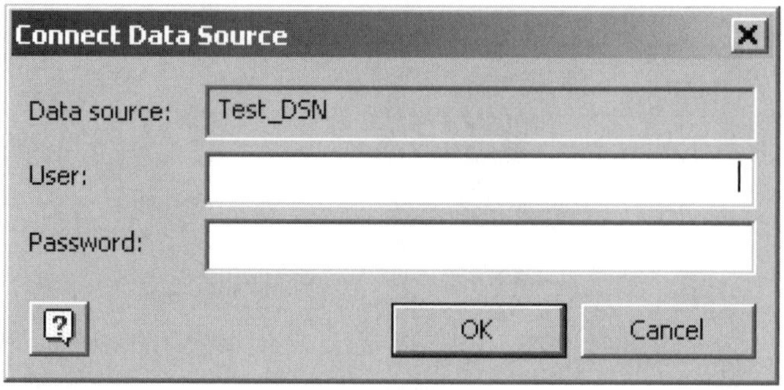

Figure 16–8   Database Connection Prompt.

DSN is defined, either supply a username and password or leave the fields blank and click OK.

4. Once you have successfully connected, VEA displays a message saying that it is comparing the physical schema with the reverse engineered model. You may find this message a little confusing, since you have not yet specifically asked VEA to reverse engineer the physical database. However, VEA did extract an image of the database immediately after you first generated the physical schema in section 16.2. When the compare is finished, you should see a screen like Figure 16–9.

How can there be "no conflicts" when you know for a fact that the physical schema doesn't have the new Patient_Drug_Allergy table, and that

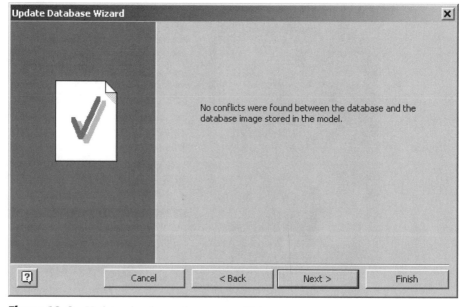

Figure 16–9   Update wizard page three, no conflicts.

CountryName in the physical schema is only 30 characters long instead of the new 44 characters?

The message "no conflicts" does not refer to a comparison between the physical schema and the current model, but between the physical schema and an image of the last known state of the physical schema, which VEA extracted and stored in the current model during the initial physical schema generation. Because the physical schema has not been changed since the initial generation, it matches VEA's database image, and there is no conflict. This comparison will be explained further in section 16.6.

5. Page four of the update wizard (Figure 16–10) shows a list of the model changes that are about to be generated into the database. This list gives the user a last chance to confirm that the changes are correct before updating the database. Click Next to continue.

6. VEA will validate the model for platform specific rules and report the results in the final page of the update wizard (Figure 16–11). Click Finish to update the database.

7. View the generated SQL script (screen shot not shown), and save the script to *something other than the default filename*. You will need to look at the script for the discussion of data migration in section 16.8.

8. Use SQL Server Enterprise Manager to verify that the physical database has been changed.

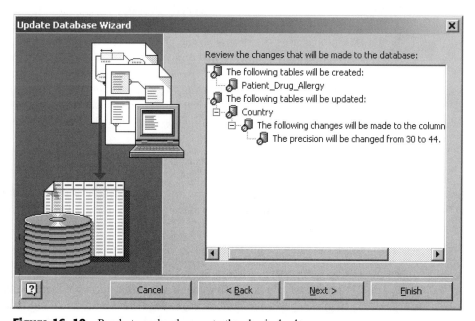

Figure 16–10 Ready to make changes to the physical schema.

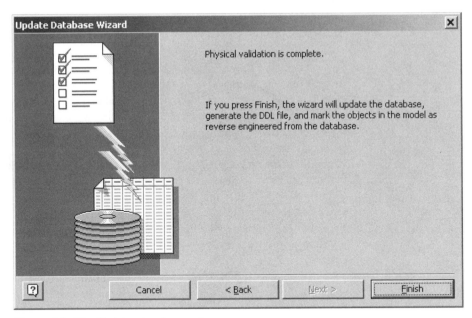

Figure 16–11   Update wizard, page five.

16.5   Refreshing Logical Models with Physical Schema Changes

VEA's "Refresh" feature allows modelers to capture changes that were made at the physical database level and automatically incorporate them into the model. You will find it more effective to change a physical schema by first changing the logical model and then propagating the change to the physical schema. As it is, people in even the most disciplined environments make physical schema changes that bypass the data model.

To show the refresh feature in action, we must first introduce some changes into the physical schema of which the logical model is unaware. Let's simulate a situation where somebody changed the length of one column, and added an entirely new column without telling the data modeler:

1. Using SQL Server Enterprise Manager, change the length of the FamilyName column in the Patient table from 30 to 35.
2. Using SQL Server Enterprise Manager, add a column called PhoneNr to the Patient table. Assign the column a data type of varchar(14), and make the column nullable.

To refresh the database model diagram, follow these steps:

1. Choose Database > Model > Refresh from the main menu.
2. Connect to your database using the DSN that you used in the previous example.
3. VEA compares the current physical schema with its stored image of the last known state of the physical schema. The image was last stored in the model

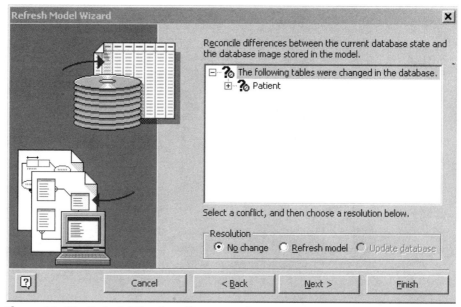

Figure 16–12 Refresh Wizard conflicts, tree collapsed.

during the update that you performed in section 16.4. In that image, FamilyName was defined as varchar(30), and PhoneNr did not exist, leading to a conflict in the Patient table as shown in Figure 16–12.

4. Expanding the tree in the conflict listing (Figure 16–13) shows that there are actually two conflicts, the new PhoneNr column, and the changed length for the existing column FamilyName.

5. The wizard allows you to resolve conflicts on an individual basis, or en masse. To resolve an individual conflict, highlight it and select the Refresh model radio button. To resolve a group of conflicts, highlight the root node for that group and choose the Refresh model radio button. When you choose the Refresh model radio button, the question marks will disappear for the resolved conflicts, as shown in Figure 16–14.

6. The final page of the refresh wizard (Figure 16–15) gives you chance to confirm changes before updating the logical model. Click Finish to update the database model diagram.

7. Your database model diagram now includes the column PhoneNr in the Patient table, and the column FamilyName has been lengthened as shown in Figure 16–16.

8. Save the database model diagram, and when prompted to migrate changes, answer Yes. This migration will "push" the new PhoneNr object and the updated FamilyName length back into the ORM source model.

9. If you wish to confirm the migration, open the ORM source model, right click on the Patient object, and choose Show Relationships from the context menu.

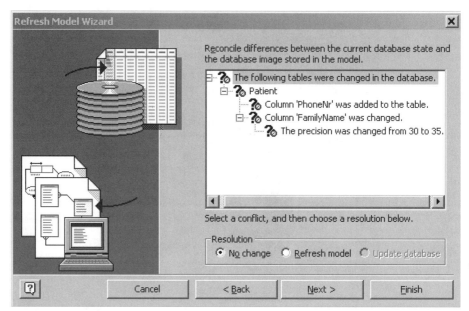

Figure 16–13   Refresh Wizard conflicts, tree expanded.

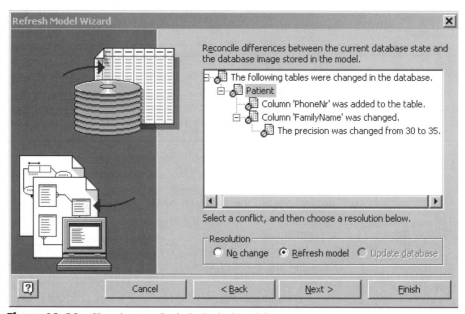

Figure 16–14   Choosing to refresh the logical model.

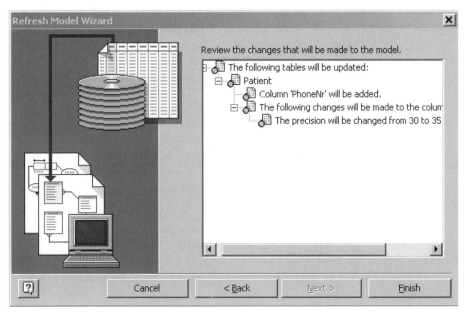

Figure 16–15 About to update the model.

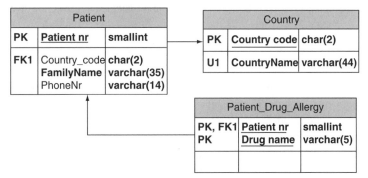

Figure 16–16 Refreshed database model diagram.

The graphical representation of the new fact "Patient has PhoneNr" will be automatically placed on the diagram.

16.6 Three-Way Synchronization

From the previous two sections, it may appear that the Update Wizard is designed solely to propagate model changes to the physical schema, while the Refresh Wizard is designed to propagate changes from the physical schema back to the logical model.

Actually, the Update Wizard can handle bi-directional changes in a single operation. This operation is known as *three-way synchronization*.

One may reasonably ask, "If the wizard is synchronizing the physical schema and the logical model, why is it called 'three-way synchronization' instead of 'two-way synchronization'?" Perhaps a more accurate description would be "three way comparison, yielding two way synchronization". To reliably synchronize the model and the physical schema, VEA must compare three things: The previous state of the physical schema (which should match the previous state of the logical model), the current state of the logical model, and the current state of the physical schema.

Synchronization involves managing the transition of multiple objects from one state to another. As long as the physical schema cannot be changed through means other than the Update Wizard, things are straightforward. Assuming a newly created model, here is the sequence of steps:

1. Use the Generate Wizard to create a physical schema from the model. The physical schema and the model are both in state A.
2. Modify your model. The model is in a new state (call it M for modified).
3. Use the Update Wizard to change the physical schema. Via its database driver and an ODBC DSN, the tool issues DDL commands to change the state of the physical schema from state A to state M.

However, the physical schema *can* be changed through other means. Let's insert a step 2.5 and assume that someone made changes to the physical schema using database administration tools. Now the physical schema is *not* in state A, but in an unknown state X.

If, in step four, the tool merely issues DDL based upon the transition from state A to state M, the results will be unpredictable. The DDL might work if state X is not too much different from state A, or the DDL may fail completely. Even if the DDL succeeds, the physical schema will still not be in state M, but in some new state that is a mix of state M and state X. Worse, the new mixed state may break applications that depend on the database. No one will know exactly what the new state is, so fixing theproblem will be very difficult. Reliable synchronization requires the model to comprehend the physical schema's full state just prior to synchronization.

The solution is for VEA to compare the physical schema's current state (X) with physical schema's previous state A, which is also the previous state of the logical model. Conflicts between state X and state A must be resolved by adjusting the physical schema, the model, or both. Only after all conflicts are resolved so that the model fully comprehends the physical schema can the tool issue the appropriate commands to reliably synchronize the schemas.

Figure 16–17 shows a graphical representation of the major steps.

In step A of Figure 16–17, the physical schema has information that is unknown to the logical model and vice versa. Upon conflict resolution in step B, the logical model knows everything about the physical schema, though the physical schema may not fully comprehend the logical model. With the conflicts resolved, the tool can issue the proper DDL to reliably synchronize the physical schema with the logical model (step C).

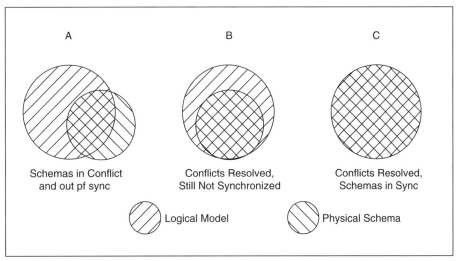

A   B   C

Schemas in Conflict Conflicts Resolved, Conflicts Resolved,
and out pf sync   Still Not Synchronized Schemas in Sync

Logical Model   Physical Schema

Figure 16–17 Resolving conflicts and synchronizing Schemas.

There is one big problem with this solution: The critical comparison of the previous physical schema and logical model state (A) and the current physical schema state (X) cannot be done because state A no longer exists. The physical schema is in state X and the model is in state M. Visio avoids this problem by storing an image of state A in the model immediately after it first generates the physical schema. Now that all the pieces are in place, here is the new sequence of steps:

1. Use the Generate Wizard to create a physical schema from the model. The physical schema and the model are now both in state A.

1.5 VEA extracts an image of state A from the physical schema and stores the image in the model file.

2. Modify your model. The model is now in state M, but the stored image remains in state A.

2.5 Someone else changes the physical schema. The physical schema is now in state X.

3. Invoke the Update Wizard to change the physical schema.

3.5 The Update Wizard compares state A and state X and reports all conflicts. For each conflict, you choose to either update the model or to update the physical schema. The logical model now fully comprehends the state of the physical schema.

3.6 Through its database driver and an ODBC DSN, the tool issues DDL commands to synchronize the physical schema with the logical model.

3.7 As a final step, VEA automatically extracts an image of the new physical schema, and replaces the stored image of state A with this new image. VEA is now ready for the next time you use the Update Wizard.

Now that you've slogged your way through the abstract example of three-way synchronization, let's see it in action. Since you just refreshed your model, it is in the same state (call it state A) as the physical schema. VEA has stored an image of state A in your model:

1. Use SQL Server Enterprise Manager to modify the physical schema.
   a. Drop the table Patient_Drug_Allergy.
   b. Lengthen the column Patient.PhoneNr from 14 to 20 characters.
   The physical schema is now in state X.
2. Now modify your model:
   a. In section 16.2, you purposely made the data length for the Drug object too short. Correct this "mistake" by changing the physical data type of the Drug object from varchar(5) to varchar(30) in the ORM source model.
   b. You decide that FamilyName should only have a length of 30 after all. Change the length in the ORM source model from 35 to 30.
3. Rebuild the project to get an updated database model diagram. (If you are prompted to migrate changes, remember the general rule about *not* migrating changes when building a project). The logical model is now in state M, but the stored image is still in state A.
4. Invoke the Update Wizard by choosing Database > Update from the main menu. Your screen should look like Figure 16–6. Select the Update Database checkbox and click the Next button.
5. Highlight the appropriate DSN, and connect to your database. See Figure 16–7 and Figure 16–8 for screenshots.
6. VEA compares the original state of the physical schema and logical model (A) with the new state of the physical schema (X), and reports the conflicts. In Figure 16–18, the tree has been expanded to show the detail.
7. Assume that the lengthening of PhoneNr from 14 to 20 was correct, but that the dropping of the Patient_Drug_Allergy was incorrect. You thus want to update the model to reflect the longer length for PhoneNr but you want to put the dropped table back into the physical schema.
   a. Highlight the node that that says The precision was changed from 14 to 20 (under the node that says Column 'PhoneNr' was changed) and select the Refresh model radio button (Figure 16–19). The question marks next to the codes dealing with changes to the patient table are replaced with icons of documents, indicating that you have elected to resolve this conflict by updating your model. Question marks remain for Patient_Drug_Allergy because this conflict is still unresolved.
   b. Highlight the node that says Patient_Drug_Allergy and select the Update Database radio button (Figure 16–20). The question marks are replaced with database icons, indicating that you have chosen to resolve this conflict through a database update. Click the Next button
8. The next page of the wizard confirms the changes that will be made to the model. In Figure 16–21 the tree has been expanded to make the detail visible. Click Next to update the model and continue. Your logical model now fully comprehends the physical schema (you just reached step B in Figure 16–17).

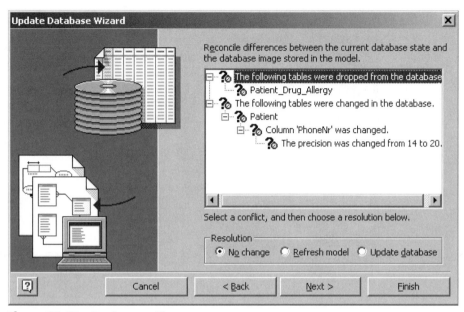

Figure 16–18   Database conflicts.

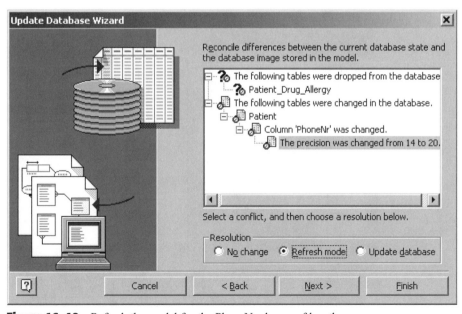

Figure 16–19   Refresh the model for the PhoneNr change of length.

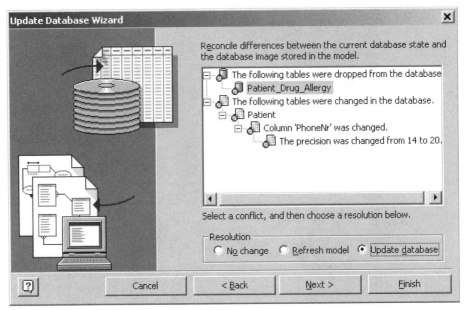

Figure 16–20   Update the database with the Patient_Drug_Allergy table.

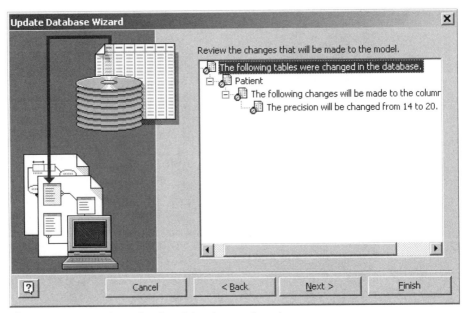

Figure 16–21   Update Wizard model update confirmation.

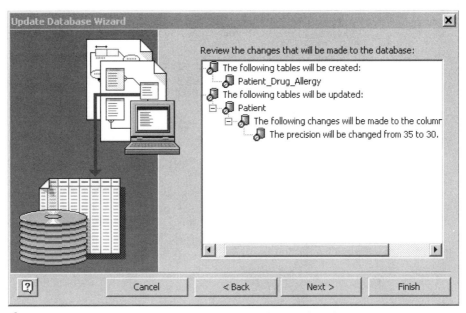

Figure 16–22 Update Wizard physical database update confirmation.

9. The wizard can now issue the proper commands to synchronize the physical schema with the logical model. Figure 16–22 shows the changes that will be made to the database.

Note that you made changes only to the ORM source model and, yet the tool will issue commands to the database to actually create a table. The three-way synchronization feature recognized that the table Patient_Drug_Allergy had been dropped from the physical level. Instead of trying to change a non-existent object, the Wizard issues a CREATE TABLE statement. Click Finish and your physical schema will be synchronized with your logical model. Remember to save your logical model and answer Yes to the migration question.

16.7 Code Synchronization and Transfer

When you create a physical schema from your logical model (see chapter 11), VEA automatically produces the DDL necessary for creating tables and views. However, most databases provide their own procedural language for writing functions and procedures. You can write stored procedures to enforce constraints that cannot be handled by key structures, or to enforce business rules.

Contrary to the advice of many web application design books and self proclaimed application design experts, executing business logic in stored procedures is often an excellent idea. Writing business logic in stored procedures does *not* violate n-tier architecture, and well written procedures will not become "entangled" with the database.

It is important to keep business logic in a separate layer, but the physical place where that logic resides is not a guiding principal of n-tier architecture. Instead of executing all business logic in a physically separate application tier that must constantly query and write to the database as it processes business logic, it often makes sense write those rules into procedures right on the database. The application server merely supplies the correct arguments while invoking the procedure. All the heavy lifting is done by code that has local access to the data in a secure environment on a very powerful machine.

Even if you don't buy into the concept of using stored procedures to enforce business rules, over time you will end up writing significant amounts of code for things like archive triggers, complex views and the like. The VEA Synchronization and Transfer features can help you manage your code.

Code Synchronization

Thankfully code synchronization has nothing to do with three-way synchronization, so the explanation will be much simpler, and it won't require any diagrams.

Many organizations tightly manage the database code written by their database administrators and developers. In these workplaces, any database code must first be put into a script that follows standard formats and tested for accuracy. Once the script is known to work, it is stored under source code control. Often, the basic DDL is separated from the trigger and procedure code.

This extra management work may sound bureaucratic, but it often makes a lot of sense. Moving among environments (development, test, and production) is much easier and less error prone if all the objects are scripted first. Restoring after a crash or setting up another environment is much easier if different versions of the scripts are clearly identifiable. As a side effect of these policies, you often have to provide trigger and procedure scripts in separate files that can be managed apart from the main data model.

The need to keep your code in separate files can lead to a quandary: On the one hand, your database code needs to reside in separate files, and on the other hand, the most natural place to store and work on your code is in the modeling tool. Code synchronization and mirror files and solve this issue.

A mirror file is a plain-text file that resides outside your model. You associate the mirror file with database code objects in VEA. Once the mirror file and database code object are associated, VEA will synchronize the mirror file and database code object on demand. The synchronization can go in either direction, file to code object, or code object to file. Let's take a look at an example:

1. If it isn't already running, open your Patient_Simple_Build file.
2. If you don't see the Code window at the bottom of the screen, select Database > View > Code from the main menu.
3. Click the New button in the Code window (Figure 16–23) to open the code editor.

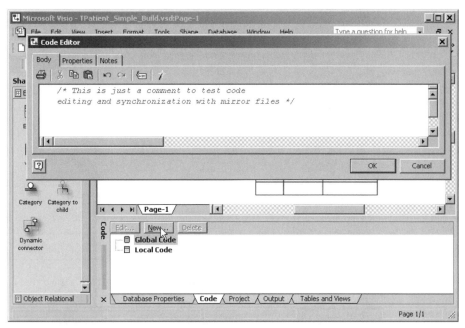

Figure 16–23   Invoking the code editor.

4. Put anything in the textbox on the Body pane of the editor. You don't have to write a real procedure to see how mirroring and code synchronization work.

5. Switch to the Properties pane of the code editor (Figure 16–24). Provide a name for your code object in the Name text box. For this test, the Type doesn't matter, so accept the default choice. Put a file name in the Mirror file text box. Notice that the mirror file name and the name of the code object are completely independent, making it easy to adhere to file naming standards even if they differ from database object naming standards. Click OK to close the code editor

6. So far you have specified the mirror file but not created it. To actually create the file, choose Database > Code > Synchronize from the main menu to invoke the code synchronization window (Figure 16–25). Highlight the code object you just created and click the Update Mirror Files button. The first time you click this button the mirror file will be created and populated with the body of your code object. Subsequent clicks will merely update the existing file. The Update Model Now button copies the contents of the associated mirror file into the body of the code object. Both operations completely overwrite the target.

7. As soon as you click one of the Update buttons, the list on the synchronization window will be replaced by a message (Figure 16–26). The list on the synchronization window is only populated with code objects whose body differs from the content of their mirror files. If you make a change to the code object or its mirror file, that object should be automatically put back on the list. The Refresh button forces VEA to look at all code objects and mirror files. Keep this model open for the next example.

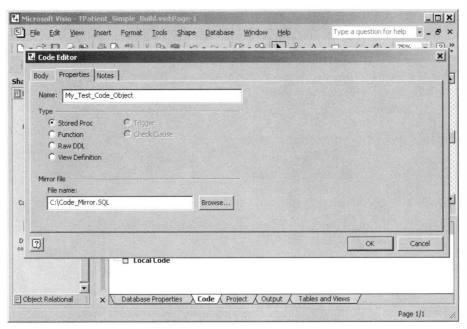

Figure 16–24   Code editor properties pane.

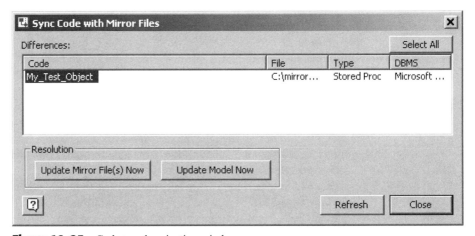

Figure 16–25   Code synchronization window.

Code Transfer

Use this feature if you must have the same data model support more than one server. In most work situations, this single model, multiple back end scenario would be extremely rare.

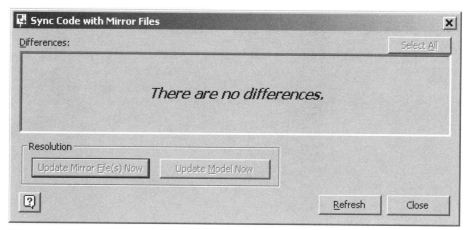

Figure 16–26   Code synchronization window after sync operation.

Code objects are tied to the default VEA database driver. If you change from say, the MS SQL Server drive to the Oracle Server driver, your code objects will "disappear." The code objects will still be in the model, they are just not available with the alternate driver. This makes sense, because Oracle PL/SQL code is significantly different from TSQL.

VEA gives you the option to selectively copy (or move if you so desire), code objects from one environment to another. Let's say you are re-hosting an Oracle database onto MS SQL Server. You might start by reverse engineering the existing database and all the procedure and trigger code. You would then switch to the MS SQL Server driver to adapt the tables. However, once you switched drivers, you would notice that all the trigger and procedure code stayed with the Oracle driver, and is not available to you.

Using Code Transfer, you can copy the Oracle code into the MS SQL Server version of the model. From that point, you can keep the code separate and work on converting the Oracle code to SQL Server. Fortunately, the Code Transfer feature is a lot easier to use than it is to explain, so let's take a look:

1. While still in your model from the previous example, change the default VEA database driver by choosing Database > Options > Drivers from the main menu. Highlight the Oracle Server selection and click OK (Figure 16–27).
2. Look in the Code window to confirm that your code object has "disappeared."
3. Invoke the Code Transfer window by choosing Database > Code > Transfer from the main menu.
4. Highlight MS SQL Server in the Source DBMS text box and Oracle Server in the Destination DBMS text box. (Figure 16–28). Choose the Copy radio button in the upper right corner. Click OK to make the transfer
5. Your code object is now transferred, and looking in the Code window will confirm it.

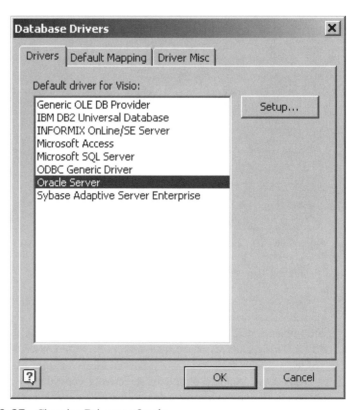

Figure 16–27 Changing Drivers to Oracle.

> *Note:* Remember three important points when using Code Transfer:
> 1. The default option for code transfer is Move. Make sure to change this to Copy if you want to leave the source code object undisturbed.
> 2. If you had a mirror file specified for the code object under another database driver, the specification is removed from the target code object upon transfer. This is good, because you don't want to update mirror files meant for SQL server with Oracle code and vice versa.
> 3. You are not actually connecting to any database servers when performing a Code Transfer. You are merely making the code available under more than one database driver.

16.8 Data Migration

It's time to dig out the DDL script that you saved in step seven of section 16.4. As you recall, you generated that script the first time you used the Update Wizard to propagate a change from the logical model to the physical schema. The script modified the existing country table by lengthening the column from 30 to 44 characters. If you can't find the script on your computer, don't despair, because the salient portion is reproduced in

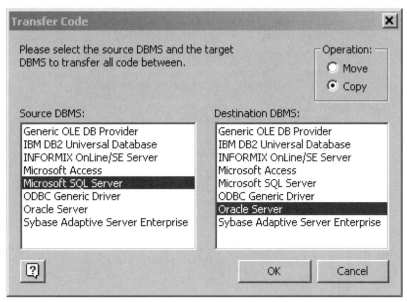

Figure 16–28   Code transfer window.

Figure 16–29. To save space, the "go" command and extra blank lines between each SQL statement have been removed.

The purpose of this script is to modify a column in an existing table. Some database engines allow a column to be lengthened by a simple ALTER TABLE statement, but some engines require that the table be dropped and rebuilt with the new desired column length. The VEA tool is not tied to a specific database engine, so the designers have chosen to have the script drop and re-create the table, which will work with any database server. The VEA generated script is designed to preserve any data in the existing table.

Lines one and two of the script drop the foreign key constraint in the Patient table that points to Country Lines four through eleven of the script create a backup table called Country_IMO and insert the rows from the current table into the backup table.

Line 13 drops the current table. The DROP TABLE statement would have failed if the foreign key were not removed from the Patient table in lines one and two. Lines 15 through 22 create a new Country table with the correct data length for CountryName, and insert the rows from the backup table. Line 24 drops the backup table because it is no longer needed. Finally, the foreign key in the Patient table is restored in line 31.

VEA's automatic data migration can save you a lot of work, but there are some important caveats to remember:

1. Be careful when performing this operation on large tables.
   a. VEA makes an exact copy of the table, and duplicates each existing row in the backup table. If the existing table has millions of rows, there is a good

```
Edit2*                                                                    _□×
 1 alter table "dbo"."Patient"
 2        drop constraint "Country_Patient_FK1"
 3
 4 create table "dbo"."Country_IMO" (
 5        "Country_code" char(2) not null,
 6        "CountryName" varchar(30) not null)
 7
 8 insert into "dbo"."Country_IMO" ("Country_code", "CountryName")
 9    select "dbo"."Country"."Country_code",
10            "dbo"."Country"."CountryName"
11    from "dbo"."Country"
12
13 drop table "dbo"."Country"
14
15 create table "dbo"."Country" (
16        "Country_code" char(2) not null,
17        "CountryName" varchar(44) not null) ON 'PRIMARY'
18
19 insert into "dbo"."Country" ("Country_code", "CountryName")
20    select "dbo"."Country_IMO"."Country_code",
21            "dbo"."Country_IMO"."CountryName"
22    from "dbo"."Country_IMO"
23
24 drop table "dbo"."Country_IMO"
25
26 alter table "dbo"."Patient"
27        add constraint "Country_Patient_FK1" foreign key (
28                "Country_code")
29        references "dbo"."Country" (
30                "Country_code") on update no action on delete no action
31
```

Figure 16–29 Fragment of a change script.

chance you will run into disk space issues on the server during the INSERT. If you are working in the middle of the night, you may have to page a data base administrator (DBA), and s/he will not be happy with you. You'll be tempted to make up a story about "unknown processes" bringing down the server, but don't do it. The DBA will find out the truth anyway and you'll be branded a "reckless liar" instead of just "reckless."

    b. Even if the server has plenty of disk space, the account with which you connect may be restricted in such a way as to make the insert fail. Heavy restrictions on your account are more likely if you have been branded a "reckless liar" in the past.

2. If you add mandatory (NOT NULL) columns to existing tables, there are special considerations for the INSERT statement that restores the backup data into the new table.

    a. The new table now has a not null column for which there is no backup data. In these cases, VEA will insert the literal value 'I' for numeric and textual columns, which will work fine. For date columns, VEA will insert the result of a date function in the column.

b. If the target column is the subject of a unique index, the INSERT statement that restores the backup data will fail. The only way around this is to make the changes via script instead of ODBC connection. Remove the unique index from the script and put the index on later, when you can get the real data.

c. If the new column is mandatory *and* a foreign key, you need to do some preparation prior to running the update. You have a few choices to handle this situation.

    i. Edit the script to remove the NOT NULL qualification for the new column. Also remove the code that uses a literal value in the INSERT statement. Run the DDL. Update the table with real data when available, and then restore the NOT NULL constraint.

    ii. Manually insert a row in the "parent" table that has 'I' as its primary key so that the INSERT of the child row will succeed. This is the only method that will still allow you to use an ODBC connection and bypass the script.

    iii. Edit the script to either remove or disable the foreign key constraint that covers the target column. The INSERT of the literal value will then work. After you UPDATE the table with real data, restore the foreign key.

16.9 DDL Script vs. Automated Update

With the exception of the last section, this chapter has focused on making updates via a direct connection to the database, instead of running DDL scripts. Using a direct connection can save you a lot of time, but remember: Speed Kills!

There are many cases where using a script is preferable to an automated update. First among these cases are any changes to a production database. Using any type of automated tool that issues DDL to modify the schema of a production database is very risky. Only software salesman and outplacement consultants trying to drum up new business will tell you differently.

Always use a script that you have thoroughly tested to modify a production database. It goes without saying that you do the modifications during a planned time when the database will be unavailable to users. You should also consider writing a "back out" script that will restore the database to its original state if something goes wrong with your changes.

Modifications to Production are not the only concern. Even changes in the Development environment can benefit from scripting. While you are making the actual modifications to the physical schema in the Development environment, software coding has to stop. For most projects, this means two to ten people will not work during the changes. A well executed schema change should take only minutes, but problems can turn those minutes into hours. Ten people wasting half a day is an expensive proposition. Using a script that you have thoroughly tested is a good way to guarantee that the changes go smoothly and quickly.

VEA can generate new database scripts without ever connecting a database, but to generate scripts for modifying a database, VEA must connect to a server. On the surface, it appears that you cannot benefit from VEA's Update Wizard technology without letting the tool update your database automatically.

Actually, there's great news. It's quite easy to set up things so that the Update Wizard generates all your change scripts, but you still execute the scripts yourself after testing. All you need in MS SQL Server terms is two small databases, called "Model" and "Scratch." The equivalent Oracle term for what you need is "account."

Once you have set up your new databases (or accounts), follow these steps:

1. VEA will never connect to anything but the Model database. When working on your model, use the Update Wizard and an ODBC connection to manage your physical schema.
2. When the first version is of your schema is ready, use VEA to generate a DDL script of the schema.
3. Run the script in the (empty) Scratch environment as a test.
4. When satisfied with step 3, run the script in Development and Test. In larger shops, you can give the script to dba and s/he will run it. The dba can also modify the script to account for different physical sizing in Development and Test.
5. When make additions or changes to data model, don't allow the Update Wizard to actually modify the schema in the Model database until you get agreement from the developers that the new model is correct.
6. Once you have the agreement, use the Update Wizard to update your schema via an ODBC connection to the Model database. Have VEA produce an SQL script when is makes the changes. This script is your schema modification script.
7. Export the schema from the Development environment. If the database has only a small amount of data, include the data in your export.
8. Clean out the Scratch database.
9. Import the Development schema into the empty Scratch database.
   a. (Conditional) If you had to export the Development schema without data, you *must* put representative data into the Scratch database. An empty schema is *not* a good test. Some modification scripts will succeed with an empty schema, but fail with a populated one.
10. Run the script you created in step 6 against the Scratch environment.
11. If you experience any problems, repeat steps 8 – 11 until the script runs perfectly and gives the correct results.
12. Agree on a 15 minute window during which everyone will stay out of the schema in the Development environment.
13. Run the perfected script against the schema in the development environment. If you did your testing properly, you'll always stay well within the 15 minute window.
14. Repeat steps 5 through 13 for subsequent changes.

These steps may seem somewhat involved, but the actual execution is very smooth and quick. The biggest advantages are:

1. The Update Wizard writes the basic change scripts for you, saving a lot of work.
2. You retain the safety, flexibility, and reproducibility of scripted changes.
3. All testing occurs in steps (8 through 11) that don't affect anyone else.
4. Most importantly, you *know* that script will work when you run it in step 13, because you have tested it thoroughly.

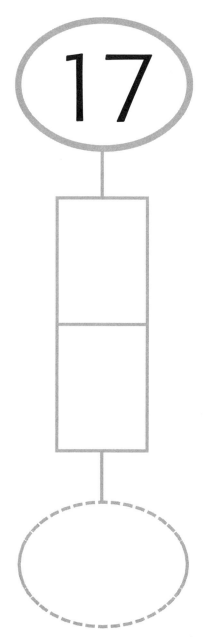

Other Features and Best Practices

17.1 Model Reviews and Presentations
17.2 Librarianship
17.3 Distributing your Database Models

This chapter covers several areas of importance, including how to get an ORM project started, model navigation, annotations, backgrounds, the Visio Reader, shape protection, and several other topics. Many of these topics are useful in extending the richness and features that Visio as a platform brings to the modeling team.

17.1   Model Reviews and Presentations

Presentations: Purpose

Before you start preparing the material for your presentation, take some time to think about the result you want to achieve and how best to achieve it. For example, a management presentation to propose a database modeling project will not be the same as a discussion with a domain expert group to define the facts and entities in their working area. The following paragraphs summarize these two scenarios; a management presentation to get approval for a database modeling project and a typical domain expert fact review that would take place during the project.

Scenario 1: Presenting a Database Modeling Proposal

Suppose that you want to get approval for a database modeling project. How do you go about it? Do you eulogize about the power of database modeling and ORM or should you take a different approach? In this first scenario, you will learn about the fundamentals of getting approval for your database modeling project. You can use this scenario for your own project by changing the content but keeping the structure.

Let's discuss the parameters for your presentation. Plan for 30 minutes. Executives have a short span of attention! Seven slides will allow an average of three minutes per slide, plus ten minutes discussion time. So what can you say about a topic in 3 minutes? If you talk at the rate of one word per second, you get only 180 words of talk time per slide. You should balance this at 90 words for you, and 90 for audience comment. If they don't say anything, remember that finishing early gets a better audience rating! Let's now take a look at what to say on each slide.

Slide 1: State the purpose of the presentation. Say what you want your audience to agree to. Make it short. For Example: "Good afternoon. The purpose of this presentation is to get your approval to assign a budget of $0000 for a database modeling project." You can say that in 15–20 seconds. Say it, and move on to slide 2.

Slide 2: State the consequences of the problem. For example: "One of our customers has been awarded $0000 damages because of a failure in one of our products. The cause of the failure has been traced to a conflict in our product specifications. There are hidden inconsistencies in the data structure of the software that we developed to run in our products." Now if your company sells electronic tin openers and a customer won a small personal injury claim, then the budget for which you plan to ask may be small. On the other hand, if you are NASA and you just lost a $125 million spacecraft near

Mars then your project will be a bit bigger. (A true story: Mars Climate Orbiter loss: http://mars.jpl.nasa.gov/msp98/orbiter/) [Figure 17–1].

It might take you 30–40 seconds to say what you have to say on Slide 2. Say it and move immediately to slide 3.

By now you should have the undivided attention of your audience, and you are only one minute into your show! If you don't have audience focus by now, you are on the way to losing it. However, let's assume that the assembled company is now hanging on your every word and asking themselves three questions 1: "How come?" 2: "Who screwed up?" and 3: "Can they pin this thing on me?" Some people might verbalize the first two questions. Not many people will admit that they are also asking themselves the third question. If anybody goes for their cell phone at this point, you know why they're calling.

Slide 3: State the root cause of the problem. Slide 3 should summarize the answer to question 1: "How come?" You can safely ignore the other two questions because they will probably already be in the hands of Legal and Human Resources. If the person on the cell phone suddenly leaves the room, you know that they are not interested in the rest of your presentation because she now has other problems to solve.

It might take you two or three minutes to summarize the answer to "How Come?" because you have to explain the organizational procedures that caused The Problem without laying the blame on any individual or group of individuals. Such problems are usually systemic rather than personal anyway so keep well away from the witch hunt mentality. Focus on the procedures that caused The Problem because your project is going to propose new procedures to replace the procedures that caused The Problem.

Slide 4. Now that the remaining audience has a good grasp of The Problem and its root cause, they should be thinking "Oh My! What can we do about The Problem?" You answer that question with Slide 4 by reviewing the cause of The Problem and introducing The Solution which is of course your project proposal. You have to explain the difference between the way things are done today and they way you are proposing they should be done. This will probably also take up the next slide as well.

Slide 5. This should summarize The Solution, which is your database modeling project. You should end by explaining why things will be much better (The Benefits.) when The Solution is implemented.

> SEPTEMBER 30, 1999
> **Likely Cause of Orbiter Loss Found**
> The Peer review preliminary findings indicate that one team used English units (e.g., inches, feet and pounds) while the other used metric units for a key spacecraft operation. Full Story

Figure 17–1   Mars Climate Orbiter Report.

Slide 6. Use this slide to summarize the differences between your project proposal and that way things are done today. Cite examples of other projects that have succeeded by using your new method. You should aim to help your audience to see that your approach is more effective than the approach that caused The Problem you described in Slide 2. It will help to have a hyperlink in Slide 6 that lets you jump back to slide 2.

Be prepared with lots of evidence. Slide 6 is where you will need to use the power of hyperlinks, OLE, Visio layers, and all the other technical wizardries explained elsewhere in this chapter. You need to be able drill down directly from each point in Slide 6 to the detailed information that supports each of your points. You can use a hyperlink to jump to a layered Visio drawing. You can use OLE and a wheel mouse to rescale each drawing by a factor of fifty or more. This helps you to quickly zoom in and out of the detail.

Slide 6 should of course include a hyperlink to a Gantt chart showing all the details of your Project Plan. Your audience will not want to see the details of your plan; they will just want to know that you have done your homework. This is where you slow down a little for questions. If you have prepared well, you will probably be about 15 minutes into your show. However, you are going to need the extra time to answer the questions from finance that you will get when you reveal slide 7.

Slide 7. This is where you go for gold. Slide 7 should contain the question that you want the audience to answer. "Request for authorization of a database modeling project budget of $0000." In Slide 7, you should summarize the benefits of approving your project, the budget, state a delivery timescale, and ask for the money. If you have done a good job, your budget will be approved, but not before you have run the gauntlet of the obligatory grilling by finance! At this point you should be prepared for zillions of detailed questions from finance as they contemplate the consequences of restructuring the corporate budget for the 99th time since the CEO approved the annual budget just a few weeks ago. As long as Slide 7 has hyperlinks to a sophisticated multidimensional spreadsheet that has all the financial answers, you will be OK.

If you are now thinking "That was a fine explanation of a project proposal but does not have much to do with database modeling." just keep on repeating the phrase, "No Bucks; No Buck Rogers!" To be an effective database modeler, it makes sense to know how to defend your project which means knowing how to defend your budget. Remember, you may not be aware that you are competing for funds with someone like a tough production director who wants a new robot for the production line and can prove the efficiency gains—in budget terms of course.

Scenario 2: Reviewing the Facts!

OK! So you are now a database modeling project manager with a big budget and nobody but you to move things forward! Step 1 is to use some of your budget to hire an assistant to recruit your project team and to send them on courses such as Microsoft's new ORM based SQL Server database modeling course number 2090A.

See http://www.microsoft.com/TRAINCERT/SYLLABI/2090afinal.ASP

Step 2 is to get the project moving right along by getting the facts from domain experts. You can use scenario 2 as a template for this task.

Getting agreement between domain experts.

You may have to begin by persuading departmental managers to release high value individuals to attend your fact finding workshop. (Or, even to persuade the managers to attend themselves. Gasp!) If you need to justify the attendance of the people you want, then adapt the approach outlined in scenario 1. Tip: You will find it helpful to have a "Scenario 1" presentation tucked away in your laptop ready for instant deployment. You never know when it might be needed! Let's assume that you managed to convene a fact finding meeting. What's the best way to run it?

Slide 1: Introduction: The three questions. Thank everyone for attending and invite each person to make a self-introduction. Give your audience a few moments to prepare by giving each person a card with the three questions you want them to answer: "What is my name?", "Which department am I from?", and "What do I hope to achieve by attending this meeting?". You will find this to be a very effective ice breaker – even if the people already know each other.

Slide 2: The group assignment. Use this slide to state the business problem, for example: "We just lost a $125 million spacecraft due to inconsistencies in facts and data definitions. We are here to help to ensure that such an event is not repeated."

Slide 3: Get the facts. Facilitate a discussion on how things are done today. Start by explaining what a "fact" is and how you go about defining one (see Chapters 4 and 5). Hand out a worked example on a single sheet of paper and walk everyone through the process of defining a fact. Make sure that you emphasize the importance of fact examples and object definitions. Use a second sheet of paper to explain a few simple constraints. It might take an hour or more before everyone "Gets it."

Next, organize your audience into teams of two. Then hand out five sheets of paper that look like the example you just used, but that have blanks to be filled in. Tell your audience that the next break will come after they have collectively agreed on five fact types. As each fact type is agreed, add it to your model. It helps to have your laptop hooked up to a large screen projector so that every member of the audience can clearly see you add the new fact type and can give their agreement before you store the latest version of the model with a new name. Repeat this fact finding procedure for the rest of the meeting. Have a 10 minute break every hour so that you can organize the fact types into pages. When you reconvene, begin by presenting a summary of the model as it now is.

You can adapt this approach to review existing facts. To review facts, prepare reports before the meeting (see Chapters 9 and 15) and hand the reports out as the basis for discussion. Invite the members of your audience to explain how their part of the organization uses and maintains the facts. Use questions to draw attention to potential inconsistencies. For example: your financial department may have lots of information about "accounts" that refers to bank accounts. However, the sales manager, whilst still concerned about bank accounts (his own for instance) may be more accustomed to using the word "Account" to mean a customer as used in "Account manager." As the facilitator, you can choose to referee a long battle for ownership of the word "Account" or you can use ORM domains to establish two separate ORM object types such as "CustomerAccount" and "BankAccount" and get agreement on that.

If you are unable to reach agreement and both parties want to continue to use an identical term to mean different things (the homonym problem) then write some text in the Database Properties Notes field to describe the situation and the action that has been taken. Then use the Database Properties "Name Space" function to give a unique system identity to each of the two usages.

Review one fact at a time and continue until you get agreement on the definition of all the facts. Take a 5 minute break every hour. Continue until each member of your audience has agreed on the definitions that should be written into the Database Properties "Notes." field. If you have a large audience it may take 5 minutes, 15 minutes or even more to get agreement on each fact, so try to limit fact finding reviews to a maximum of ten people.

The duration of the review will depend on the number of people in your audience, your skills as a facilitator, the effectiveness of your preparation, and the number of facts you want to review. You can use a ballpark estimate of 40 fact types a day for a fact review but set a lower target for fact discovery meetings. For example, it might take you two or more days to review a 5NF database model with 100 tables. Remember to select the audience so that you have those who understand the facts and those who can approve any changes to the facts. They may not always be the same people!

Support each fact review with printed reports from VEA (see Chapters 9 and 15). This will allow the members of your meeting to make notes and to think. When each fact is agreed, update your model immediately. At the end of the meeting, print a copy of the updated reports and store your updated model in a tool such as Visual SourceSafe. If there are business consequences, such as a change to corporate policy, sales documentation or application software updates then be aware that the change may commit your organization to significant expenditure in order to harmonize terms between departments and to implement the changes into existing computer applications. It's a good idea to get ready for the next finance grilling by updating your Scenario 1 support material.

For each fact review, you will need relevant database model diagrams and verbalized reports. You might consider making a standard "one fact" PowerPoint presentation that you can reuse for each fact by hyper-linking the appropriate diagrams into each slide. If you have a large screen projector then you can use OLE and a wheel mouse to click on a Visio database model object in your PowerPoint slide and drill down to the detail. Adding hyperlinks and layers to structure your material will help to reduce the time it takes to discuss each fact.

Presentations: Designing Your Material

What's in a page?

First, you have to rethink what you mean by a "page." With paper documents, you have no alternative but to use separate physical pages. With Visio, you have much more flex-

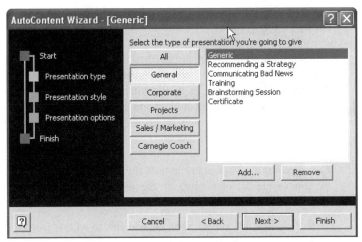

Figure 17–2 Microsoft PowerPoint AutoContent Wizard.

ibility. The main question is not about "pages" but about what you want to say and how best to say it.

The diagrams for a model may be spread over several Visio pages. Think of a page as a placeholder for a concept you want to explain or a point you want to make. So the way you decide what to put on a page is by thinking about your audience and what you want to say to them. If you are short of ideas, try starting with the AutoContent Wizard in Microsoft PowerPoint as shown in Figure 17–2.

When you have chosen the main headings and sequence for your presentation you can begin to develop and organize your Visio database model material.

You should use each theme in your PowerPoint slides as a focal point for the hyperlinks to your layered Visio database model diagrams. Designing the PowerPoint show first will provide the context you need to decide how to layer your supporting database model diagrams.

Whether you use PowerPoint or not, you still have to structure your Database Models using Visio pages. You may have already done this as part of your database model development process. Pagination is explained in Chapter 3 and in Visio Help.

Layers
You can use layers to create a deep structure through which you can navigate during a presentation. You can hide such things as annotations you created by adding shapes from other stencils. You can easily set up layers, assign shapes to each layer and then show or hide the layers as required. Use Visio Help and some experimentation to develop your skills in using layers for database modeling. Layers give you a way of structuring your database models to meet your presentation needs. If you put too many shapes on a page, the drawing becomes harder to understand.

You can use Visio layers to create a deep structure in your database model. You can hide things such as annotations until you need them. You can assign database model components to each layer and then show or hide the layer to fit in with your PowerPoint show.

To set up a layers. Layers are defined in the Layers Properties Window which is found in the main menu (View > Layer Properties). See Figure 17–3.
Remember this location, as this is where you also select which layers to make visible. To create a new layer, select New and enter a layer name (see Figure 17–4).

You can add as many new layers as you need to support your presentation strategy. This example shows four layers:

Layer example. This example uses the first page of the Patient conceptual model and the four layers defined above. To create the Patient All Layer:

Select all shapes for this layer.
Right-Click any object, then choose Format > Layer from the context menu.
Select the Patient All layer (see Figure 17–6).
Select "OK".

Figure 17–3   Main Menu—View—Layer Properties.

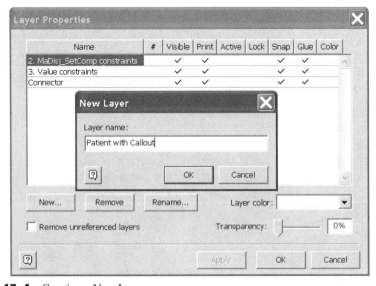

Figure 17–4   Creating a New Layer.

Table 17-1 Layering the patient model.

Layer	Layer Scope	Things to include
1	Patient All	All shapes on the page.
2	Patient Only	Patient object and the callout.
3	Patient Related Objects	Patient Only and All objects on the page – no roles.
4	Patient Object Roles	Patient Only. Patient Related Objects. Selected Roles Only.

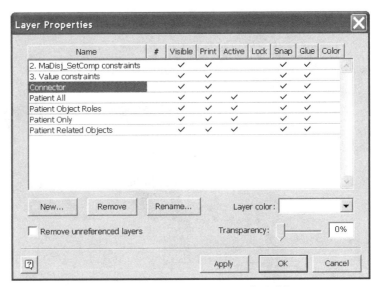

Figure 17-5 All defined layers for the Patient Conceptual Model.

This sequence is repeated for each layer, only the selection of objects and the assigned layer change.

To create the Patient Only layer, select the Patient, Callout, and the connection line shapes. Take care when selecting shapes because there are more individual shapes on the page than you may realize. Assign all four layers to these shapes. This is the smallest layer (view), however, these shapes are also part of each higher level in the structure.

To create the Patient Related Objects layer, select all the ORM object shapes then assign these objects to all except the Patient Only layer. The lower level is not assigned, however, this layer and all higher levels are assigned.

To assign shapes to the Patient Object Role layer, select the fact types of interest for this layer, select all the role boxes, connection lines and the external constraint, and then assign this to the Patient Object Role level and Patient All Layer.

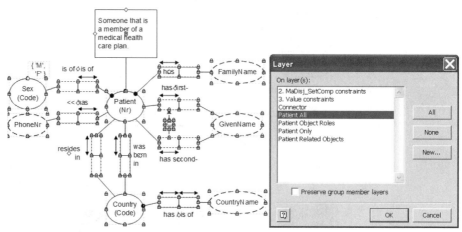

Figure 17–6   Creating the Patient All Layer.

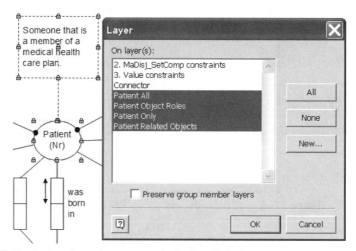

Figure 17–7   Assign shapes instances to the Patient Only Layer.

Viewing by layer example. Once the layers are defined and the shapes are assigned to the layer, you can view the drawing layer by layer. The easiest way to select the view is to right-click on the drawing and choose View > Layers. The Layer Properties window opens for you to select the layer you want to view. To display a layer, check the layer. To hide a layer, uncheck the layer. In Figure 17–10, the Patient Only is the only layer that is visible. Click on Apply to see the effect while leaving the Layer Properties window open.

Now make the Patient Related Object visible as well (Figure 17–11). Select Apply again.

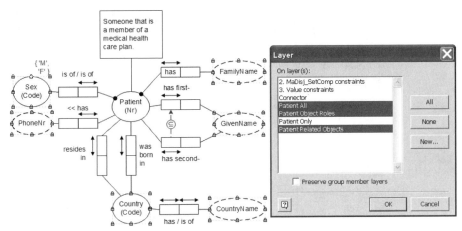

Figure 17–8 Assign shapes to the Patient Related Objects Layer.

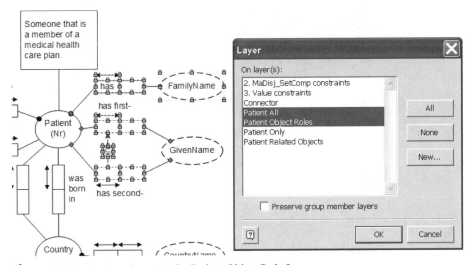

Figure 17–9 Assign shapes to the Patient Object Role Layer.

Now make the Patient Object Role visible as well (Figure 17–12). Select Apply again.

To view all you have two choices. You can select the Patient All layer and then click on Apply, or you can uncheck all except for Patient All and then Apply. See Figure 17–13.

You need to think carefully about your layering strategy before you assign shapes to a layer. You can use a hierarchical structure, as in this example, or you can make a flat, subject area structure. Layers are a general Visio feature and are not unique to database models. You can also use these techniques to structure a Logical Model. This may help with IDEF0 diagrams.

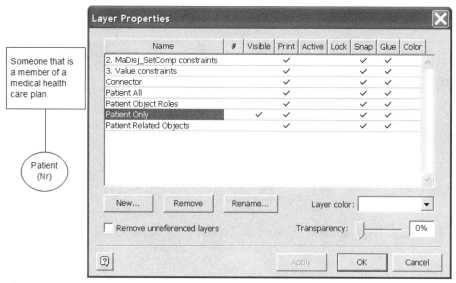

Figure 17–10   Patient Only Layer.

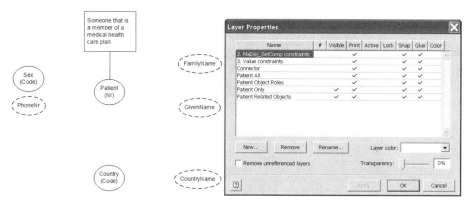

Figure 17–11   Patient Related Objects Layer.

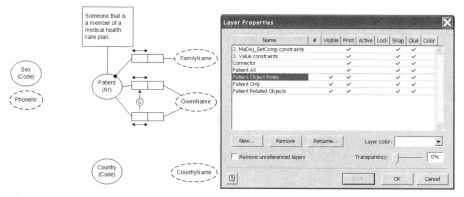

Figure 17–12   Patient Object Role Layer.

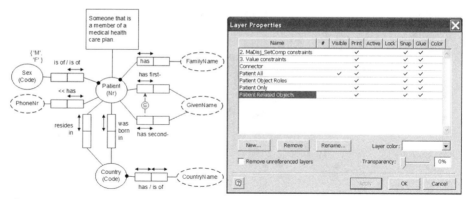

Figure 17-13 Patient All Layer.

You should design a stable layer structure *before* you add shapes to the layers. If you don't do this then you may spend a lot of time editing layers rather than assigning shapes. You can use colors in each layer but make sure that you use color wheel principles mentioned elsewhere in this chapter.

Using Visio custom properties

Many Visio drawing elements have pre-defined custom properties, and you can also create new custom properties. The ORM and Entity Relationship stencil shapes typically do not have predefined custom properties.

To create a custom property, you right click the shape and select Shape → Custom Properties. You will see the message "No custom properties exist, would you like to create customer properties now?" Select "Yes."

The example shown in Figure 17–14 adds a custom property to help you to make a note of when this entity was approved by the review team. To create several properties select "New" and enter the information for the other properties one by one.

Select "OK" when you are done creating custom properties. Going back to the shape on the drawing, right click on the shape, then select custom properties. Now a custom properties window appears and you can enter data into the new property as shown in Figure 17–15. For example, you can enter the approval date from your fact review as explained in Scenario 1 above. The "Define" option opens the custom property definition.

Adding hyperlinks

You can hyperlink to other pages in the same drawing, other pages in a different drawing, to other file types, and directly to objects on the web. Our example link is an internet address *www.orm.net*.

To set up a hyperlink, first select the shape to host the hyperlink then from the main menu choose View > Hyperlinks to open the hyperlink dialog box shown in Figure 17–16. You can use Address Browse to browse your computer, a computer on the network or

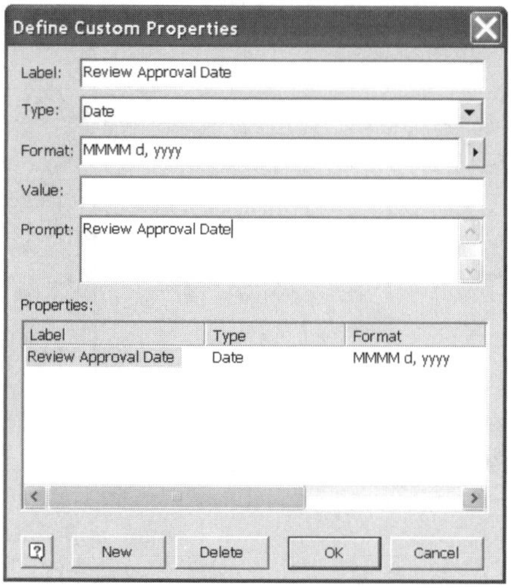

Figure 17–14   Creating a custom property.

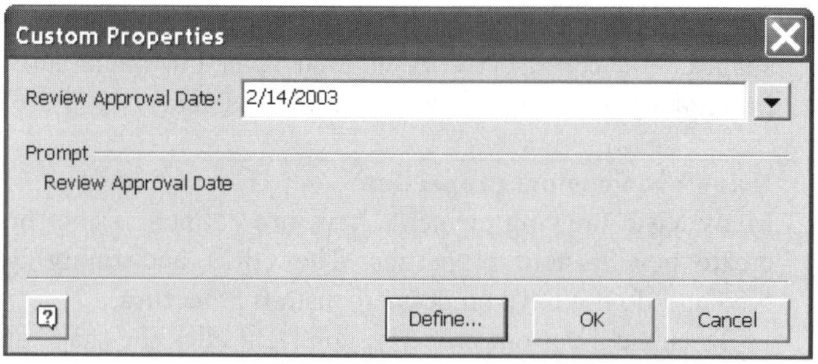

Figure 17–15   Viewing custom properties.

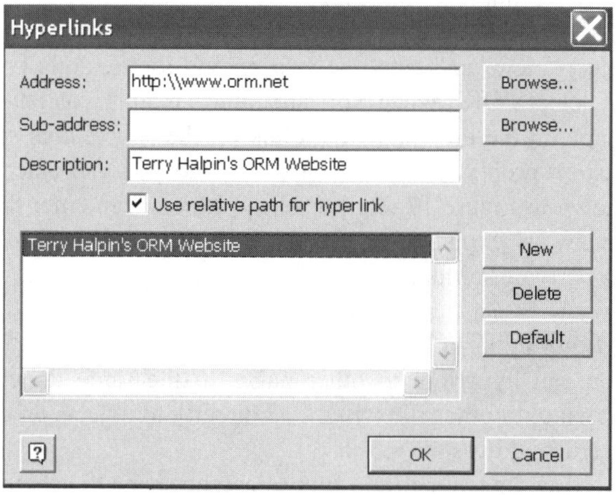

Figure 17–16   Hyperlink Definition Window.

the internet. Sub-Address browse is constrained by the Address Browse and displays the parts of the address to which you can make a direct link. For example, the sub-address can be a page in a Visio drawing, a tagged paragraph in MS Word or one of many other possibilities. If there is no sub-address then there are no linkable components in your target document. You can use any shape as the source for a hyperlink, however, you can only sub link if your target object supports sub linking.

To hyperlink to another page within the same drawing you only need to enter a page name in the Sub-address. The Address is not required.

To hyperlink to another Visio drawing, enter the file path/name in the Address and the specific page name, if desired, in the Sub-address. The file path/name can be to your machine or to any networked computer to which you have access permission.

Sub-addressing capability depends on what the target file type supports. You may be limited to a link to the beginning of the file. For example, when linking to MS Word, you can link to the file. You may or may not be able to link to a specific location in the file. Selecting Sub-address returns known link targets within the file. You can link to a specific spot if the author provided tags which support linking.

To link to an internet address, browse until you locate the target address. Then copy the address using Ctrl+C, and paste it into the hyperlink address using Ctrl+V.

You can hyperlink to other pages in the same drawing, to a page in another drawing or to most other documents on the web.

Annotating Visio diagrams with shapes

You can enhance your database diagrams with illustrative graphics by using Visio's other stencils. To add additional stencils choose File > Stencil and select your stencil from the menu. For example the Annotation Stencil is located at File > Stencils > Visio Extras > Annotations. When selected, the new stencil will appear in the open stencil list. To use an individual stencil, click on its header to make it the active stencil. You may find it best to choose your stencils after you have made your list of presentation objectives and you know exactly what you want to say. On the other hand, browsing stencils can sometimes help you to clarify your ideas about what you want to say.

In Figure 17–17(a) the block shapes stencil was used to note that these two tables are sourced from the marketing division. In Figure 17–17(b) an icon from the callout stencil was used to note why there is a hardware table. In Figure 17–17(c) the category note is from the annotations stencil and explains how Item is typed as a Hardware Item.

You can add UML shapes from the UML stencil, but you cannot modify them directly. If you want to embellish a UML shape, use a shape from the block diagram stencil.

Using other Visio stencils

Visio has many stencils. To use another stencil, choose File > Stencils from the main menu and browse until you find the stencil you want. The stencil is added to your open stencil stack, which is usually located on the left side of the drawing, as shown in Figure 17–18. Click on a stencil header to see and use shapes from the stencil.

Some stencils have intelligent shape behavior. These shapes have shape behavior. These shapes have associated behavioral code. When using these shapes in a drawing that is not of that specific type, you can use the image of the shape, but no intelligent

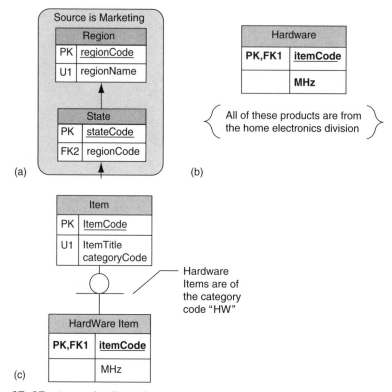

Figure 17–17   Annotation Examples.

behavior is possible in your drawing. It is merely an image. UML and Network shapes with embedded intelligence will provide a shape, but not the associated behaviors that work in their own category. The ORM Diagram has ORM shapes but no modeling functions. The Express-G template has shapes for the Express-G notation (ER) but no modeling functions.

Some ORM constraints are not visible on the drawing surface. They are present in the constraints for the object, but no image is shown on the page. You can simulate the constraint on the page by using the appropriate shape from an ORM diagram stencil. The Express-G template contains shapes for drawing ER diagrams in the Express-G notation but does not have any intelligent shapes. Express-G is the graphical component of the Express formal information requirements specification language as described in ISO standard 10303-11. Express and Express-G are components of STEP (Standard for the Exchange of Product Model Data), an international standard for the computer-interpretable representation and exchange of product data.

Foreground and background

By default, all Visio pages are foreground pages. If you want to create a background to put a background feature on every foreground page you must begin by creating

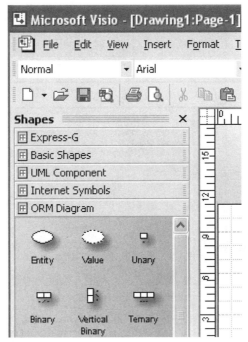

Figure 17–18 Visio Stencil Stack.

foreground page that contains all the background shapes that you want to use. A divisional logo is placed on the upper left of a foreground page (Figure 17–19).

When you are done adding shapes, choose File > Page Setup > Page Properties and set the page as a background. Enter a name for your new background page and click OK.

To apply the background page go to the page and again return to File > Page Setup > Page Properties and assign the background page, in Figure 17–20 the background page name is set to "Background." Click OK to finish.

You must apply a background to each foreground page on a page by page basis (Figure 17–21). You can add many shapes and properties to a background page, for example, a fill color, images, and text. The shapes on the background page will appear on each foreground page in the same spatial position as they appear on the background page. Take care to ensure that you place the background shapes where they will not

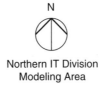

N

Northern IT Division
Modeling Area

Figure 17–19 Logo in the upper left corner of page.

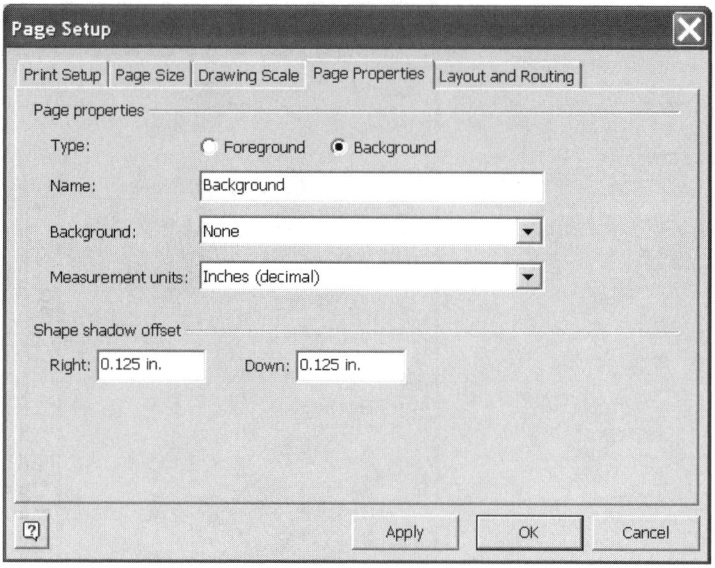

Figure 17–20   Setting the page as background.

interfere with the shapes on any of your foreground pages. If you are making a lot of pages, you will find it helpful to set structural standards for all foreground pages. For example, if you always want a background logo with some text along the top of each foreground page, then design all foreground pages to start below your own "upper margin" line.

Using color

Color helps to differentiate objects on the drawing surface. You can color any Visio shape in any of your database diagrams by right clicking the shape and choosing Format from the menu. Color can add structure or create chaos. Color selection is a complex process, and you should apply color wheel principles to get the right effect. You can find a color wheel explanation at *http://hort.ifas.ufl.edu/TEACH/floral/color.htm*.

The color wheel has three categories: primary, secondary, and tertiary. The three primary colors are red, yellow, and blue. These colors are used to create all other colors. When you combine two primary colors, three secondary colors are formed. You can make one of the six tertiary colors by combining a primary and an adjacent secondary color. Different colors are different wavelengths of light. A "clash" between two colors happens when the two light waves combine to overload the optical system of your eye. If you want to make extensive use of colors in your diagrams, it will help if you thoroughly understand the color wheel principles and then choose colors to clarify your messages.

Presentations: Delivering your Presentation

Coping with audience attitudes.   Some people prefer to look at drawings; others are more comfortable with words. You have to be prepared for both.

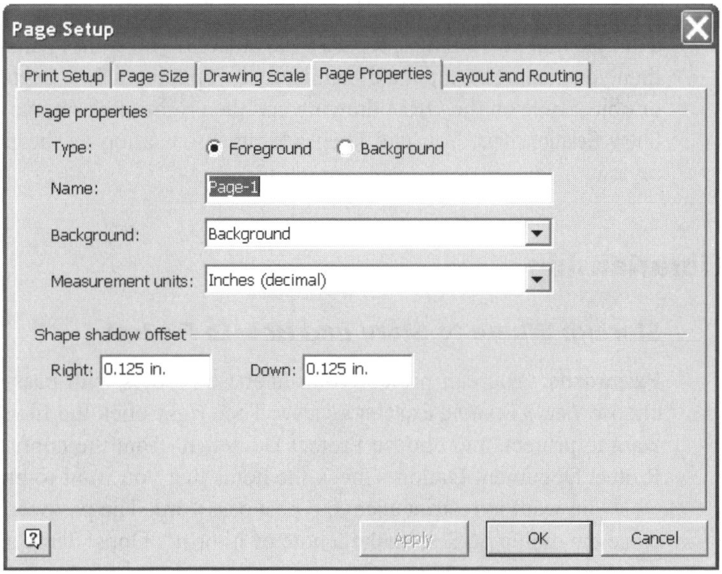

Figure 17–21   Assign the background to the foreground page.

Those who like drawings. You can use drawings for review after some short training of the review team. Usually this is a train-as-you-go plan. In our experience, this has never caused and delays or issues with reviews. Actually, the reviewers usually prefer the diagrams once they realize they are diagrams of the sentences. The diagrams with an active verbalized window create a fast way to see both. Using a projector also keeps everyone on the same page. It is also possible to make changes while in the review, assuring everyone that the change is in place. The lack of paper copies reduces preparation time.

Those who like words. You can use words for those sessions where the reviewers are unfamiliar with the diagram notations or have a strong leaning for text. These reviews do tend to go slower. Creating an electronic version of the reports is one way to keep everyone on the same page during the review. Again, projecting this helps. This also limits dynamic changes as when using actual models. To use words, use the verbalizer or one of the report options discussed in Chapters 9 and 15.

Preparing both drawings and words. Use the verbalization function to discuss entities, facts and constraints. Use ORM or ER diagrams to give the big picture. Diagrams help everyone to get the big picture and Visio is an excellent tool to help you to design and to deliver your material. Since the ORM drawing is one model and the logical model is separate, you can open both models and toggle between them. Making changes to the ORM model can be reflected in the logical model with a simple rebuild. This often can be done very quickly, satisfying people who prefer one drawing notation over the other.

During the show. During a presentation, you might want to answer a question with an example that you did not prepare in advance. If you want to answer questions on the fly, then you can create a page dynamically by opening a new page, place a single fact type or object type on the ORM drawing and then right-click on one of the objects and select Show Relationships. You can keep adding information to the page as you continue to review.

17.2 Librarianship

Storing: Where to Store and How to Protect

Passwords. You can protect your database models with passwords. To protect a file, choose View > Drawing Explorer Window. Then right-click the filename of the drawing you want to protect, and choose Protect Document from the context menu. This opens the Protect Document Dialog. Check the items that you want to protect.

If you want to restrict access, type a password. The password is not visible after you close the dialog box, so make a note of it, or it's Oops! Time again.

Lock shapes against deletion. Locking aspects of drawing shapes can prevent accidents, and control resizing or the movement of shapes. This feature cannot present some that has file update permissions from unlocking some aspect of the drawing, but it does help to manage these aspects.

Select the shape or shapes that you want to protect.

On the Format menu, click Protection.

Indicate what you wish to protect. In Figure 17–22 the shapes are protected against deletion. No modeler or reviewer can accidentally delete the region fact type without first removing the protection. To remove the protection, simply return to this window and remove the protection.

Select "OK."

Any attempt to delete the "Region Name" object type results in the warning message shown in Figure 17–23.

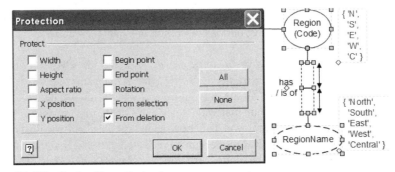

Figure 17–22 Setting Shape Protection.

> ⚠ Shape protection and/or layer properties prevent complete execution of this command.

Figure 17–23   Visio Warning – stops user from violating a protection.

Visio File Types

In various places in Visio, you will see one or more of the six file types shown in Table 17–2 but you can's use them all directly from within the VEA database solution.

Naming Conventions

You should establish naming conventions for files, objects, columns, tables, and just about any other group of things to which you want to refer. File naming is important because Visio saves all database drawings using file type *.vsd* and you will want to clearly separate your ORM Source Model files from your Logical Model files. For example, suppose you create an ORM Source Model and save it as "Test." Then you build a logical model and save the logical model as "Test". Oops! You just lost your ORM Source Model.

Naming conventions can be complex. The point to bear in mind is that you should use one! To get started, you can use a simple method such at the one used in this book's examples. We have named each model with a suffix to indicate the model type. For example, "Patient_CS" means Patient Conceptual Schema, and "Patient_LS" means Patient Logical Schema. You can find lots of advice about naming convention principles and practices in many places on the web.

Version Control

Database models are valuable documents, so you should set up your own version control system. If you use a tool such as Microsoft Visual SourceSafe, then you can manage versions a file-at-a-time. Visio has the standard Undo/Redo commands, but if you are designing many database models you will need more than this simple feature. You can find out more about Visual SourceSafe at *http://msdn.microsoft.com/ssafe/*. The Visual SourceSafe home page is shown in Figure 17–24.

Table 17–2   Visio file types.

Drawing Type	Screen and Printer	For Use with XML
Drawing	vsd	vsx
Stencil	vss	vdx
Template	vst	vtx

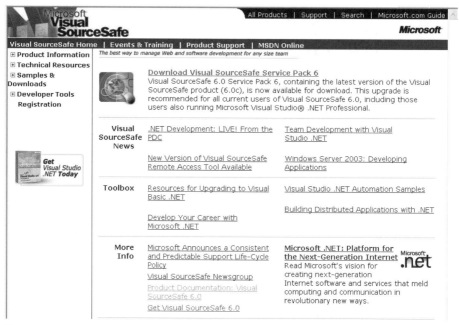

Figure 17–24   Visual SourceSafe.

Model Browsing

Large pages or models that involve many pages are navigated by selecting a fact type or object type in an ORM model, or a table in a logical data model. To find a fact type in an ORM drawing, select the Fact Types tab of the Business Rules window, right-click the fact type, and select Find Fact in Drawing from the context menu (Figure 17–25). This positions you at the first entered instance of the fact type. This will not position you at any duplicate instances of the fact type. This means if you are on a page that has a duplicate instance of the fact type on the drawing, it will take you the pages where the first instance was created, even though an instance is visible right in front of you.

This next example illustrates the same concept using an object type. Right-click an object type in the Object Types pane of the Business Rules window, and then choose Find Object Type in Drawing from the context menu (Figure 17–26).

To locate a table in logical model drawing, open the Tables and Views window by choosing Database > View > Tables and Views from the main menu (Figure 17–27). Then double-click on the table or view name to locate the first instance.

VisioModeler 3.1

The VisioModeler version of the ORM tool is a free, unsupported product from Microsoft. Some modelers are still using this version, while others use it as way to investigate the features of ORM. It can be down loaded from *http://www.microsoft.com/downloads/release.asp?ReleaseID=27489*.

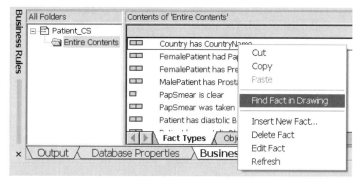

Figure 17–25 Find a fact type in the drawing.

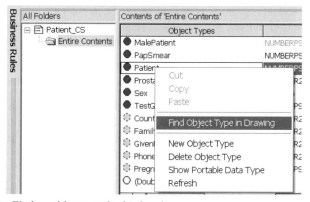

Figure 17–26 Find an object type in the drawing.

Figure 17–27 Find a table in the drawing.

XML

You can extract ORM and Logical Model information as XML. To make an XML extract, you can use a free third-party add-in called Orthogonal toolbox. This is downloadable from the toolbox area at www.OrthogonalSoftware.com. This add-in extracts all the information exposed by the COM API for the VEA's database modeling engine.

This COM API is currently unsupported by Microsoft, and has a few limitations, but is still quite useful. The installation of Orthogonal Toolbox is very simple and adds a main menu item to your Visio application.

17.3   Distributing your Database Models

Web Pages

You can save your database models as web pages by opening a database model and choosing File > Save as Web Page. You will then see a standard folder save window. The name of your file will appear in the file name box with the extension ".htm". To save the file, click on Save.

You can publish ORM Source Model files, ER Source Model files and Database Model Diagram files as web pages. To publish a model diagram, click on the "Publish" button and you will see the Save as Web Page Dialog shown in Figure 17–28. Use this tabbed dialog box to format your database model for viewing as a web page.

Visio Reader

You can use the Visio Reader to share database models over the internet. Since the Visio Reader is a free and self-installing download, you don't have to worry about buying, installing, and managing a Visual Studio. Net license for everyone who wants to see your database models.

Caution: Don't install the Visio Reader on a machine that already has Visio installed because the reader then becomes the default program for viewing Visio files.

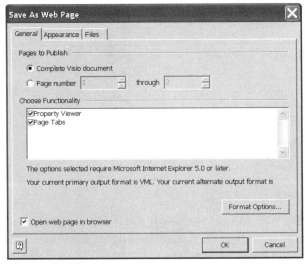

Figure 17–28   Save as Web Page.

You can download and install the Visio reader from the following web address. *http://office.microsoft.com/downloads/2002/vviewer.aspx.* To add Visio Reader to your installed version of Internet Explorer, just follow the installation instructions. Note that you need Internet Explorer Version 5 or later.

You can use Visio Reader to open and browse Visio files (VSD or VDX). When you use the Visio Reader you will see the toolbar shown in Figure 17–29.

When you use the Visio Reader to view your database models over the internet, all the hyperlinks in your model documents remain active, so you can quickly create a powerful communications facility. However, if you don't use an effective naming convention or layers, you will end up with a chaotic jumble of files. Remember the PAP[4] principle: Preparation And Planning Prevent Pathetic Performance!

Reporting

As discussed in Chapters 9 and 15, there are several reports from an ORM or logical model that are useful for reviews. These reports are saved as Rich Text Files. Rich Text files can then be saved as web pages making the distribution of matching Visio drawings and reports possible.

Reports are accessible from the Database menu option Reports. In our simple example, a fact type report is selected from the Patient conceptual model using only the default options. Keep in mind that these reports also contain any examples and notes provided by the modeling team. So are excellent for reviews. As a matter of good practice, complete reports are the fastest way to get user confirmation of the model. The model is also a specification, so keep the specification up-to-date, and keep it as rich as possible with content.

You can filter the report to get a meaningful sub-report for a specific review (see Figure 17–31). Determine the information (attributes) that will be displayed, then sort and control the presentation issues, headers, and pagination.

This example reports information about each fact type in the model. By default, simple diagrams of the fact types are also presented, as shown in Figure 17–32. Only internal uniqueness and simple mandatory constraints can be displayed on these simple

1. About Microsoft Visio Viewer 2002
2. Drawing page selection
3. Zoom in
4. Zoom out
5. Zoom page
6. Zoom to %
7. Open this drawing in Visio (only active if Microsoft Visio is installed on your computer)
8. Drawing shape properties & display properties
9. Help (includes usage tips)

Figure 17–29 Visio Reader toolbar.

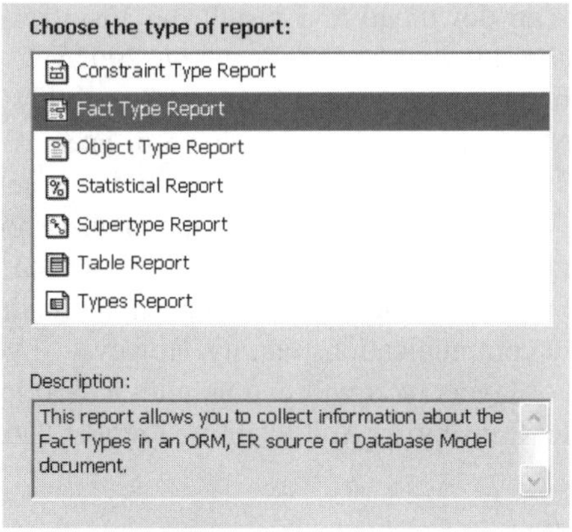

Choose the type of report:
Constraint Type Report
Fact Type Report
Object Type Report
Statistical Report
Supertype Report
Table Report
Types Report
Description:
This report allows you to collect information about the Fact Types in an ORM, ER source or Database Model document.

Figure 17–30 Selecting a Fact Type Report.

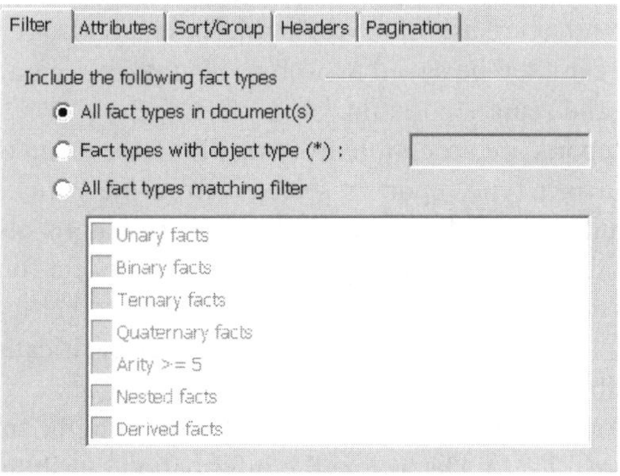

Filter
Attributes
Sort/Group
Headers
Pagination
Include the following fact types
All fact types in document(s)
Fact types with object type (*) :
All fact types matching filter
Unary facts
Binary facts
Ternary facts
Quaternary facts
Arity >= 5
Nested facts
Derived facts

Figure 17–31 All fact types are selected by default.

1
Patient
(Nr)
is in / includes
Text Group
(Nr)

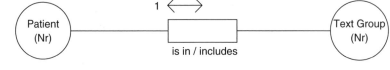

Record:	3
Fact:	Patient is in Test Group
Inverse fact:	Test Group includes Patient
Mapping option:	Does not result in a composite type
Constraints:	2 1: Each Patient is in at most one Test Group. 2: Each Test Group that occurs in Patient is in Test Group occurs there at least 5 times.
External rules:	None
Examples:	None

Figure 17–32 Sample of a default Fact Type Report.

diagrams. However, all constraints are verbalized. In this example, the frequency constraint that each test group includes at least five patients is verbalized, even though it does not appear on the report diagram. Although not displayed diagrammatically in the report, this constraint is displayed as ">=5" on the TestGroup role in the actual ORM diagram for the model.

In this example, the frequency constraint verbalization, though unambiguous, is a little awkward. Its meaning can be clarified by including examples to back it up, and by including a better verbalization as a note (e.g., "Each test group includes at least five patients"). This makes it easier for the domain expert to check whether the constraint is correct. For instance, maybe the frequency constraint should actually be: Each test group includes at most five patients (<=5). In general however, the automatic verbalization provided by the tool is easy to understand, and reports of this type provide a very useful means of validating business rules with the domain experts

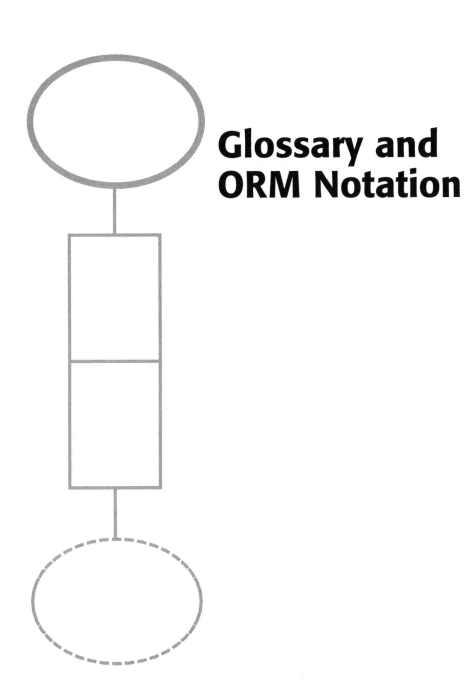

Glossary and ORM Notation

This glossary lists key terms and symbols used in the conceptual and logical database modeling solutions within Microsoft Visio for Enterprise Architects. A brief explanation of the terms and symbols is included. A more complete list of terms may be found in the index, and a thorough explanation of the terminology and underlying methodologies may be found in Halpin (2001), from which some of the notation glossaries have been adapted with permission.

5NF	Fifth Normal Form–a high level of relational normalization.
Application domain	That portion of the world about which information is recorded in the application. Also known as Universe of Discourse.
Arity	The number of roles in a predicate. Arity 1 is termed "unary," arity 2 is termed "binary," and so on.
Attribute	A property of an entity in the Entity-Relationship modeling approach.
Bag	See multiset.
Base type	A primitive data type from which other data types may be defined. Example: char.
Binary fact	[ORM] A fact with two roles in its predicate.
Cardinality	Classification of a binary relationship: one-to one (1:1), one-to-many (1:n), many-to-one (n:1), or many-to-many (m:n).
Catalog	A vendor-specific dictionary of an existing relational database.
Category entity	[IDEF1X] An entity whose instances form a subset of another entity (generic entity). Also known as a subtype entity.
Child entity	[IDEF1X] The entity receiving a foreign key. A child entity receives a foreign key from a parent entity. See also parent entity.
Complex type	A complex type combines one or more existing data types to create a new data type.
Composite object type	[ORM] An entity type whose identification scheme involves at least two components. Either a co-referenced or nested entity type.
Conceptual model	A formal definition of the information in an application domain independent of the way that the data will be physically implemented.
Conceptual view	Information about data articulated in simple natural concepts. See also external view, logical view, physical view
Co-referenced object	[ORM] An object that is identified by two or more roles spanned by an external uniqueness constraint. Example: the City that has the CityName "Newcastle" and is located in the Country "Australia."
Co-role	[ORM] Another role in the same predicate.
Data migration	Moving data from one physical database to another.
Database	A set of related tables.
Database driver	A utility that converts a logical model into a format recognized by a specific database product.
Database re-engineering	A series of processes (reverse engineering, conceptual refinement, forward engineering, and data migration) resulting in the modification of a physical database.
DBMS	Database management system. Software designed for storing, manipulating and retrieving data.
DCL	Data control language. A subset of SQL used to control database access authorization. Examples: Grant, Revoke.

DDL	Data definition language. A subset of SQL used to create, change, and delete one or more database objects. Example: Create Table.
Dependent entity	[IDEF1X] An entity whose primary key includes one or more foreign key attributes. See also independent entity.
Derivation rule	[ORM] A rule that is used to derive a fact.
Derived and stored	[ORM] This setting creates a permanent column when you generate a physical database, to store the results of the derivation.
Derived fact type	[ORM] A fact type whose instances are derived from a logical or mathematical calculation involving other fact types.
Discriminator	An attribute in a generic (supertype) entity that is used to determine that category to which an instance belongs.
Distinct type	A data type based on an existing data type with the same representation but different from an existing data type.
DML	Data manipulation language. A subset of SQL used to query, insert, update, or delete database objects.
Domain	The set of all possible values of a named concept. A data type alias of a built-in, collection, or unnamed row type.
Domain expert	A person who has a good understanding of the application domain.
DSN	Data Source Name. A logical name for a database. A DSN is created by a user, and associated with a particular ODBC driver. Visio uses DSNs to connect to databases.
Elementary fact	[ORM] A fact that cannot be split into two or more facts and still retain the original meaning.
Entity	[ERM] A "thing" about which data is to be stored. The logical modeling solution treats an entity as a table.
Entity	[ORM] An object that is identified by relating it to other objects. Not a value. Example: the Country that has CountryCode 'US'.
ER or ERM	Entity-Relationship modeling. A database design technique that models facts using either attributes or associations.
External element	[ORM] An object type or fact type that is defined in a different model, and is reused in your current model.
External view	A view of data created for specific users. Example: a sales report.
Fact	[ORM] A fact instance, but sometimes used as shorthand for fact type. Example: Employee '100' works for Department 'CS' is a fact instance for the fact type Employee works for Department.
Fact type	[ORM] Kind of fact, including object types and predicate. Example: Employee works for Department.
Foreign key	In the relational model, a column or combination of columns whose entries must also exist in the population of a primary key.
FORML	Formal Object-Role Modeling Language.
Forward engineering	Transforming a higher level schema into a lower level schema. Conceptual to Logical, and/or Logical to Physical.
Functional role	[ORM] A role spanned by a simple internal uniqueness constraint.
Generation	A process that creates a DDL script from a logical model and optionally passes it on to a physical database.
Generic entity	[IDEF1X] An entity whose instances are classified as one or more category entities. Also known as a supertype entity.
HTML	Hypertext Markup Language

IDEF0	A process modeling notation standard.
IDEF1X	A data modeling notation standard.
Identifying relationship	[IDEF1X] A relationship in which the primary key attributes of the parent entity form part of the primary key of the child.
Independent entity	[IDEF1X] An entity whose primary key contains no foreign key attributes.
Independent entity type	[ORM] An entity type with whose instances may exist without participating in any fact.
Index mark	[ORM] An annotation on a conceptual model that identifies roles to be mapped to indexed columns in the physical database.
List	An ordered collection of elements that allows duplicate elements. Each element in the collection has an ordinal position.
Logical model	A description of a relational database structure, including relational tables, constraints, triggers and stored procedures.
Logical view	Data that is shown in a normalized form of a relational model and shows the logical relationships between tables.
Mapping	The process that converts a conceptual model to a logical model.
Metadata	Data that describes a model.
Model	Technically, a schema (structure) plus its instances (data). Informally, "model" is often used as a synonym for "schema."
Model diagram	A diagram of a model. The diagram might not show all the details of the underlying model.
Multiset	An unordered collection of elements that can have duplicate values. Also known as bag.
Name space	[ORM] A scope in which a name identifies an object. If two elements in a model have the same name, then you may assign them different name spaces to differentiate them.
Nested entity type	[ORM] A relationship type that plays some role. Also called objectified relationship type or objectified association.
Non-identifying relationship	[IDEF1X] A relationship in which the primary key attributes of the parent entity become non-key attributes of the child.
Normalization	A technique by which attributes are grouped into relations so as to avoid update anomalies, mainly by eliminating redundancy.
Object	[ORM] Thing of interest. An entity or value. Strictly, an object instance, though sometimes used as shorthand for object type.
Object type	[ORM] A kind of object. Example: Person.
Objectified relationship	[ORM] See nested entity type.
Object-Role Modeling	[ORM] A conceptual modeling method that views the application domain as a collection of objects playing roles.
ODBC	Open Database Connectivity.
OLE	Object linking and embedding
Optimization	The application of techniques to enhance performance.
ORM	Object-Role Modeling.
Parent entity	The entity contributing a foreign key to a child entity.
Physical schema	The structure of a database as stored in the catalog of a specific DBMS. Also called physical database schema.
Physical view	A database design for a specific DBMS, including physical data types and indexes.
Population	All instances of a fact type. You can use a sample population to check or determine constraints.
Predicate	[ORM] A proposition with object-holes in it. Examples: ... smokes; ... works for ....

Primary key	A relational column or column combination whose entries may appear in only one row of the table, thus identifying each row.
Quaternary fact	[ORM] A fact with four roles in its predicate.
RDBMS	Relational Database Management System. In this book, the term DBMS is often used as a synonym for RDBMS.
Re-engineering	See database re-engineering.
Reference mode	[ORM] Manner in which a single value references an entity. Example: Code.
Referential integrity	A relational database characteristic that requires foreign key values of the referencing (child) table either to be null or to match the primary key values of the referenced (parent) table.
Relation	A named table with a set of named columns and populated by a set of unnamed rows.
Relational database	A database that appears to the user as a collection of relations.
Relational model	A logical data model invented by Dr. E.F. Codd, in which all facts are stored in relations. Associations between relations are made by name rather than by pre-declared access paths. Data can be manipulated a set at a time, using operations such as join.
Reverse engineering	An existing physical database is used to construct a logical or conceptual model.
Role	[ORM] A part played by an object type within a predicate.
Role sequence	[ORM] Two or more roles selected in a particular order from one or more predicates. See also predicate, role, set constraint.
RTF	Rich Text Format. A portable file type for documents.
Schema	The structure of a model.
Set	An unordered collection of unique elements.
SQL	A standardized language for managing data in a relational database. Each database vendor uses a different dialect of SQL.
Stored procedure	A callable procedure stored in the catalog for repeated use by one or more applications.
Subtype	[ORM] An object type whose instances all belong to another object type.
Supertype	[ORM] An object type that includes one or more subtypes.
Ternary fact	[ORM] A fact containing three roles.
Trigger	[ORM] Procedural code that may be fired when a specific table is subject to an insert, update, or delete event.
Unary fact	[ORM] A fact whose predicate contains only one role.
Universe of Discourse	The aspects of the world that we want to define in our model. Also known as application domain.
Value	[ORM] An unchangeable, lexical object such as a character string or a number. Example: the CountryCode 'US'.

ORM Notation

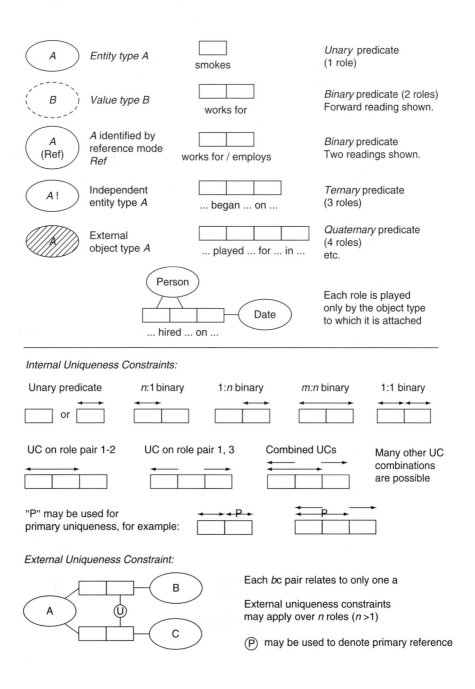

A	Entity type A	
B	Value type B	
A (Ref)	A identified by reference mode Ref	
A !	Independent entity type A	
A	External object type A	

smokes — *Unary* predicate (1 role)

works for — *Binary* predicate (2 roles) Forward reading shown.

works for / employs — *Binary* predicate Two readings shown.

... began ... on ... — *Ternary* predicate (3 roles)

... played ... for ... in ... — *Quaternary* predicate (4 roles) etc.

Person — Date — ... hired ... on ...

Each role is played only by the object type to which it is attached

---

Internal Uniqueness Constraints:

Unary predicate — or

n:1 binary

1:*n* binary

m:n binary

1:1 binary

UC on role pair 1-2

UC on role pair 1, 3

Combined UCs

Many other UC combinations are possible

"P" may be used for primary uniqueness, for example:

External Uniqueness Constraint:

A — U — B — C

Each *bc* pair relates to only one *a*

External uniqueness constraints may apply over *n* roles (*n* >1)

P may be used to denote primary reference

395

Simple mandatory role constraint: Role *r is mandatory* for population of *A*

Inclusive-or constraint: (disjunctive-mandatory)
Disjunction of roles is mandatory for population of *A*.
Each *a* in pop(*A*) plays at least one of roles r_1 .. r_n
where *n* > 1.
Case shown is for *n* = 2.

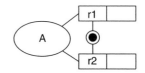

The constrained roles may occur in predicates of any arity.

Objectified association (nested entity type)
Relationship type *R* is objectified as entity type *A*.
Nesting may be applied to an association that
either has a spanning UC or is a 1:1 association.

Value constraints indicate possible values or value ranges, or both.

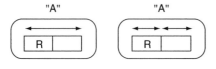

Subset constraints:

(a) Each object that plays *r2* also plays *r1*

(b) Each object-pair playing *r3*, *r4* also plays *r1*, *r2*

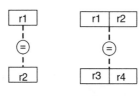

Equality constraints:

Populations must be equal

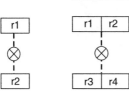

Exclusion constraints:

Populations must be mutually exclusive

Exclusive-or constraint:
Each object in the population of A
plays exactly one of r1, r2.

Combined inclusive-or and exclusion constraints.

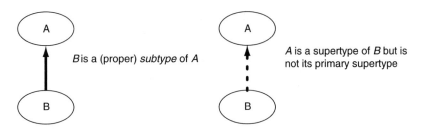

B is a (proper) *subtype* of *A*

A is a supertype of *B* but is not its primary supertype

In principle, the following constraints on subtypes are implied by subtype definitions and other constraints. Currently however, VEA supports neither formal subtype definitions, nor these subtyping constraints.

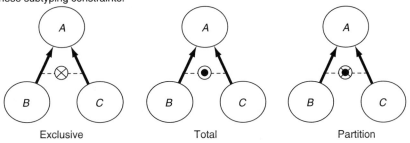

Exclusive   Total   Partition

Frequency constraints:

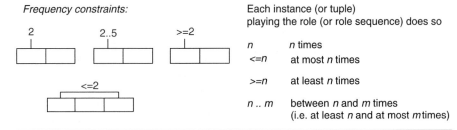

Each instance (or tuple) playing the role (or role sequence) does so

n	*n* times
<=n	at most *n* times
>=n	at least *n* times
n .. m	between *n* and *m* times (i.e. at least *n* and at most *m* times)

Ring constraints:

°*ir*	irreflexive	°*ans*	antisymmetric
°*as*	asymmetric	°*ac*	acyclic
°*it*	intransitive	°*sym*	symmetric

Derived fact types:

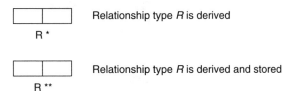

Relationship type *R* is derived

Relationship type *R* is derived and stored

Default Logical Model Notation

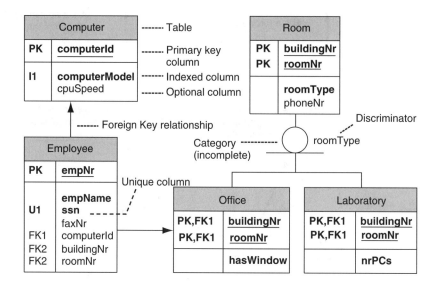

------- Table

------- Primary key
        column

------- Indexed column

------- Optional column

------- Foreign Key relationship

Discriminator

Complete categories are displayed with a double bar:

Various display options exist. The following example renders the
Employee-Computer subschema without compartment lines, but
with data types and a foreign key relationship name:

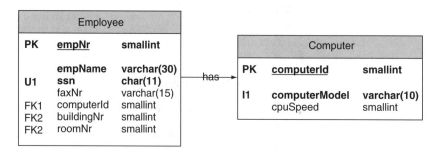

Crows-foot Notation for foreign key relationships

----O<	----O+	----|<	----||-
0 or more	0 or 1	1 or more	exactly 1

IDEF1X notation

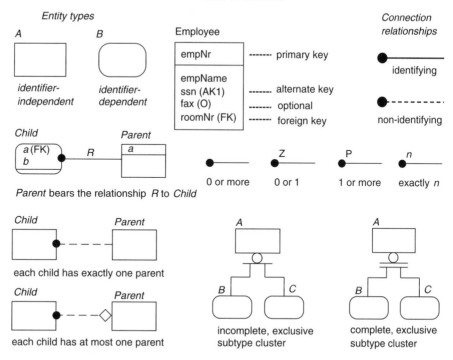

Parent bears the relationship *R* to *Child*

each child has exactly one parent

each child has at most one parent

incomplete, exclusive
subtype cluster

complete, exclusive
subtype cluster

For example, the logical model shown earlier is rendered below in IDEF1X notation:

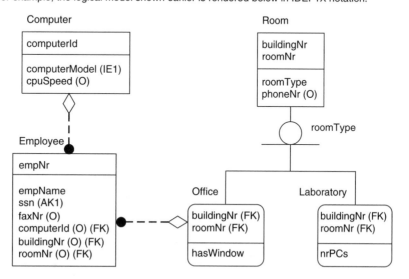

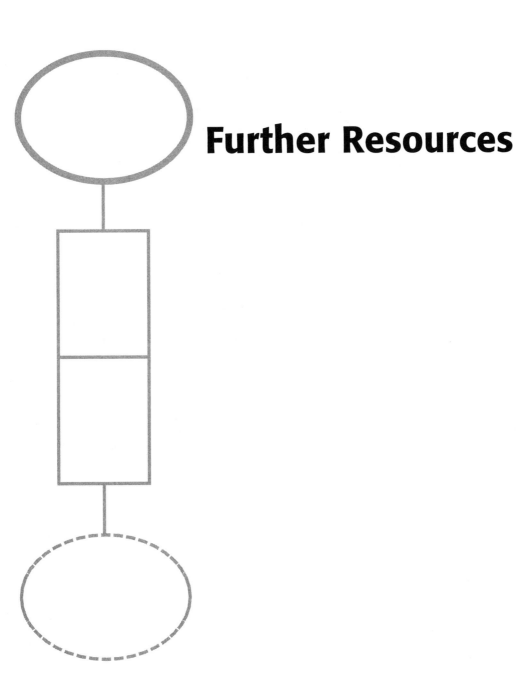

Further Resources

This section provides information about further resources for the modeling solutions within Microsoft Visio for Enterprise Architects, including sample models, downloadable files, references, and useful websites.

Sample Models

Many of the examples discussed in this book are based at least in part on the following sample models that may be downloaded from http://www.orm.net/sampleModels.html.

Patient_CS.vsd	Conceptual schema for a medical patient application
Patient_LS.vsd	Logical schema mapped from the Patient_CS.vsd
BPtest2_CS.vsd	Alternative conceptual schema for blood pressure tests
BPtest2_LS.vsd	Logical schema mapped from BPtest2_CS.vsd
BPtest3_CS.vsd	Another alternative schema for blood pressure tests
BPtest3_LS.vsd	Logical schema mapped from BPtest3_CS.vsd
Sales_CS.vsd	Conceptual schema for sales invoice application
Sales_LS.vsd	Logical schema mapped from Sales_CS.vsd

The schema diagrams for the above models are reproduced here. Download the files to inspect other aspects of the models, such as notes, data types, and mapping settings for name generation.

Patient_CS.vsd: Personal page

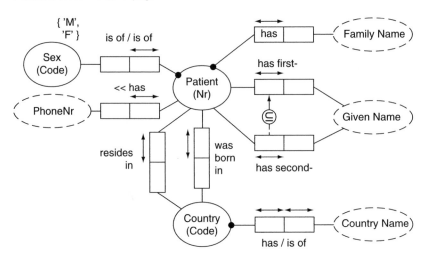

Patient_CS.vsd: Subtyping page

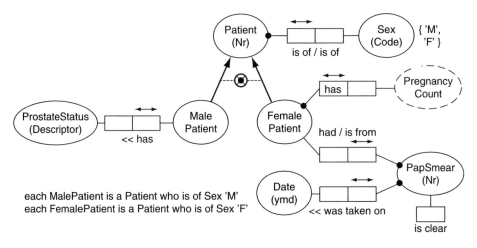

each MalePatient is a Patient who is of Sex 'M'
each FemalePatient is a Patient who is of Sex 'F'

Patient_CS.vsd: BPtests page

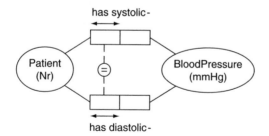

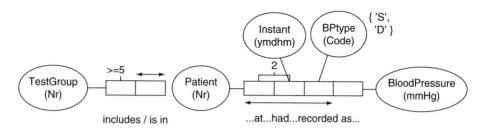

Patient_LS.vsd

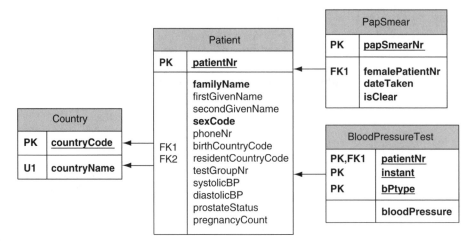

BPtest2_CS.vsd

BPtest2_LS.vsd

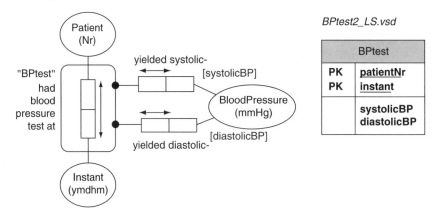

BPtest3_CS.vsd

BPtest3_LS.vsd

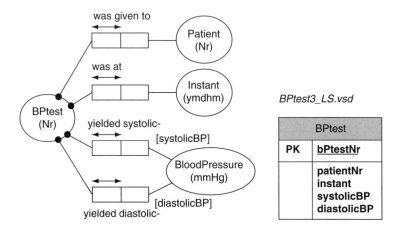

Sales_CS.vsd

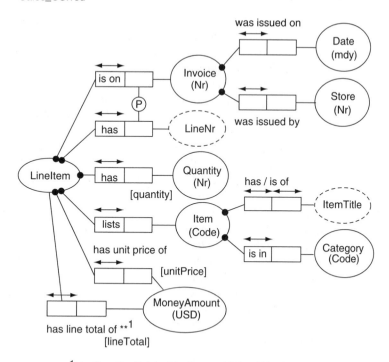

[1]LineItem.lineTotal = LineItem.unitPrice * LineItem.quantity

Sales_LS.vsd

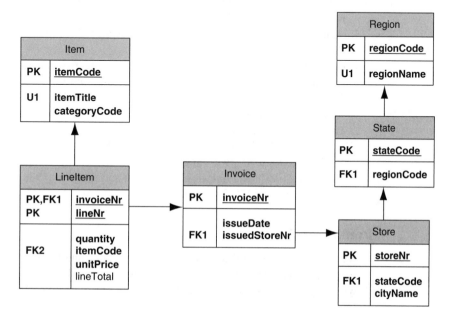

References

Bruce, T. (1992). *Designing Quality Databases: Practical Information Management and IDEFIX,* Dorset House, New York.

Finkelstein, C. (1998). Information engineering methodology. In *Handbook on Architectures of Information Systems,* eds. P. Bernus, K. Mertins & G. Schmidt, Springer-Verlag, Berlin, pp. 405–427.

van Griethuysen, J.J., ed. (1982). *Concepts and terminology for the conceptual schema and the information base,* ISO TC97/SC5/WG3, Eindhoven.

Halpin, T.A. (1999). 'Object Role Modeling: an overview', online at www.orm.net.

Halpin, T.A. (2000). Supplementing UML with concepts from ORM, In *Unified Modeling Language: Systems Analysis, Design and Development Issues,* Eds. K. Siau & T. Halpin, Idea Group Publishing Company, Hershey, PA.

Halpin, T.A. (2001). *Information Modeling and Relational Databases,* Morgan Kaufmann Publishers, San Francisco, CA. (ISBN 1-55860-672-6).

IEEE (1999). *IEEE standard for conceptual modeling language syntax and semantics for IDEFIX$_{97}$ (IDEF$_{object}$),* IEEE Standard 1320.2-1998, IEEE, New York.

Kent, W. (1983). A simple guide to five normal forms in relational database theory, *CACM* 26:2, pp 120–125.

Microsoft Corporation (2001). *Developing Microsoft Visio Solutions,* Microsoft Press, Redmond, WA. (ISBN: 0735613532).

Microsoft Corporation (2001). *Microsoft Visio Version 2002 Inside Out,* Microsoft Press, Redmond, WA. (ISBN: 0735612854).

Mullins, C. S. (2002). *Database Administration: The Complete Guide to Practices and Procedures,* Addison-Wesley, Boston MA.

NIST (1993). *Integration definition for information modeling (IDEFIX),* FIPS Publication 184, National Institute of Standards and Technology, www.sdct.itl.nist.gov/~ftp/ideflx.trf.

Resources Online (2001). *Microsoft Visio Version 2002 Step by Step,* Microsoft Press, Redmond, WA. (ISBN: 0735613028.)

Ritson, P.R. and Halpin, T.A. (1993). Mapping integrity constraints to a relational schema, *Proceedings of the 4th ACIS,* Brisbane (Sep.), pp. 381–400.

Sundblad, S. and Sundblad, P. (2002). *Design Patterns for Scalable Microsoft .NET Applications,* Sundblad & Sundblad ADB-Arkitektur AB, Uppsala, Sweden. Electronic version available online at http:// www.2xsundblad.com/.

Wideman, G. (2001). *Microsoft Visio 2002 Developer's Survival Pack,* Trafford Publishing, Victoria, BC, Canada.

Zachman, J. (1987). A framework for information systems architecture, *IBM Systems Journal* 26:3, pp. 276–292.

Useful Websites

www.orm.net: Many ORM articles, product details, and links.

www.inconcept.com: InConcept ORM consultancy and user group.

www.inconcept.com/JCM/index.html. Journal of Conceptual Modeling.

www.ormcentral.com. COM API details for ORM and Logical Database Modeling solutions, and other ORM details.

www.orthogonalsoftware.com/products.html. Free download of Orthogonal Toolbox, which provides an XML layer add-on to the database modeling COM API.

http:// www.microsoft.com/office/visio/. Main site for Visio – lots of useful links.

http:// office.microsoft.com/downloads/2002/visref.aspx. Visio Shortcut reference.

http:// msdn.microsoft.com/library/default.asp?url=/library/enus/dnvisio02/html/ visdbcomp.asp. Visio modeling product comparisons.

www.microsoft.com/downloads/release.asp?ReleaseID=37591&area=search&ordi- nal=7. VEA SR1 download. (superceded by Visual Studio 2003 release)

http:// support.microsoft.com/. Microsoft official site for general support and knowl- edge base articles.

www.msdn.microsoft.com. Microsoft Software Developer Network site.

www.microsoft.com/TRAINCERT/SYLLABI/2090AFINAL.ASP. Microsoft offi- cial three-day course 2090A on using Visio for Enterprise Architects for database modeling.

http:// msdn.microsoft.com/theshow/. The 25th .NET Show (video on ORM)

http:// msdn.microsoft.com/downloads/default.asp?URL=/downloads/sample.asp? url=/msdn-files/027/001/894/MsdnCompositeDoc.xml. Visio 2002 SDK down- load.

http:// msdn.microsoft.com/vstudio/techinfo/articles/developerproductivity/orm.asp. Quick overview of ORM as implemented in Visual Studio .NET Enterprise Architect.

http:// msdn.microsoft.com/library/en-us/dv_vstechart. html/vstchvsea_ormoverview. asp. Overview of Object Role Modeling.

http:// msdn.microsoft.com/vstudio/productinfo/features/eafeatures.asp. Features overview for Visual Studio .NET Enterprise Architect.

http:// msdn.microsoft.com/vstudio/productinfo/roadmap.asp. Product roadmap for Visual Studio.

http:// msdn.microsoft.com/vstudio/howtobuy/pricing.asp. Prices for Visual Studio .NET Editions.

http:// www.mkp.com/. Morgan Kaufmann books website.

Index

Page numbers in *italics* indicate figures; *italic page numbers followed by t indicate tables.*